尾田栄一郎

Here's volume 10. It's been two years since I started this series. Two years...two years... Back then Sazae-san, who's 24, was only 24... Oh, now that I think about it, I'm now the same age as Sazae-san. But it seems like I used to be the same age as Katsuo-kun. Who will it be next? Norisuke-kun? Taiko-san? Tara-san? It makes me laugh to say "Tara-san." Or "Ikura-san." What am I going on about? Anyway, I'm the same as ever—not working, just drawing manga.

-Eiichiro Oda, 1999

Editor's note: The aforementioned names belong to ageless characters from the beloved cartoon series, *Sazae-san*.

Eiichiro Oda began his manga career at the age of 17, when his one-shot cowboy manga **Wanted!** won second place in the coveted Tezuka manga awards. Oda went on to work as an assistant to some of the biggest manga artists in the industry, including Nobuhiro Watsuki, before winning the Hop Step Award for new artists. His pirate adventure **One Piece**, which debuted in **Weekly Shonen Jump** in 1997, quickly became one of the most popular manga in Japan.

**ONE PIECE VOL. 10
EAST BLUE PART 10**

SHONEN JUMP Manga Edition

This volume contains material that was originally
published in English in **SHONEN JUMP** #36–38.

STORY AND ART BY EIICHIRO ODA

English Adaptation/Lance Caselman
Translation/Naoko Amemiya
Touch-up Art & Lettering/Mark McMurray
Additional Touch-up/Josh Simpson
Design/Sean Lee
Editor/Yuki Takagaki

ONE PIECE © 1997 by Eiichiro Oda. All rights reserved.
First published in Japan in 1997 by SHUEISHA Inc., Tokyo.
English translation rights arranged by SHUEISHA Inc.

Printed in Italy

Published by VIZ Media, LLC
P.O. Box 77010
San Francisco, CA 94107

25
First printing, April 2006
Twenty-fifth printing, July 2024

viz.com

SHONEN JUMP MANGA

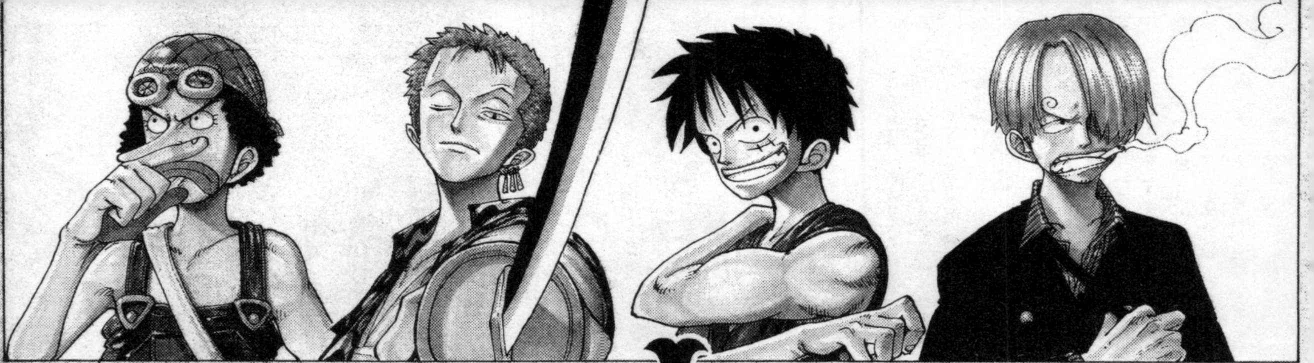

ONE PIECE #10 "OK, Let's STAND UP!"

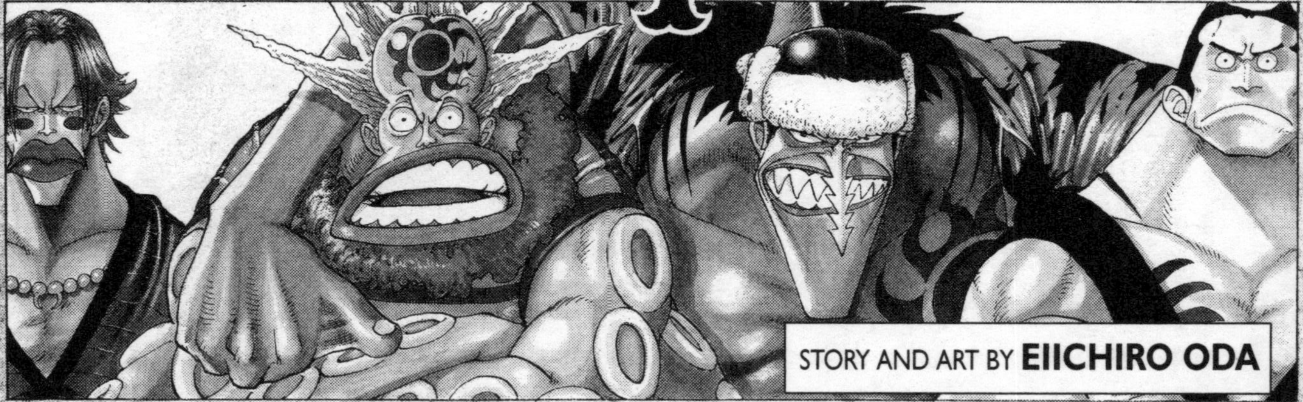

STORY AND ART BY **EIICHIRO ODA**

Genzo

Nojiko

"Red-Haired" Shanks

THE STORY OF ONE PIECE
Volume 10

Monkey D. Luffy started out as just a kid with a dream — and that dream was to become the greatest pirate in history! Stirred by the tales of pirate "Red-Haired" Shanks, Luffy vowed to become a pirate himself. That was before the enchanted Devil Fruit gave Luffy the power to stretch like rubber, at the cost of being unable to swim — a serious handicap for an aspiring sea dog. Undeterred, Luffy set out to sea and recruited some crewmates: lying sharpshooter Usopp, master swordsman Zolo, and treasure-hunting thief Nami.

Luffy and his shipmates have finally defeated Don Krieg and his pirates and added the high-kicking cook Sanji to their crew. At last it seems they can finally set sail for the Grand Line—until they discover that their navigator, Nami, has deserted! Zolo and Usopp sail after her and come upon an island under the tyrannical rule of the fiendish Fish-Man Pirates and their leader, Captain "Saw-Tooth" Arlong. Worse still, Nami is in cahoots with them.

Luffy and the others reach the island, but despite what they hear about Nami they refuse to believe it. They come to understand Nami's hatred of pirates when they learn from her foster sister, Nojiko, that their adoptive mother, Belle-Mère, was killed by Arlong. They discover, too, that Nami has been hoarding her loot to buy Coco Village back from Arlong. Nami, who has been fighting a solitary battle for so long, finally asks Luffy for help.

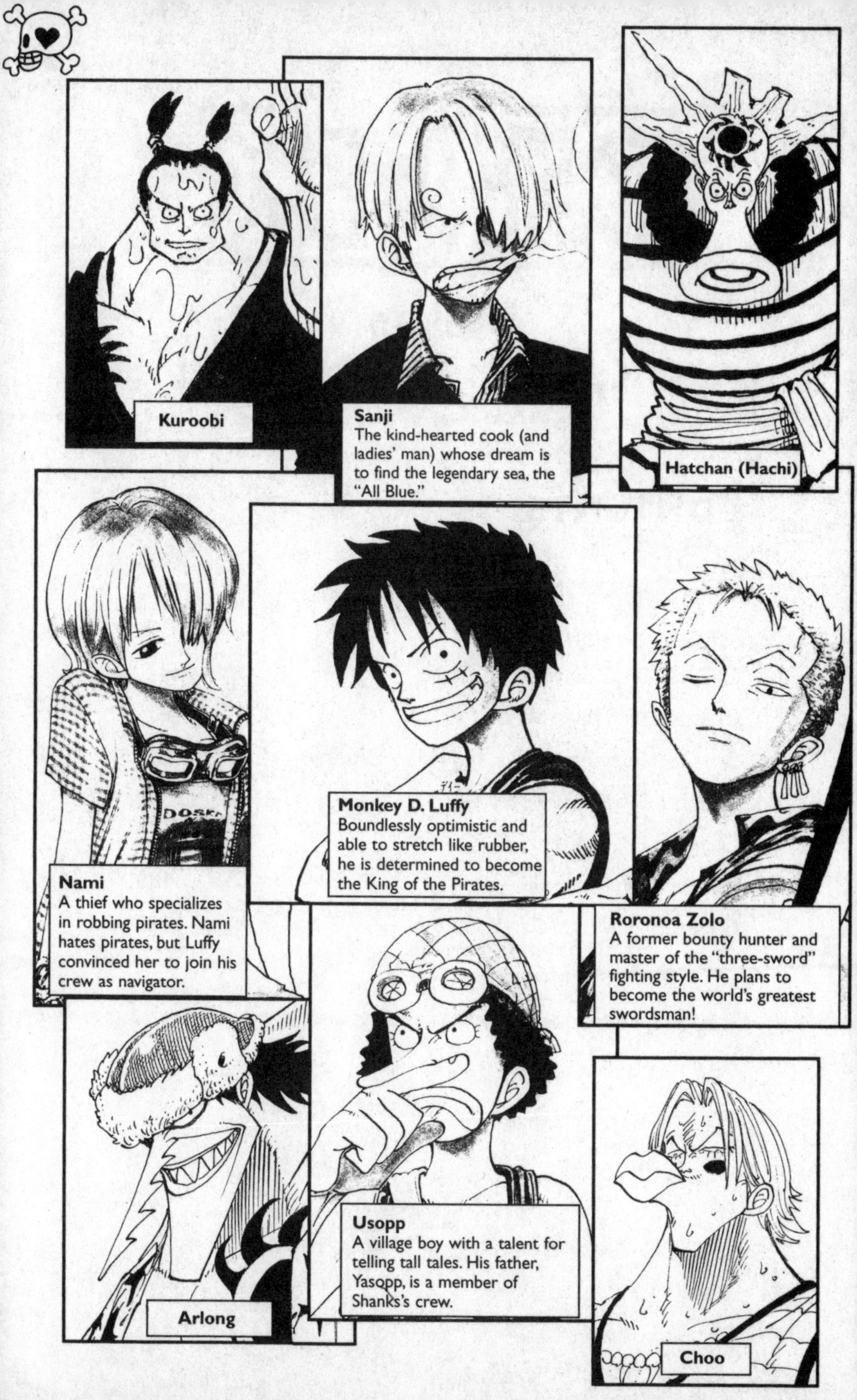

Hatchan (Hachi)
Sanji
The kind-hearted cook (and ladies' man) whose dream is to find the legendary sea, the "All Blue."
Kuroobi
Roronoa Zolo
A former bounty hunter and master of the "three-sword" fighting style. He plans to become the world's greatest swordsman!
Monkey D. Luffy
Boundlessly optimistic and able to stretch like rubber, he is determined to become the King of the Pirates.
Nami
A thief who specializes in robbing pirates. Nami hates pirates, but Luffy convinced her to join his crew as navigator.
Choo
Usopp
A village boy with a talent for telling tall tales. His father, Yasopp, is a member of Shanks's crew.
Arlong

Vol. 10
OK, Let's STAND UP!

CONTENTS

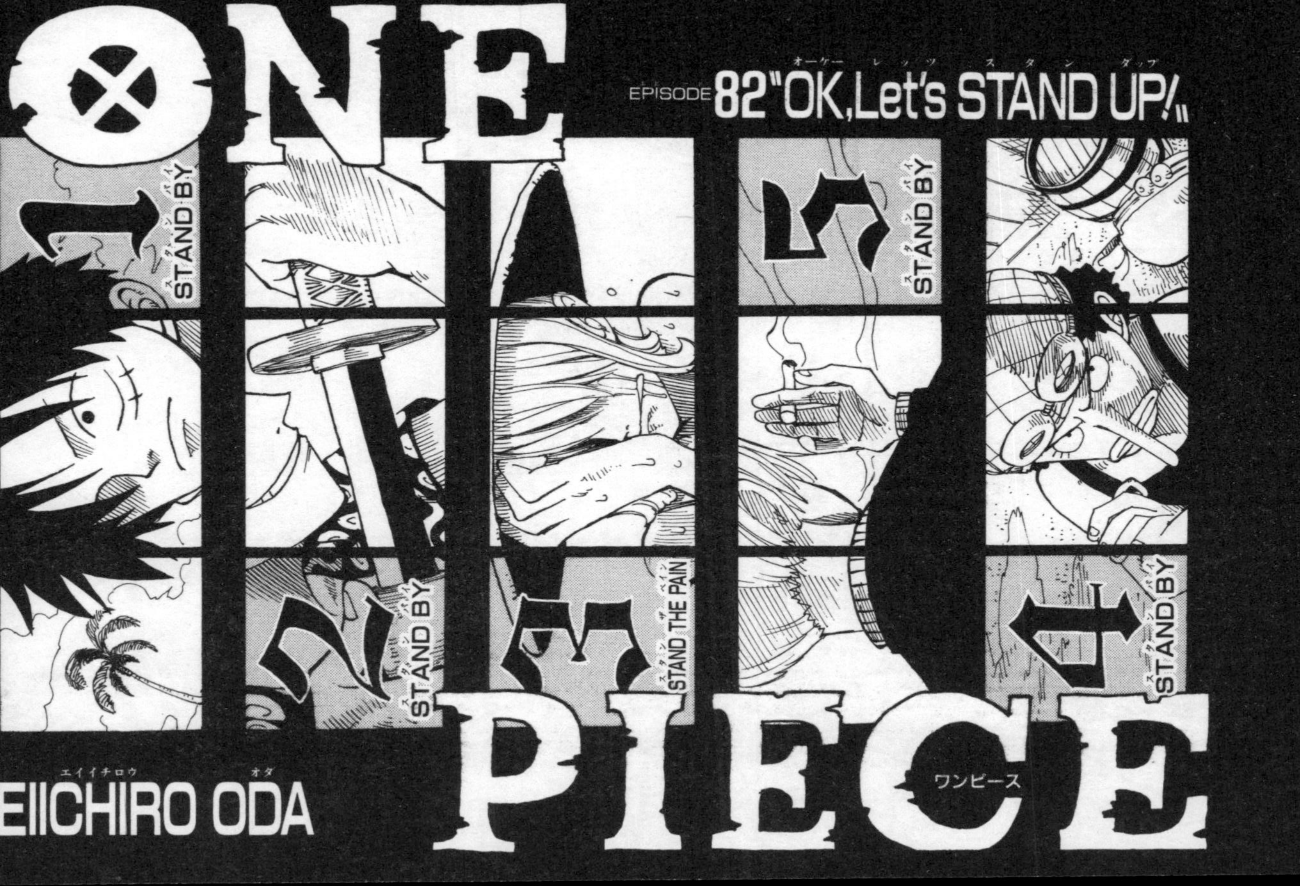
ONE PIECE
ワンピース
EPISODE 82 "OK, Let's STAND UP!"
オーケー レッツ スタンダップ
1 STAND BY
スタンバイ
2 STAND BY
スタンバイ
3 STAND THE PAIN
スタンザペイン
4 STAND BY
スタンバイ
5 STAND BY
スタンバイ
EIICHIRO ODA
エイイチロウ オダ

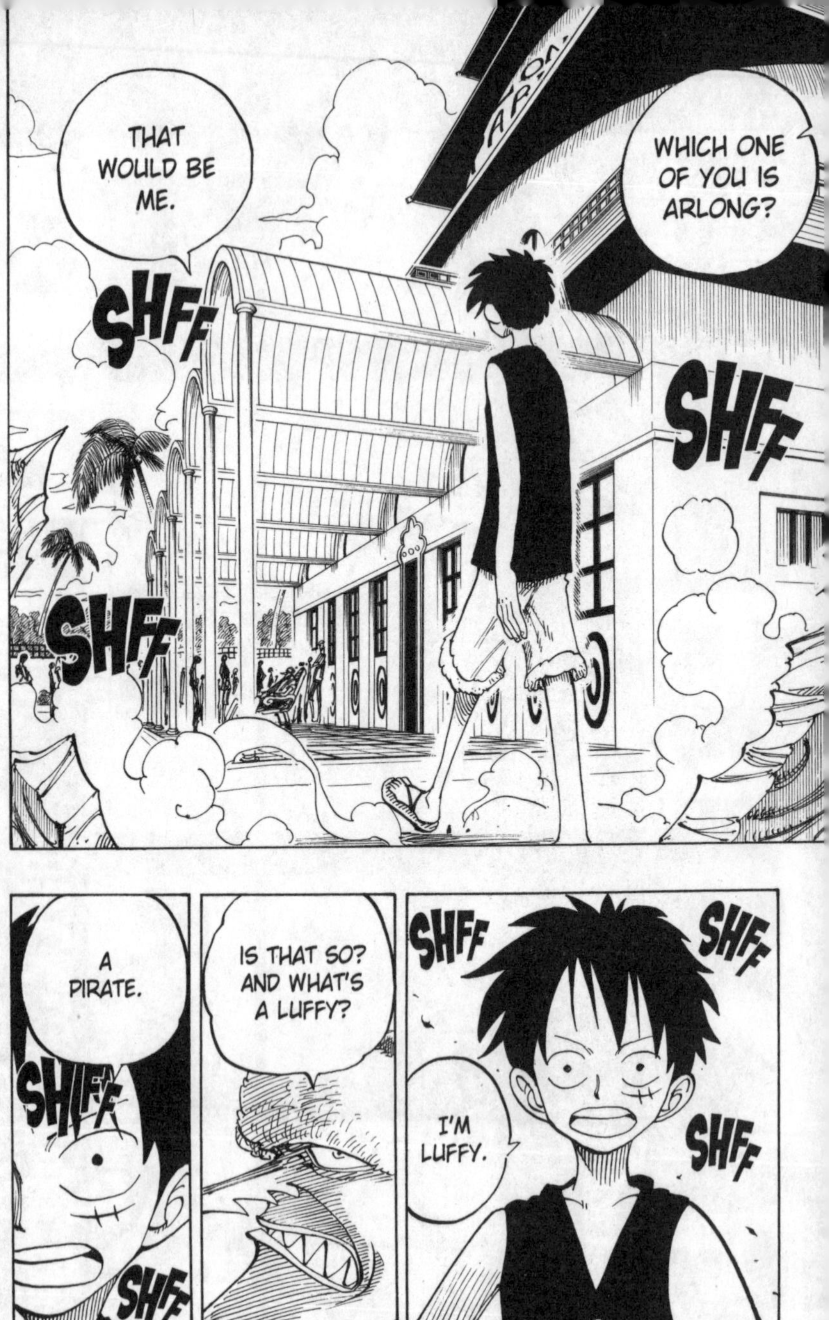
WHICH ONE OF YOU IS ARLONG?
THAT WOULD BE ME.
SHFF
SHFF
SHFF
SHFF
SHFF
I'M LUFFY.
SHFF
IS THAT SO? AND WHAT'S A LUFFY?
A PIRATE.
SHFF
SHFF

READ THIS WAY

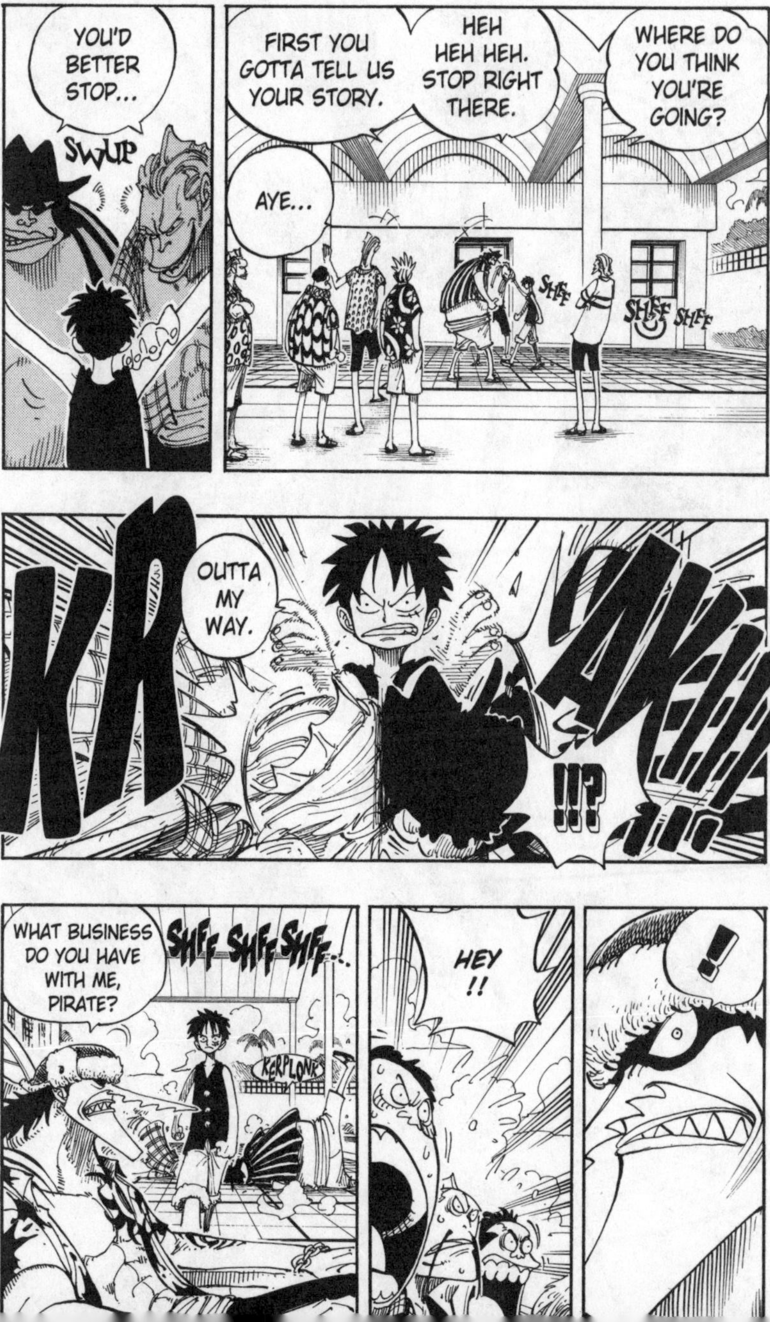
WHERE DO YOU THINK YOU'RE GOING?
HEH HEH HEH. STOP RIGHT THERE.
FIRST YOU GOTTA TELL US YOUR STORY.
AYE...
SHFF
SHFF SHFF
YOU'D BETTER STOP...
SWUP
KR
OUTTA MY WAY.
!!?
!
HEY !!
WHAT BUSINESS DO YOU HAVE WITH ME, PIRATE?
SHFF SHFF SHFF...
KERPLONK

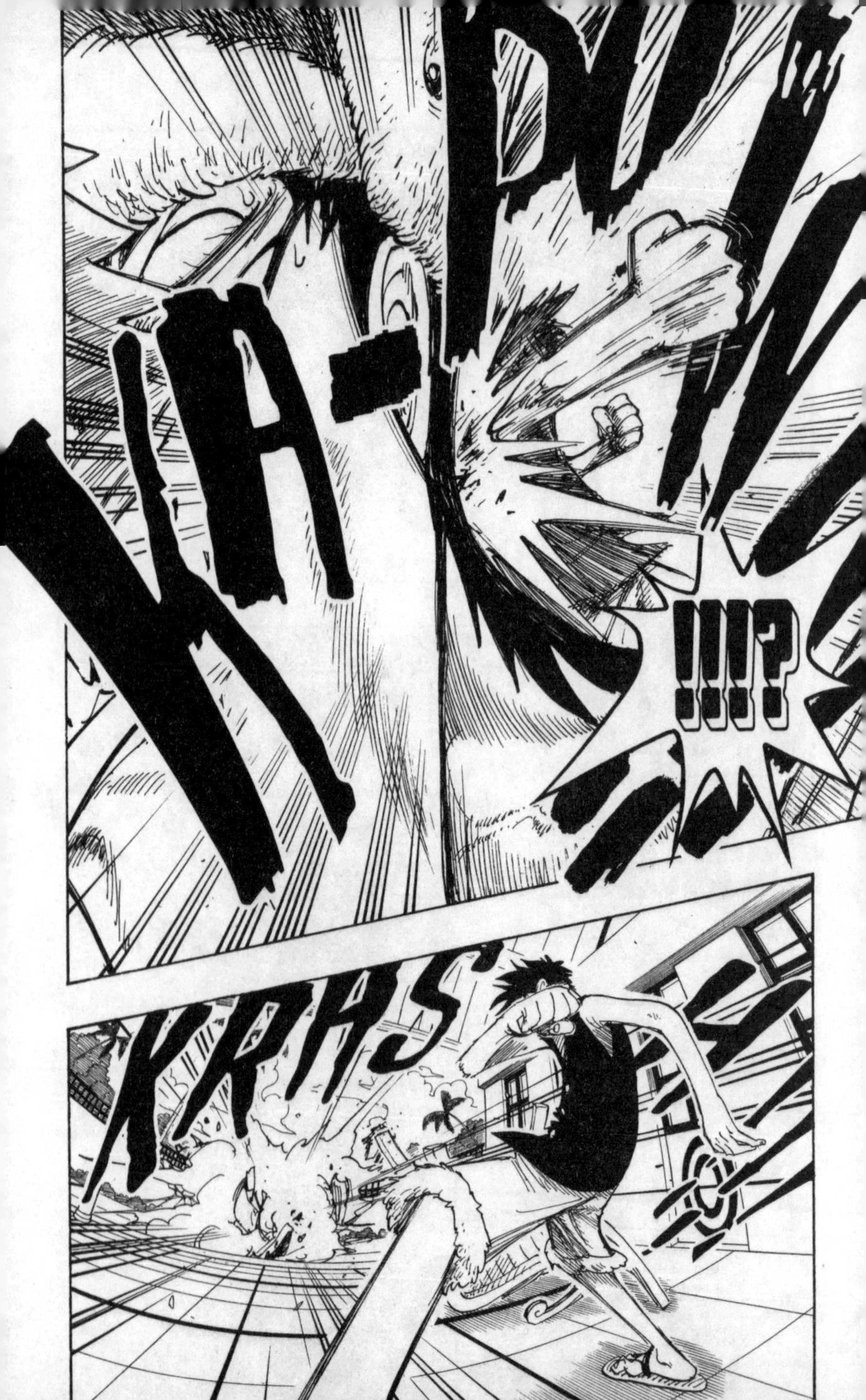
KA-
!!!?

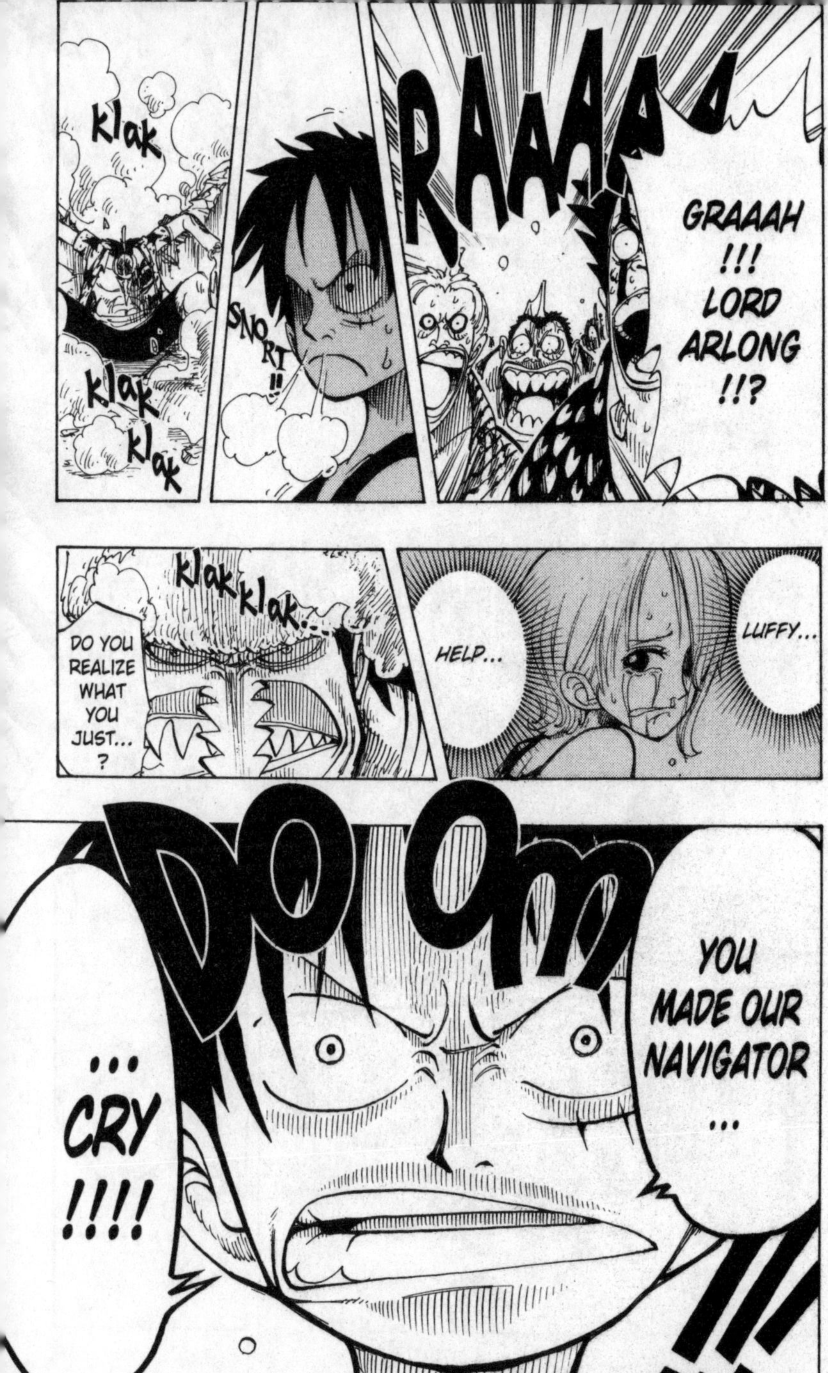
RAAAA
GRAAAH!!! LORD ARLONG!!?
SNORT!!
klak
klak
klak
LUFFY...
HELP...
klak klak...
DO YOU REALIZE WHAT YOU JUST...?
DOOM
YOU MADE OUR NAVIGATOR...
...CRY!!!!

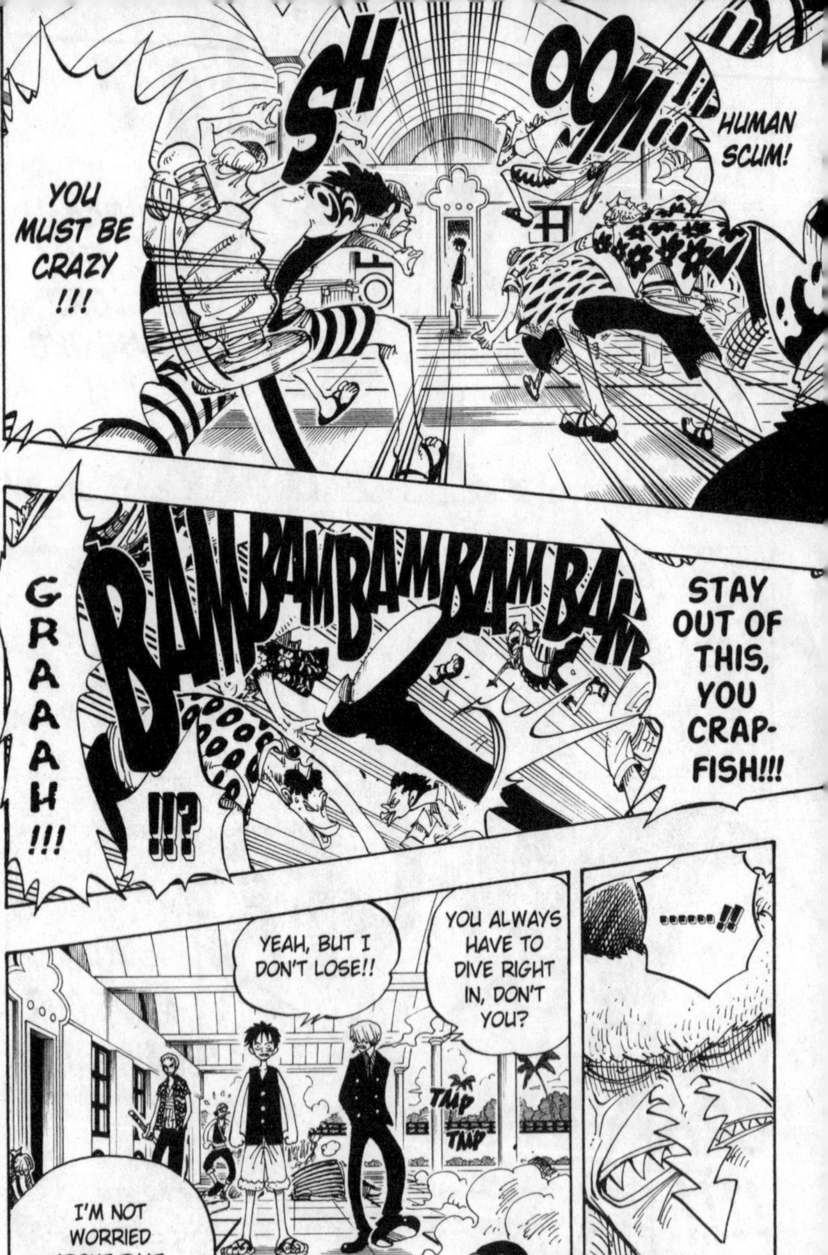
HUMAN SCUM!
SH
OOM!!
YOU MUST BE CRAZY!!!
STAY OUT OF THIS, YOU CRAP-FISH!!!
BAMBAMBAMBAMBAM
!!?
GRAAAAH!!!
......!!
YOU ALWAYS HAVE TO DIVE RIGHT IN, DON'T YOU?
YEAH, BUT I DON'T LOSE!!
TMP
TMP
I'M NOT WORRIED ABOUT THAT, DUMMY!!

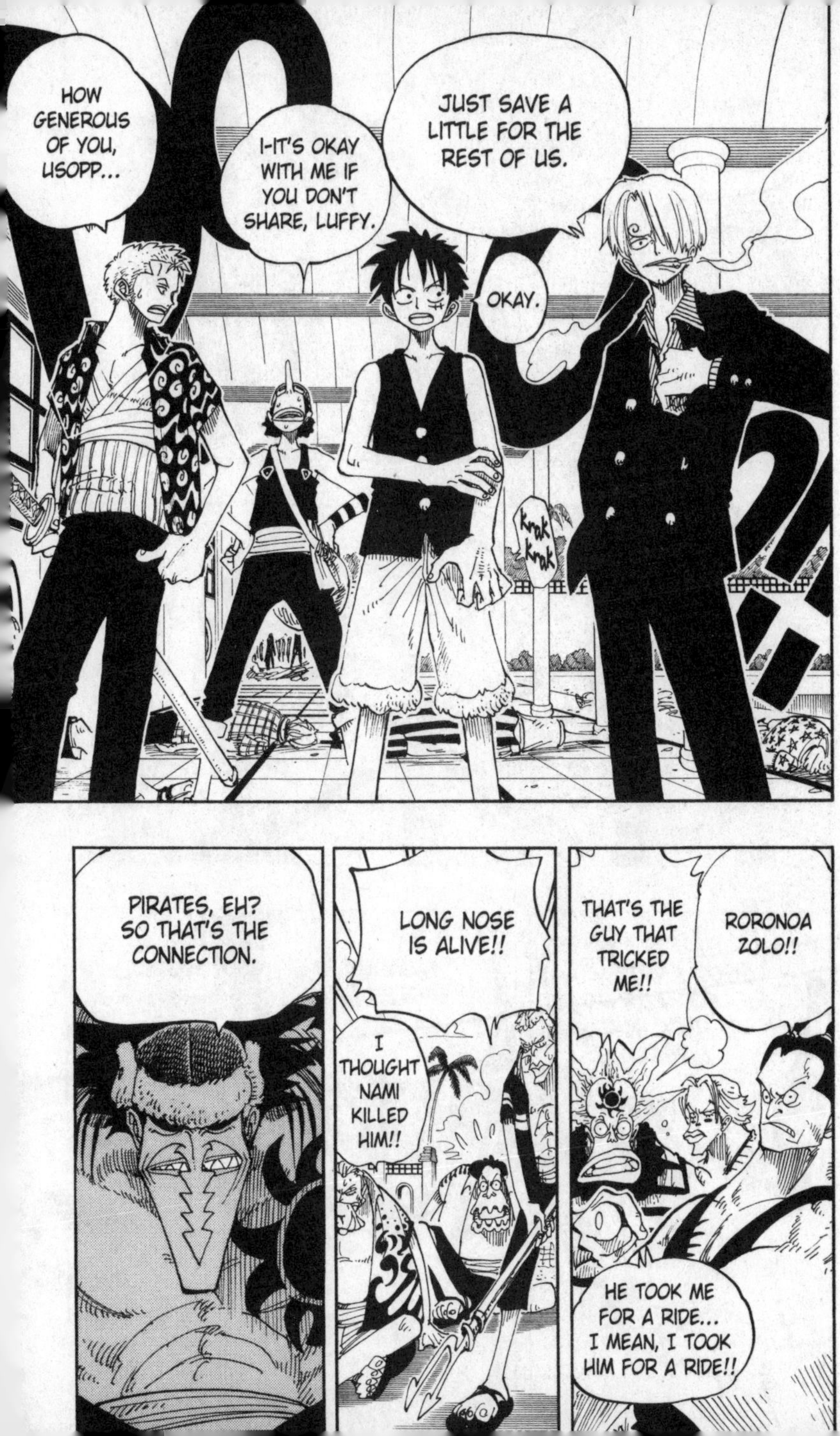
JUST SAVE A LITTLE FOR THE REST OF US.
OKAY.
I-IT'S OKAY WITH ME IF YOU DON'T SHARE, LUFFY.
HOW GENEROUS OF YOU, USOPP...
krak krak
RORONOA ZOLO!!
THAT'S THE GUY THAT TRICKED ME!!
HE TOOK ME FOR A RIDE... I MEAN, I TOOK HIM FOR A RIDE!!
LONG NOSE IS ALIVE!!
I THOUGHT NAMI KILLED HIM!!
PIRATES, EH? SO THAT'S THE CONNECTION.

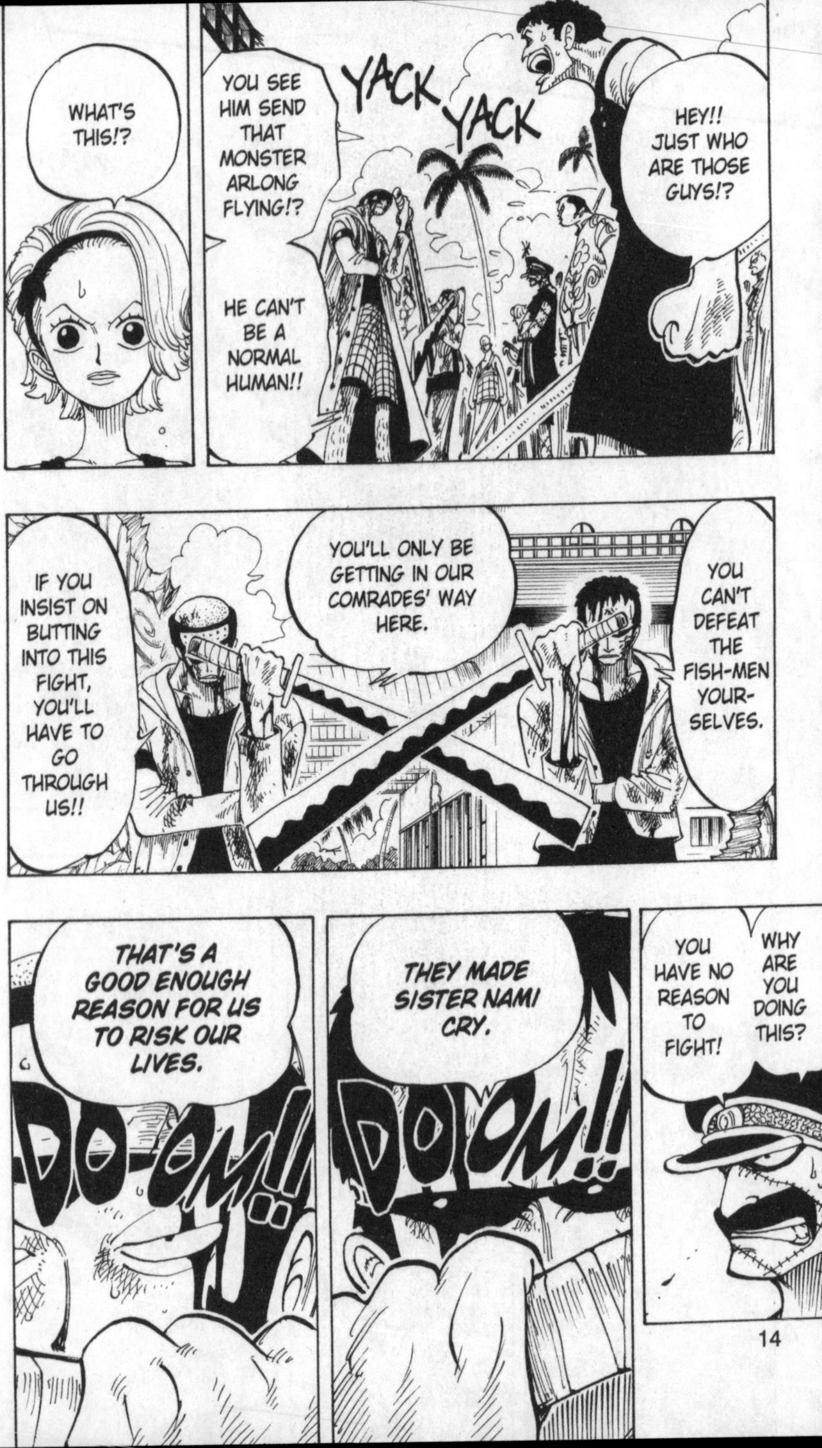
HEY!! JUST WHO ARE THOSE GUYS!?
YACK YACK
YOU SEE HIM SEND THAT MONSTER ARLONG FLYING!?
HE CAN'T BE A NORMAL HUMAN!!
WHAT'S THIS!?
YOU CAN'T DEFEAT THE FISH-MEN YOUR-SELVES.
YOU'LL ONLY BE GETTING IN OUR COMRADES' WAY HERE.
IF YOU INSIST ON BUTTING INTO THIS FIGHT, YOU'LL HAVE TO GO THROUGH US!!
WHY ARE YOU DOING THIS?
YOU HAVE NO REASON TO FIGHT!
THEY MADE SISTER NAMI CRY.
DOOM!!
THAT'S A GOOD ENOUGH REASON FOR US TO RISK OUR LIVES.
DO-OM!!

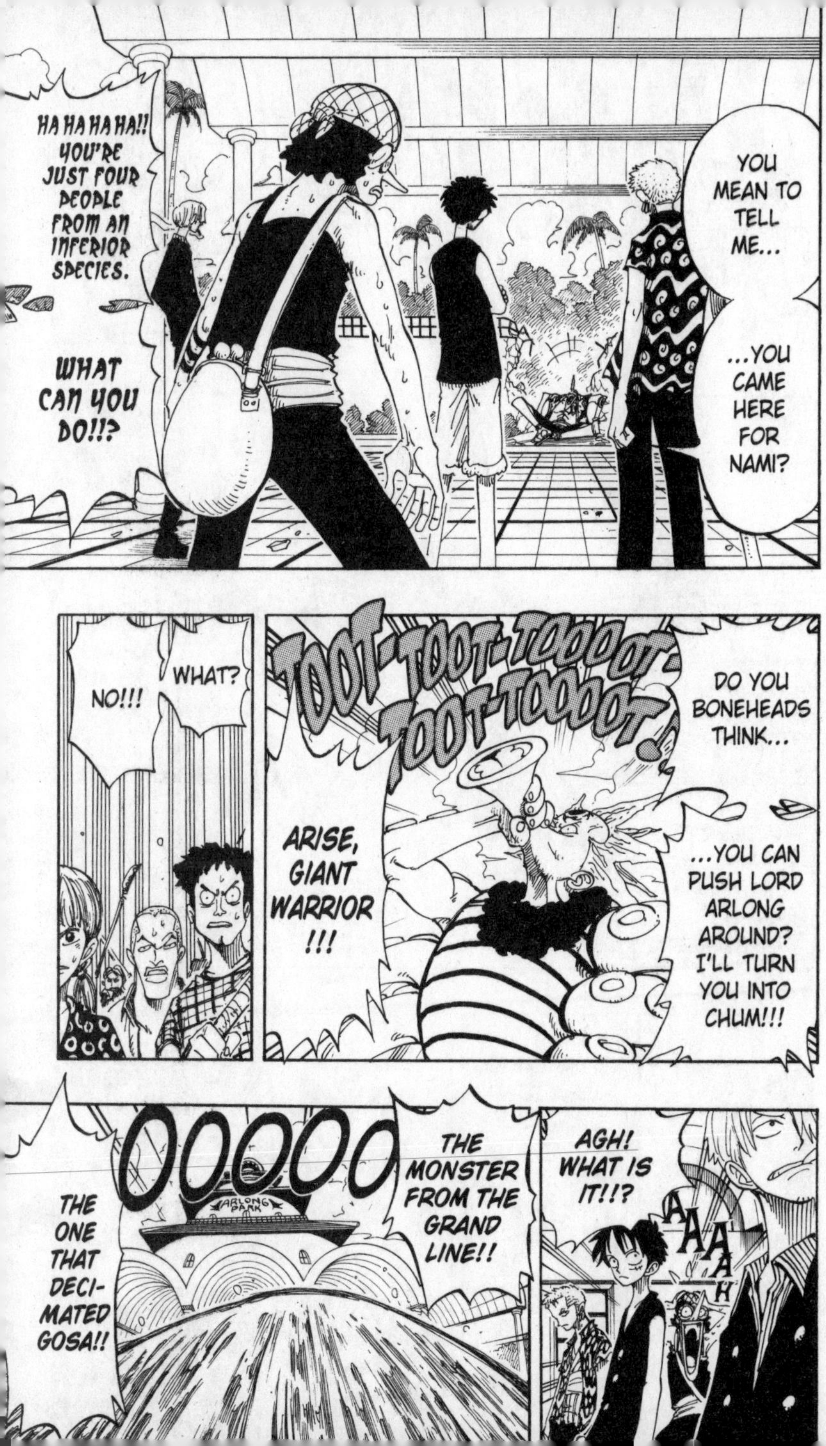
YOU MEAN TO TELL ME...
...YOU CAME HERE FOR NAMI?
HA HA HA HA!! YOU'RE JUST FOUR PEOPLE FROM AN INFERIOR SPECIES.
WHAT CAN YOU DO!!?
DO YOU BONEHEADS THINK...
...YOU CAN PUSH LORD ARLONG AROUND? I'LL TURN YOU INTO CHUM!!!
TOOT-TOOT-TOOOOT-TOOT-TOOOOT
ARISE, GIANT WARRIOR!!!
WHAT?
NO!!!
AGH! WHAT IS IT!!?
AAAAH
OOOOO
ARLONG PARK
THE MONSTER FROM THE GRAND LINE!!
THE ONE THAT DECIMATED GOSA!!

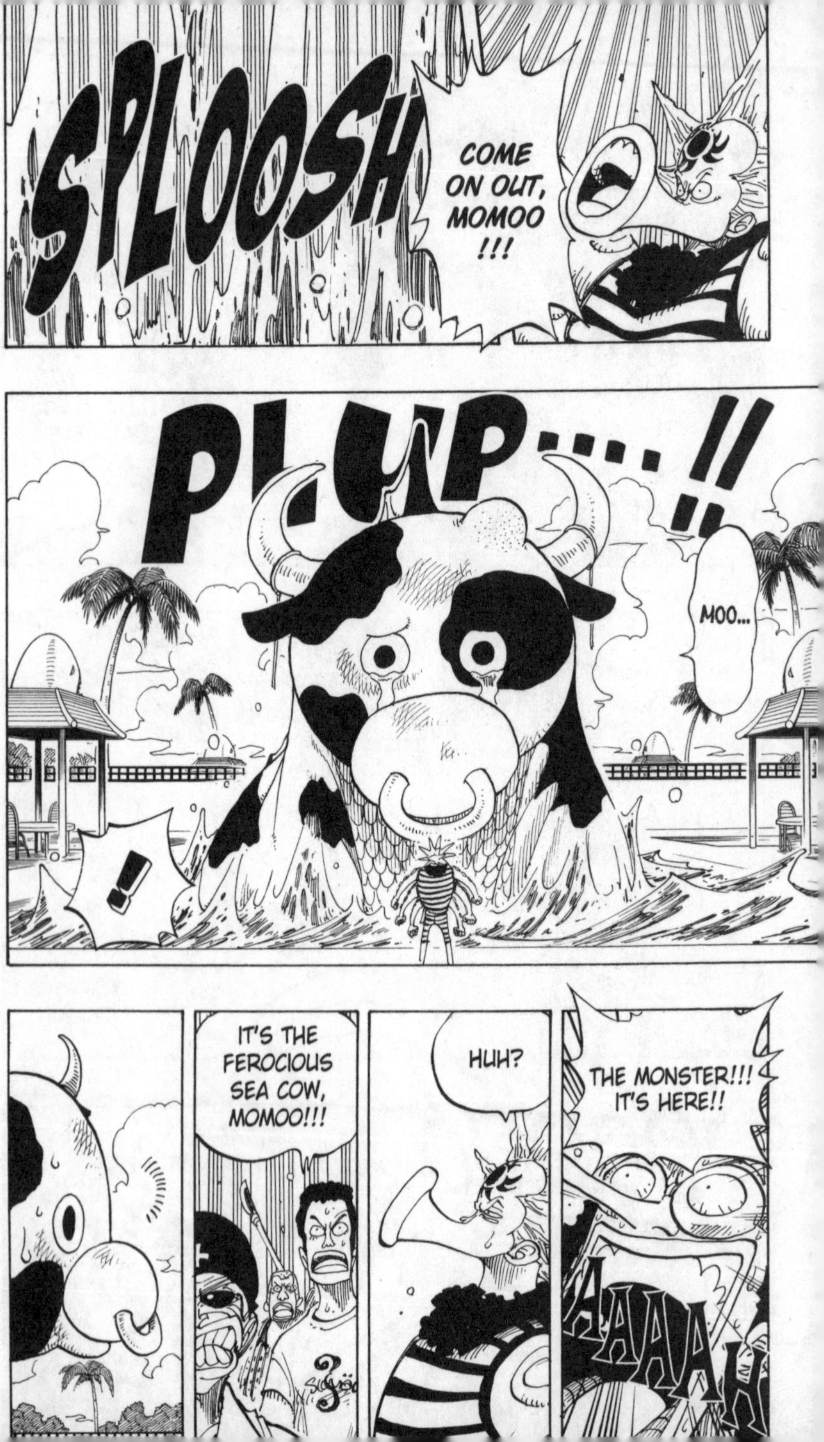
SPLOOSH
COME ON OUT, MOMOO !!!
PLUP...!!
MOO...
!
THE MONSTER!!! IT'S HERE!!
HUH?
IT'S THE FEROCIOUS SEA COW, MOMOO!!!
AAAAH

OH, IT'S JUST HIM.

SO HE WORKS FOR THESE GUYS.

!!!

FLINCH!!

WHERE ARE YOU GOING!!?

WAIT, MOMOO!!

MOO-HOO!!!

WHAT DO YOU THINK YOU'RE DOING?

MOMOO?

...I WON'T STOP YOU.

WELL, IF YOU WANT TO RUN AWAY...

SHLAKE!!

shake shake

shake shake

GO AHEAD, MOMOO.

HERE HE COMES !!!!

MOOOOOO!!!!

SPLLASH!!!

19

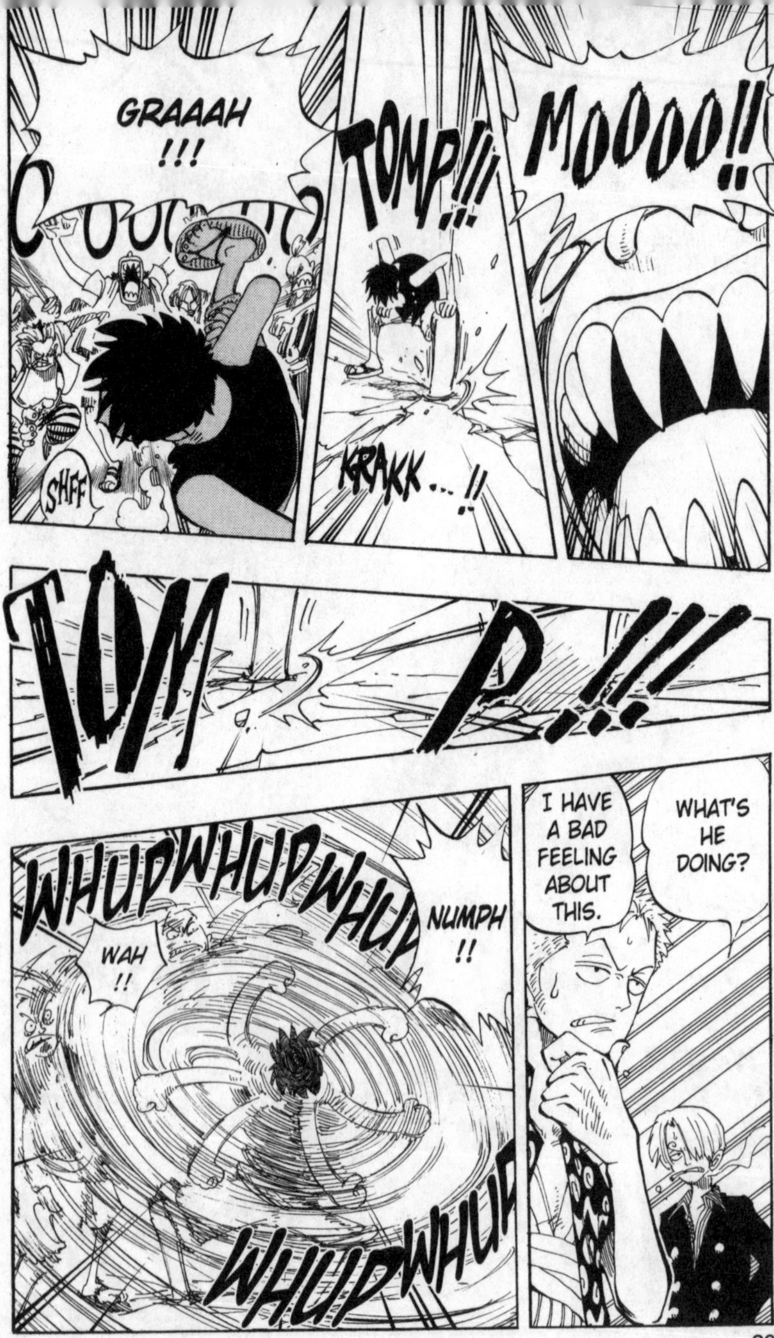
MOOOOO!!
TOMP!!!
KRAKK...!!
GRAAAH !!!
SHFF
TOMP!!!
WHAT'S HE DOING?
I HAVE A BAD FEELING ABOUT THIS.
WHUPWHUPWHUP
NUMPH !!
WAH !!
WHUPWHUP

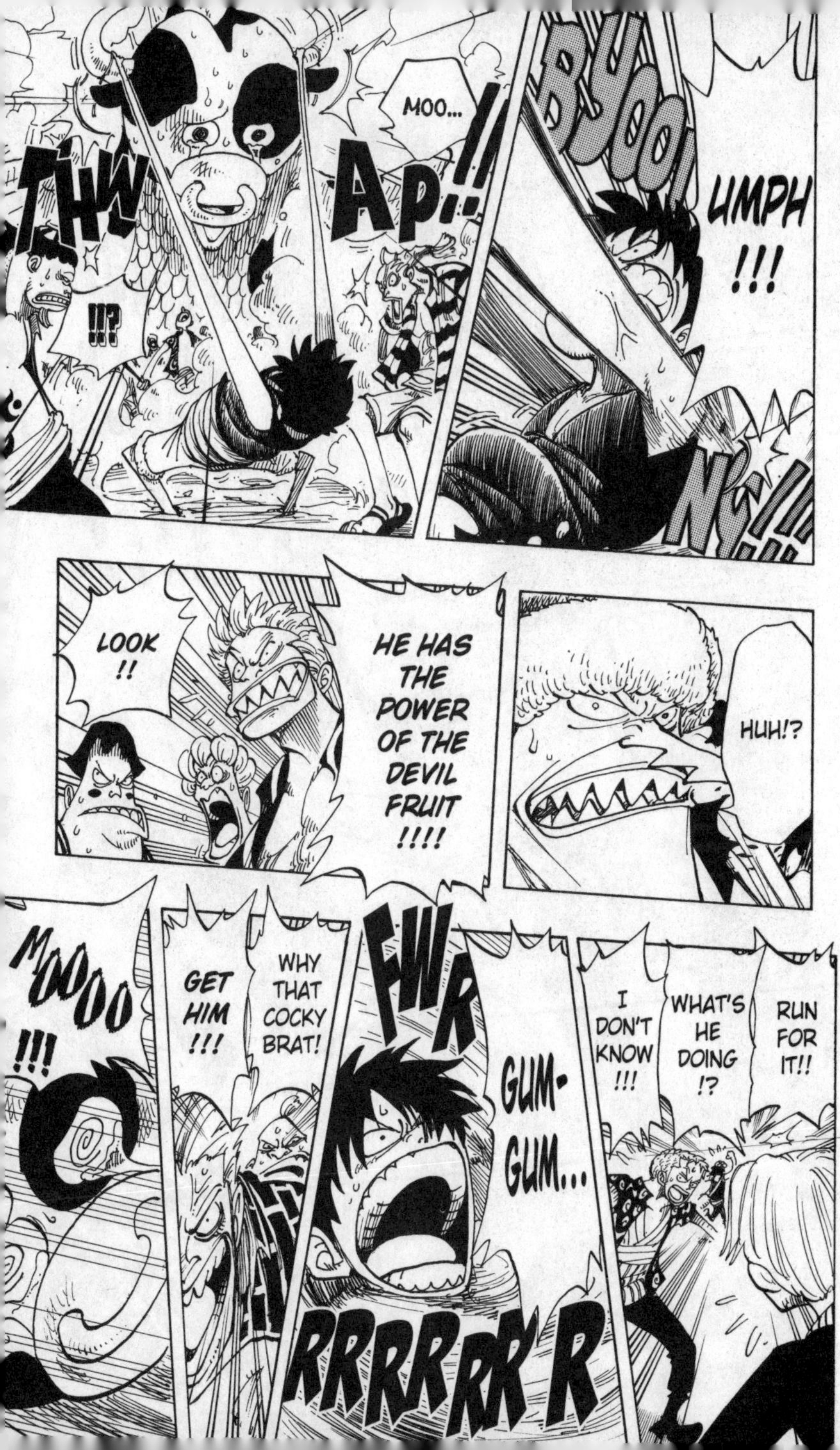

BYOO
UMPH !!!
N!!!
MOO...
THWAP!!
!!?
HUH!?
HE HAS THE POWER OF THE DEVIL FRUIT !!!!
LOOK !!
RUN FOR IT!!
WHAT'S HE DOING !?
I DON'T KNOW !!!
GUM-GUM...
FWR
RRRRRRK R
WHY THAT COCKY BRAT!
GET HIM !!!
MOOOO !!!

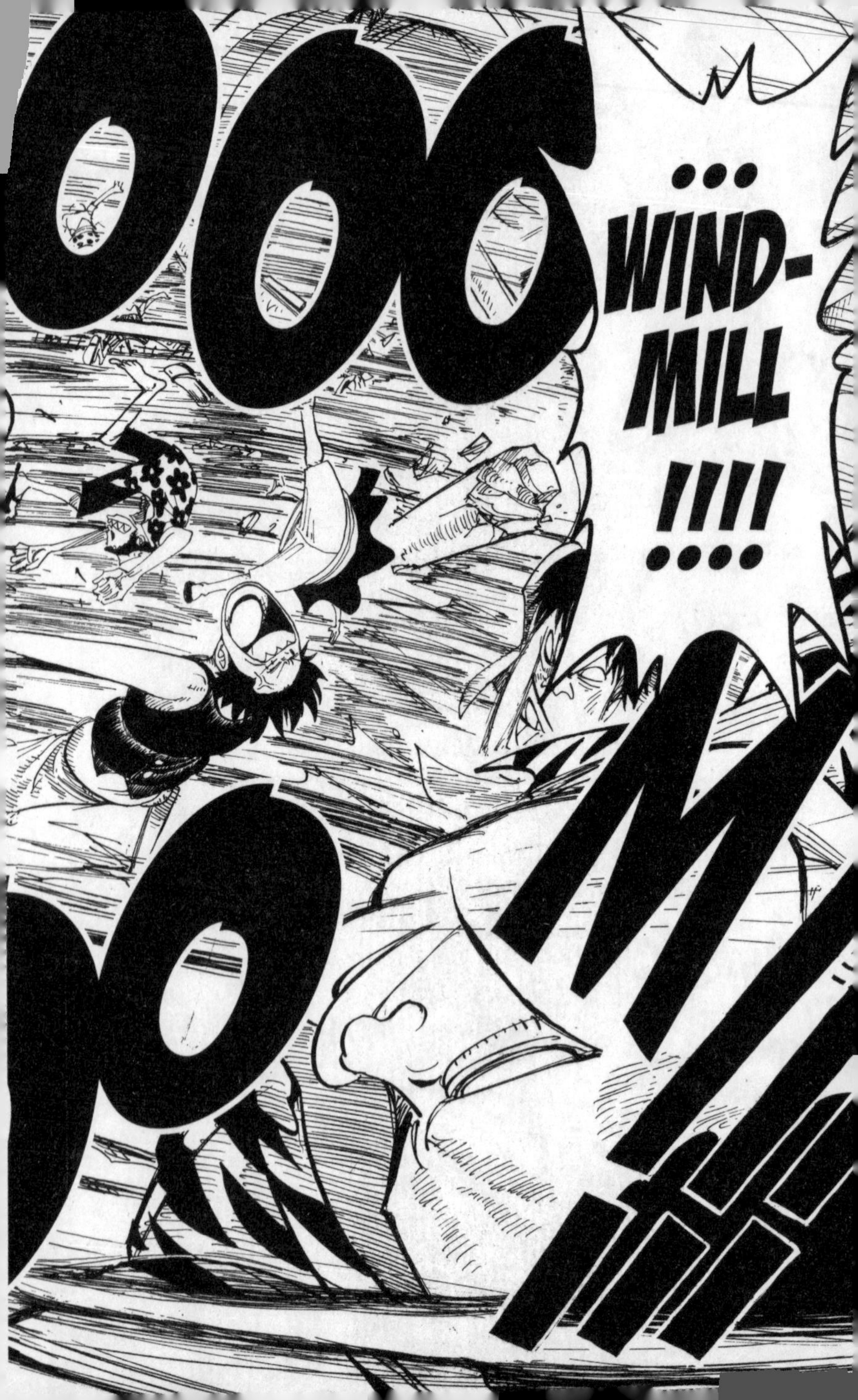
...WIND-MILL!!!!....

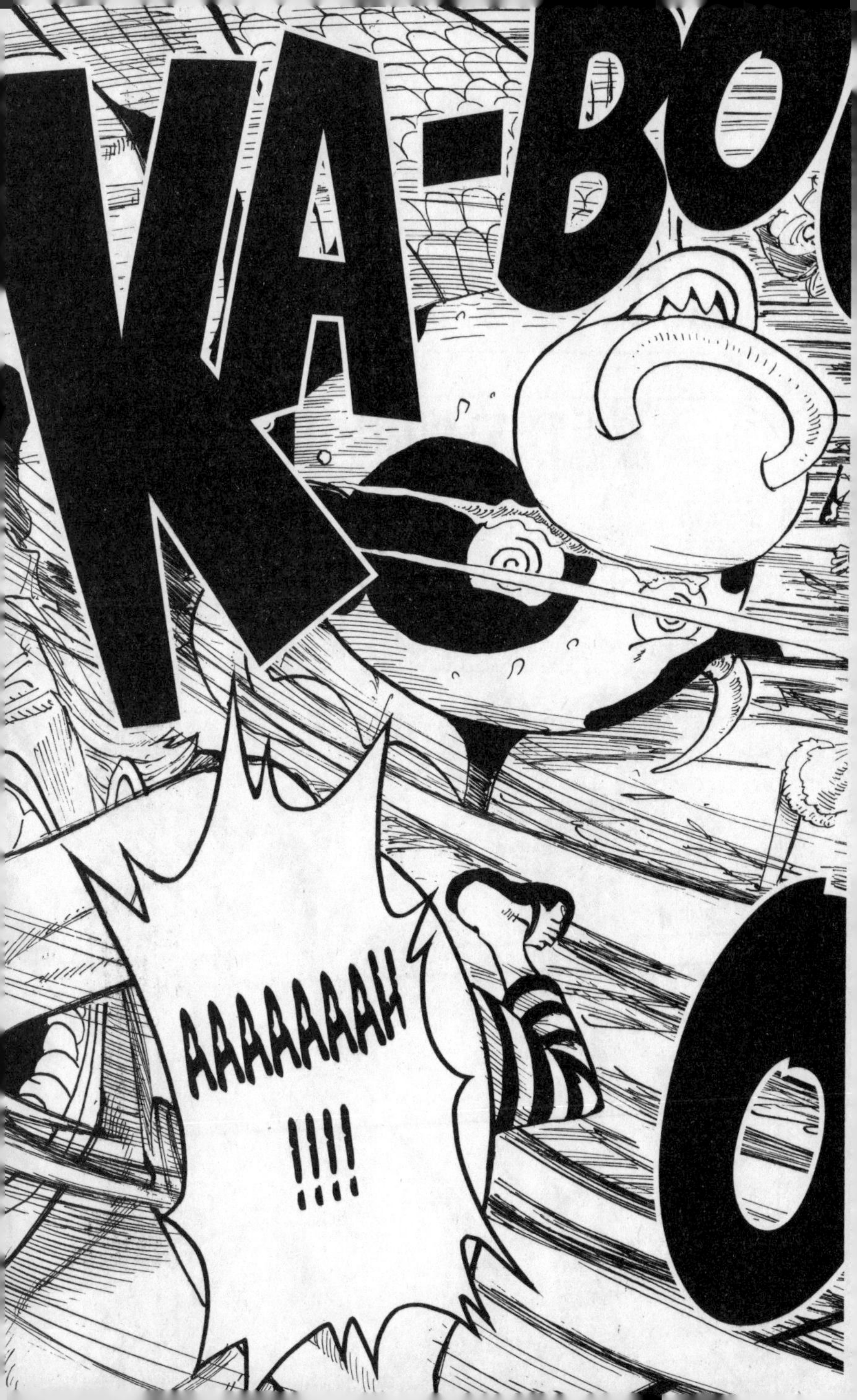
KA-BOOM
AAAAAAH
!!!!

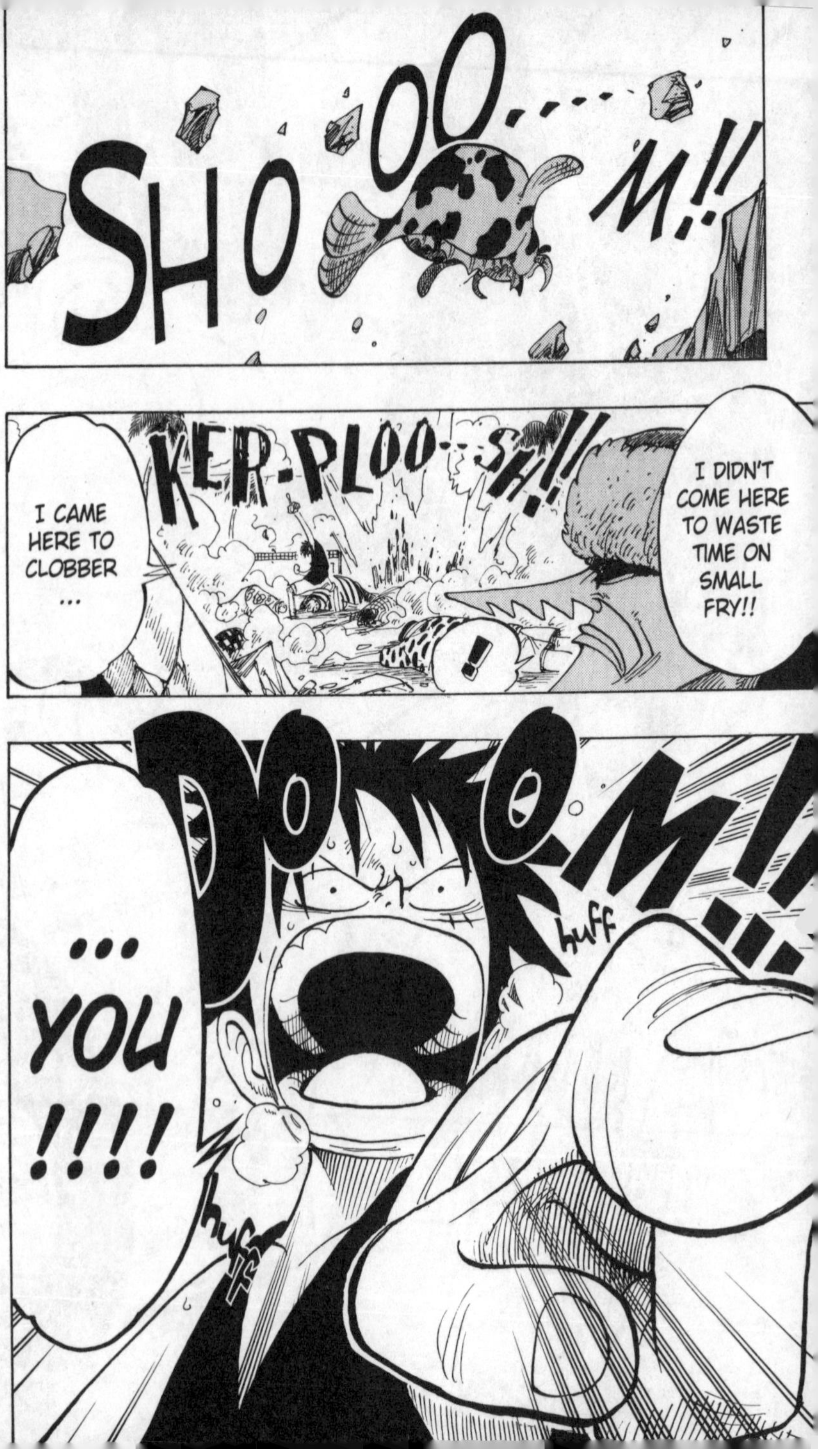
SHOOOO...M!!
KER-PLOO--SH!!
I DIDN'T COME HERE TO WASTE TIME ON SMALL FRY!!
I CAME HERE TO CLOBBER ...
!
DOOOM!!!
huff
... YOU !!!!
huff

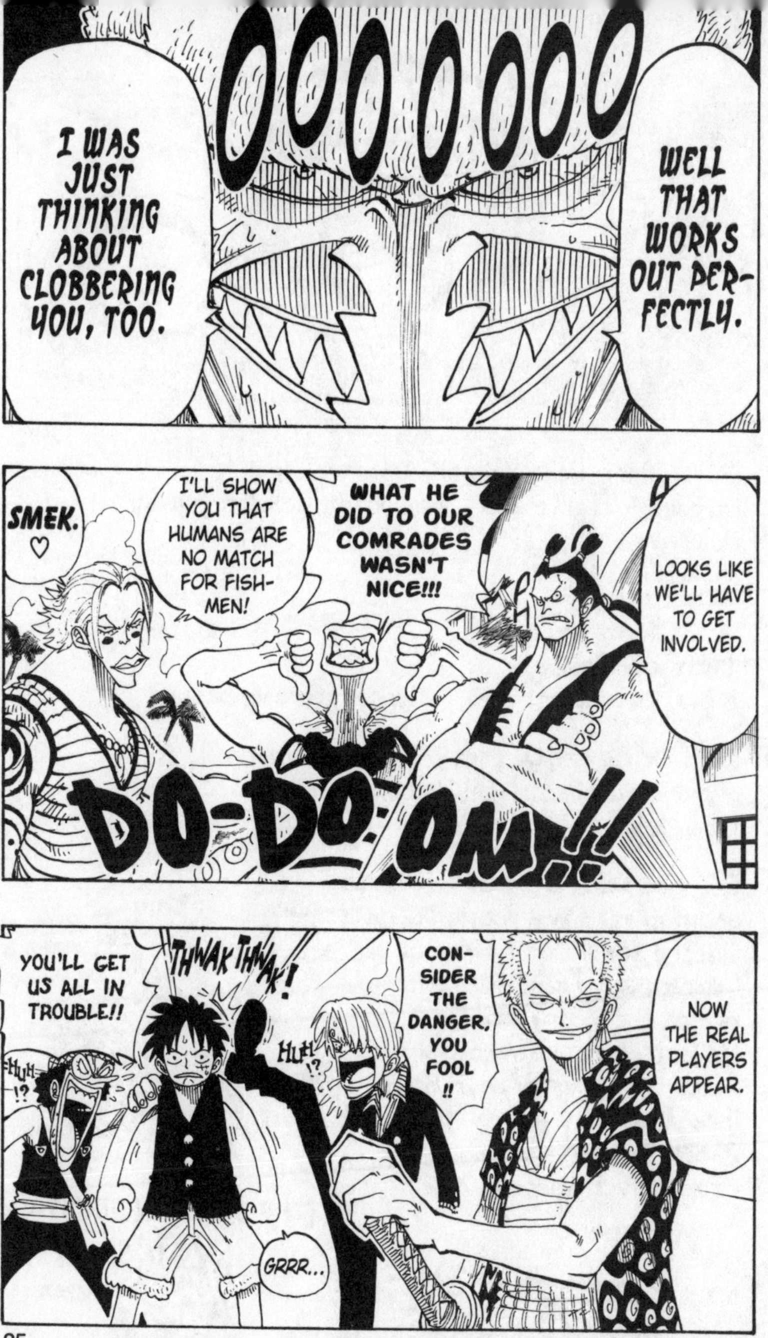
OOOOOOO
WELL THAT WORKS OUT PER-FECTLY.
I WAS JUST THINKING ABOUT CLOBBERING YOU, TOO.
LOOKS LIKE WE'LL HAVE TO GET INVOLVED.
WHAT HE DID TO OUR COMRADES WASN'T NICE!!!
I'LL SHOW YOU THAT HUMANS ARE NO MATCH FOR FISH-MEN!
SMEK. ♡
DO-DO-OM!!
NOW THE REAL PLAYERS APPEAR.
CON-SIDER THE DANGER, YOU FOOL!!
HUH!?
THWAK THWAK!
YOU'LL GET US ALL IN TROUBLE!!
HUH!?
GRRR...

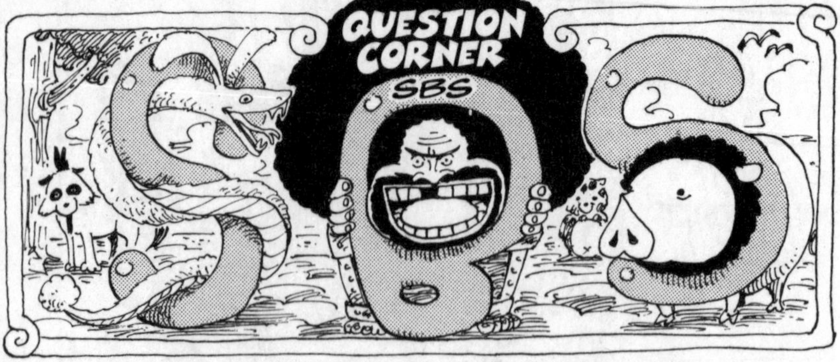
QUESTION CORNER
SBS

Q: This is Timmy Ueda of the SBS Takeover Gang!
I'm going to begin the SBS Question Corner before you do, Oda Sensei!!
SBS will now begin!!

A: Agh! Oh no, you did it!
Darn you, Timmy.
Now I can't do it! Well, I guess it's already begun.

Q: Hello, Oda Sensei. On page 92 of volume 8, in panel 6, it says "Find Panda Man," but I can't find him. Where is he?

A: Oh, that. I got a lot of postcards about that. Some people found him and some didn't. First of all, I didn't even expect people to notice those tiny words. Nevertheless, I'll give the answer. Inside the lower circle, it does indeed say, "Find Panda Man!!!" And Panda Man can be seen in the circle at the upper right.

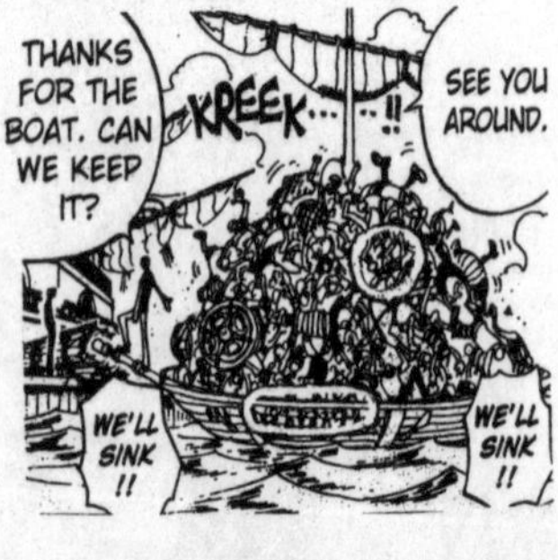
SEE YOU AROUND.
KREEK
!!
THANKS FOR THE BOAT. CAN WE KEEP IT?
WE'LL SINK !!
WE'LL SINK !!

(THE SCENE IN QUESTION)

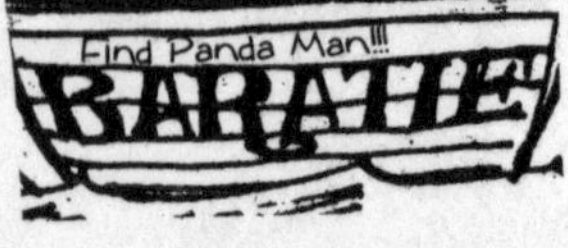
Find Panda Man!!!
BARATIE

⬅ Close-up, lower left

Close-up, upper right ➡

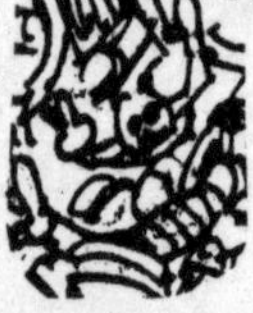

⬅ He's making a peace sign.

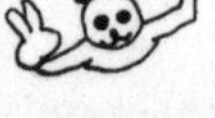

Chapter 83: LUFFY IN BLACK

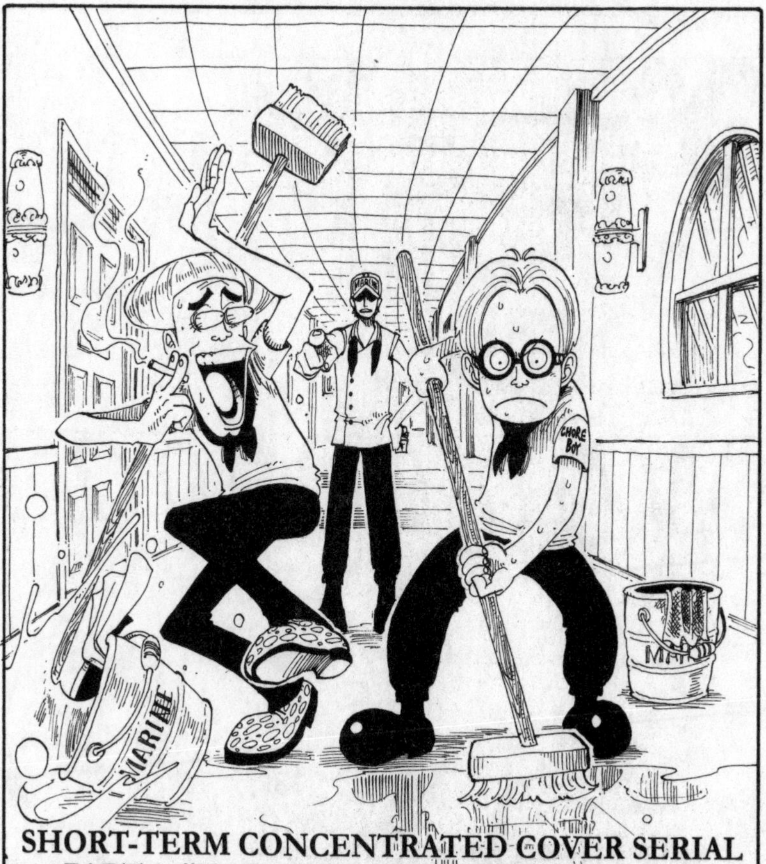
CHORE BOY
MARINE

SHORT-TERM CONCENTRATED COVER SERIAL
PART 2: "KOBY AND HELMEPPO–LATER"

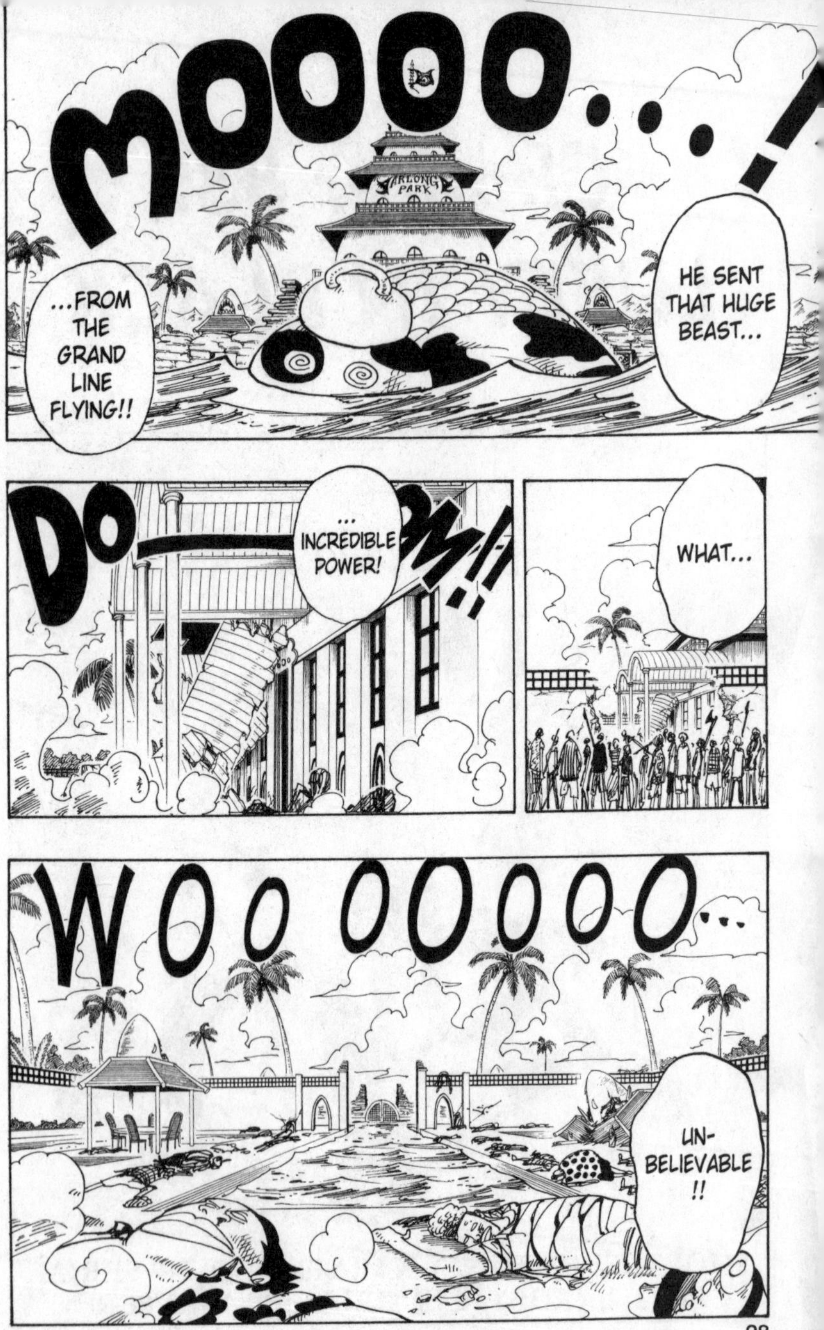
MOOOO...!!
HE SENT THAT HUGE BEAST...
...FROM THE GRAND LINE FLYING!!
WHAT...
DO—OM!!
...INCREDIBLE POWER!
WOOOOOO...
UN-BELIEVABLE!!

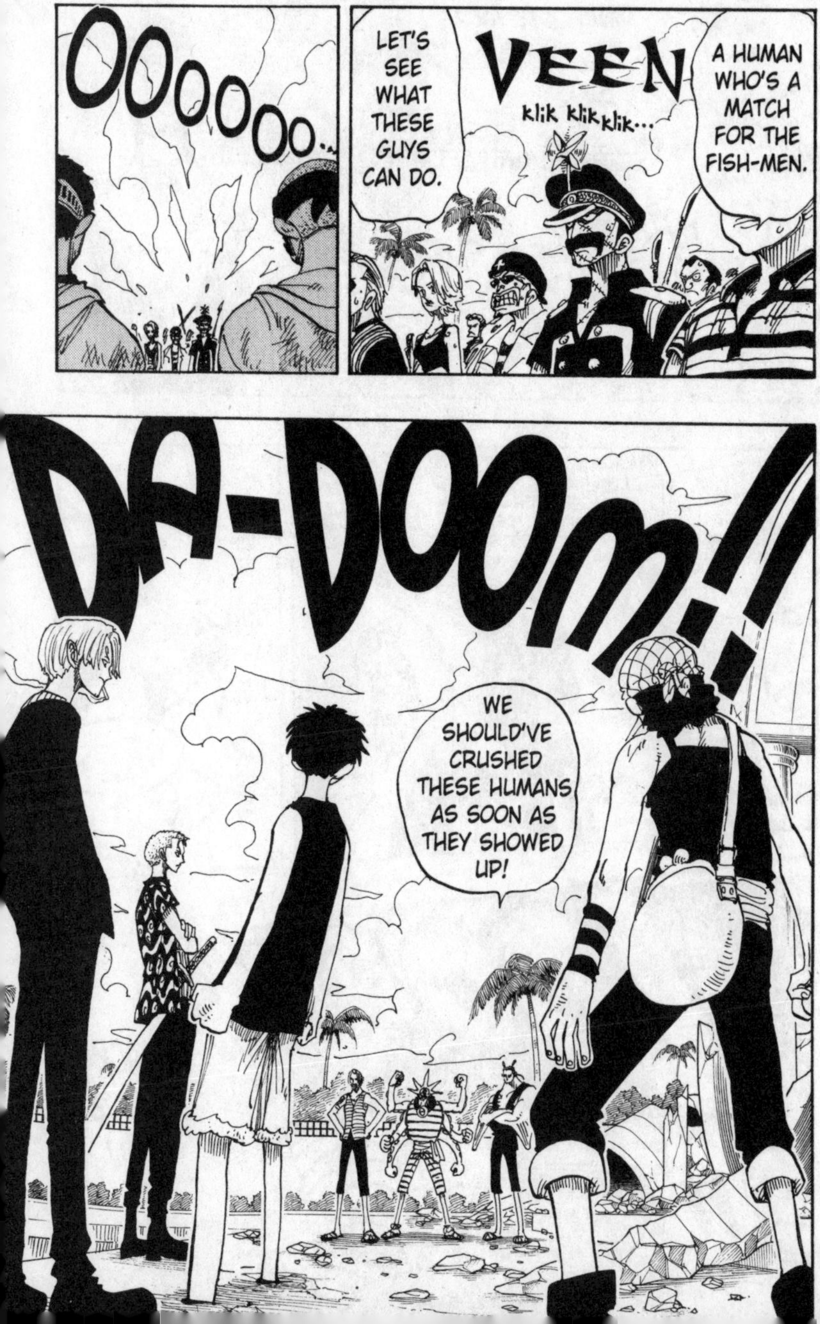
A HUMAN WHO'S A MATCH FOR THE FISH-MEN.
VEEN
klik klik klik...
LET'S SEE WHAT THESE GUYS CAN DO.
OOOOOO...
DA-DOOM!!
WE SHOULD'VE CRUSHED THESE HUMANS AS SOON AS THEY SHOWED UP!

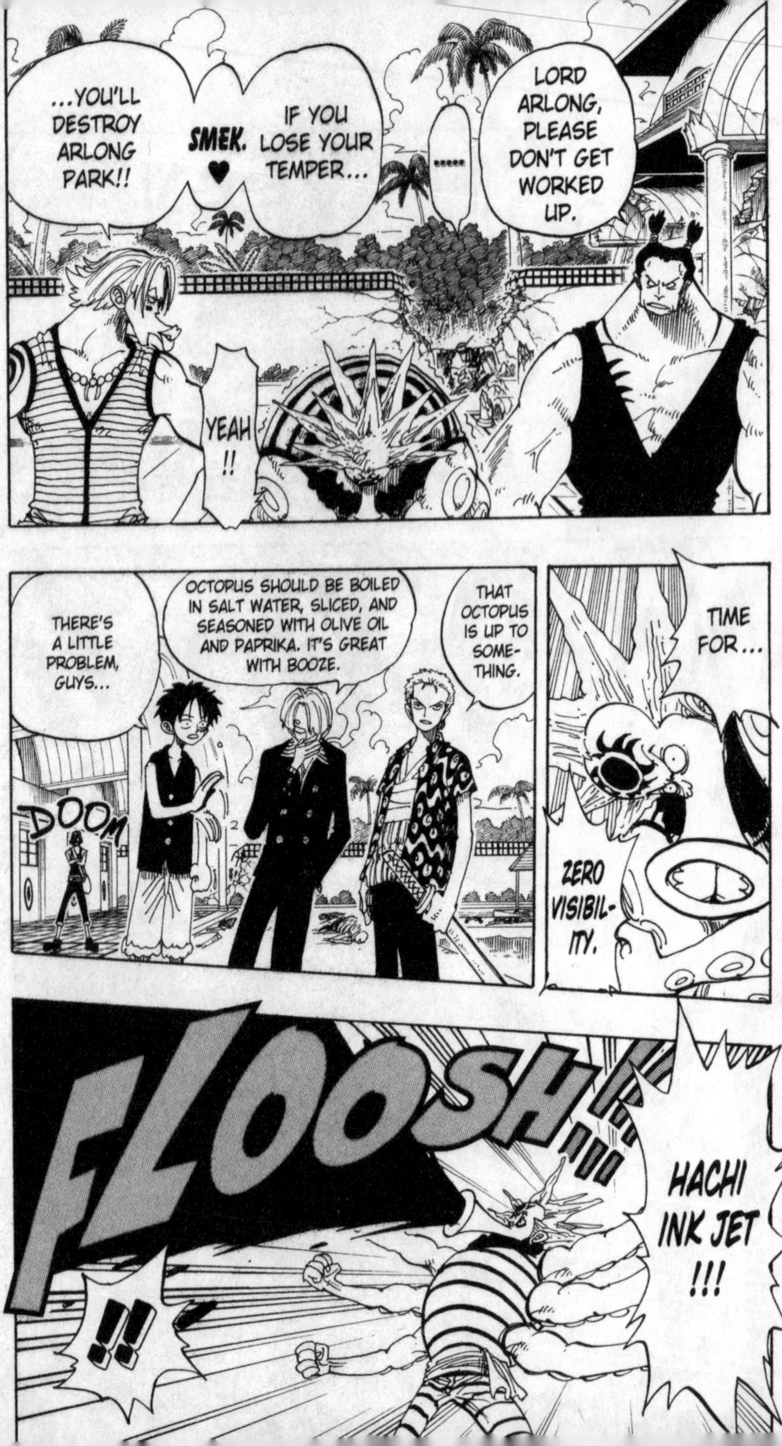
LORD ARLONG, PLEASE DON'T GET WORKED UP.
.....
IF YOU LOSE YOUR TEMPER...
SMEK. ♥
...YOU'LL DESTROY ARLONG PARK!!
YEAH!!
TIME FOR...
ZERO VISIBIL-ITY.
THAT OCTOPUS IS UP TO SOME-THING.
OCTOPUS SHOULD BE BOILED IN SALT WATER, SLICED, AND SEASONED WITH OLIVE OIL AND PAPRIKA. IT'S GREAT WITH BOOZE.
THERE'S A LITTLE PROBLEM, GUYS...
DOOM
HACHI INK JET!!!
FLOOSH!!!
!!

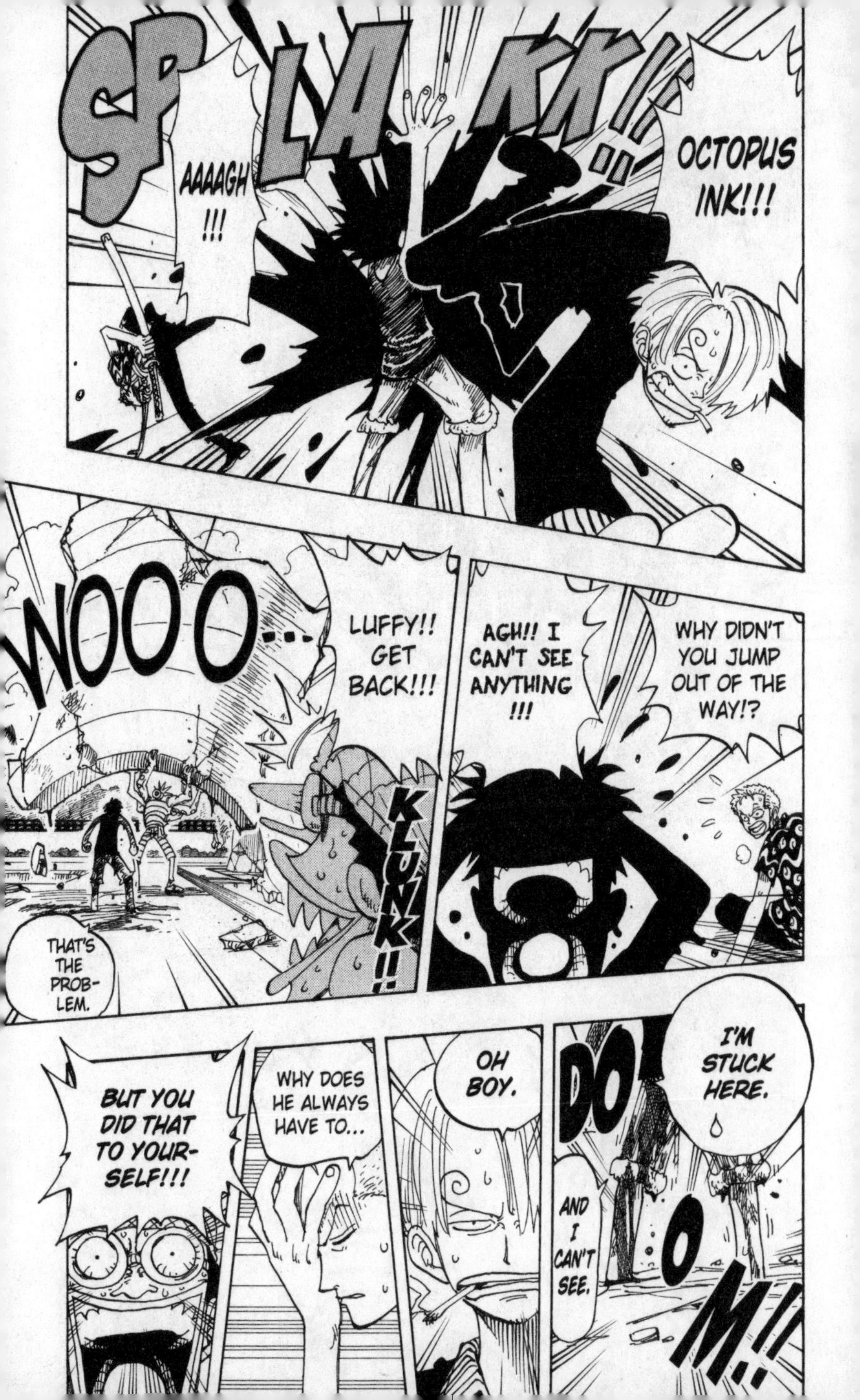
SPLAKK!!
OCTOPUS INK!!!
AAAAGH !!!
WHY DIDN'T YOU JUMP OUT OF THE WAY!?
AGH!! I CAN'T SEE ANYTHING !!!
LUFFY!! GET BACK!!!
WOOO...
KLUNK!!
THAT'S THE PROB-LEM.
I'M STUCK HERE.
DOOM!!
AND I CAN'T SEE.
OH BOY.
WHY DOES HE ALWAYS HAVE TO...
BUT YOU DID THAT TO YOUR-SELF!!!

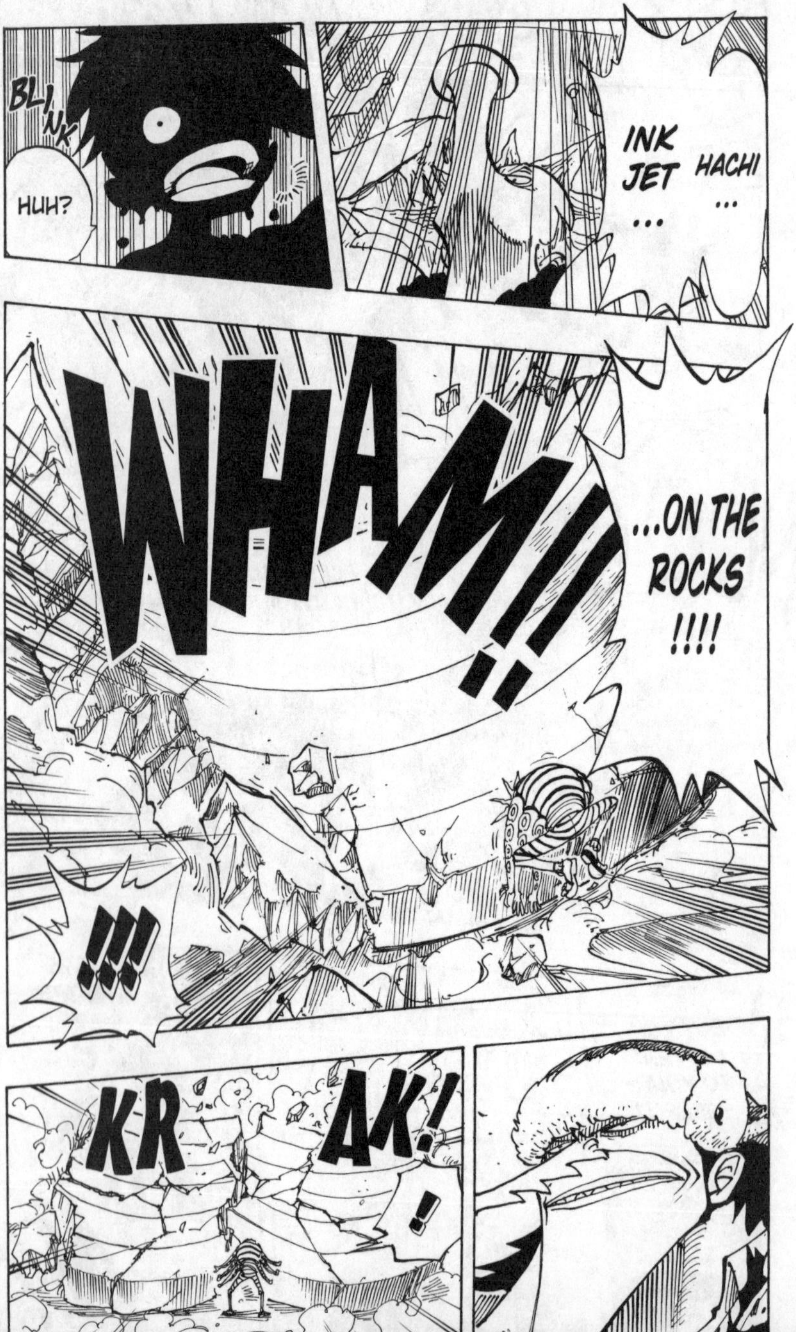
HACHI ...
INK JET ...
BLINK
HUH?
WHAM!!
...ON THE ROCKS !!!!
!!!
KRAK!!

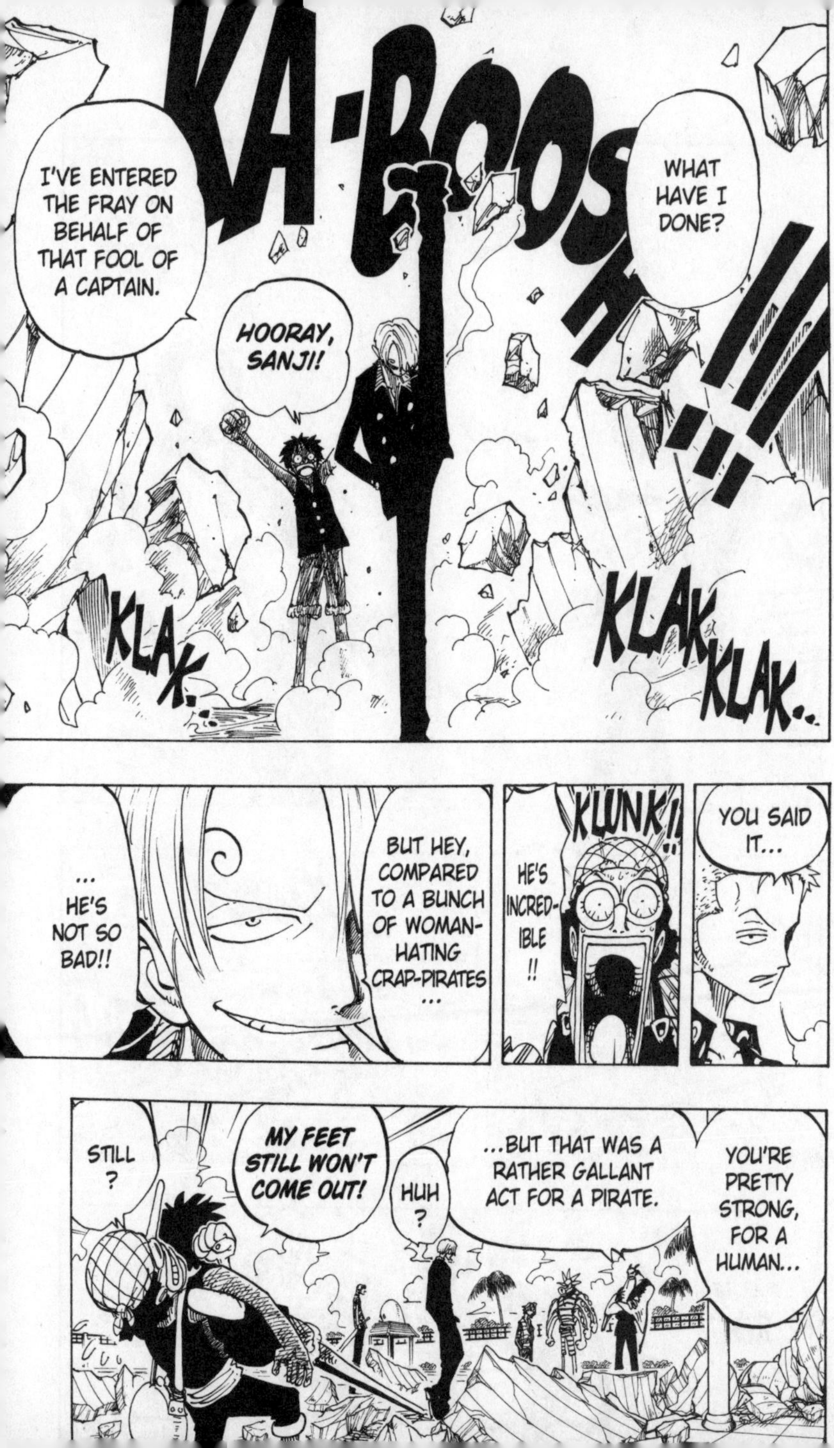
KA-BOOSH!!!
WHAT HAVE I DONE?
I'VE ENTERED THE FRAY ON BEHALF OF THAT FOOL OF A CAPTAIN.
HOORAY, SANJI!
KLAK KLAK KLAK...
KLAK.
YOU SAID IT...
KLUNK!!
HE'S INCRED-IBLE !!
BUT HEY, COMPARED TO A BUNCH OF WOMAN-HATING CRAP-PIRATES ...
... HE'S NOT SO BAD!!
YOU'RE PRETTY STRONG, FOR A HUMAN...
...BUT THAT WAS A RATHER GALLANT ACT FOR A PIRATE.
HUH ?
MY FEET STILL WON'T COME OUT!
STILL ?

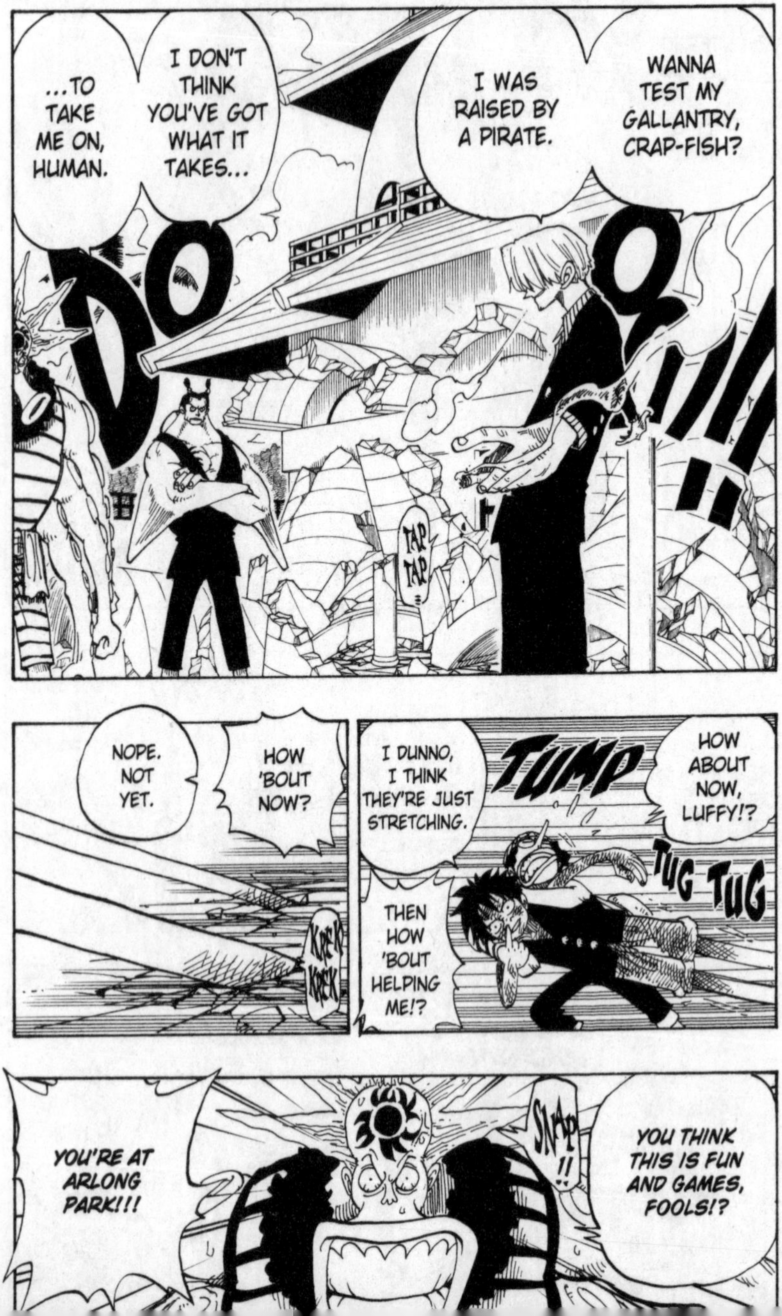
WANNA TEST MY GALLANTRY, CRAP-FISH?
I WAS RAISED BY A PIRATE.
I DON'T THINK YOU'VE GOT WHAT IT TAKES...
...TO TAKE ME ON, HUMAN.
TAP TAP
HOW ABOUT NOW, LUFFY!?
TUMP
TUG TUG
I DUNNO, I THINK THEY'RE JUST STRETCHING.
THEN HOW 'BOUT HELPING ME!?
HOW 'BOUT NOW?
NOPE. NOT YET.
KREK KREK
YOU THINK THIS IS FUN AND GAMES, FOOLS!?
SNAP!!
YOU'RE AT ARLONG PARK!!!

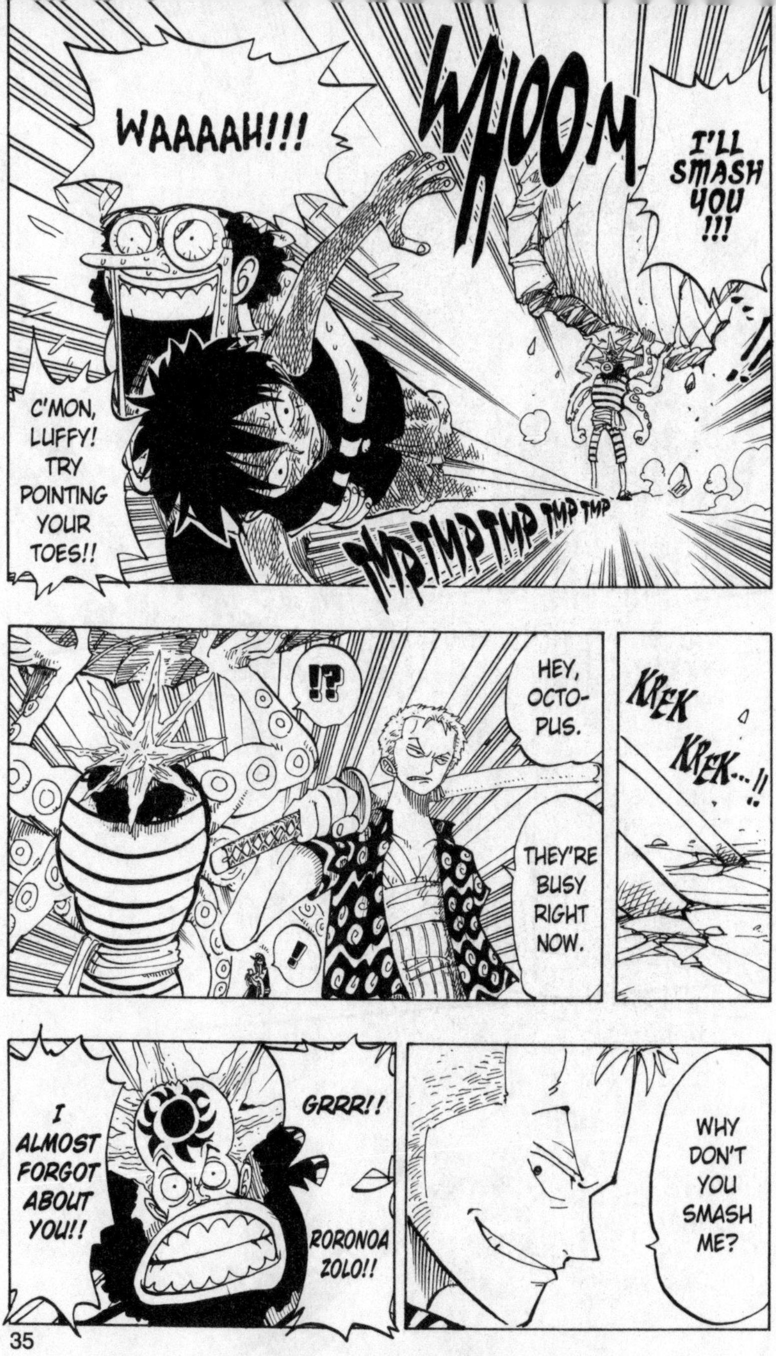
I'LL SMASH YOU!!!
WHOOM
WAAAAH!!!
C'MON, LUFFY! TRY POINTING YOUR TOES!!
TMP TMP TMP TMP TMP
KREK KREK...!!
HEY, OCTO-PUS.
THEY'RE BUSY RIGHT NOW.
!?
!
WHY DON'T YOU SMASH ME?
GRRR!!
I ALMOST FORGOT ABOUT YOU!!
RORONOA ZOLO!!

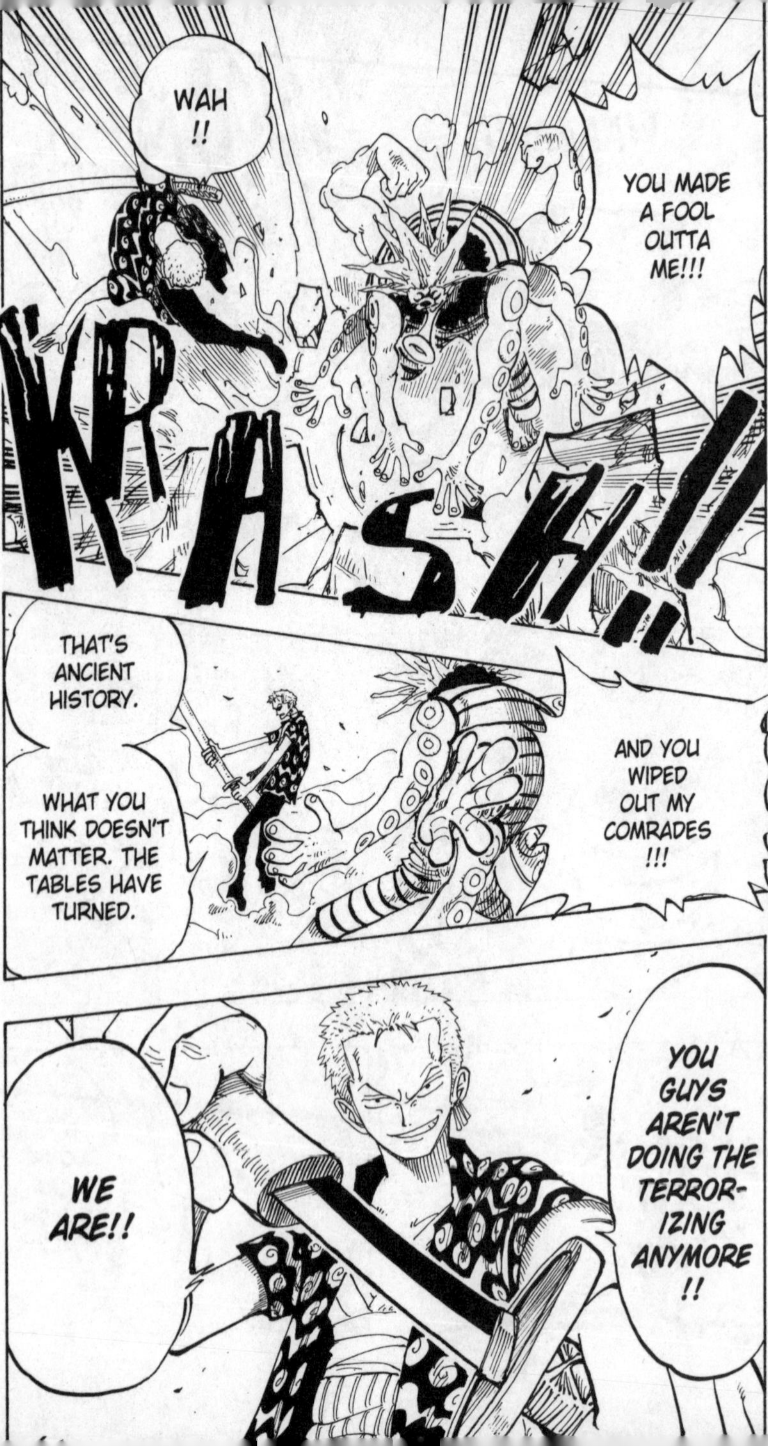
YOU MADE A FOOL OUTTA ME!!!
WAH !!
KRASH!!
AND YOU WIPED OUT MY COMRADES !!!
THAT'S ANCIENT HISTORY.
WHAT YOU THINK DOESN'T MATTER. THE TABLES HAVE TURNED.
YOU GUYS AREN'T DOING THE TERROR-IZING ANYMORE !!
WE ARE!!

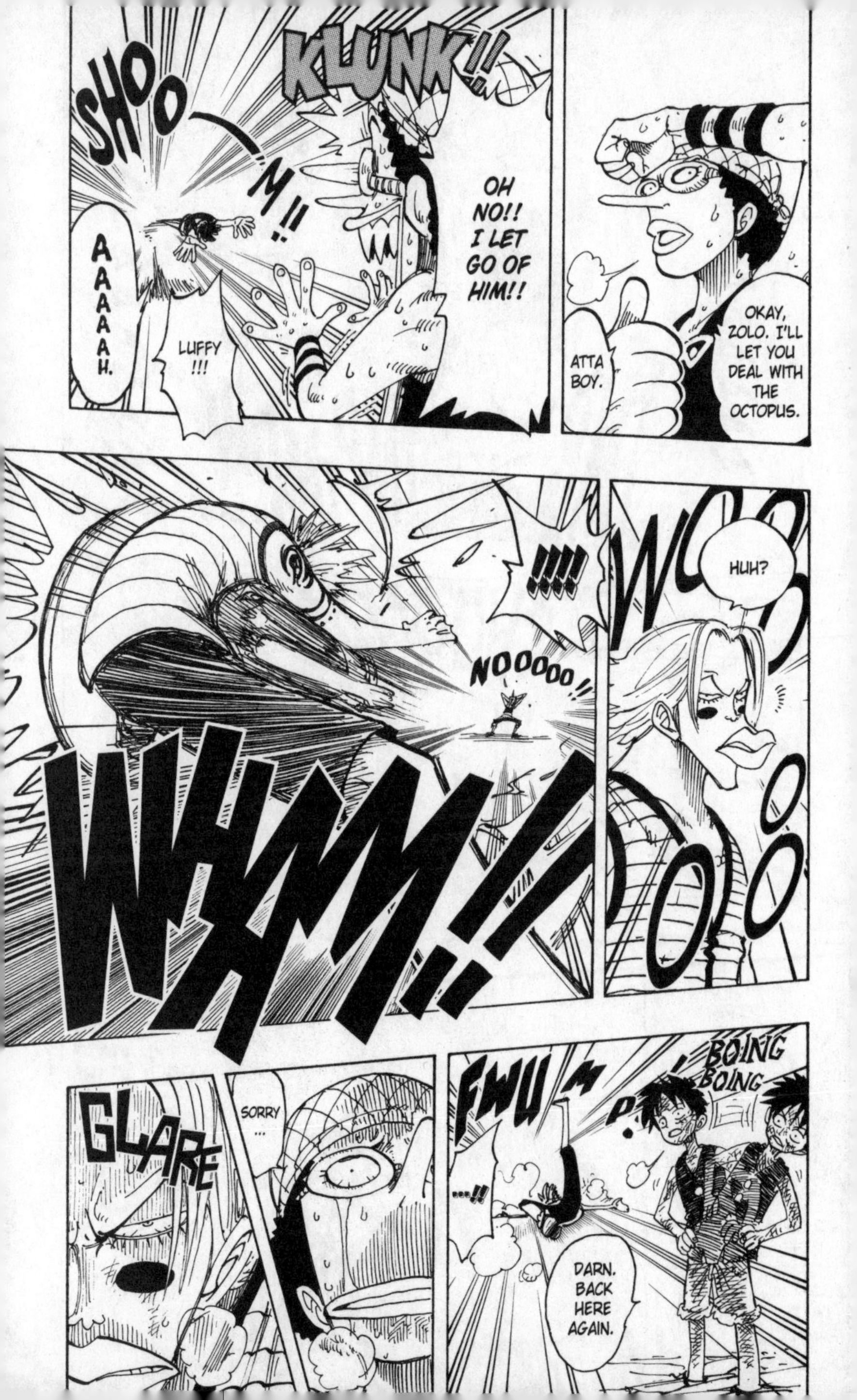
OKAY, ZOLO. I'LL LET YOU DEAL WITH THE OCTOPUS.
ATTA BOY.
KLUNK!!
OH NO!! I LET GO OF HIM!!
SHOOM!!
AAAAAAH.
LUFFY!!!
HUH?
!!!!
NOOOOO!!
WHAM!!
FWUMP
BOING BOING
...!!
DARN. BACK HERE AGAIN.
SORRY...
GLARE

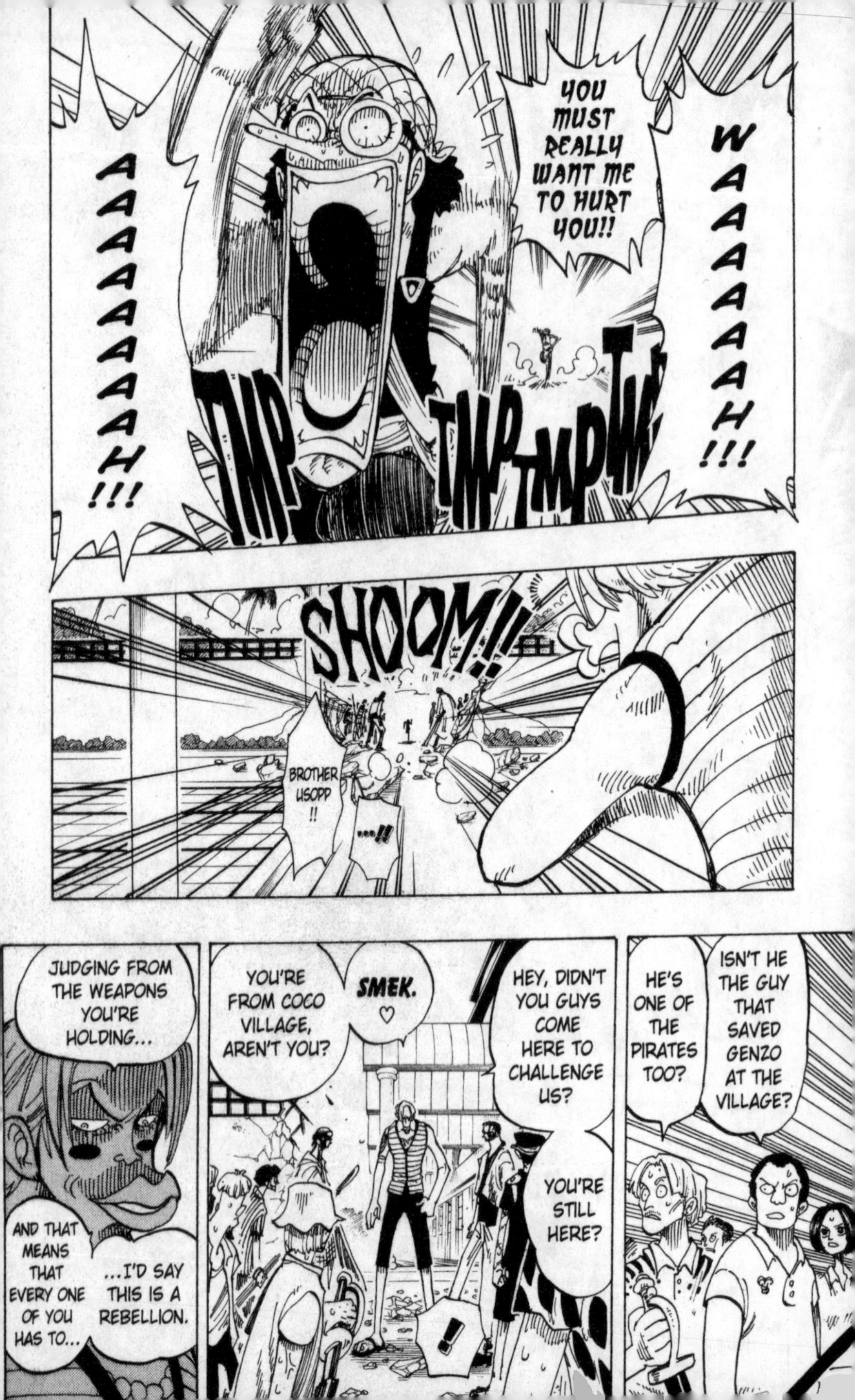
WAAAAAAAAAH!!!
YOU MUST REALLY WANT ME TO HURT YOU!!
AAAAAAAAAAH!!!
TMP
TMP
TMP
SHOOM!!
BROTHER USOPP!!
...!!
ISN'T HE THE GUY THAT SAVED GENZO AT THE VILLAGE?
HE'S ONE OF THE PIRATES TOO?
HEY, DIDN'T YOU GUYS COME HERE TO CHALLENGE US?
SMEK. ♡
YOU'RE FROM COCO VILLAGE, AREN'T YOU?
YOU'RE STILL HERE?
JUDGING FROM THE WEAPONS YOU'RE HOLDING...
...I'D SAY THIS IS A REBELLION.
AND THAT MEANS THAT EVERY ONE OF YOU HAS TO...

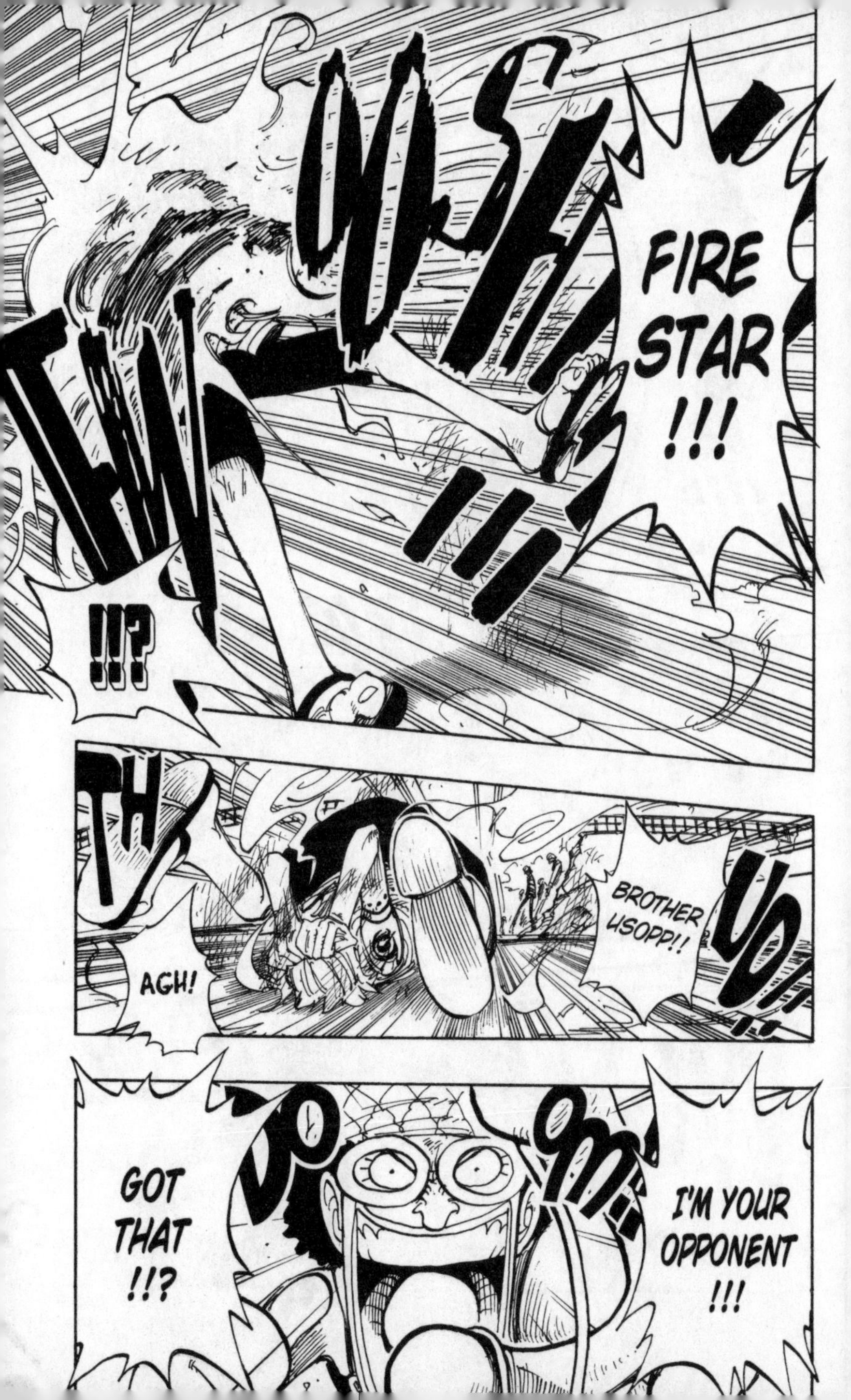
FIRE STAR !!!
!!?
BROTHER USOPP!!
AGH!
I'M YOUR OPPONENT !!!
GOT THAT !!?

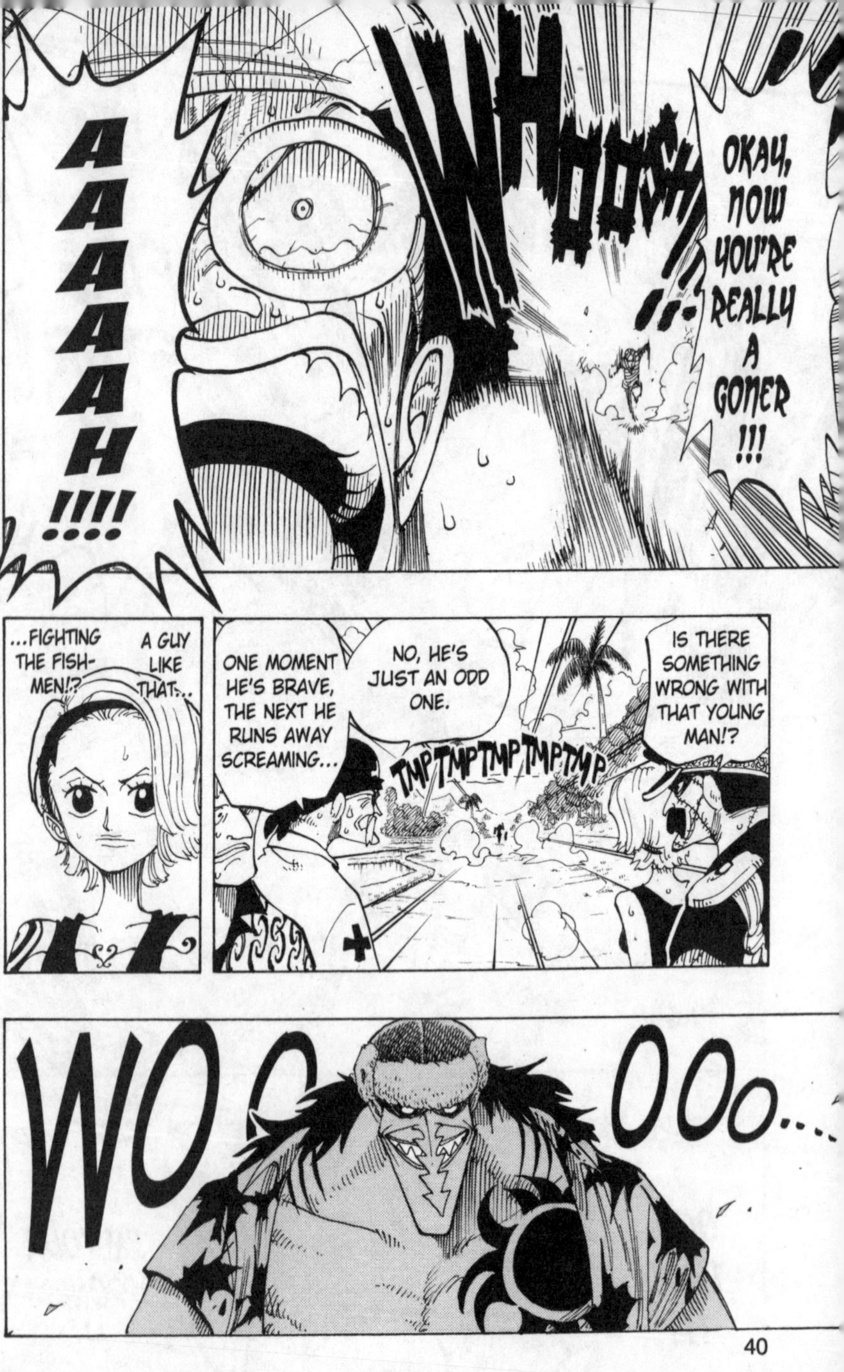
OKAY, NOW YOU'RE REALLY A GONER!!!
WHOOSH!!
AAAAAH!!!!
IS THERE SOMETHING WRONG WITH THAT YOUNG MAN!?
NO, HE'S JUST AN ODD ONE.
ONE MOMENT HE'S BRAVE, THE NEXT HE RUNS AWAY SCREAMING...
TMP TMP TMP TMP TMP
A GUY LIKE THAT...
...FIGHTING THE FISH-MEN!?
WO
OOo....

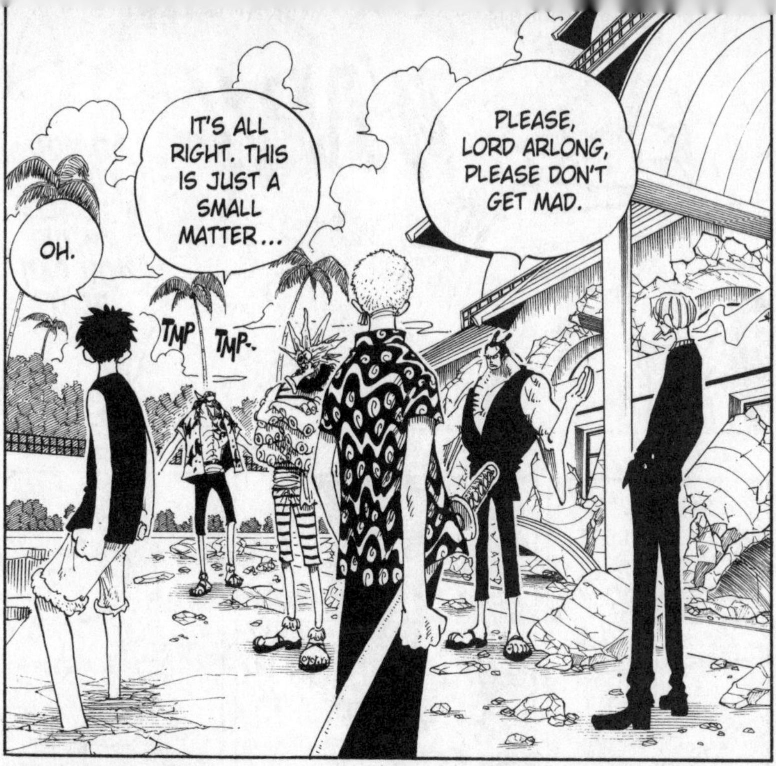
PLEASE, LORD ARLONG, PLEASE DON'T GET MAD.
IT'S ALL RIGHT. THIS IS JUST A SMALL MATTER...
OH.
TMP TMP..

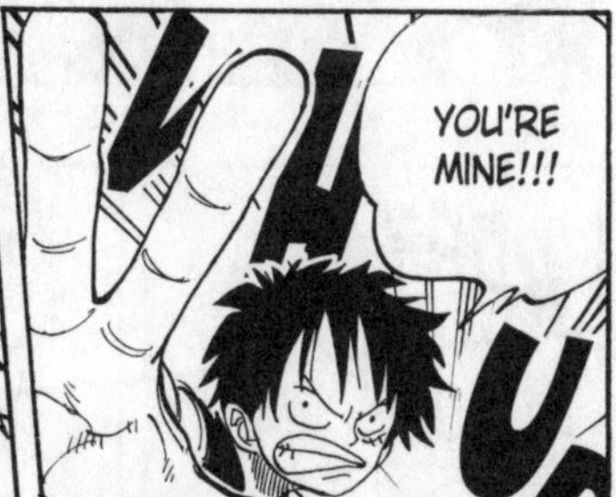
YOU'RE MINE!!!
WHUP!!

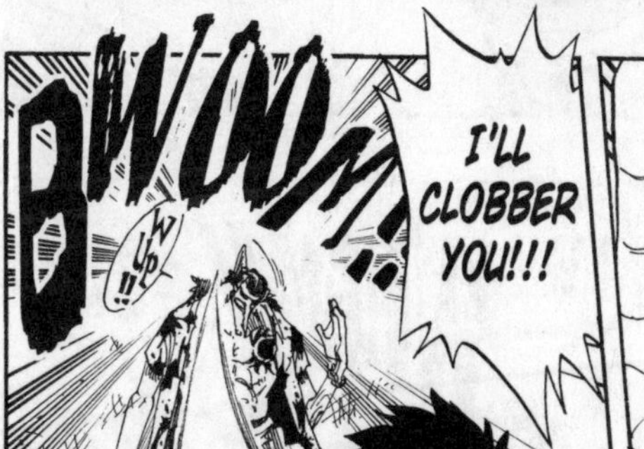
I'LL CLOBBER YOU!!!
BWOOM!!
WUP!!

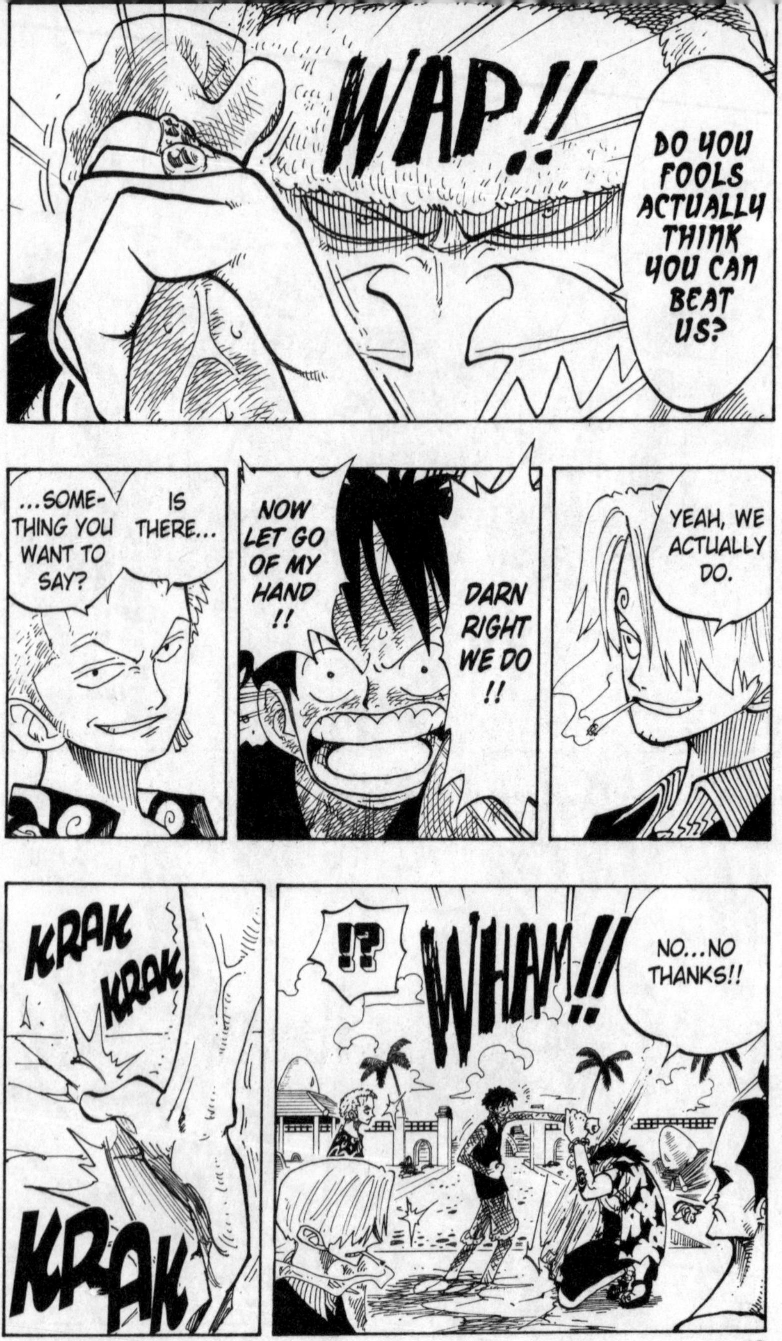
DO YOU FOOLS ACTUALLY THINK YOU CAN BEAT US?
WAP!!
YEAH, WE ACTUALLY DO.
DARN RIGHT WE DO!!
NOW LET GO OF MY HAND!!
IS THERE...
...SOME-THING YOU WANT TO SAY?
NO...NO THANKS!!
WHAM!!
!?
KRAK
KRAK
KRAK

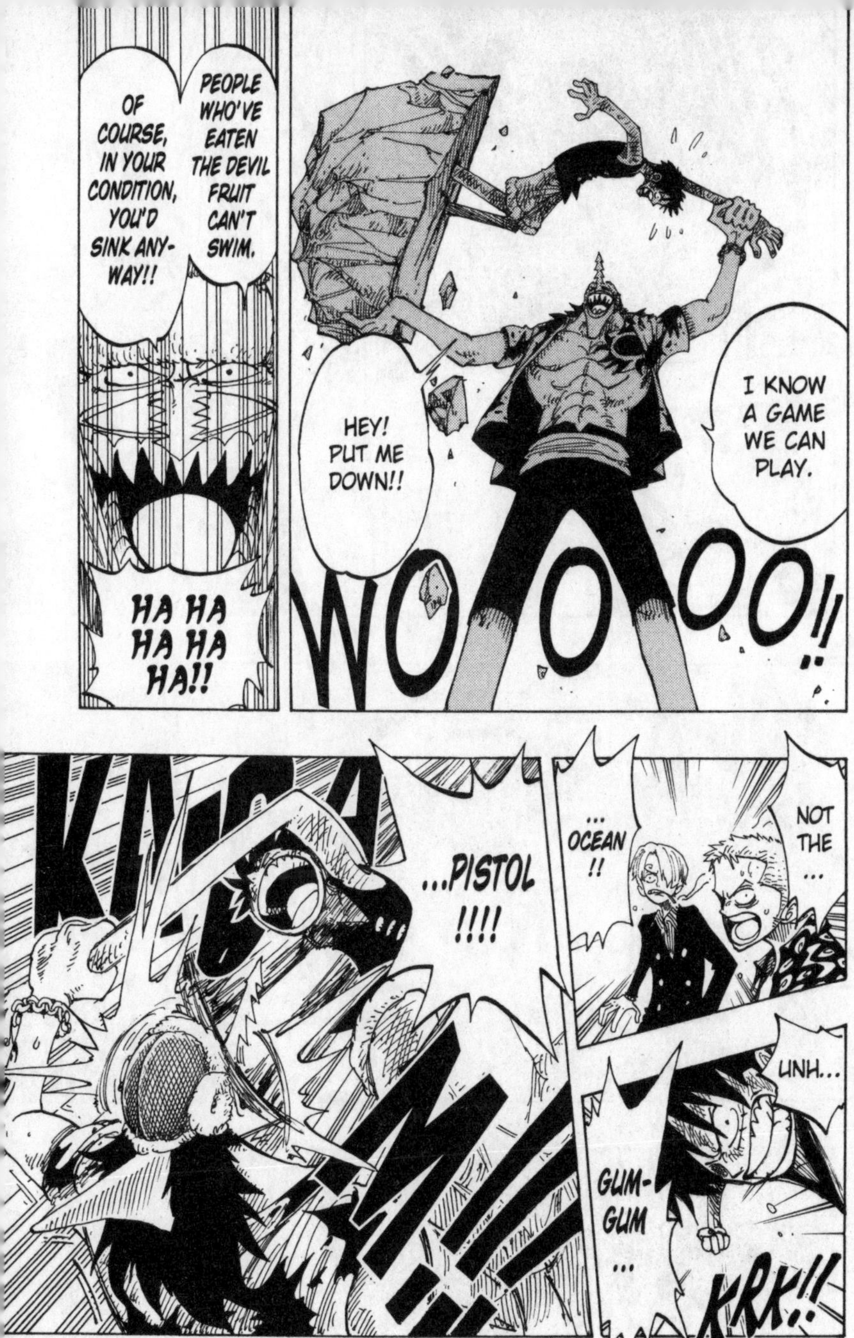
I KNOW A GAME WE CAN PLAY.
HEY! PUT ME DOWN!!
WOOOOO!!
PEOPLE WHO'VE EATEN THE DEVIL FRUIT CAN'T SWIM.
OF COURSE, IN YOUR CONDITION, YOU'D SINK ANYWAY!!
HA HA HA HA HA!!
NOT THE ...
...OCEAN!!
UNH...
GUM-GUM ...
KRK!!
...PISTOL!!!!

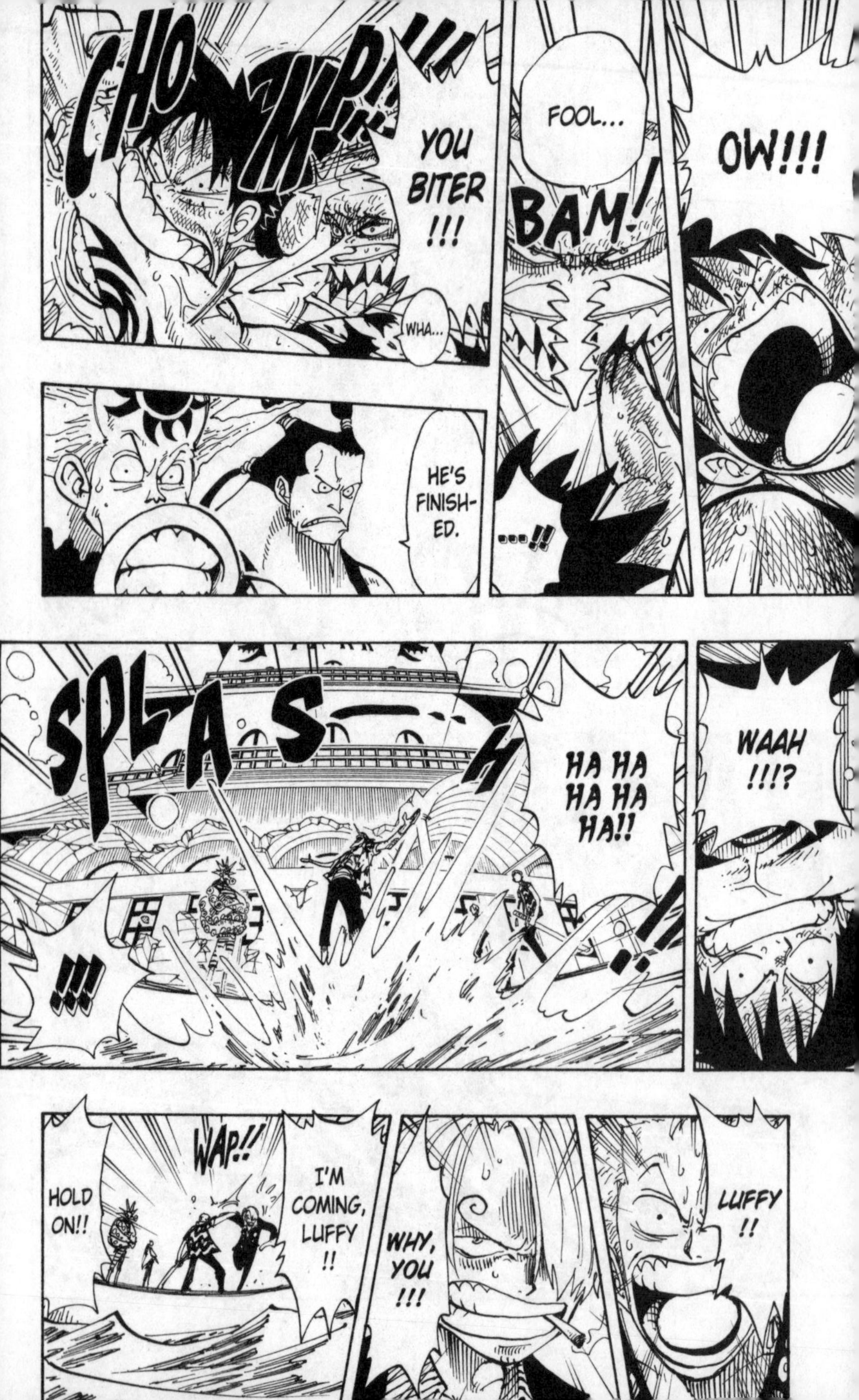
OW!!!
FOOL...
BAM!
...!!
CHOMP!!!
YOU BITER!!!
WHA...
HE'S FINISH-ED.
WAAH!!!?
HA HA HA HA HA!!
SPLASH
!!!
..!!
LUFFY!!
WHY, YOU!!!
I'M COMING, LUFFY!!
WAP!!
HOLD ON!!

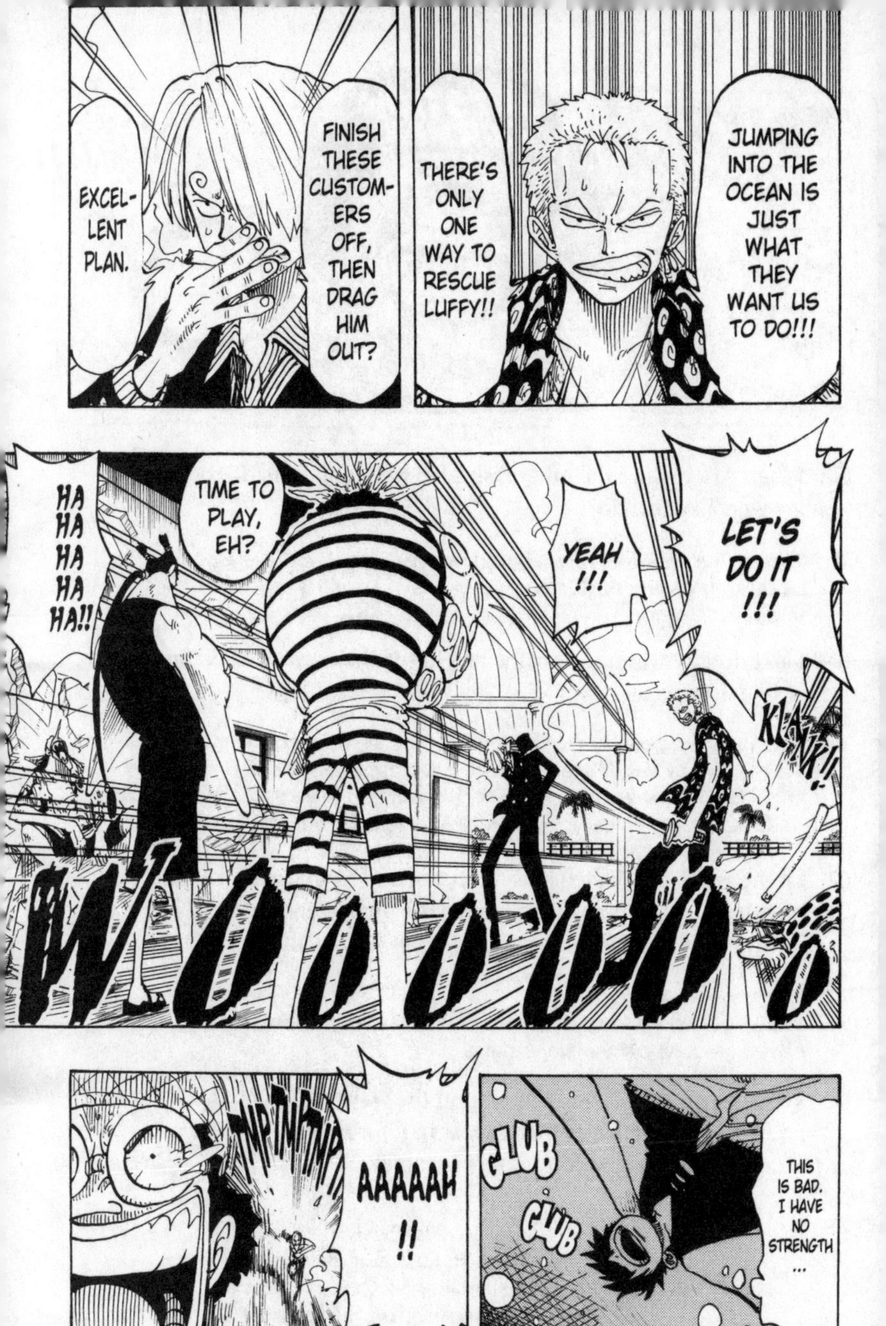
JUMPING INTO THE OCEAN IS JUST WHAT THEY WANT US TO DO!!!
THERE'S ONLY ONE WAY TO RESCUE LUFFY!!
FINISH THESE CUSTOM-ERS OFF, THEN DRAG HIM OUT?
EXCEL-LENT PLAN.
LET'S DO IT !!!
YEAH !!!
KLANK!!
TIME TO PLAY, EH?
HA HA HA HA HA!!
WOOOOOOOO
THIS IS BAD. I HAVE NO STRENGTH ...
GLUB
GLUB
AAAAAH !!
TMP TMP TMP!!

Q: When Arlong and the other Fish-Men have children, do they lay eggs like fish do?

A: (Buzz) The Fish-Men are actually mammals, so they have kids the same way humans do. Of course, that's the job of the Fish-Women

Q: I, like, totally wanna know the heights of the crew. That Nami is, like, soooo cute!

A: The main five, eh? All right. Um, first of all, Gaimon's height is... Just kidding. Okay, I'll start with the shortest. Nami's 5' 6 ½", Luffy is 5' 8," Usopp is 5' 8 ½", Sanji is a little under 5' 10," and Zolo is 5' 10." So basically, they're all like about the same height.

Q: Of the Fish-Men, Hatchan is the cutest and funniest. So what I wonder is, how come his full name is Hatchan and his nickname is Hachi? (In Japanese, "-chan" is usually part of a nickname.)

A: You know how Chinese people sometimes have Chan as a last name? It's kind of the same thing.

Q: What is that thing wrapped around the waists of Usopp and most of the pirates that appear in *One Piece*? A towel? Or are they trying to copy Zolo's haramaki?

A:

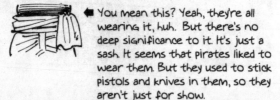

◀ You mean this? Yeah, they're all wearing it, huh. But there's no deep significance to it. It's just a sash. It seems that pirates liked to wear them. But they used to stick pistols and knives in them, so they aren't just for show.

Chapter 84:
ZOMBIE

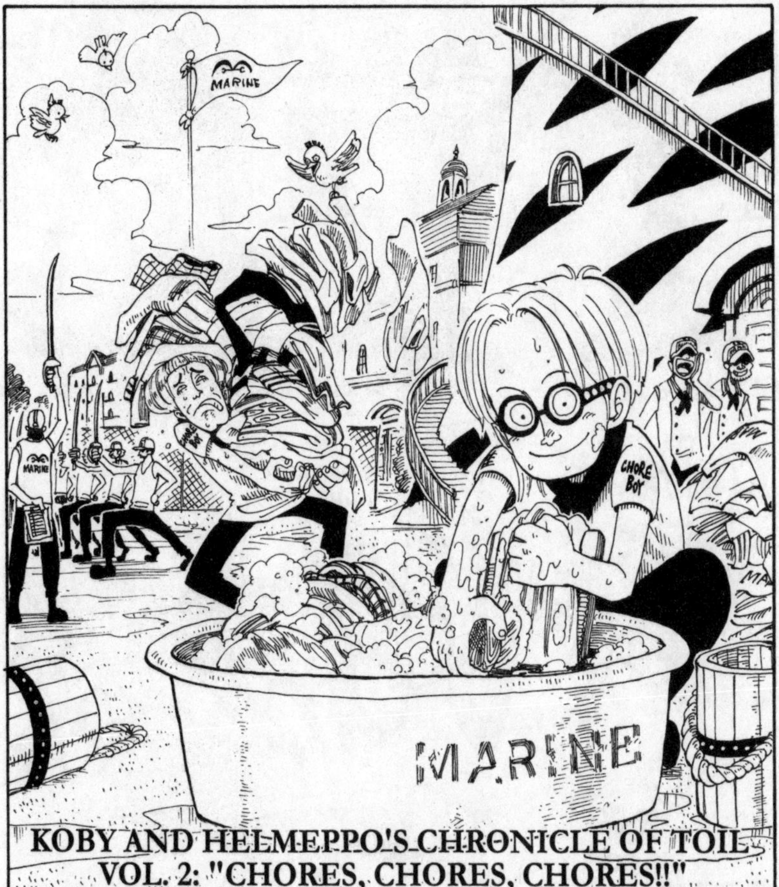
MARINE
MARINE
CHORE BOY
CHORE BOY
MARINE
MARINE

KOBY AND HELMEPPO'S CHRONICLE OF TOIL
VOL. 2: "CHORES, CHORES, CHORES!!"

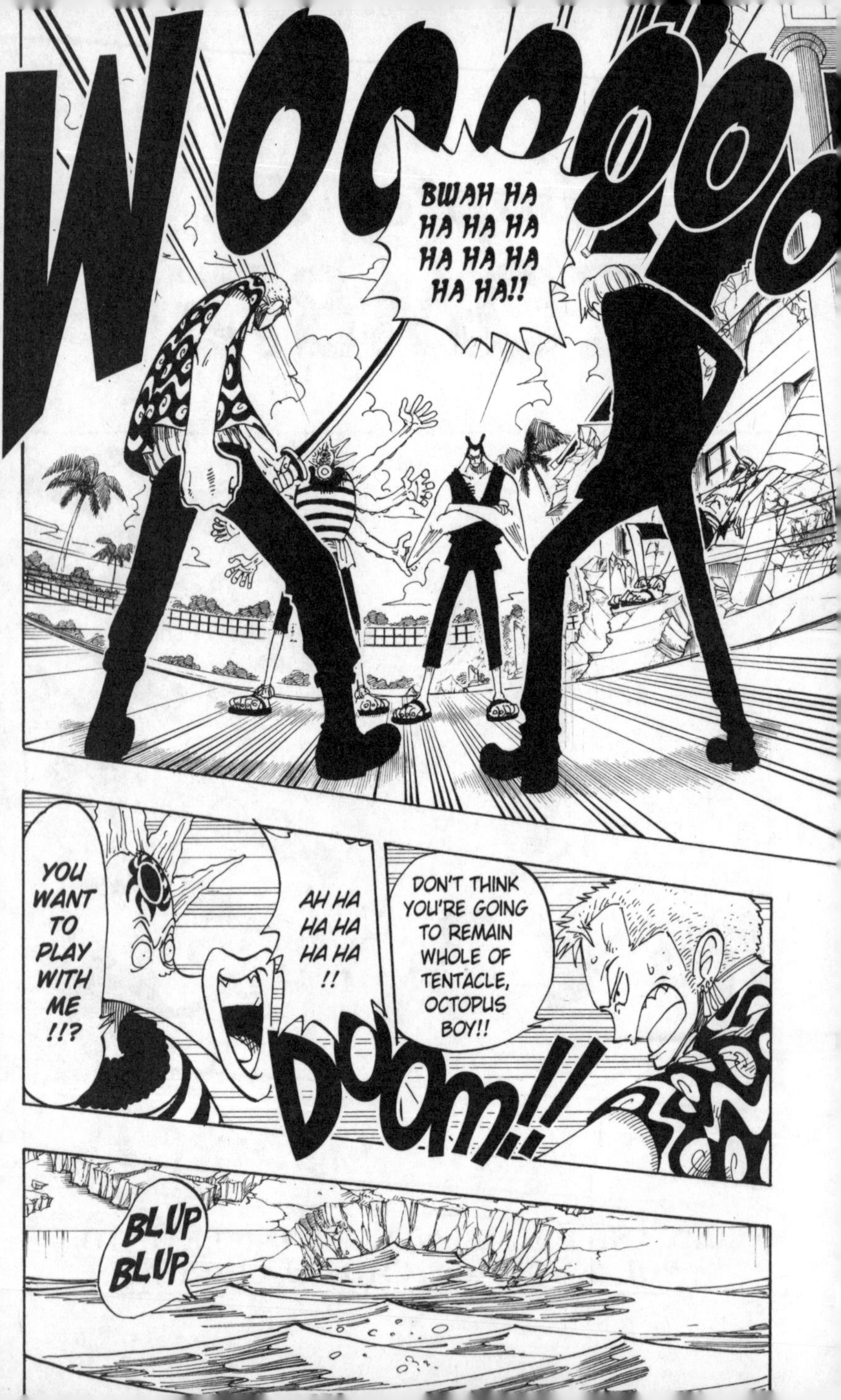
WOOOOOO
BWAH HA HA HA HA HA HA HA HA HA!!
DON'T THINK YOU'RE GOING TO REMAIN WHOLE OF TENTACLE, OCTOPUS BOY!!
AH HA HA HA HA HA !!
YOU WANT TO PLAY WITH ME !!?
DOOM!!
BLUP BLUP

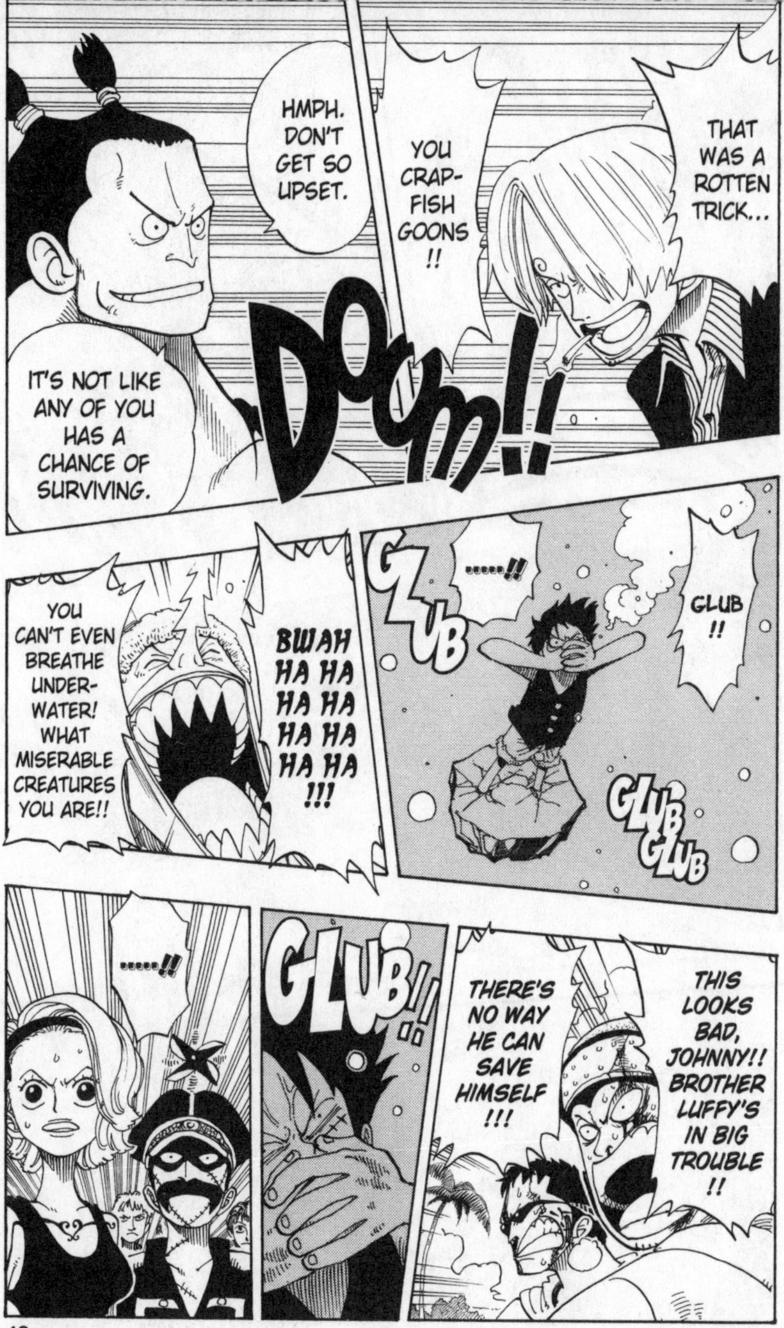
THAT WAS A ROTTEN TRICK...
YOU CRAP-FISH GOONS!!
HMPH. DON'T GET SO UPSET.
IT'S NOT LIKE ANY OF YOU HAS A CHANCE OF SURVIVING.
DOOM!!
GLUB!!
......!!
GLUB
GLUB GLUB
BWAH HA HA HA HA HA HA HA HA!!!
YOU CAN'T EVEN BREATHE UNDER-WATER! WHAT MISERABLE CREATURES YOU ARE!!
THIS LOOKS BAD, JOHNNY!! BROTHER LUFFY'S IN BIG TROUBLE!!
THERE'S NO WAY HE CAN SAVE HIMSELF!!!
GLUB!!
......!!

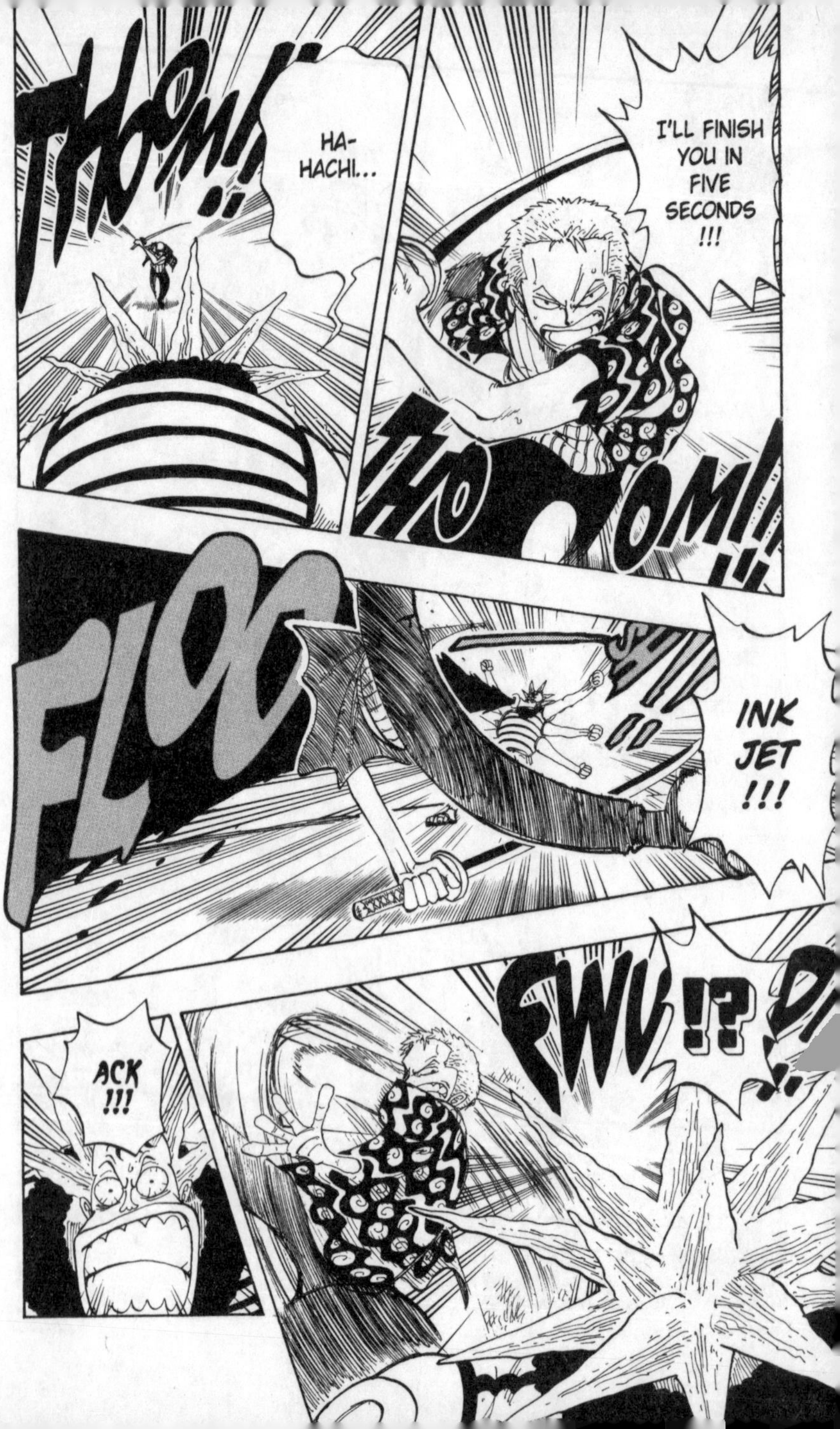
I'LL FINISH YOU IN FIVE SECONDS !!!
THOOM!!
HA-HACHI...
THOM!!
INK JET !!!
FLOO
FWU !?
ACK !!!

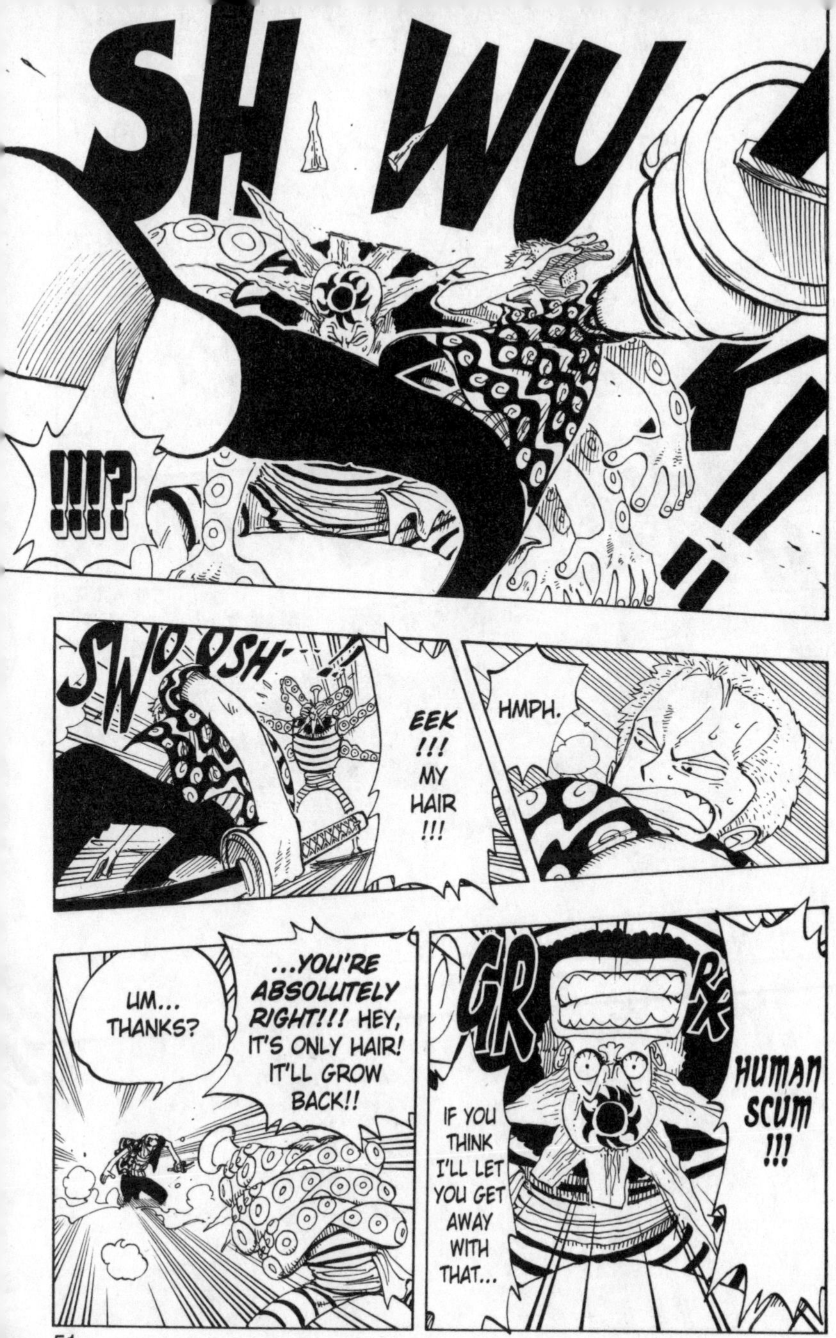
SHWUK!!
!!!?
HMPH.
SWOOSH
EEK!!! MY HAIR!!!
GRR
HUMAN SCUM!!!
IF YOU THINK I'LL LET YOU GET AWAY WITH THAT...
...YOU'RE ABSOLUTELY RIGHT!!! HEY, IT'S ONLY HAIR! IT'LL GROW BACK!!
UM... THANKS?

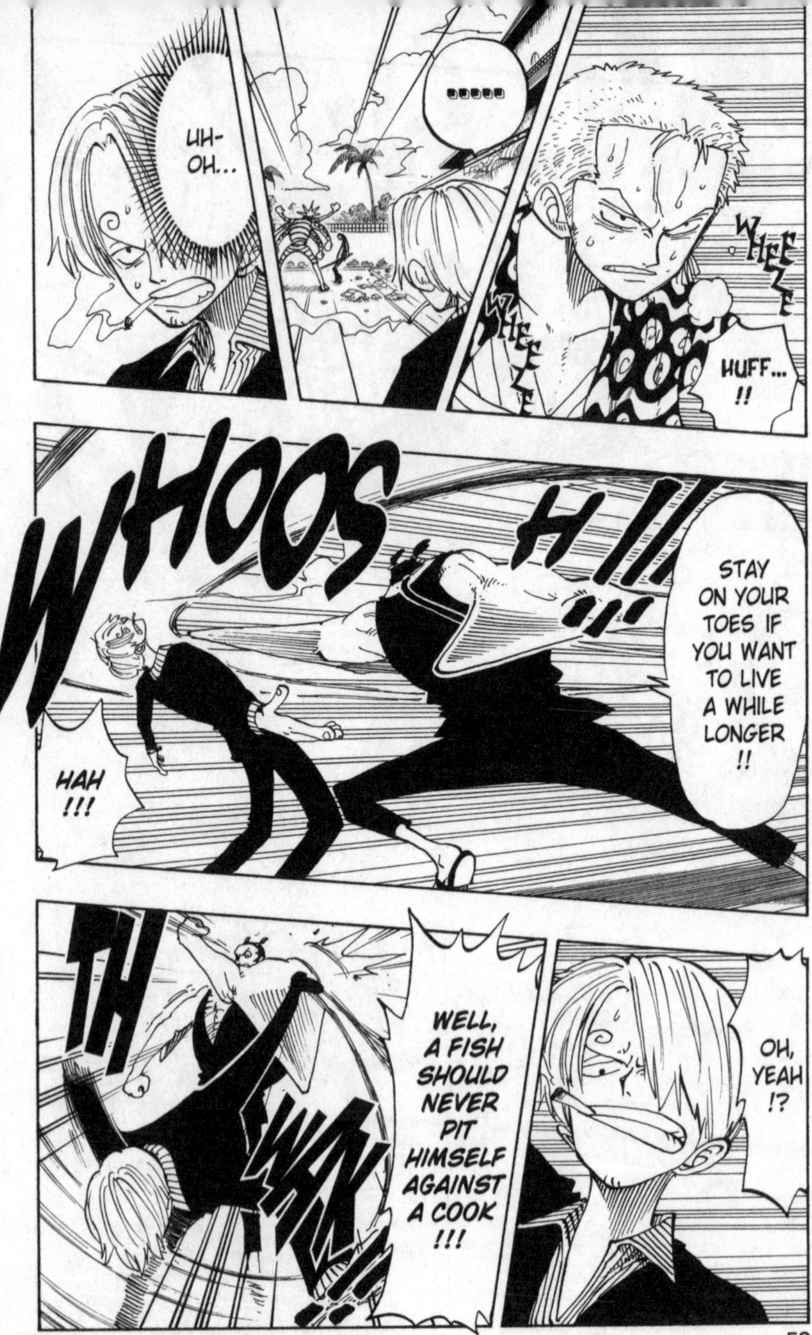
WHEEZE
HUFF... !!
WHEEZE
.....
UH-OH...
WHOOSH!!
STAY ON YOUR TOES IF YOU WANT TO LIVE A WHILE LONGER !!
HAH !!!
OH, YEAH !?
WELL, A FISH SHOULD NEVER PIT HIMSELF AGAINST A COOK !!!
THWACK!!

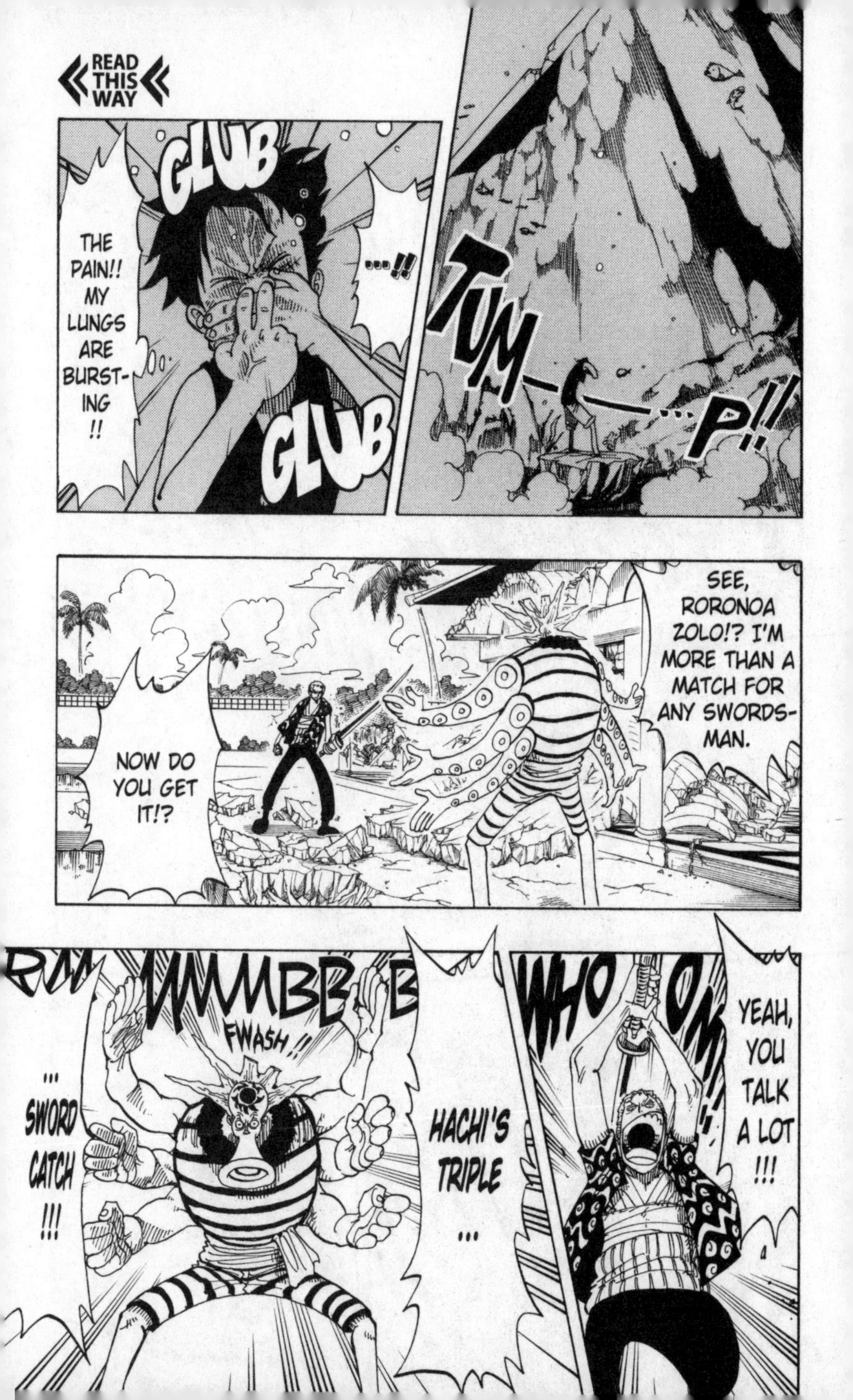
READ THIS WAY
TUM--...P!!
...!!
GLUB
THE PAIN!! MY LUNGS ARE BURST-ING!!
GLUB
SEE, RORONOA ZOLO!? I'M MORE THAN A MATCH FOR ANY SWORDS-MAN.
NOW DO YOU GET IT!?
WHOOM!!
YEAH, YOU TALK A LOT!!!
RUMMBBB
FWASH!!
HACHI'S TRIPLE...
...SWORD CATCH!!!

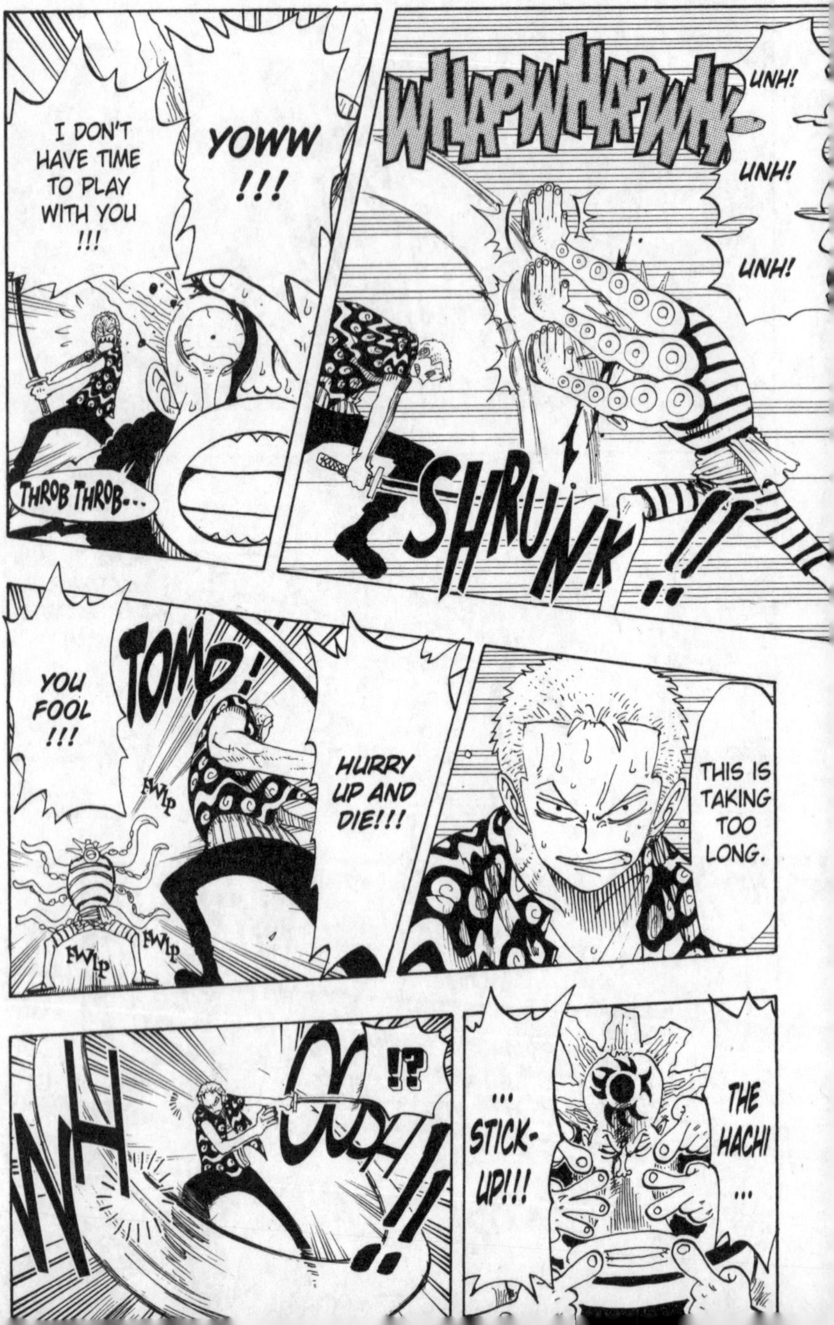

WHAPWHAPWAK-
UNH!
UNH!
UNH!
SHRUNK!!
YOWW!!!
I DON'T HAVE TIME TO PLAY WITH YOU!!!
THROB THROB...
THIS IS TAKING TOO LONG.
HURRY UP AND DIE!!!
TOMP!
YOU FOOL!!!
FWIp
FWIp
FWIp
THE HACHI...
...STICK-UP!!!
!?
OOOH!!

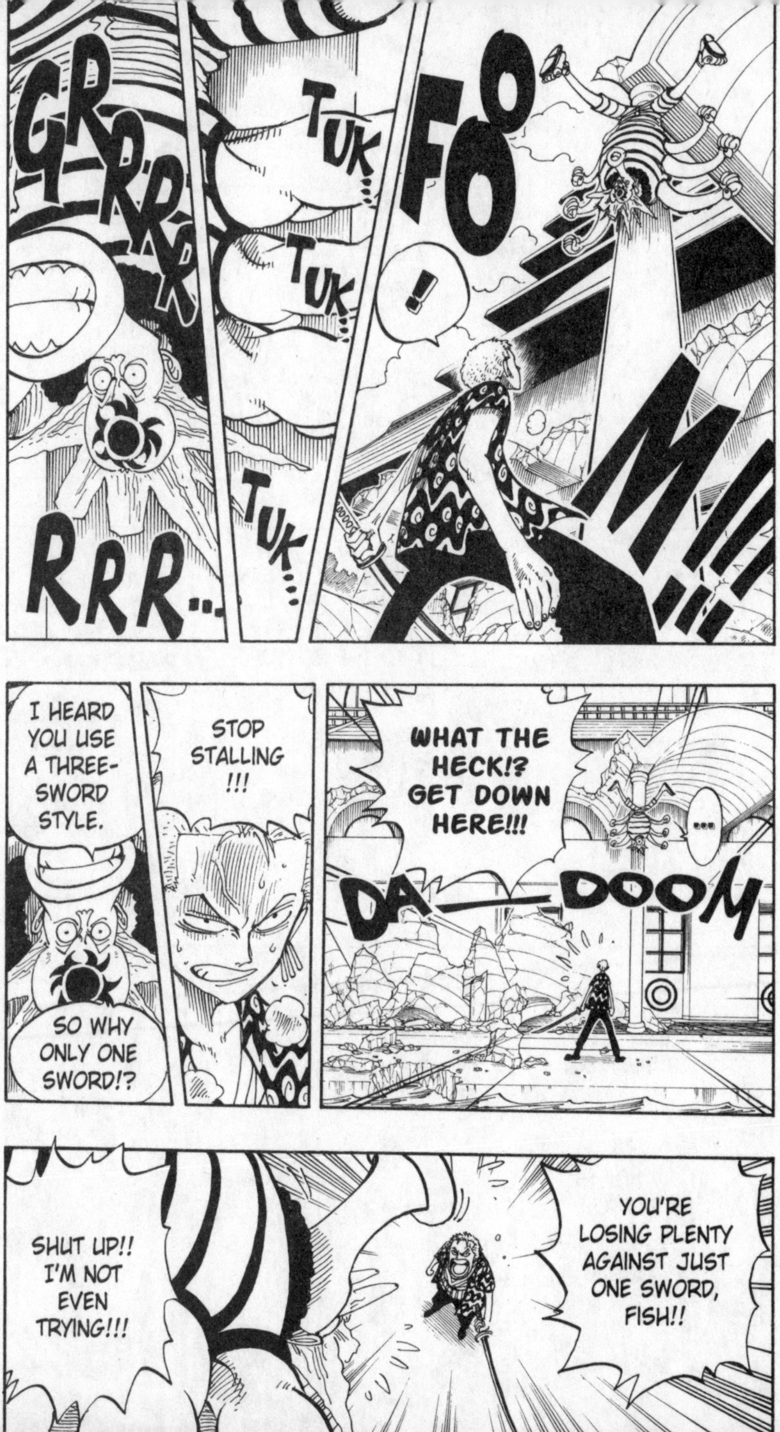
FOOOM!!!
!
TUK... TUK... TUK...
GRRRRR RRR...
WHAT THE HECK!? GET DOWN HERE!!!
...
DA—DOOM
STOP STALLING!!!
I HEARD YOU USE A THREE-SWORD STYLE.
SO WHY ONLY ONE SWORD!?
YOU'RE LOSING PLENTY AGAINST JUST ONE SWORD, FISH!!
SHUT UP!! I'M NOT EVEN TRYING!!!

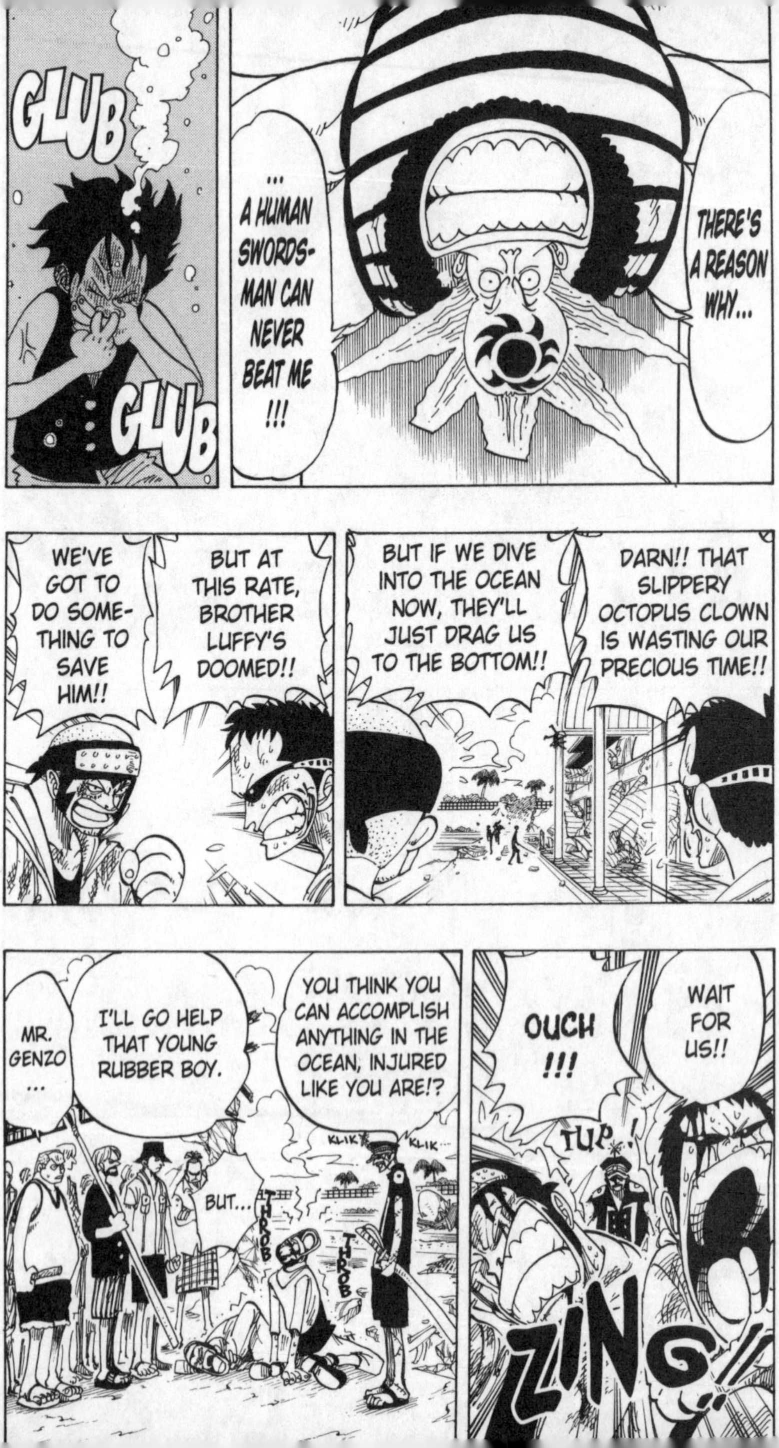
THERE'S A REASON WHY...
... A HUMAN SWORDS-MAN CAN NEVER BEAT ME !!!
GLUB
GLUB
DARN!! THAT SLIPPERY OCTOPUS CLOWN IS WASTING OUR PRECIOUS TIME!!
BUT IF WE DIVE INTO THE OCEAN NOW, THEY'LL JUST DRAG US TO THE BOTTOM!!
BUT AT THIS RATE, BROTHER LUFFY'S DOOMED!!
WE'VE GOT TO DO SOME-THING TO SAVE HIM!!
WAIT FOR US!!
OUCH !!!
TUP
ZING!!
YOU THINK YOU CAN ACCOMPLISH ANYTHING IN THE OCEAN, INJURED LIKE YOU ARE!?
KLIK KLIK...
THROB
THROB
BUT...
I'LL GO HELP THAT YOUNG RUBBER BOY.
MR. GENZO ...

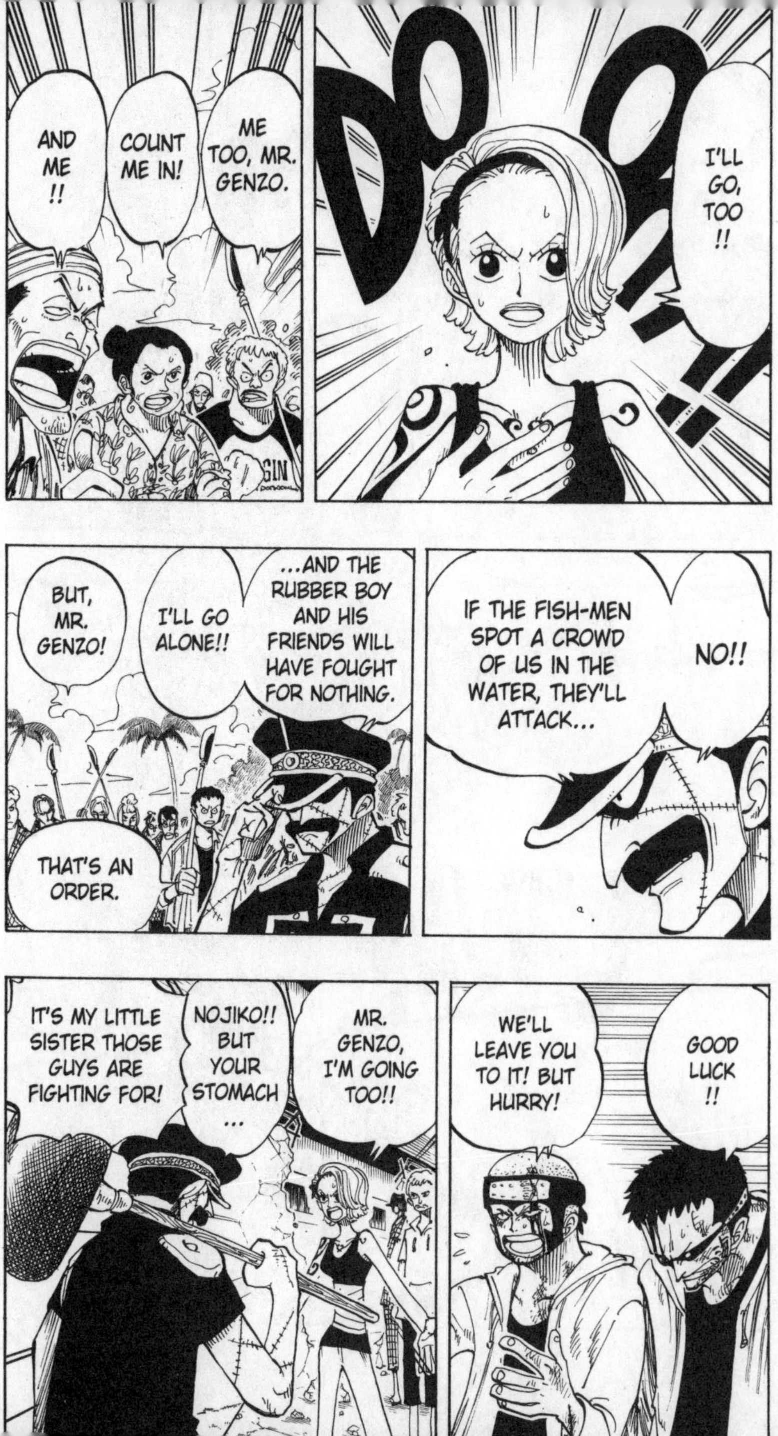
I'LL GO, TOO!!
ME TOO, MR. GENZO.
COUNT ME IN!
AND ME!!
NO!!
IF THE FISH-MEN SPOT A CROWD OF US IN THE WATER, THEY'LL ATTACK...
...AND THE RUBBER BOY AND HIS FRIENDS WILL HAVE FOUGHT FOR NOTHING.
I'LL GO ALONE!!
BUT, MR. GENZO!
THAT'S AN ORDER.
GOOD LUCK!!
WE'LL LEAVE YOU TO IT! BUT HURRY!
MR. GENZO, I'M GOING TOO!!
NOJIKO!! BUT YOUR STOMACH...
IT'S MY LITTLE SISTER THOSE GUYS ARE FIGHTING FOR!

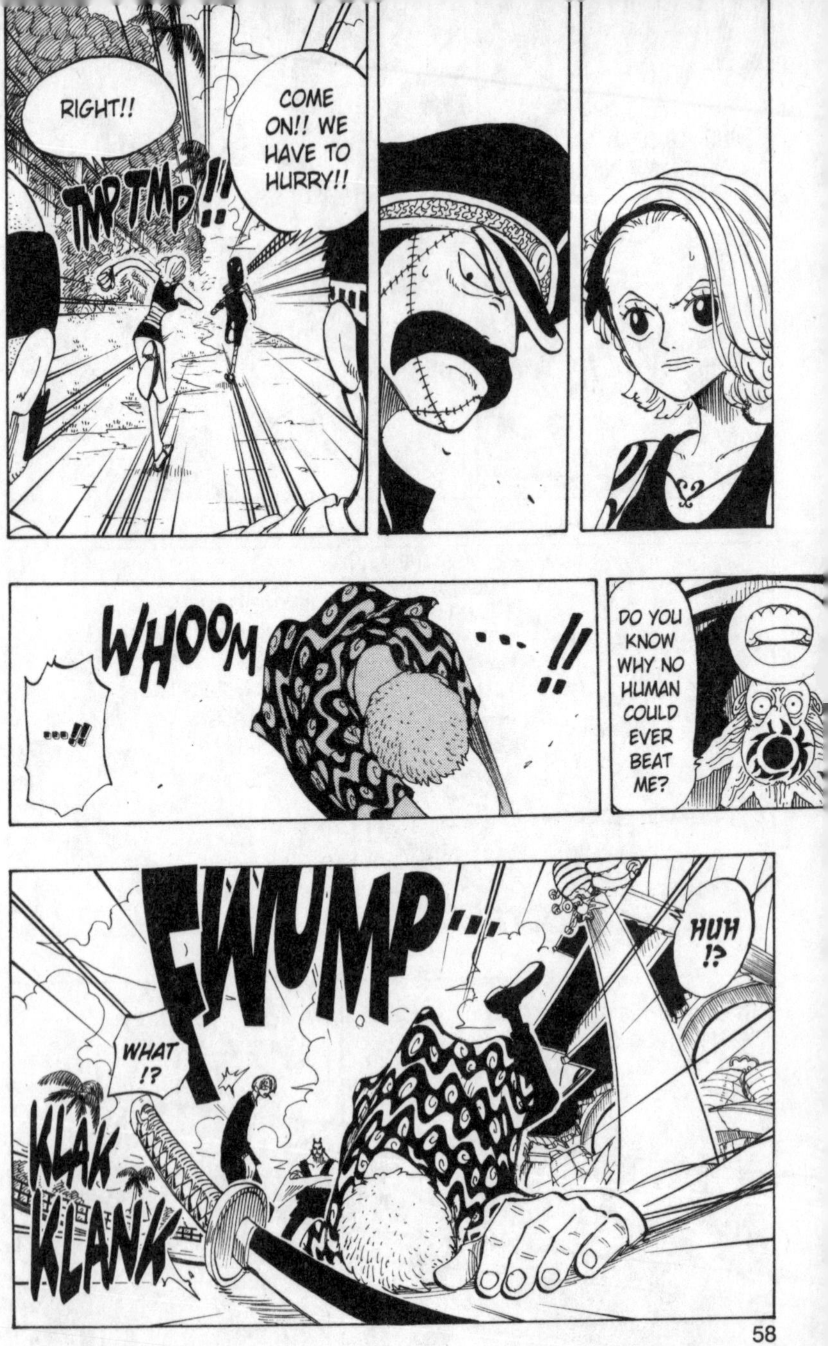
COME ON!! WE HAVE TO HURRY!!
RIGHT!!
TMP TMP!!
DO YOU KNOW WHY NO HUMAN COULD EVER BEAT ME?
...!!
WHOOM
...!!
HUH !?
FWUMP...
WHAT !?
KLAK KLANK

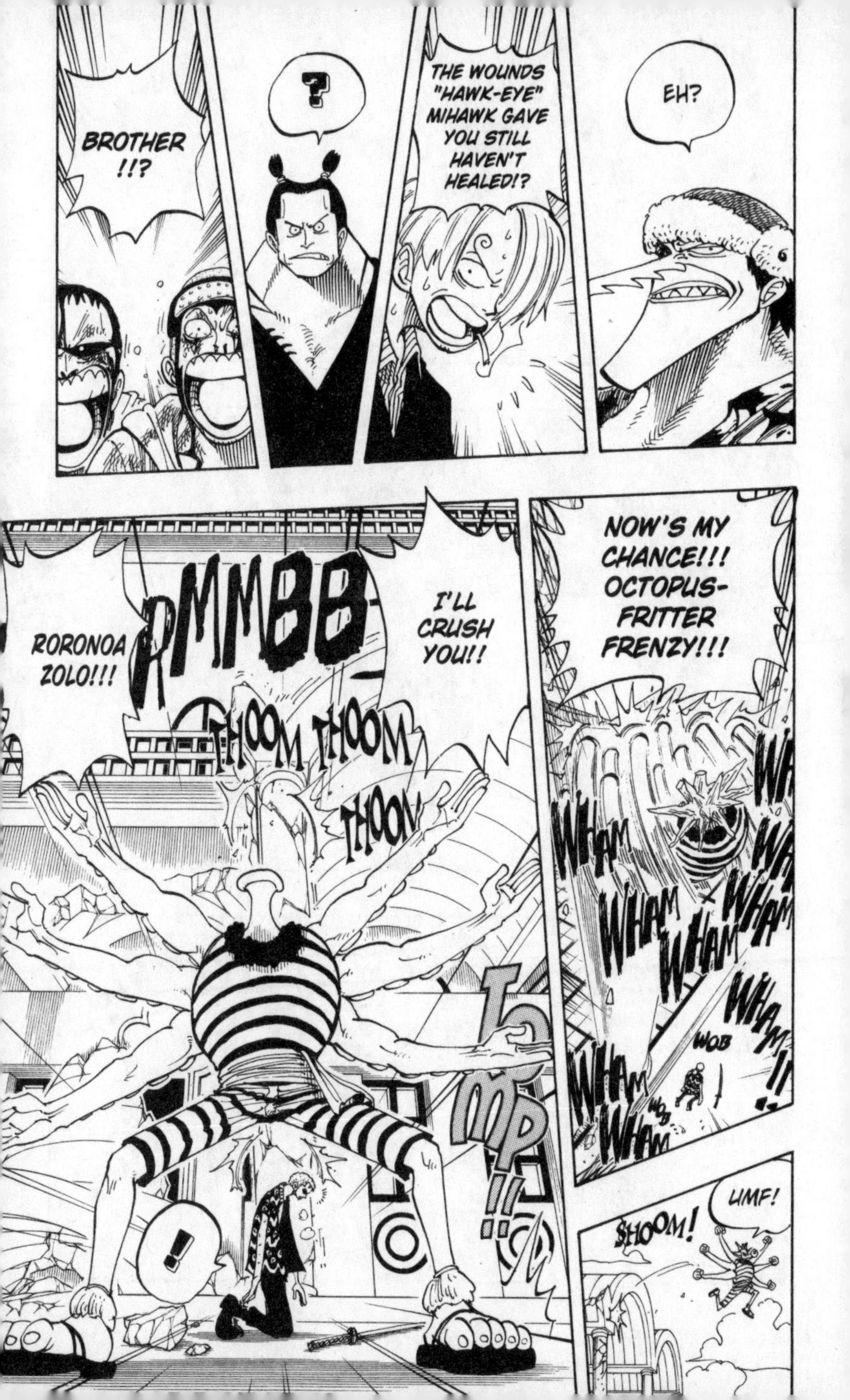
EH?
THE WOUNDS "HAWK-EYE" MIHAWK GAVE YOU STILL HAVEN'T HEALED!?
?
BROTHER !!?
NOW'S MY CHANCE!!! OCTOPUS-FRITTER FRENZY!!!
WHAM WHAM WHAM WHAM WHAM WHAM WHAM WHAM WHAM!!
WOB WOB
WHAM WHAM
UMF!
SHOOM!
RORONOA ZOLO!!!
I'LL CRUSH YOU!!
RMMBB
THOOM THOOM THOOM
TOMP!!
!

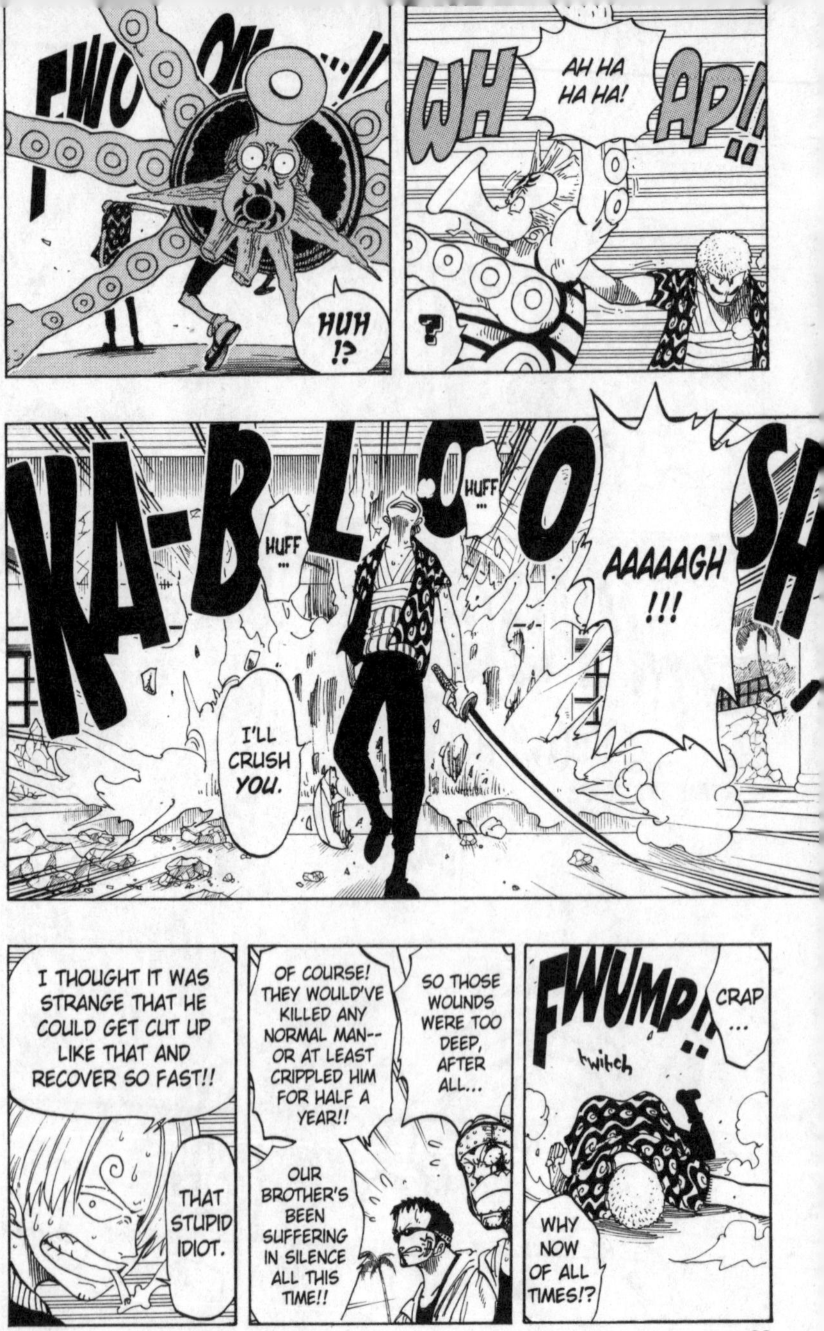
WHAP!!
AH HA HA HA!
?
FWOOOM!!
HUH!?
KA-BLOOSH
AAAAAGH!!!
HUFF...
HUFF...
I'LL CRUSH YOU.
FWUMP!!
CRAP...
twitch
WHY NOW OF ALL TIMES!?
SO THOSE WOUNDS WERE TOO DEEP, AFTER ALL...
OF COURSE! THEY WOULD'VE KILLED ANY NORMAL MAN--OR AT LEAST CRIPPLED HIM FOR HALF A YEAR!!
OUR BROTHER'S BEEN SUFFERING IN SILENCE ALL THIS TIME!!
I THOUGHT IT WAS STRANGE THAT HE COULD GET CUT UP LIKE THAT AND RECOVER SO FAST!!
THAT STUPID IDIOT.

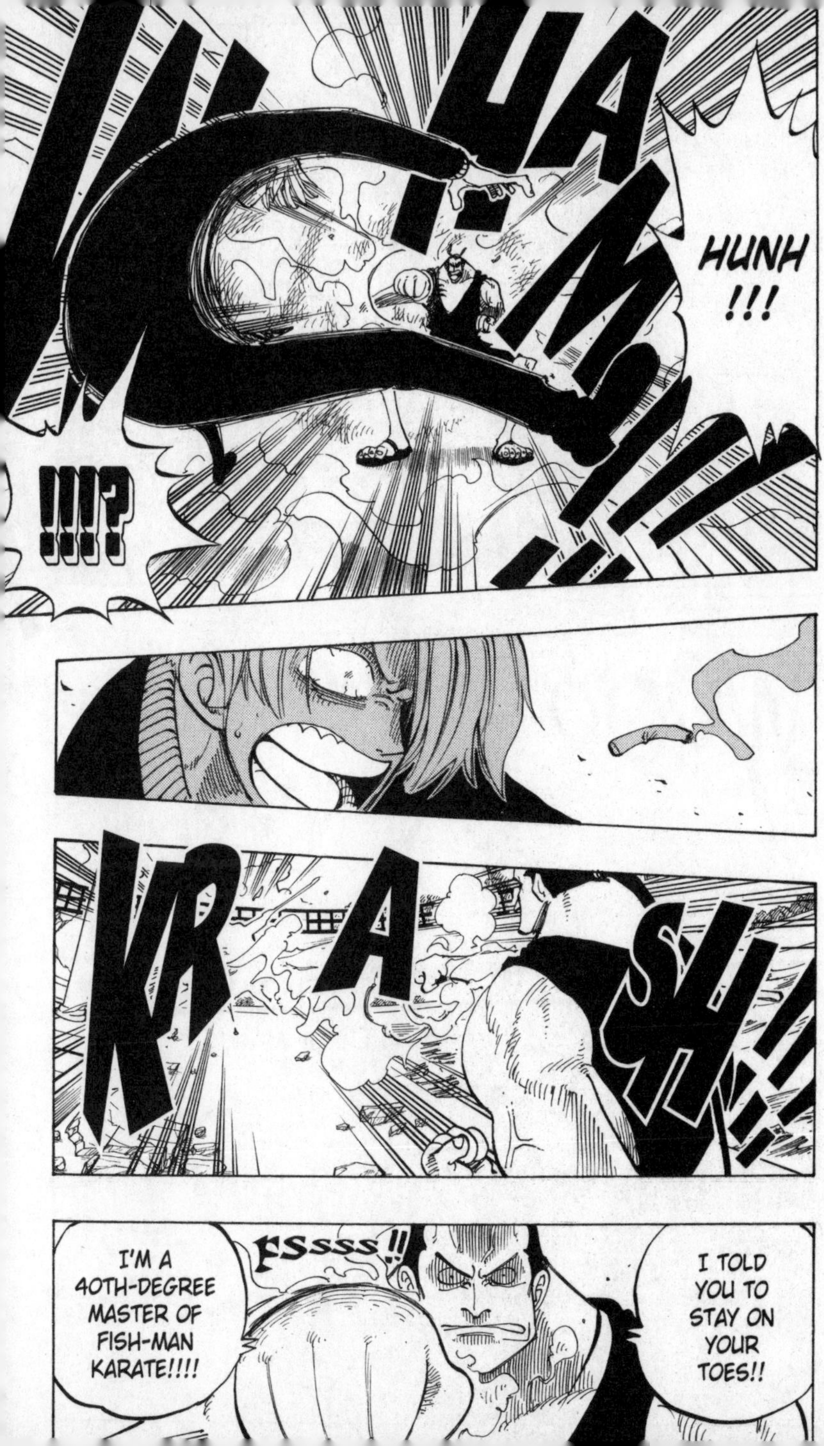
HAM!!
HUNH!!!
!!!?
KRASH!!
I TOLD YOU TO STAY ON YOUR TOES!!
FSSSS!!
I'M A 40TH-DEGREE MASTER OF FISH-MAN KARATE!!!!

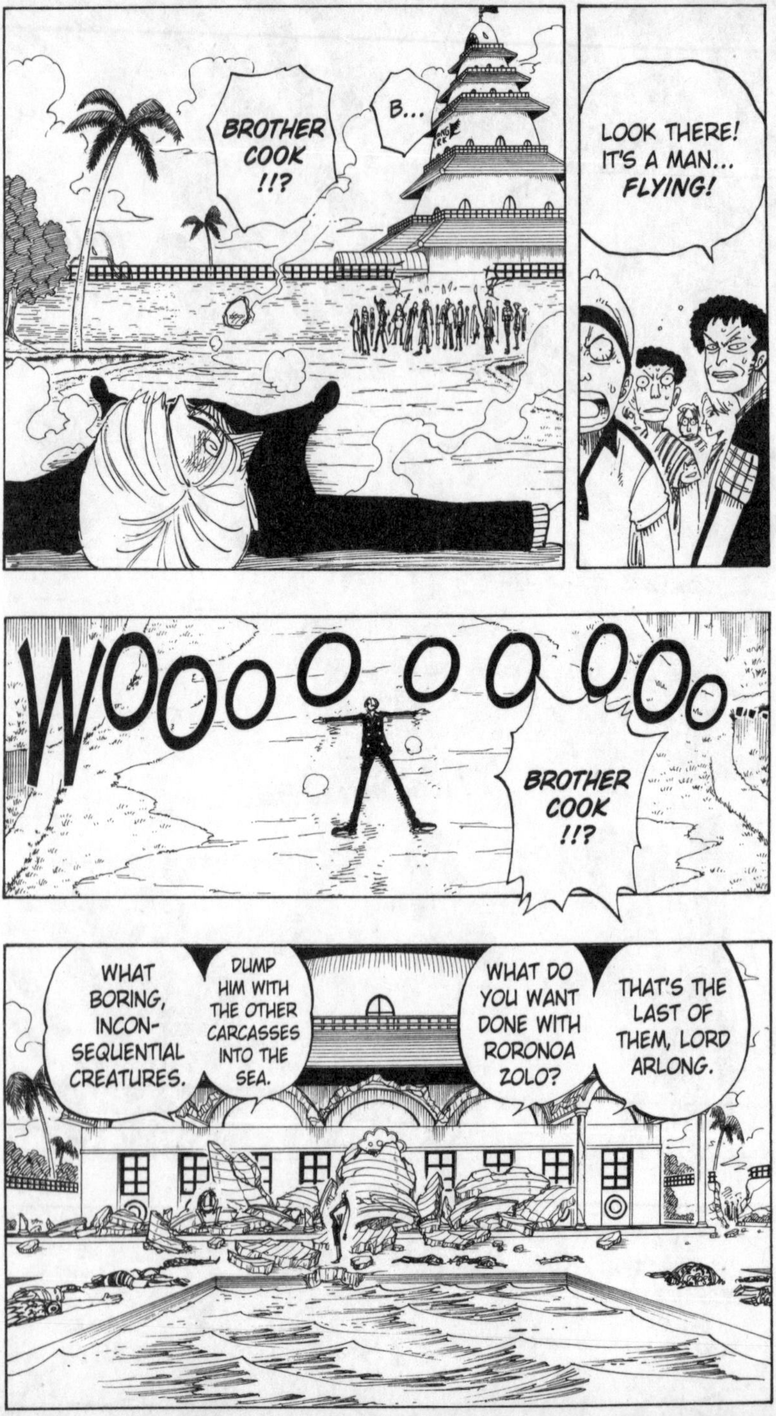
LOOK THERE! IT'S A MAN... FLYING!
B...
BROTHER COOK !!?
WOOOOOOOOOOO
BROTHER COOK !!?
THAT'S THE LAST OF THEM, LORD ARLONG.
WHAT DO YOU WANT DONE WITH RORONOA ZOLO?
DUMP HIM WITH THE OTHER CARCASSES INTO THE SEA.
WHAT BORING, INCON-SEQUENTIAL CREATURES.

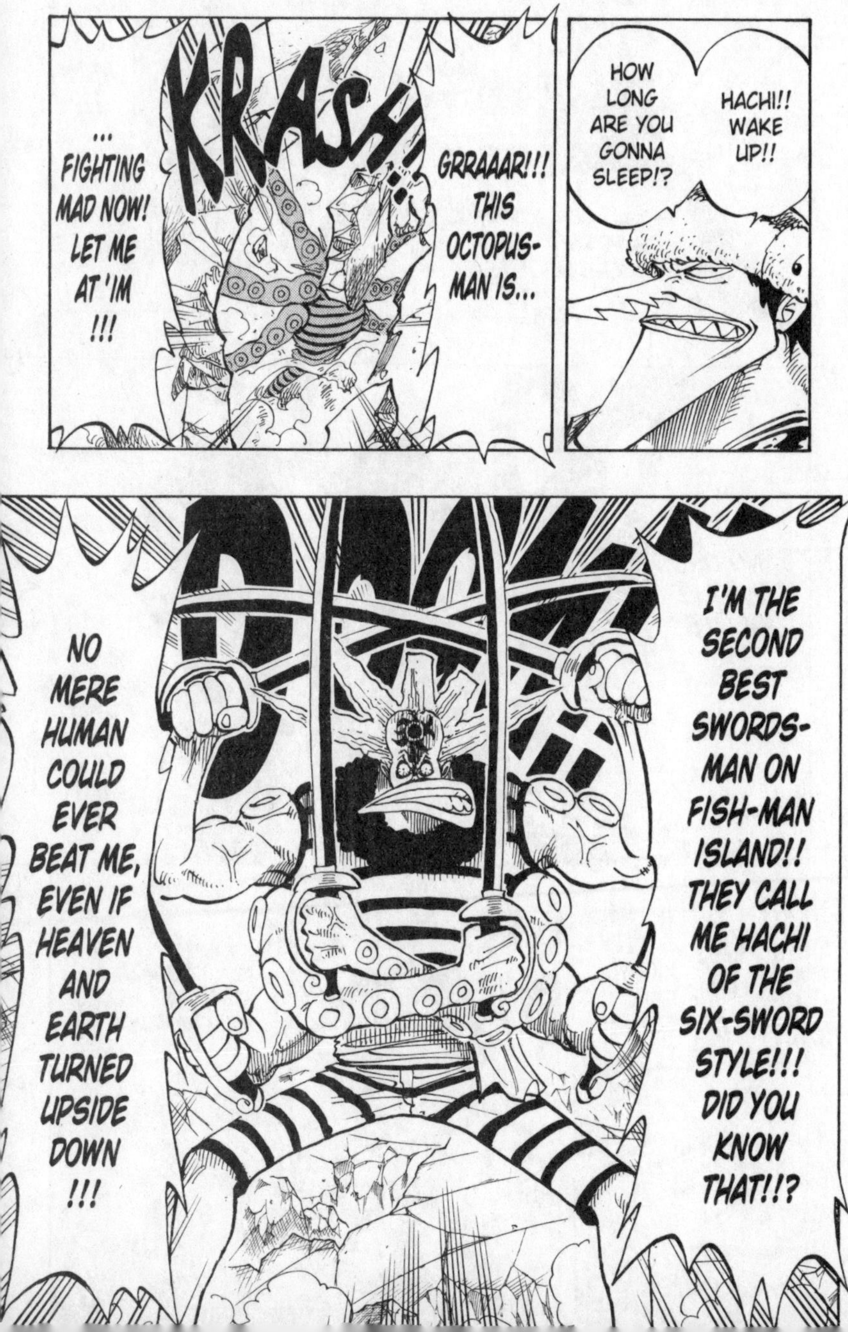
HACHI!! WAKE UP!!
HOW LONG ARE YOU GONNA SLEEP!?
KRASH
GRRAAAR!!! THIS OCTOPUS-MAN IS...
... FIGHTING MAD NOW! LET ME AT 'IM!!!
I'M THE SECOND BEST SWORDSMAN ON FISH-MAN ISLAND!! THEY CALL ME HACHI OF THE SIX-SWORD STYLE!!! DID YOU KNOW THAT!!?
NO MERE HUMAN COULD EVER BEAT ME, EVEN IF HEAVEN AND EARTH TURNED UPSIDE DOWN!!!

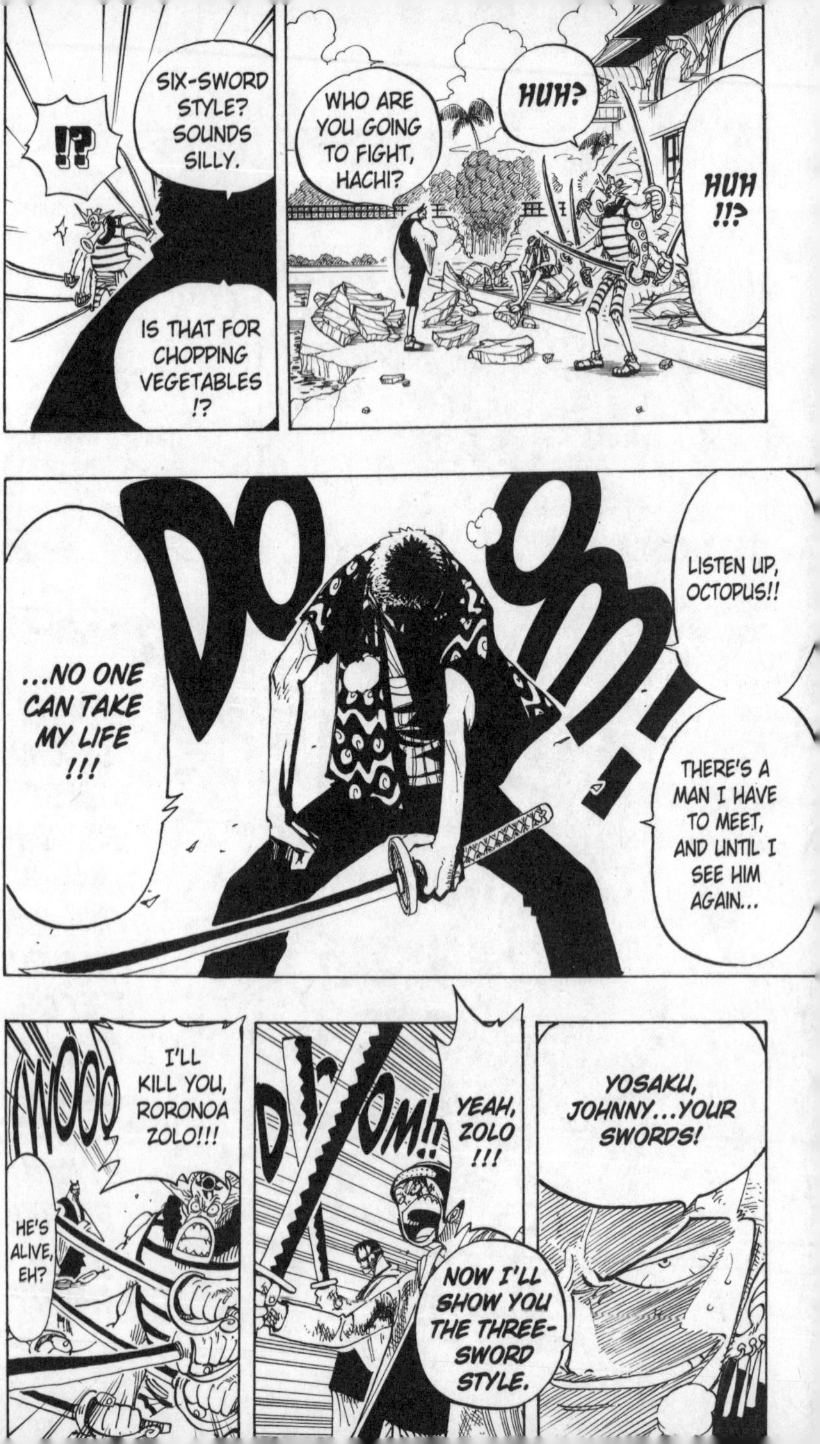
HUH?
HUH !!?
WHO ARE YOU GOING TO FIGHT, HACHI?
SIX-SWORD STYLE? SOUNDS SILLY.
!?
IS THAT FOR CHOPPING VEGETABLES !?
LISTEN UP, OCTOPUS!!
DOOM!!
THERE'S A MAN I HAVE TO MEET, AND UNTIL I SEE HIM AGAIN...
...NO ONE CAN TAKE MY LIFE !!!
YOSAKU, JOHNNY...YOUR SWORDS!
YEAH, ZOLO !!!
DOOM!!
NOW I'LL SHOW YOU THE THREE-SWORD STYLE.
I'LL KILL YOU, RORONOA ZOLO!!!
WOOO
HE'S ALIVE, EH?

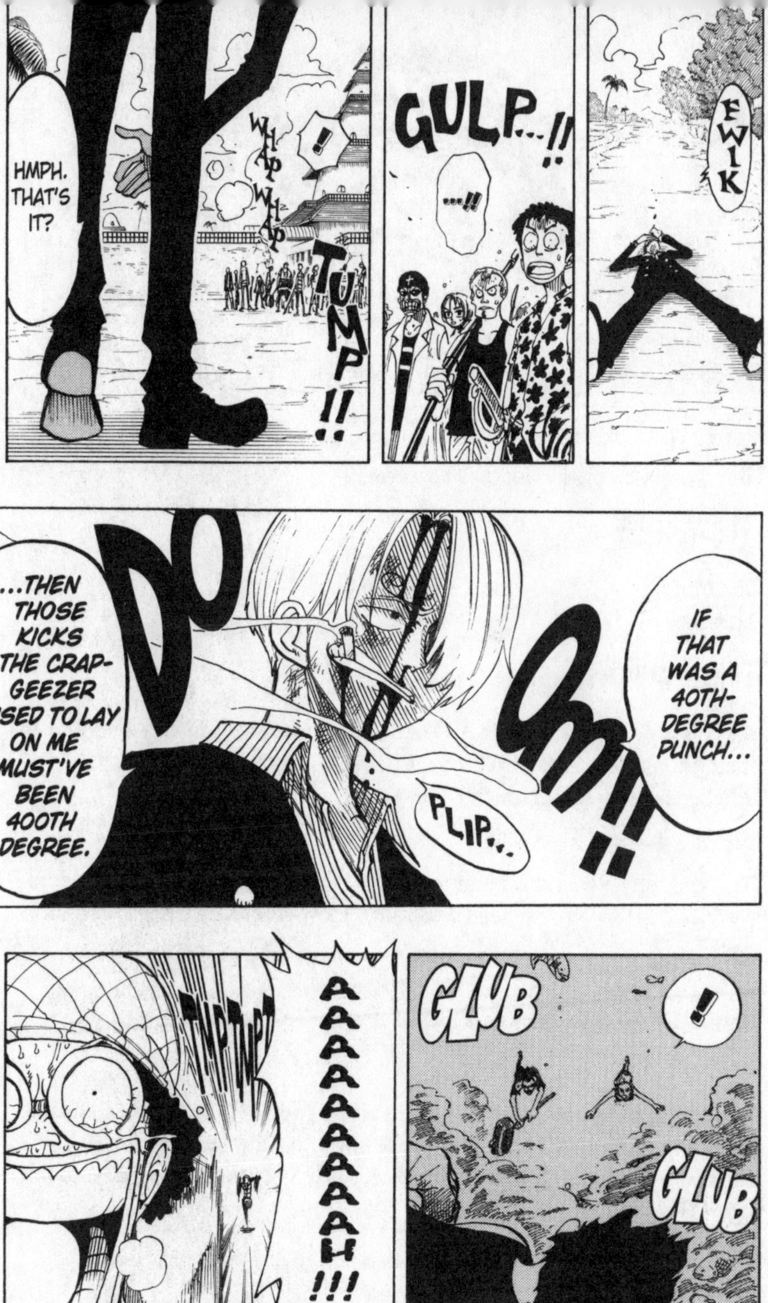
EWIK
GULP...!!
...!!
!
WHAP WHAP
TUMP!!
HMPH. THAT'S IT?
IF THAT WAS A 40TH-DEGREE PUNCH...
DOOM!!
PLIP...
...THEN THOSE KICKS THE CRAP-GEEZER USED TO LAY ON ME MUST'VE BEEN 400TH DEGREE.
GLUB
!
GLUB
AAAAAAAAAH!!!
TMP TMP

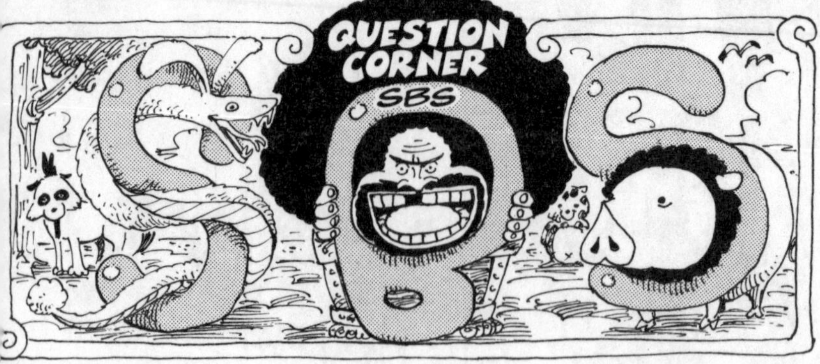
QUESTION CORNER
SBS

Q: Here goes! Oooone! Twoooo!! Threeeee!!!

A: Thump!!!!

Q: One more time! ♡ Oooone.♡ Twoooo.♡ Threeeee.♡

A: Thump!!! Oh... I'm being played.

Q: Yo! Wassup? ONE PIECE is A-OK! It's always lots of fun and a regular storm of emotions. This is my first time writing to a manga artist. ♡ Oda Sensei, you're a character I like.

A: I'm not a character.

Q: The other day a friend asked me to draw Shanks, so I did. Then suddenly my friend hit me on the head and said, "How come you drew Django!?" Am I sick?

A: Yes. It's an illness. It's "Django Drawer's Disease." You just keep drawing Django. Late-stage symptoms include drawing Django even when you're signing for deliveries, so please be careful.

Q: That thing that's perched on Zeff's head on page 121 of volume 8 is a hat, right? My mom won't believe me. She says, "It's too tall to be a hat. There must be a pole behind him." Sensei, please tell her yourself so the blockhead (age 44) will believe it.

A: Er, Mom, please listen carefully. In this world, there are facts that cannot be bent and realities from which we cannot avert our eyes. The thing that looms above Zeff's head is a "Tower of Faith" that rises up because of his spirit. It is called the "Blue Heavens-Dividing Chef's Hat!" It's true!!!!

Chapter 85: THREE SWORDS VS. SIX

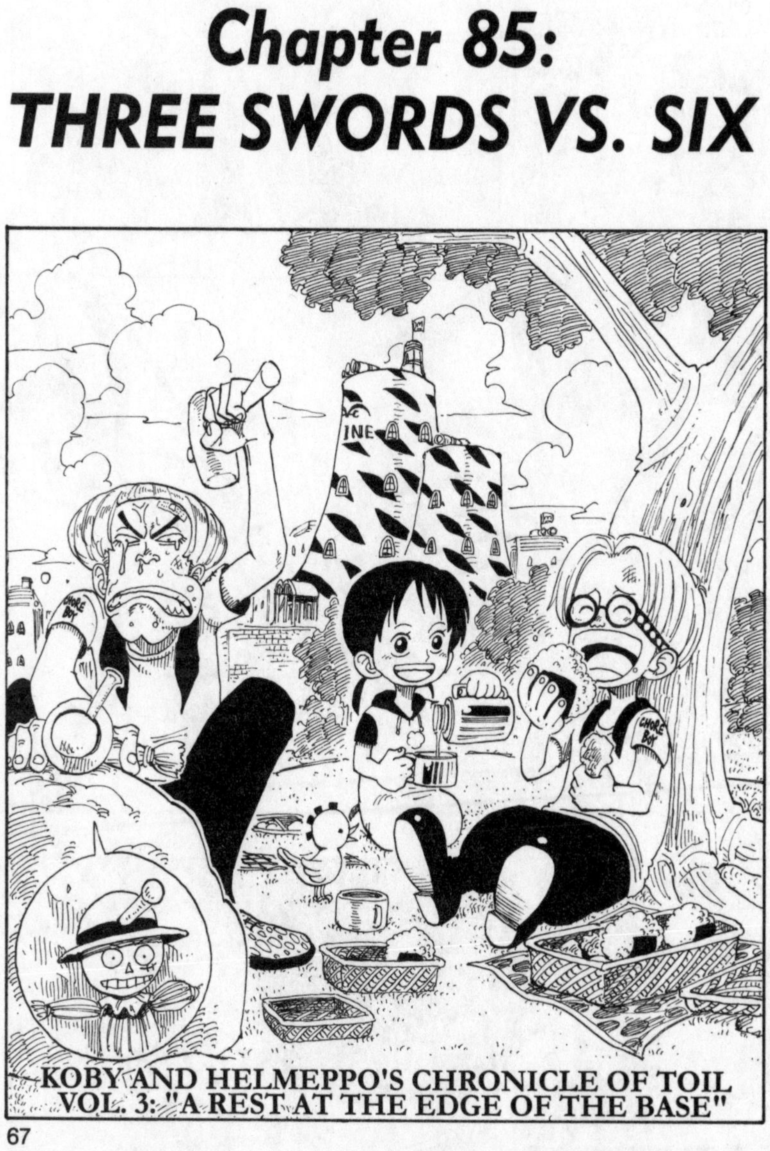
CHORE BOY
CHORE BOY

KOBY AND HELMEPPO'S CHRONICLE OF TOIL
VOL. 3: "A REST AT THE EDGE OF THE BASE"

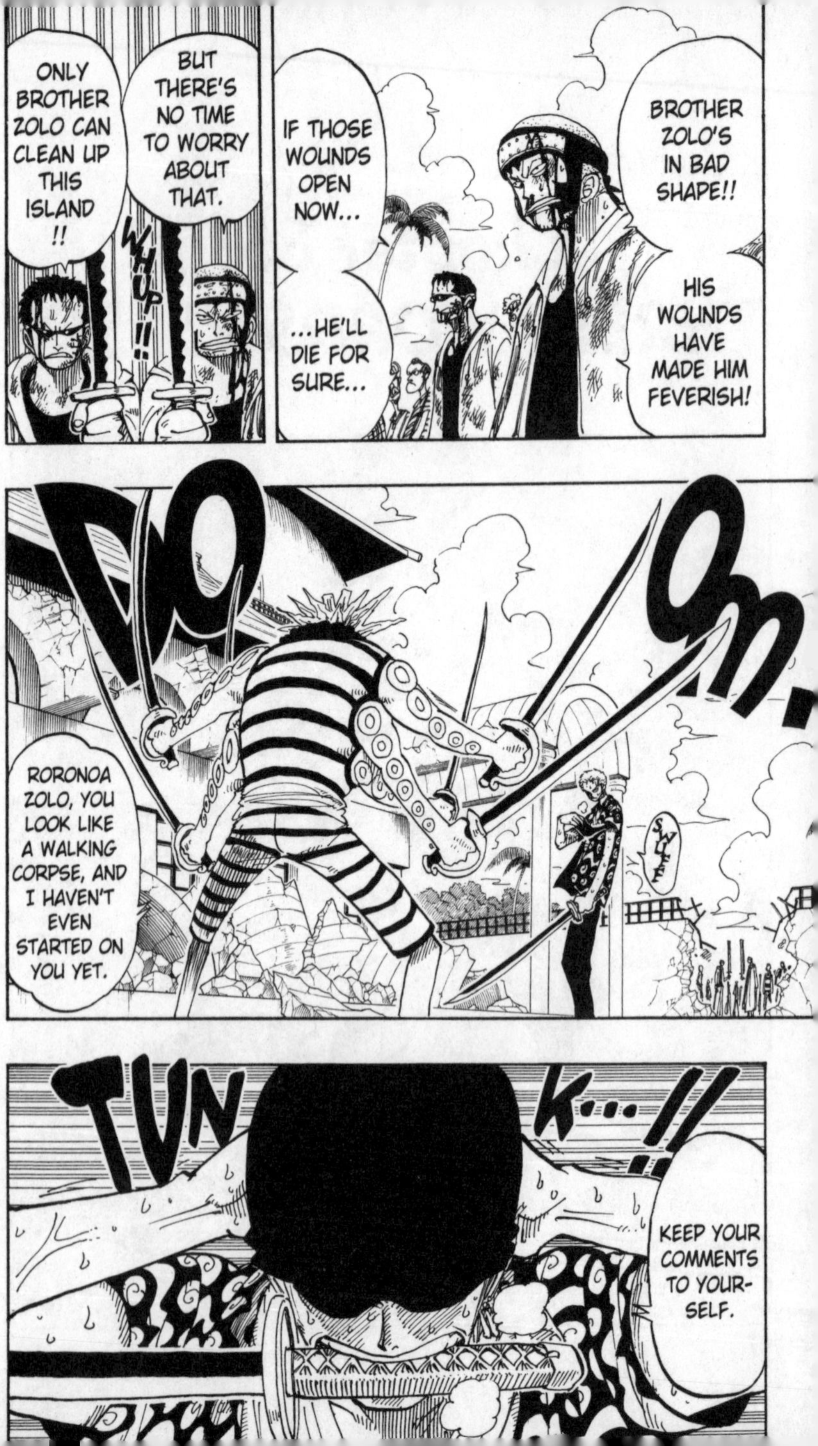
BROTHER ZOLO'S IN BAD SHAPE!!
HIS WOUNDS HAVE MADE HIM FEVERISH!
IF THOSE WOUNDS OPEN NOW...
...HE'LL DIE FOR SURE...
BUT THERE'S NO TIME TO WORRY ABOUT THAT.
ONLY BROTHER ZOLO CAN CLEAN UP THIS ISLAND!!
WHUP!!
DOOM..
RORONOA ZOLO, YOU LOOK LIKE A WALKING CORPSE, AND I HAVEN'T EVEN STARTED ON YOU YET.
SWUFF
TUNK...!!
KEEP YOUR COMMENTS TO YOURSELF.

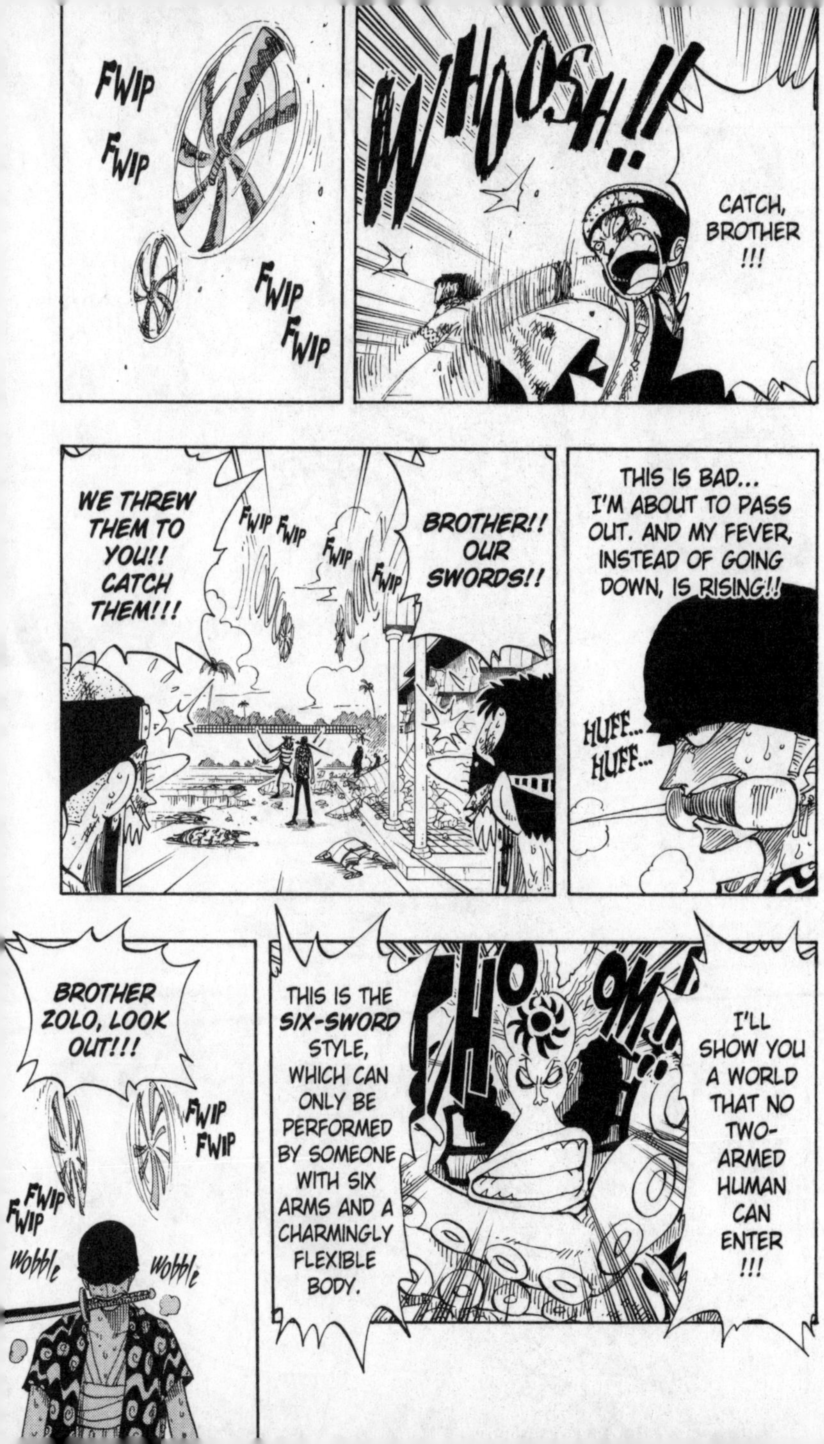
WHOOSH!!
CATCH, BROTHER!!!
FWIP
FWIP
FWIP
FWIP
THIS IS BAD... I'M ABOUT TO PASS OUT. AND MY FEVER, INSTEAD OF GOING DOWN, IS RISING!!
HUFF... HUFF...
BROTHER!! OUR SWORDS!!
FWIP FWIP
FWIP
FWIP
WE THREW THEM TO YOU!! CATCH THEM!!!
THOOM!!
I'LL SHOW YOU A WORLD THAT NO TWO-ARMED HUMAN CAN ENTER!!!
THIS IS THE SIX-SWORD STYLE, WHICH CAN ONLY BE PERFORMED BY SOMEONE WITH SIX ARMS AND A CHARMINGLY FLEXIBLE BODY.
BROTHER ZOLO, LOOK OUT!!!
FWIP FWIP
FWIP FWIP
wobble
wobble

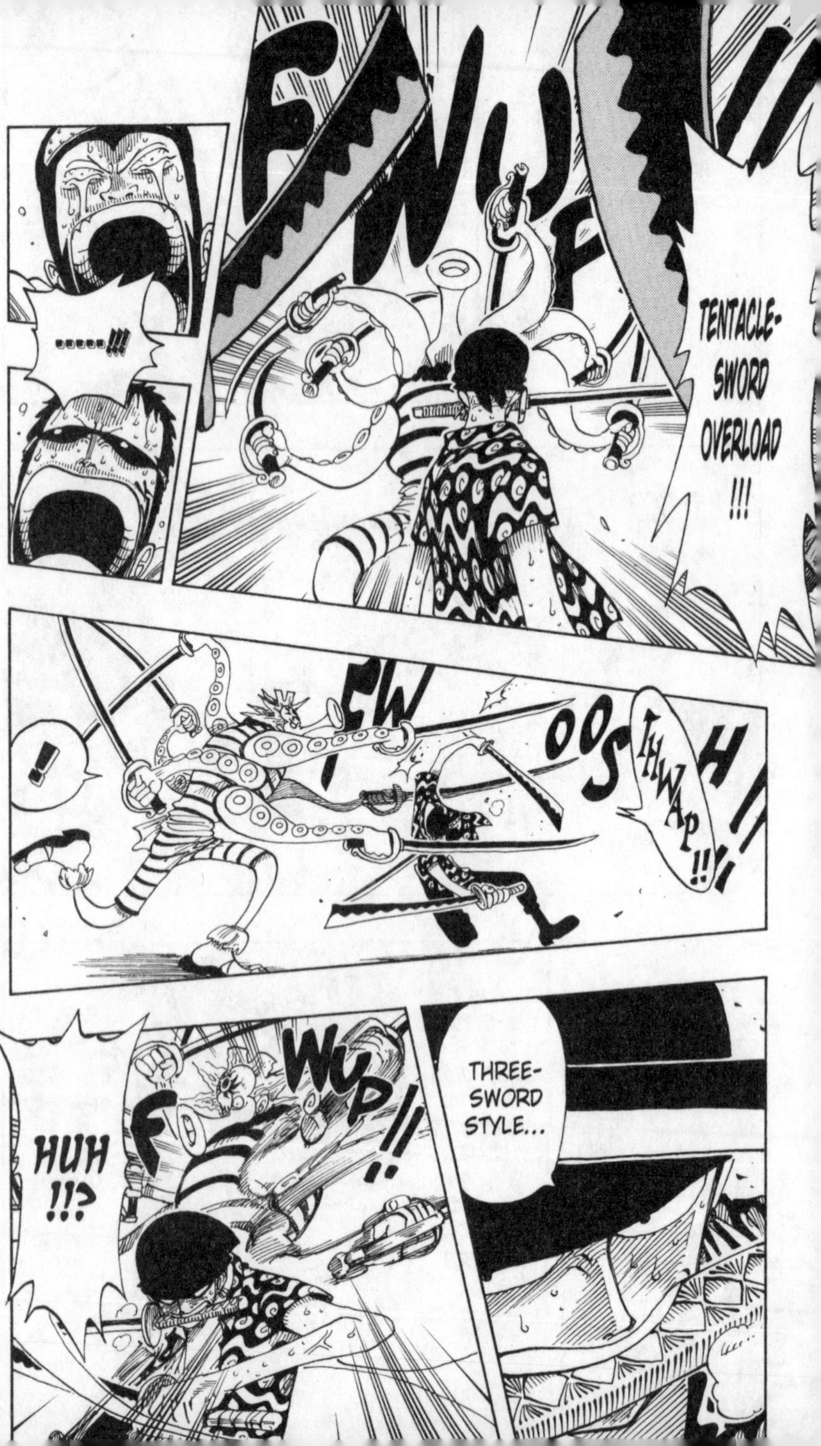
FWUF
TENTACLE-SWORD OVERLOAD !!!
.....!!!
FWOOSH
THWAP!!
!
THREE-SWORD STYLE...
FWUP!!
HUH !!?

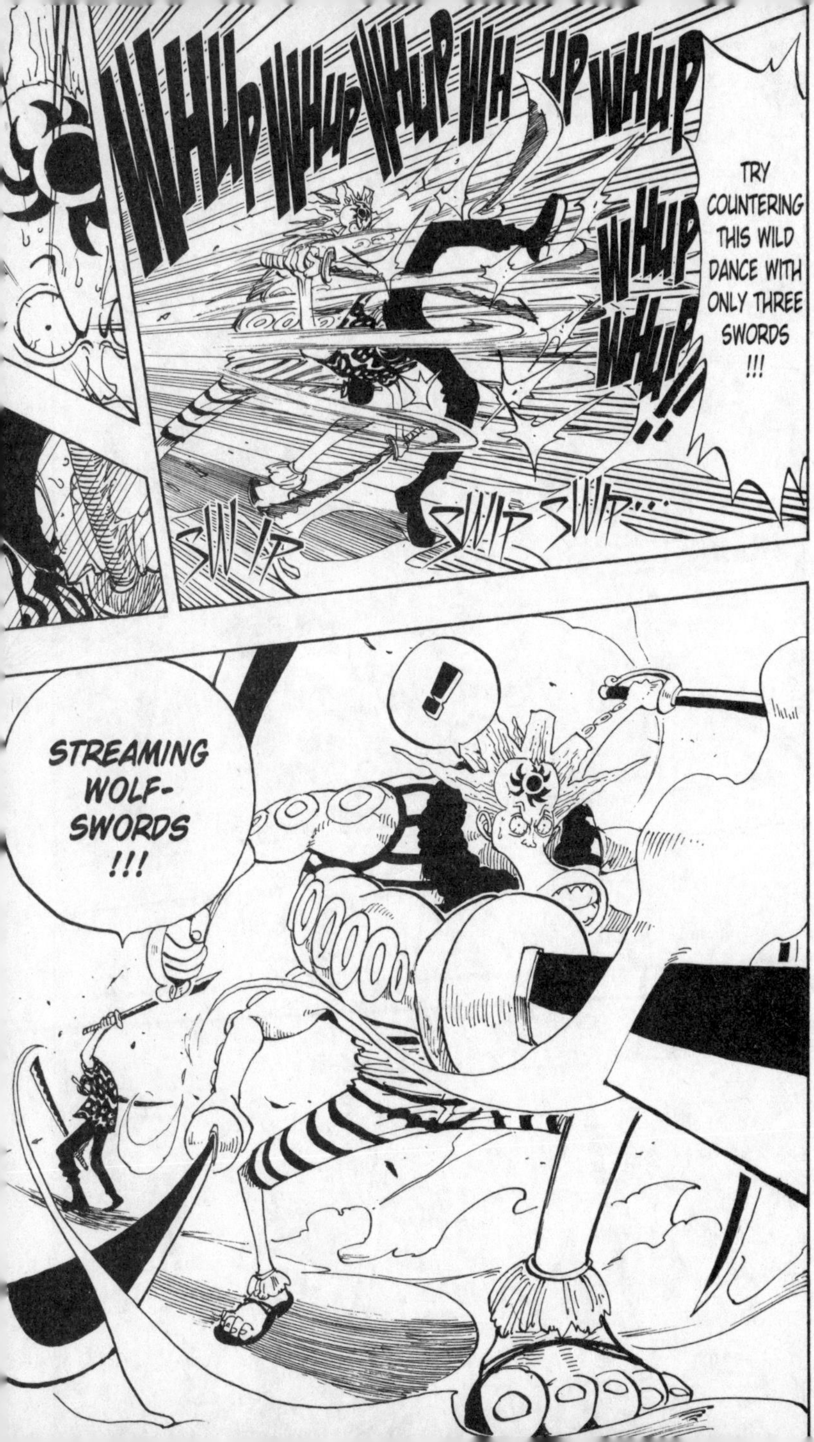
TRY COUNTERING THIS WILD DANCE WITH ONLY THREE SWORDS !!!
WHUP WHUP WHUP WH UP WHUP
WHUP WHUP!!
SWIP SWIP SWIP...
!
STREAMING WOLF-SWORDS !!!

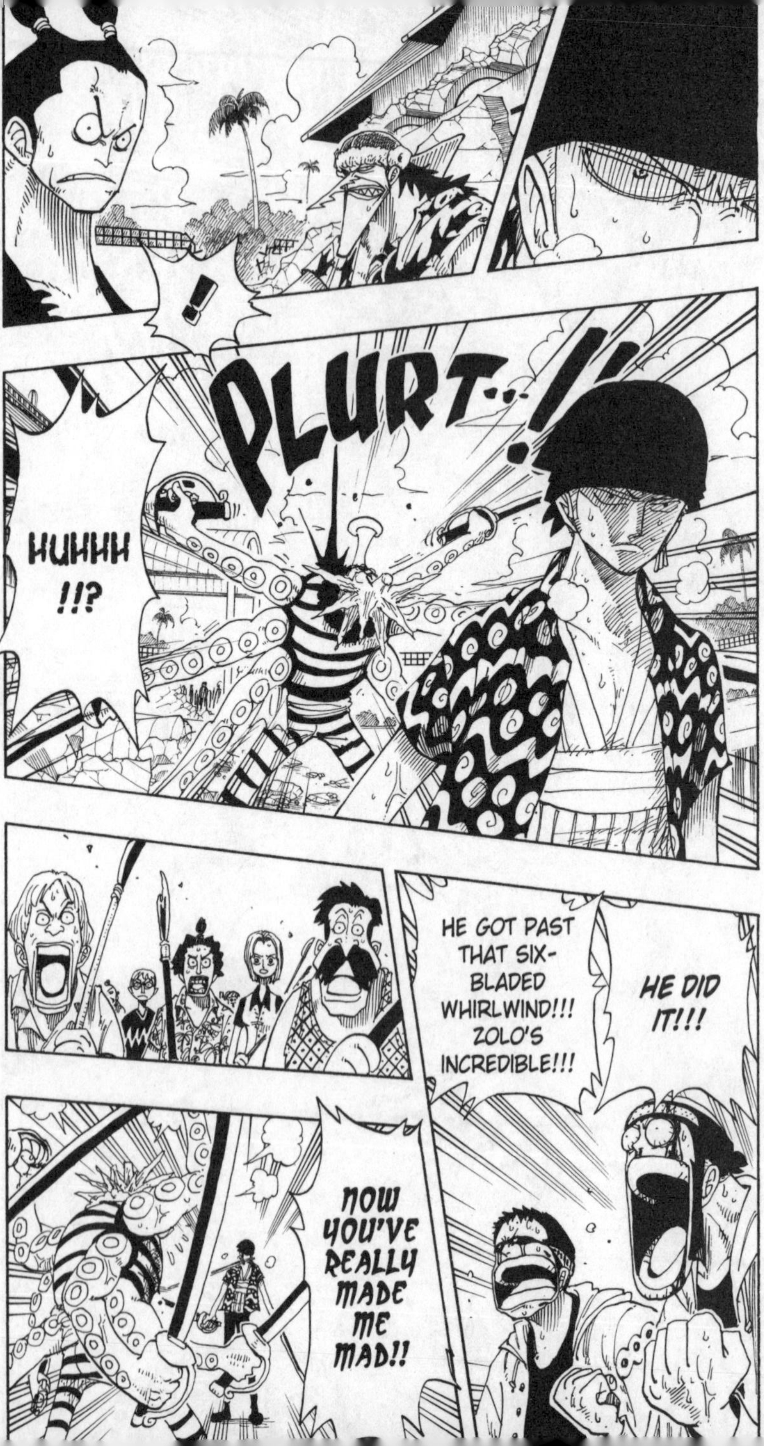
!
PLURT...!!
HUHHH !!?
HE DID IT!!!
HE GOT PAST THAT SIX-BLADED WHIRLWIND!!! ZOLO'S INCREDIBLE!!!
NOW YOU'VE REALLY MADE ME MAD!!

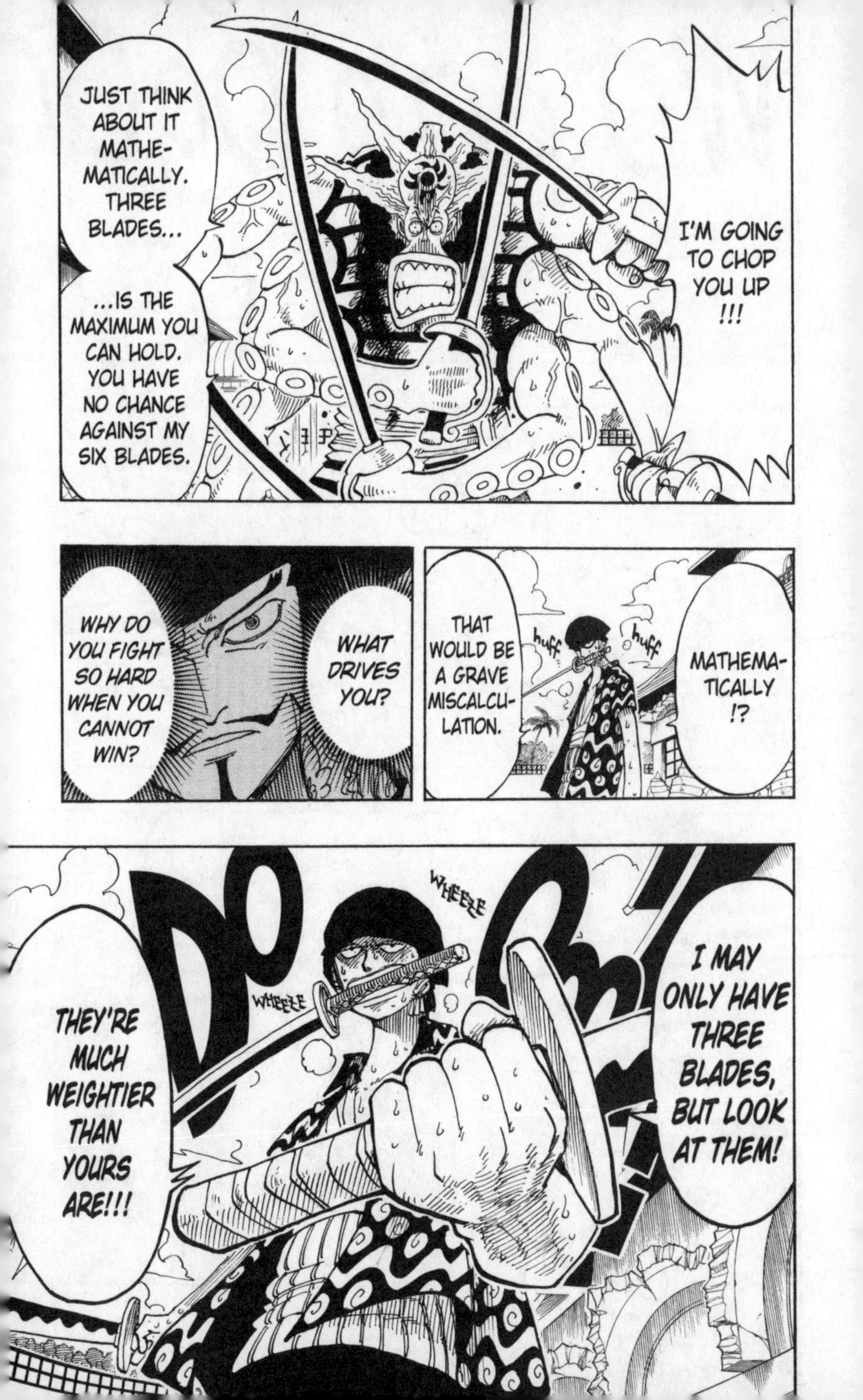
I'M GOING TO CHOP YOU UP !!!
JUST THINK ABOUT IT MATHE-MATICALLY. THREE BLADES...
...IS THE MAXIMUM YOU CAN HOLD. YOU HAVE NO CHANCE AGAINST MY SIX BLADES.
MATHEMA-TICALLY !?
huff
huff
THAT WOULD BE A GRAVE MISCALCU-LATION.
WHAT DRIVES YOU?
WHY DO YOU FIGHT SO HARD WHEN YOU CANNOT WIN?
WHEEZE
I MAY ONLY HAVE THREE BLADES, BUT LOOK AT THEM!
WHEEZE
THEY'RE MUCH WEIGHTIER THAN YOURS ARE!!!

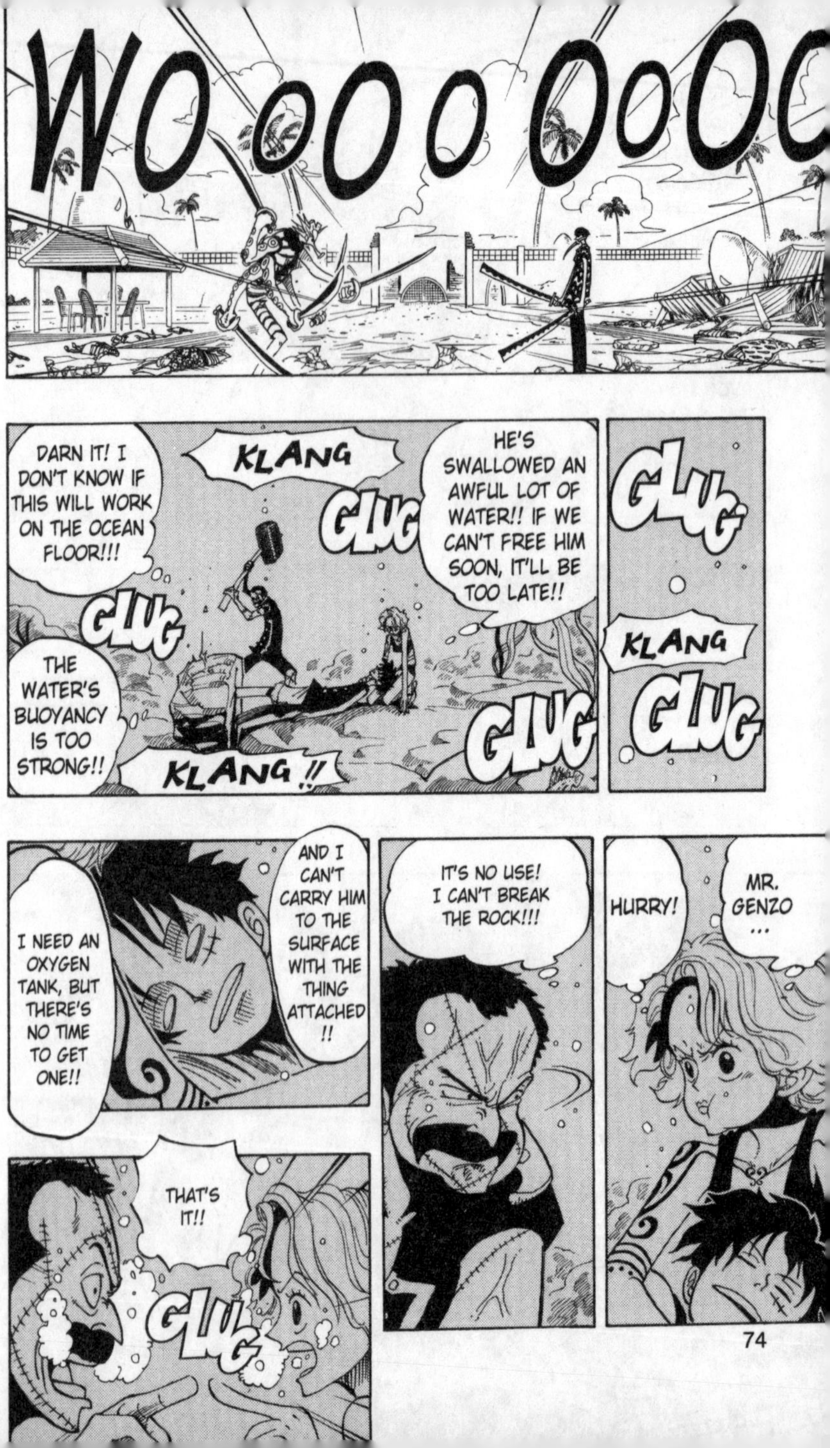
WOOOOOOOO
GLUG
KLANG
GLUG
HE'S SWALLOWED AN AWFUL LOT OF WATER!! IF WE CAN'T FREE HIM SOON, IT'LL BE TOO LATE!!
KLANG
GLUG
DARN IT! I DON'T KNOW IF THIS WILL WORK ON THE OCEAN FLOOR!!!
GLUG
GLUG
THE WATER'S BUOYANCY IS TOO STRONG!!
KLANG !!
MR. GENZO ...
HURRY!
IT'S NO USE! I CAN'T BREAK THE ROCK!!!
AND I CAN'T CARRY HIM TO THE SURFACE WITH THE THING ATTACHED !!
I NEED AN OXYGEN TANK, BUT THERE'S NO TIME TO GET ONE!!
THAT'S IT!!
GLUG

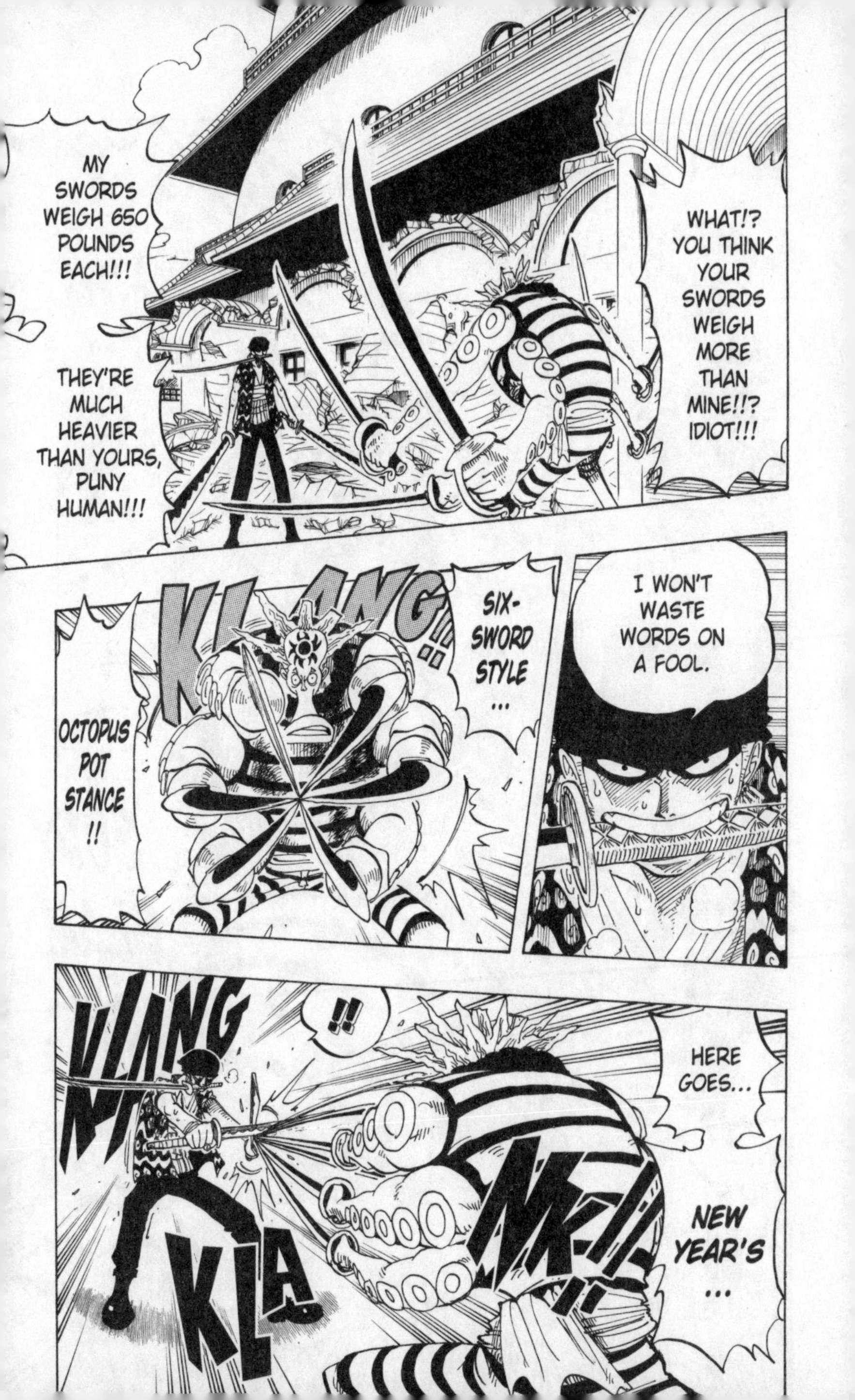
WHAT!? YOU THINK YOUR SWORDS WEIGH MORE THAN MINE!!? IDIOT!!!
MY SWORDS WEIGH 650 POUNDS EACH!!!
THEY'RE MUCH HEAVIER THAN YOURS, PUNY HUMAN!!!
I WON'T WASTE WORDS ON A FOOL.
KLANG!!
SIX-SWORD STYLE ...
OCTOPUS POT STANCE !!
HERE GOES...
!!
KLANG
NEW YEAR'S ...

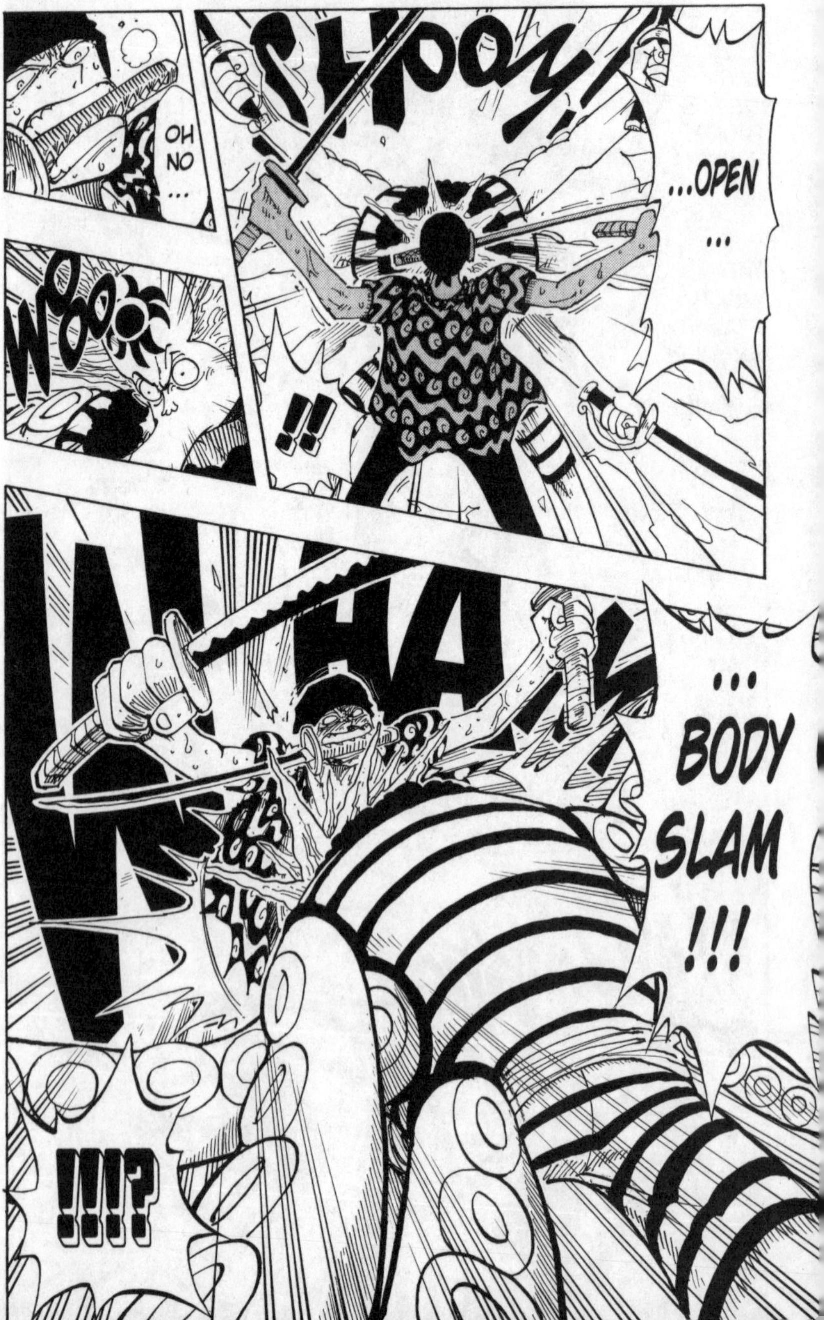
SHOOM!!
...OPEN ...
!!
OH NO ...
WOO
WHAM
... BODY SLAM !!!
!!!?

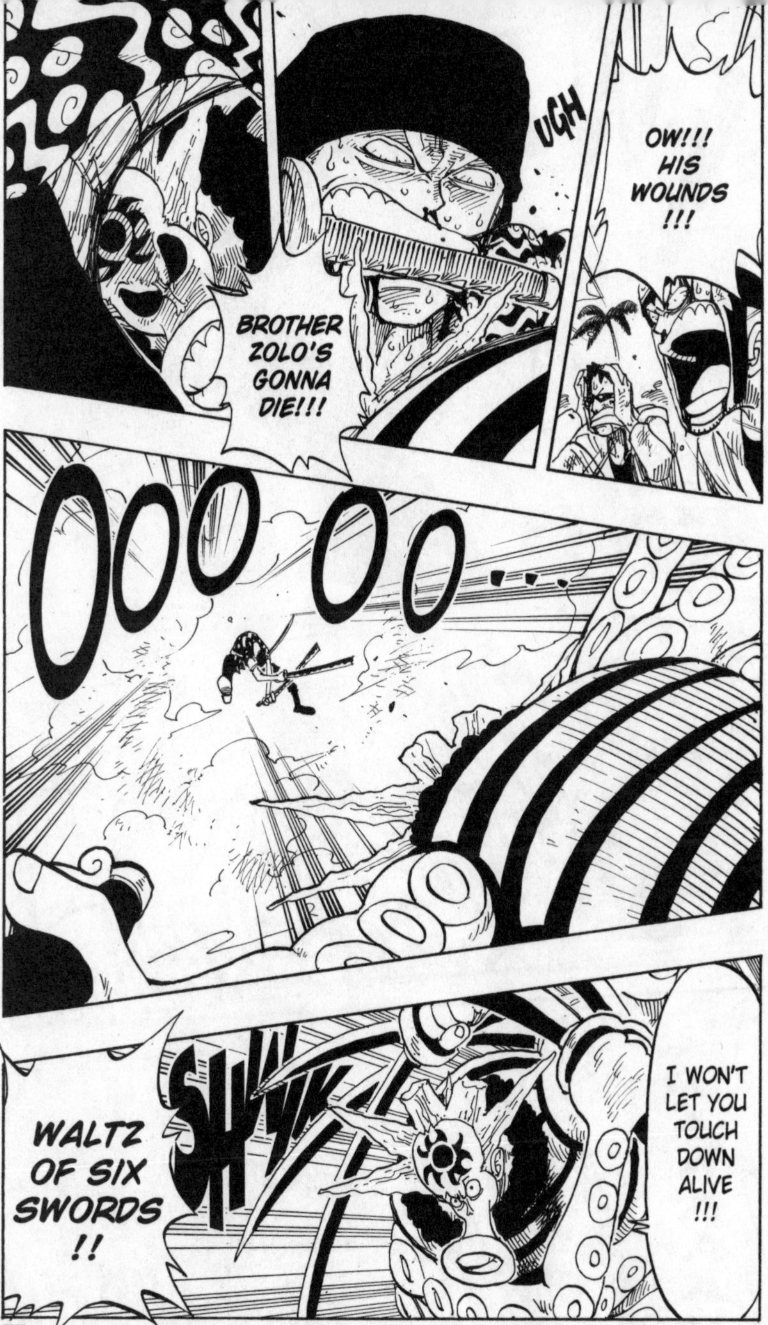
OW!!! HIS WOUNDS !!!
UGH
BROTHER ZOLO'S GONNA DIE!!!
OOO OO...
I WON'T LET YOU TOUCH DOWN ALIVE !!!
SHWK
WALTZ OF SIX SWORDS !!

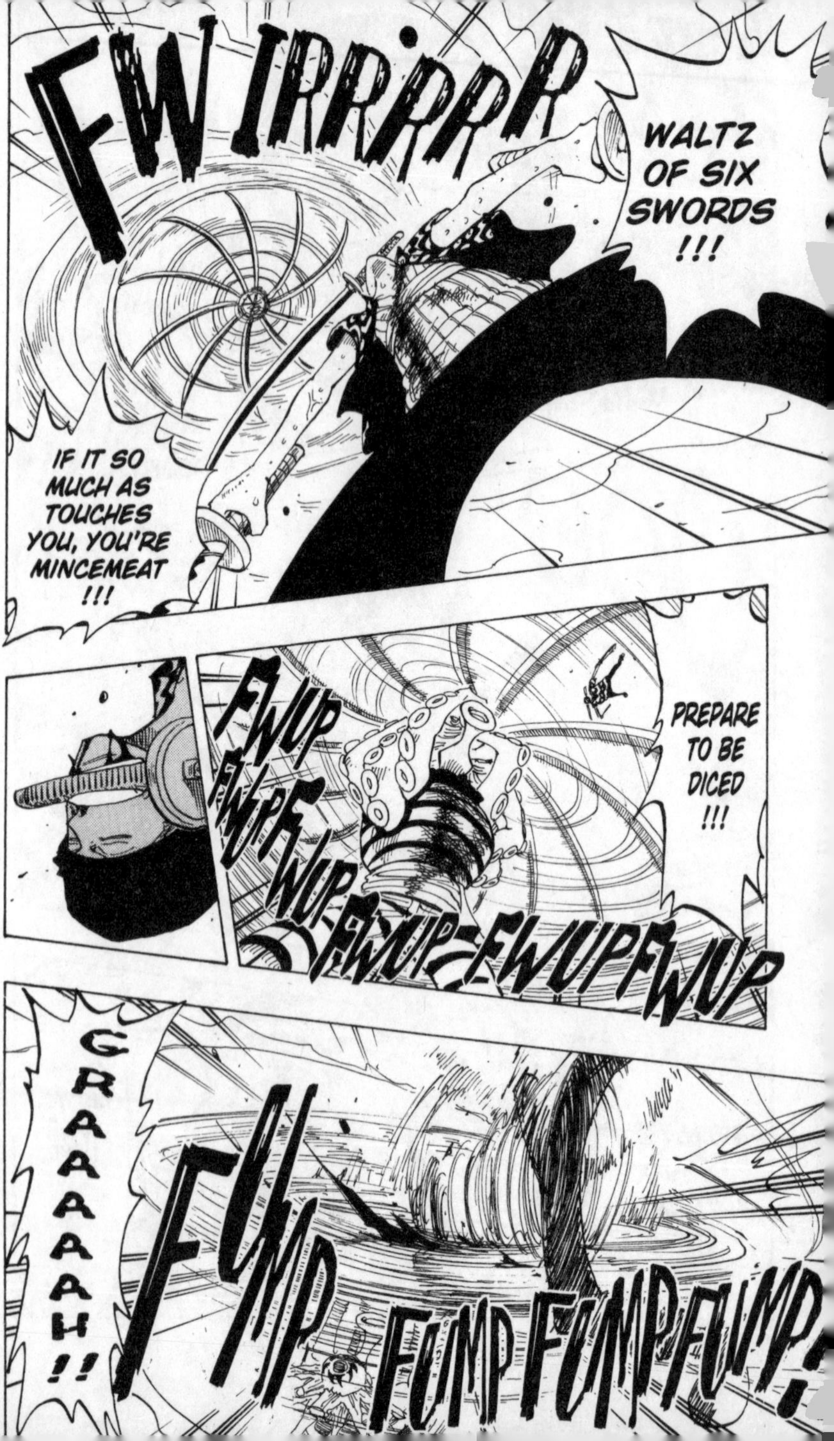
FWIRRRRRR
WALTZ OF SIX SWORDS !!!
IF IT SO MUCH AS TOUCHES YOU, YOU'RE MINCEMEAT !!!
FWUP FWUPFWUP FWUP FWUP FWUP FWUPFWUP
PREPARE TO BE DICED !!!
GRAAAAAAH!!
FUMP FUMP FUMP FUMP

READ THIS WAY

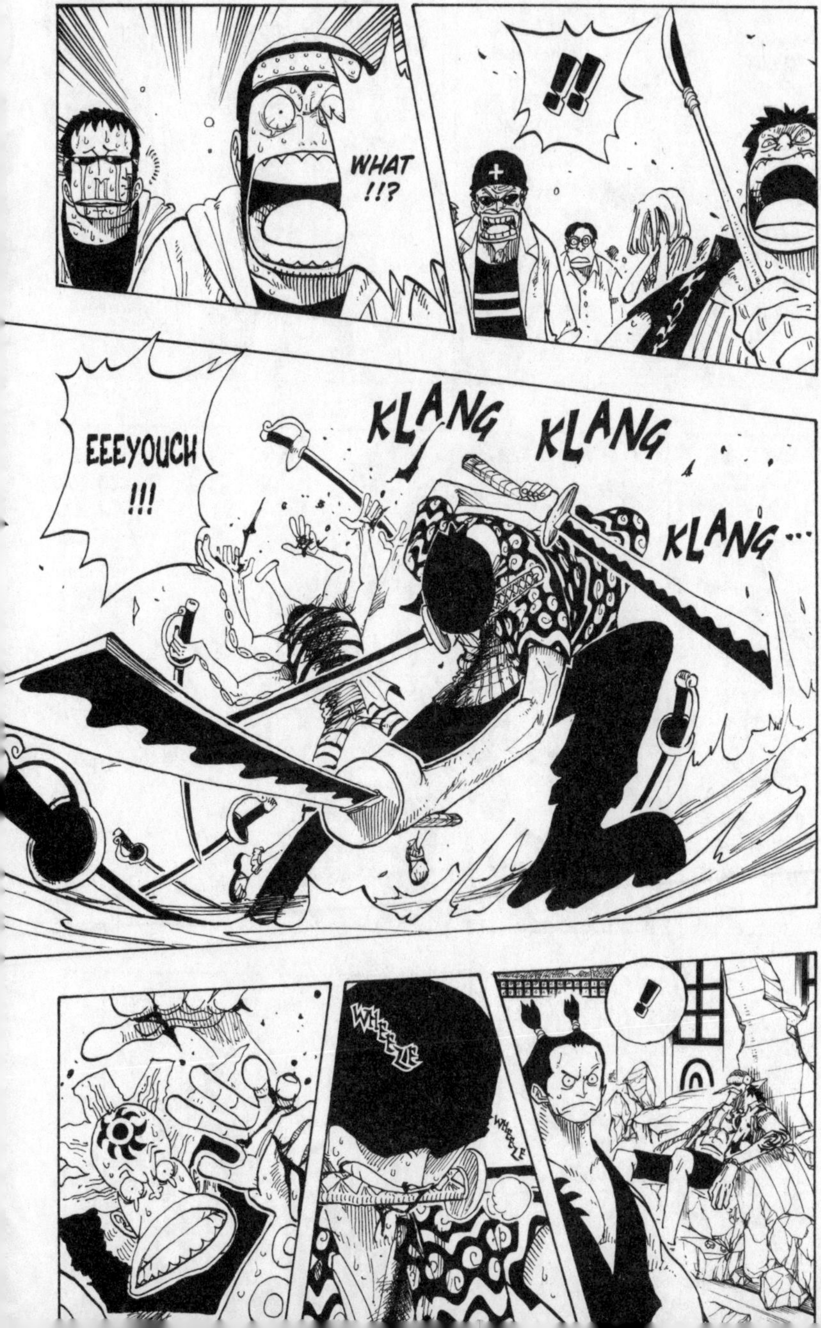
!!
WHAT !!?
KLANG KLANG
KLANG...
EEEYOUCH !!!
!

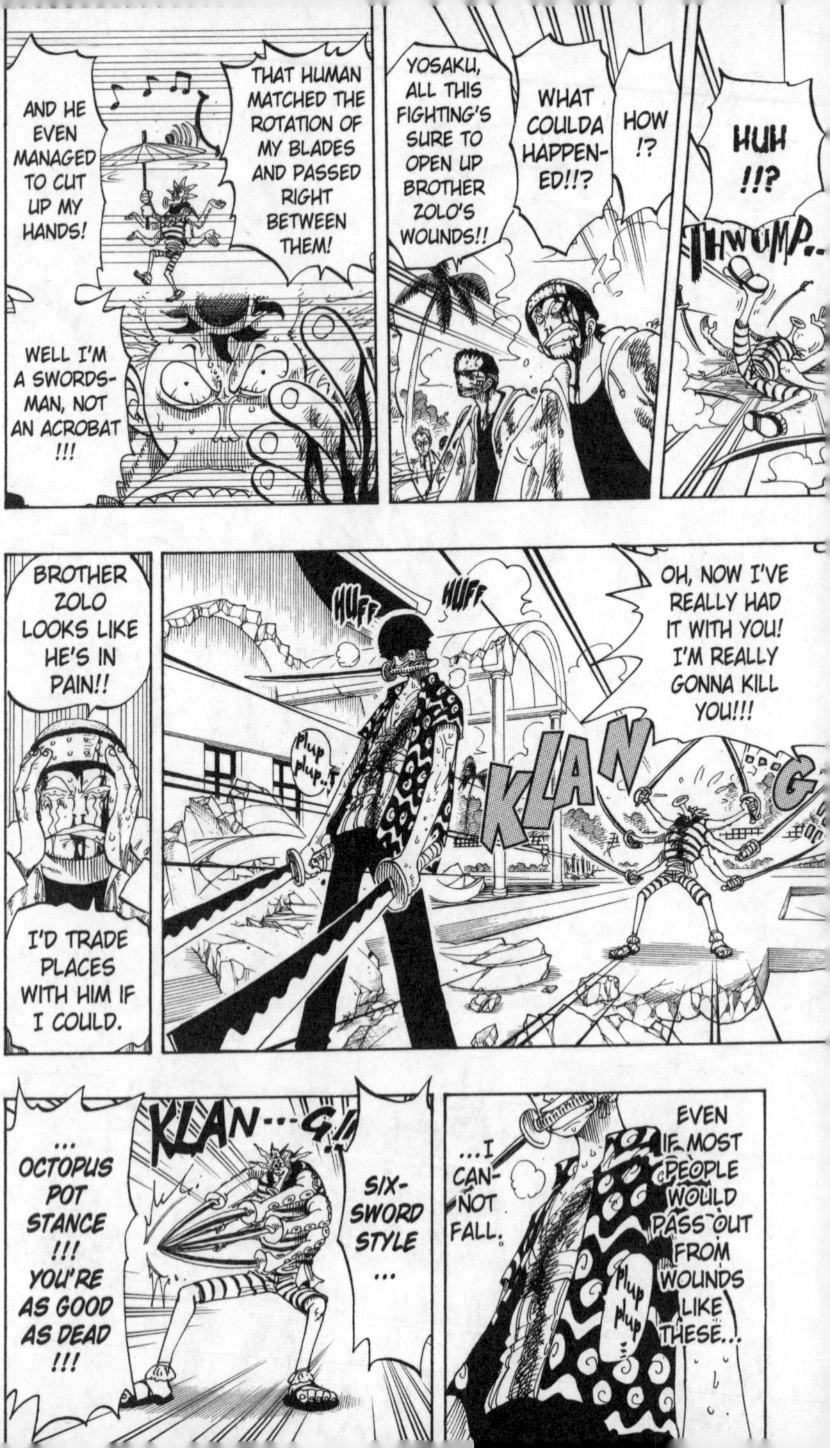
HUH !!?
THWUMP..
HOW !?
WHAT COULDA HAPPEN-ED!!?
YOSAKU, ALL THIS FIGHTING'S SURE TO OPEN UP BROTHER ZOLO'S WOUNDS!!
THAT HUMAN MATCHED THE ROTATION OF MY BLADES AND PASSED RIGHT BETWEEN THEM!
AND HE EVEN MANAGED TO CUT UP MY HANDS!
WELL I'M A SWORDS-MAN, NOT AN ACROBAT !!!
OH, NOW I'VE REALLY HAD IT WITH YOU! I'M REALLY GONNA KILL YOU!!!
KLANG
HUFF
HUFF
plup plup..
BROTHER ZOLO LOOKS LIKE HE'S IN PAIN!!
I'D TRADE PLACES WITH HIM IF I COULD.
EVEN IF MOST PEOPLE WOULD PASS OUT FROM WOUNDS LIKE THESE...
...I CAN-NOT FALL.
plup plup
SIX-SWORD STYLE ...
KLAN---G!!
... OCTOPUS POT STANCE !!! YOU'RE AS GOOD AS DEAD !!!

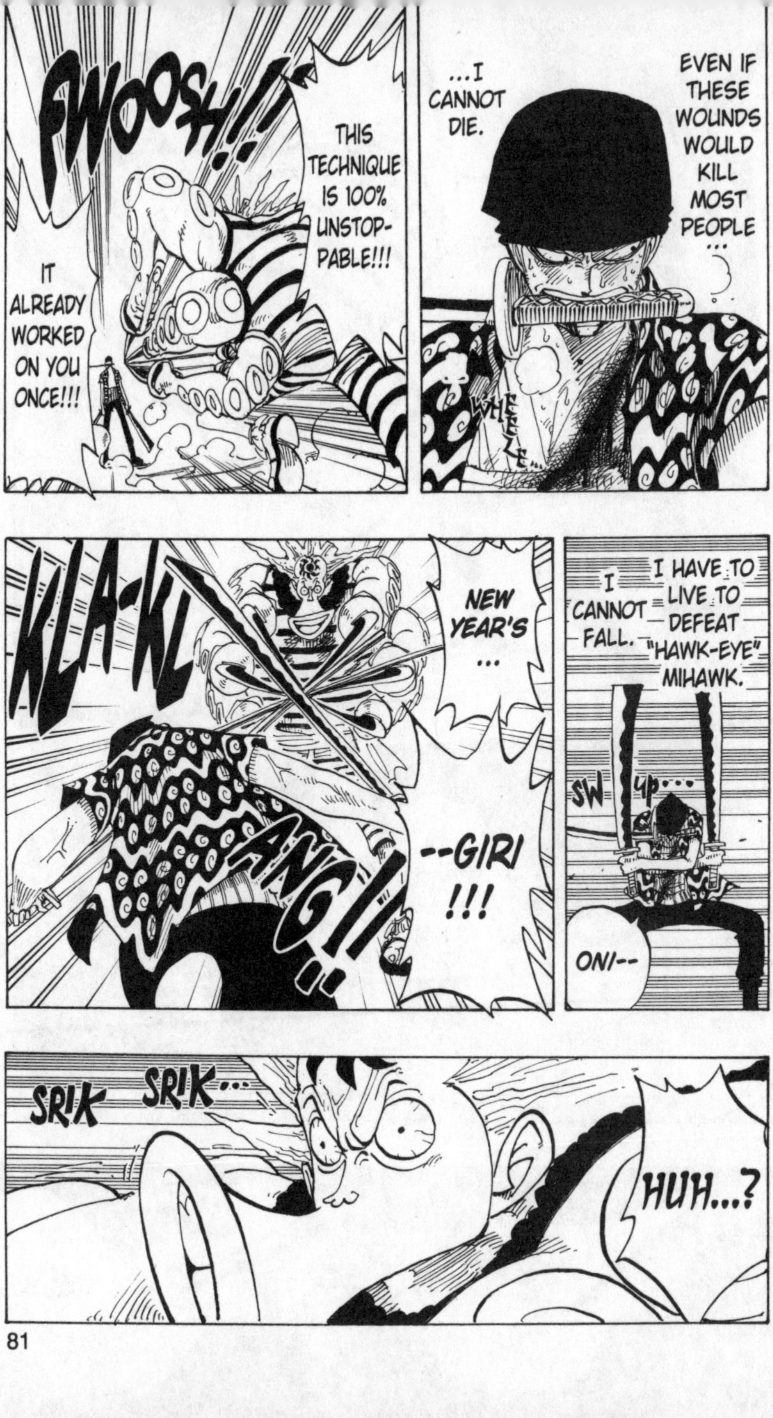
EVEN IF THESE WOUNDS WOULD KILL MOST PEOPLE ...
...I CANNOT DIE.
WHEEZE...
THIS TECHNIQUE IS 100% UNSTOP-PABLE!!!
FWOOSH!!!
IT ALREADY WORKED ON YOU ONCE!!!
I HAVE TO LIVE TO DEFEAT "HAWK-EYE" MIHAWK.
I CANNOT FALL.
SWUP...
ONI--
NEW YEAR'S ...
KLA-KLANG!!
--GIRI !!!
HUH...?
SRIK SRIK...

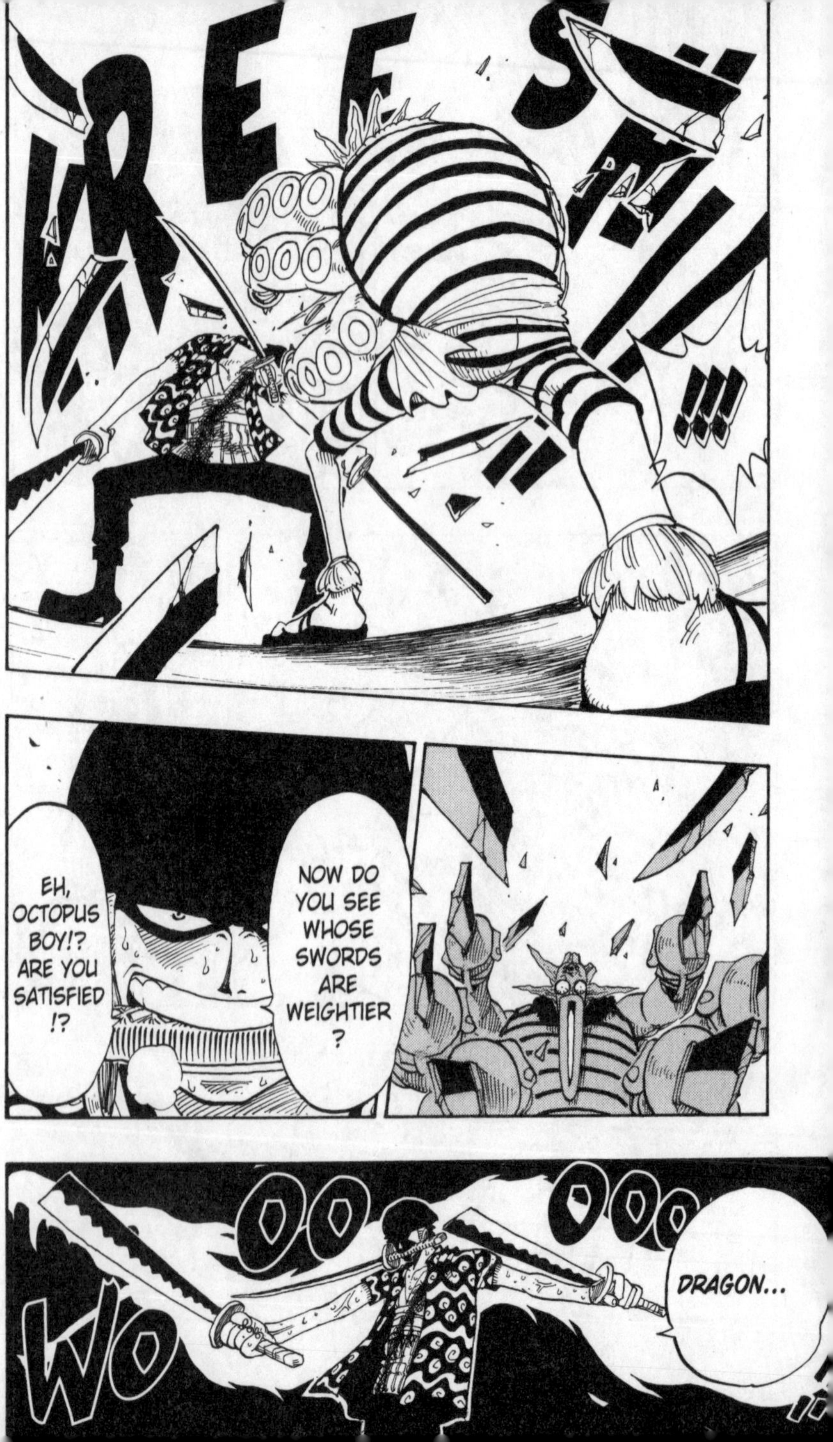
NOW DO YOU SEE WHOSE SWORDS ARE WEIGHTIER?
EH, OCTOPUS BOY!? ARE YOU SATISFIED!?
DRAGON...

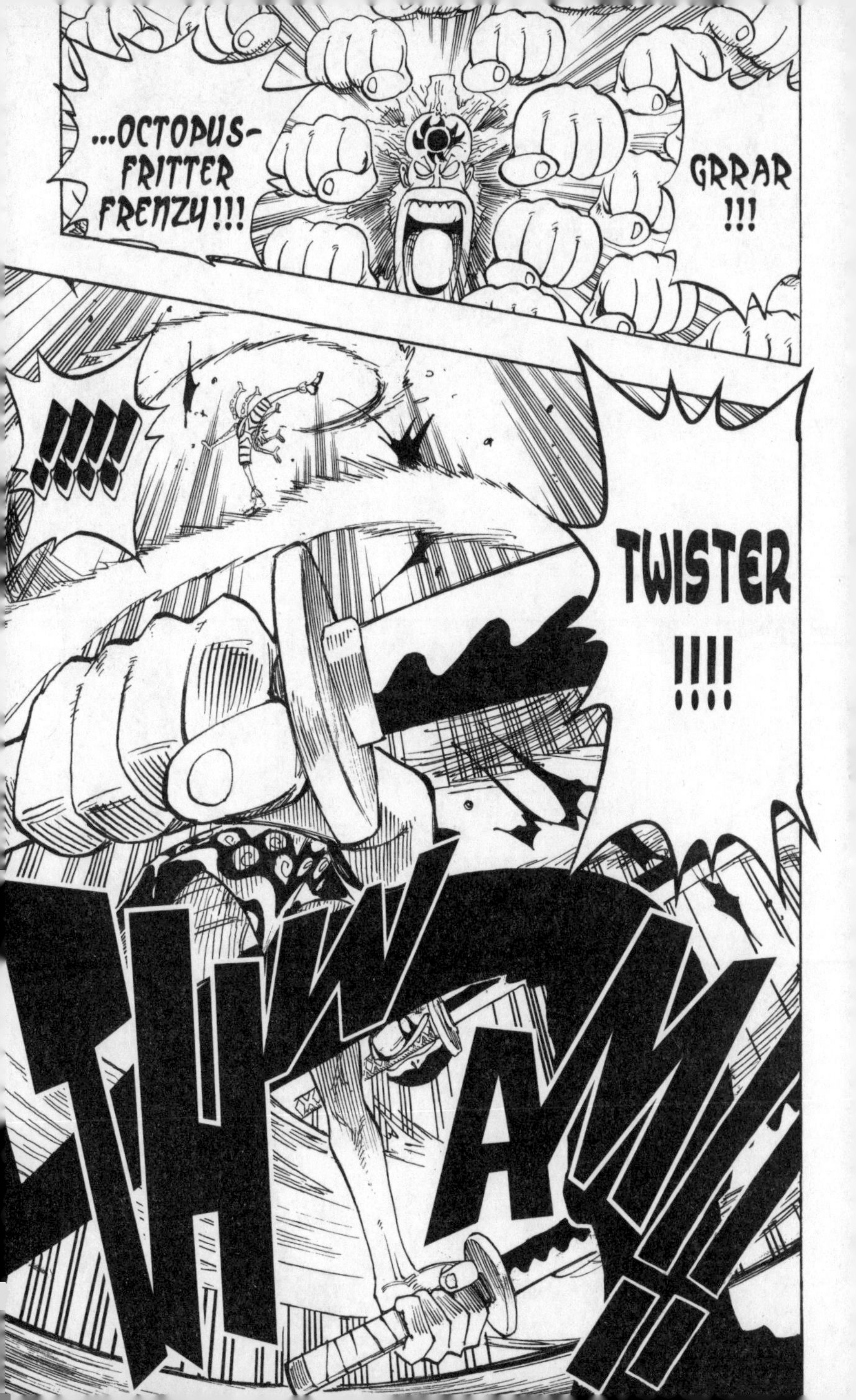
GRRAR!!!
...OCTOPUS-FRITTER FRENZY!!!
!!!!!
TWISTER!!!!
THWAM!!

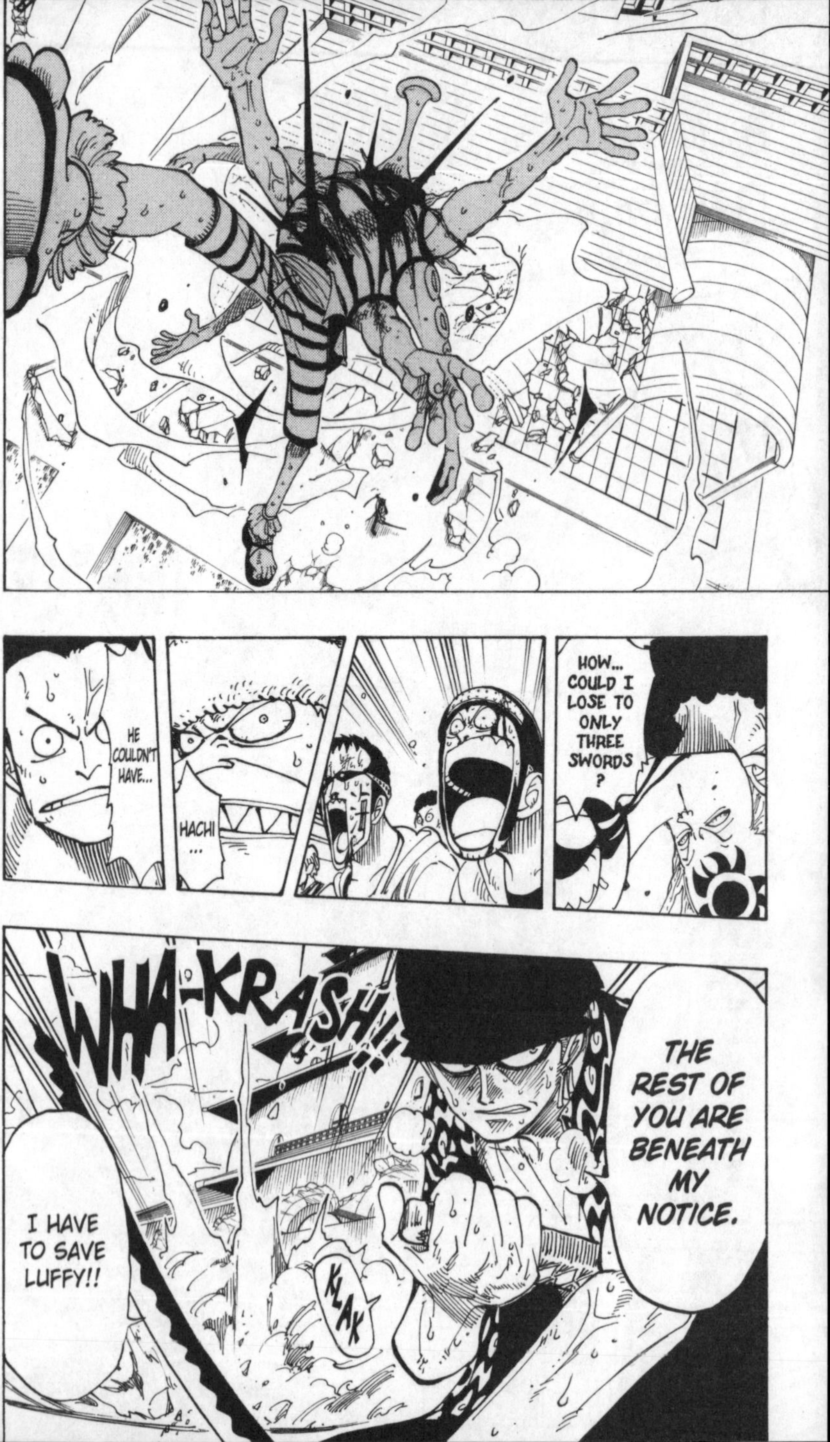
HOW... COULD I LOSE TO ONLY THREE SWORDS?
HACHI...
HE COULDN'T HAVE...
WHA-KRASH!!
THE REST OF YOU ARE BENEATH MY NOTICE.
KLAK
I HAVE TO SAVE LUFFY!!

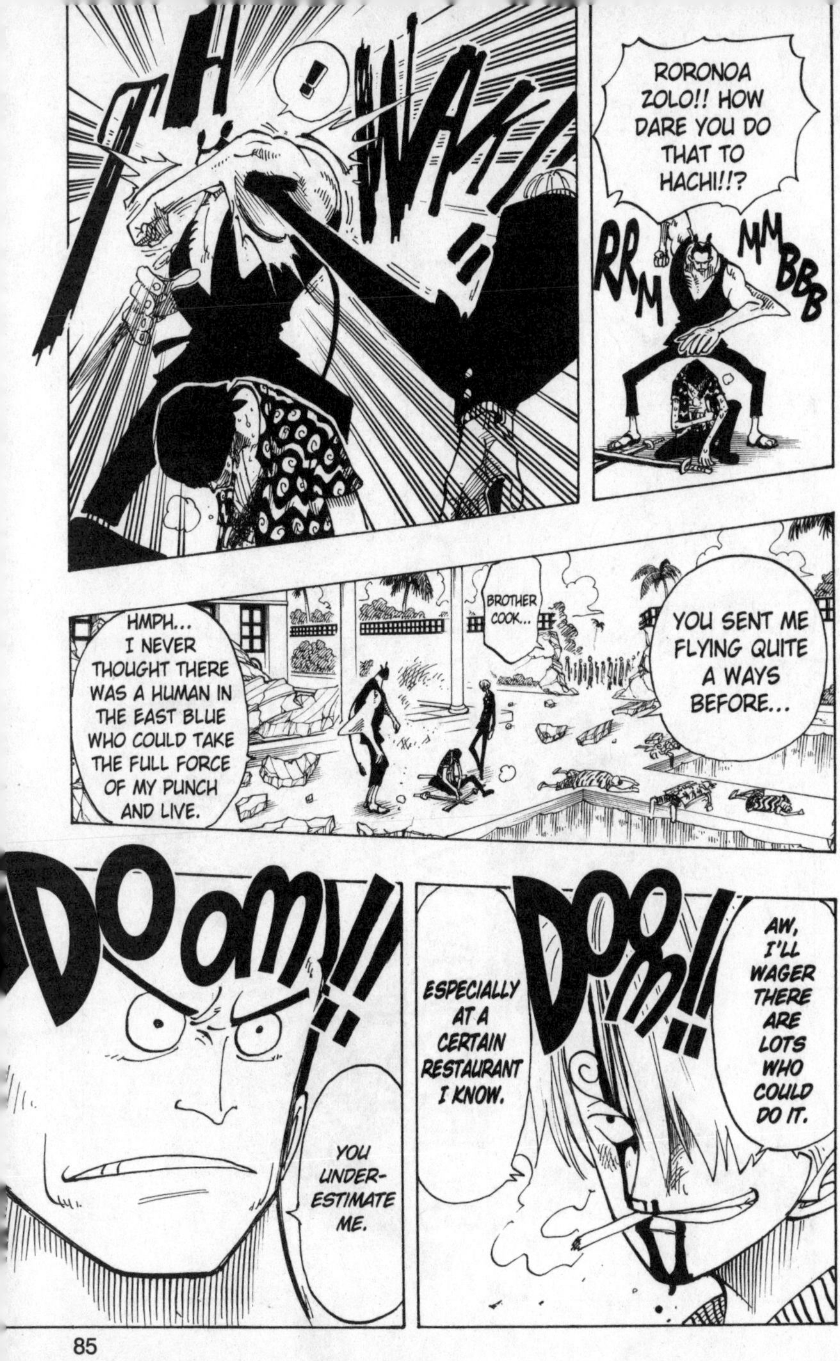
RORONOA ZOLO!! HOW DARE YOU DO THAT TO HACHI!!?
RRRMMMBBB
THWAK!!
!
YOU SENT ME FLYING QUITE A WAYS BEFORE...
BROTHER COOK...
HMPH... I NEVER THOUGHT THERE WAS A HUMAN IN THE EAST BLUE WHO COULD TAKE THE FULL FORCE OF MY PUNCH AND LIVE.
DOOM!!
AW, I'LL WAGER THERE ARE LOTS WHO COULD DO IT.
ESPECIALLY AT A CERTAIN RESTAURANT I KNOW.
DOOM!!
YOU UNDER-ESTIMATE ME.

COLORING CORNER

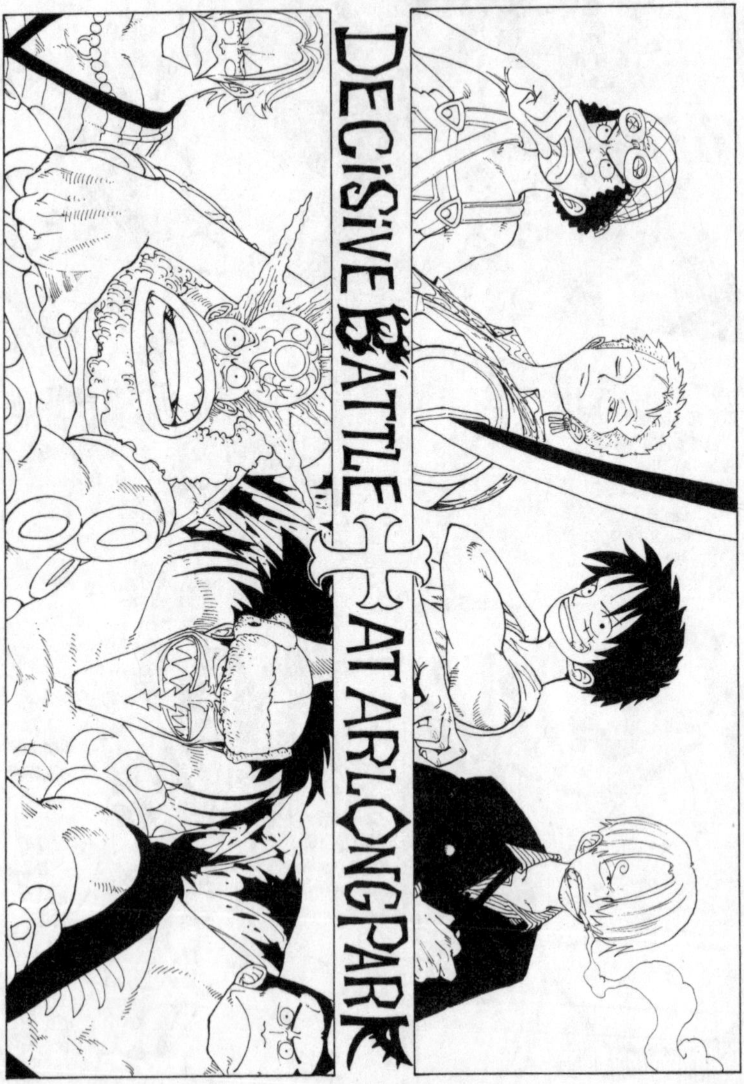
DECISIVE BATTLE AT ARLONG PARK

Chapter 86:
HEROISM VS. FISH-MAN CRUELTY

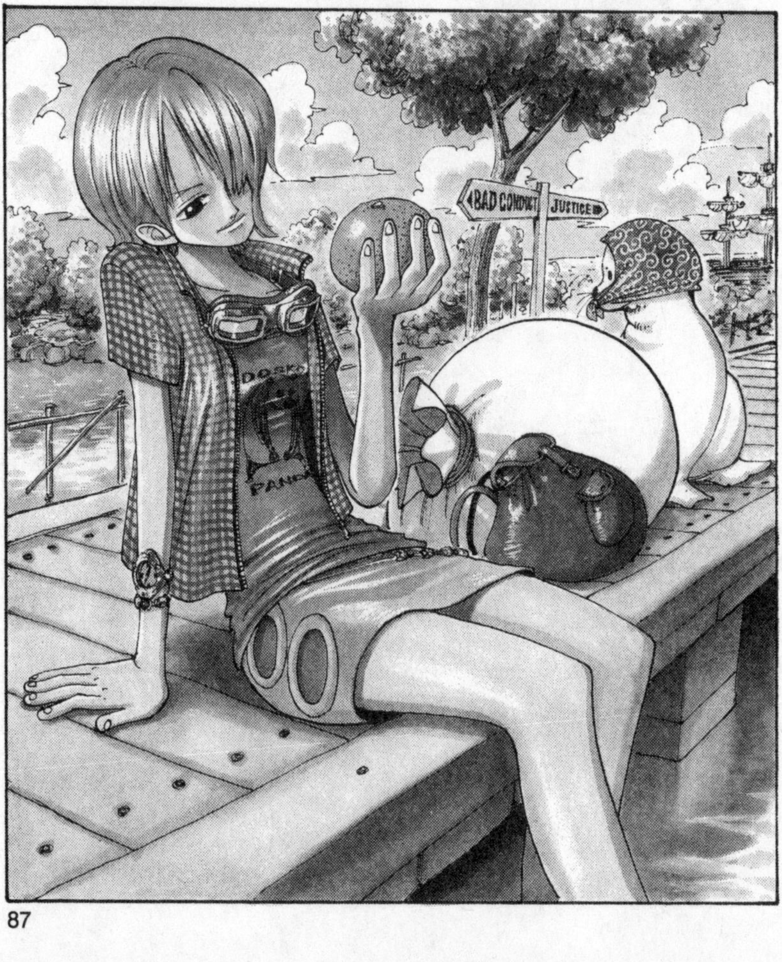
BAD CONDUCT
JUSTICE

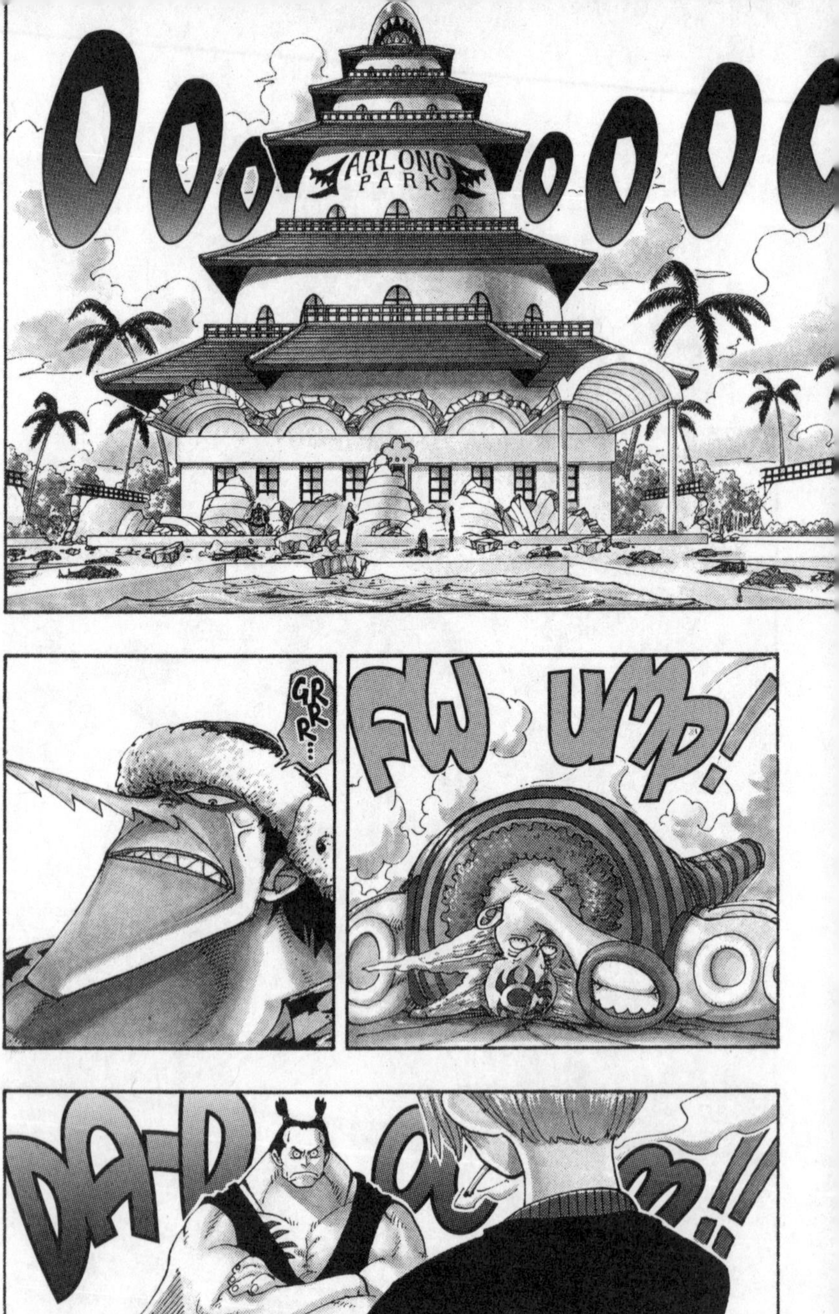
OOOOOOOOOOOO
ARLONG PARK
GRRR...
FWUMP!
DA-DOOM!!

READ THIS WAY

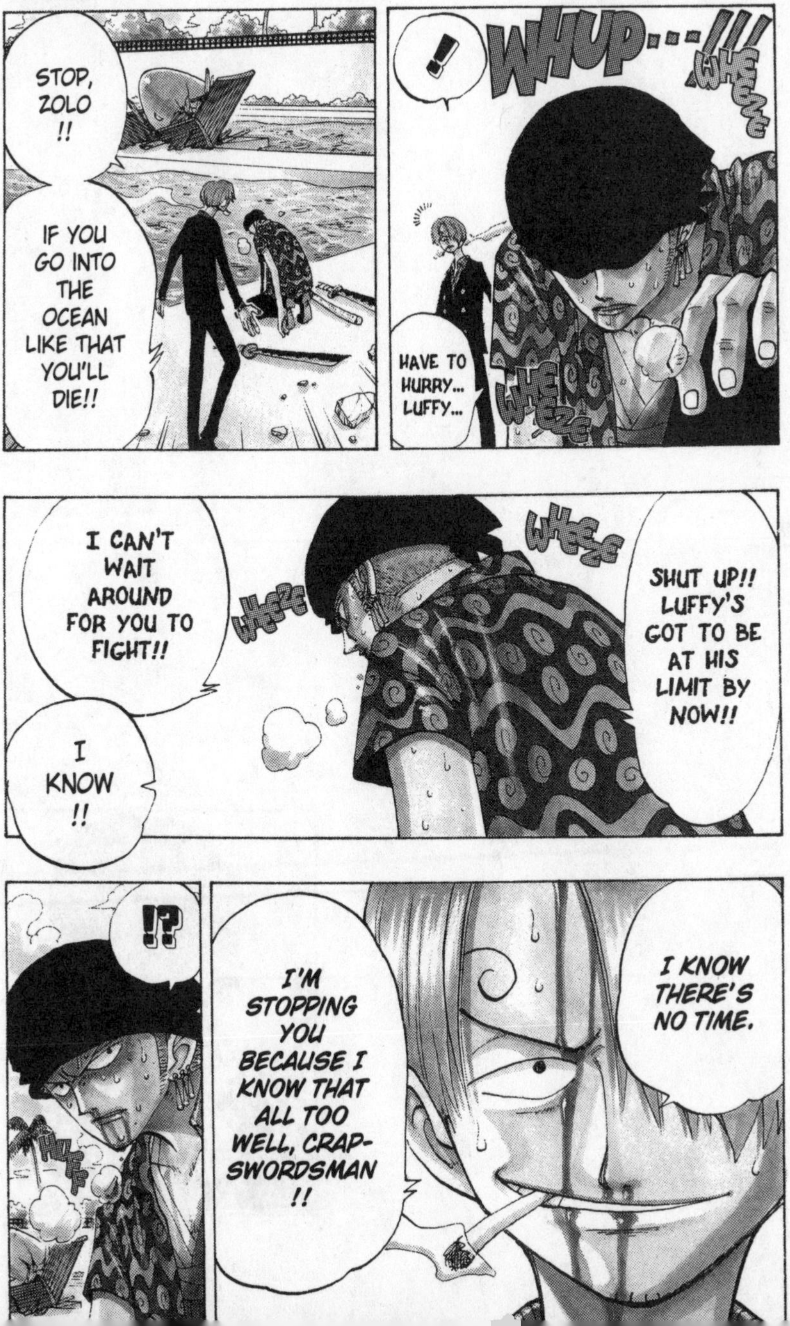
!
WHUP...!!!
WHEEZE
HAVE TO HURRY... LUFFY...
WHEEZE
STOP, ZOLO !!
IF YOU GO INTO THE OCEAN LIKE THAT YOU'LL DIE!!
WHEEZE
SHUT UP!! LUFFY'S GOT TO BE AT HIS LIMIT BY NOW!!
WHEEZE
I CAN'T WAIT AROUND FOR YOU TO FIGHT!!
I KNOW !!
I KNOW THERE'S NO TIME.
I'M STOPPING YOU BECAUSE I KNOW THAT ALL TOO WELL, CRAP-SWORDSMAN !!
!?
HUFF

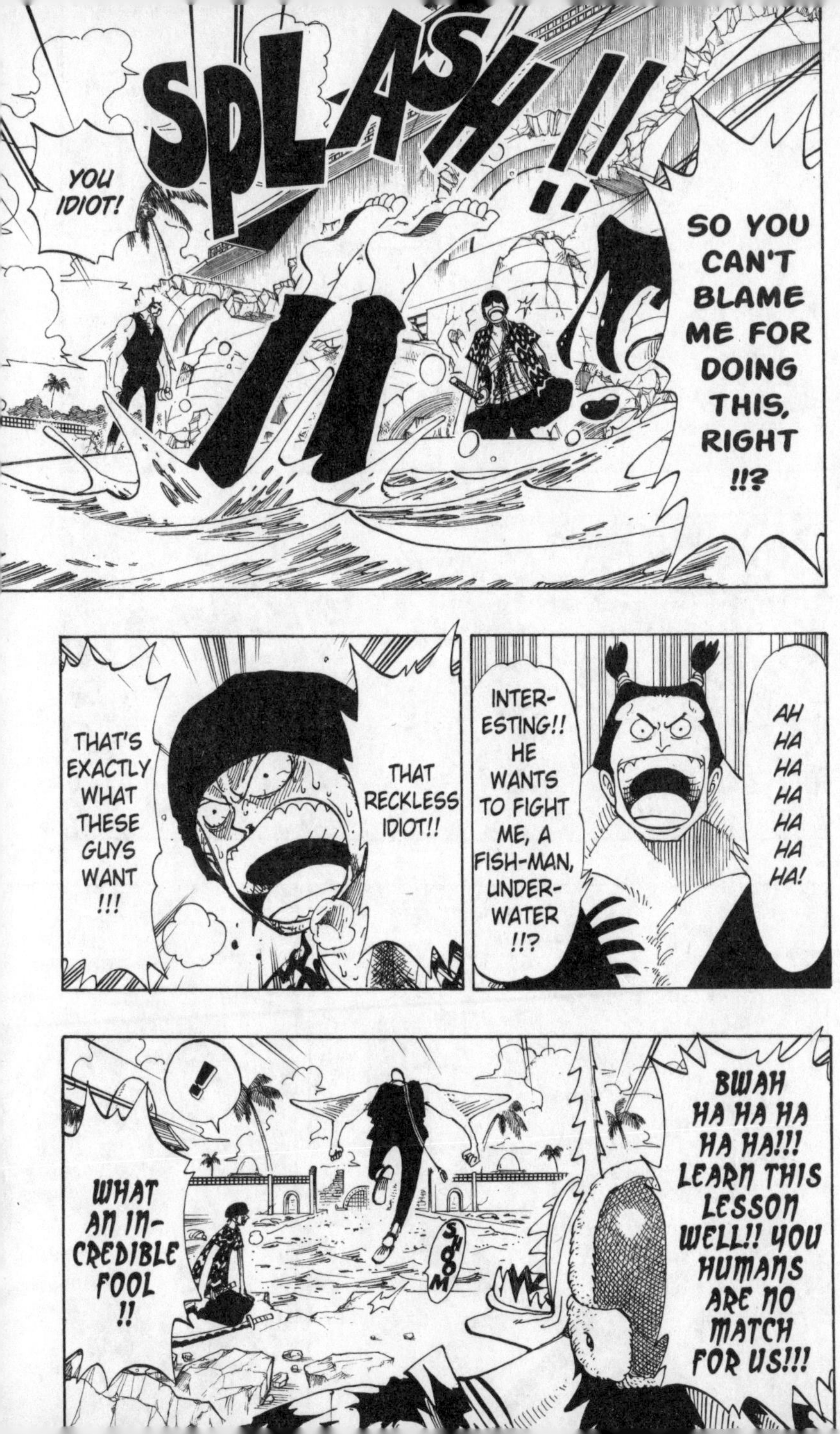
SPLASH!!
SO YOU CAN'T BLAME ME FOR DOING THIS, RIGHT!!?
YOU IDIOT!
AH HA HA HA HA HA HA!
INTERESTING!! HE WANTS TO FIGHT ME, A FISH-MAN, UNDERWATER!!?
THAT RECKLESS IDIOT!!
THAT'S EXACTLY WHAT THESE GUYS WANT!!!
BWAH HA HA HA HA HA!!! LEARN THIS LESSON WELL!! YOU HUMANS ARE NO MATCH FOR US!!!
SHOOM
!
WHAT AN INCREDIBLE FOOL!!

WHAT!? ISN'T THAT...

...THE VILLAGE HEADMAN !!?

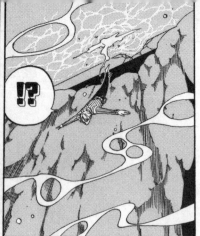

!?

DOOM!!

GLUB

GLUB

IS THAT LUFFY'S STRETCHED NECK!?

HURRY, BEFORE MY BREATH RUNS OUT...

WUMP

WUMP

PLEASE LET US BE IN TIME!!!

C'MON, BREATHE!!

WHUMP

WHUMP

...WITH THIS STRETCHY NECK OF YOURS, YOU COULD AT LEAST COUGH UP WATER AND BREATHE!!

I'M SORRY!! I DON'T HAVE THE STRENGTH TO BRING UP YOUR WHOLE BODY, BUT...

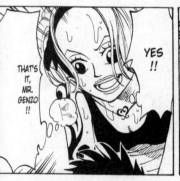

THAT'S IT, MR. GENZO !!

YES !!

PLOOSH

WHUMP

WHUMP

...AND LEAVE THE REST TO THE OLD MAN!!

GLUB GLUB

THEN I JUST HAVE TO SHATTER THE ROCK WITH A KICK...

GLUB

GLUB

GOOD. NOW EVEN WITH HIS FEET IN THE ROCK, HE CAN AT LEAST BREATHE !!

FISH-MAN KARATE ...

FOREARM SLEDGE !!!

!!?

HMPH, IT'S THOSE WORMS FROM COCO VILLAGE! BUT THEY'RE WASTING THEIR TIME !!

BLOOP!!

...!!!

!!?

I'LL DROWN YOU RIGHT NOW !!!

GLUB GLUB GLUB

DO YOU REALLY THINK YOUR EFFORTS...

...WILL BUY YOU ANY MORE TIME IN THIS WORLD !?

I'VE BEEN SPOTTED BY A FISH-MAN!!

GLUB

OH NO !!

GLUB

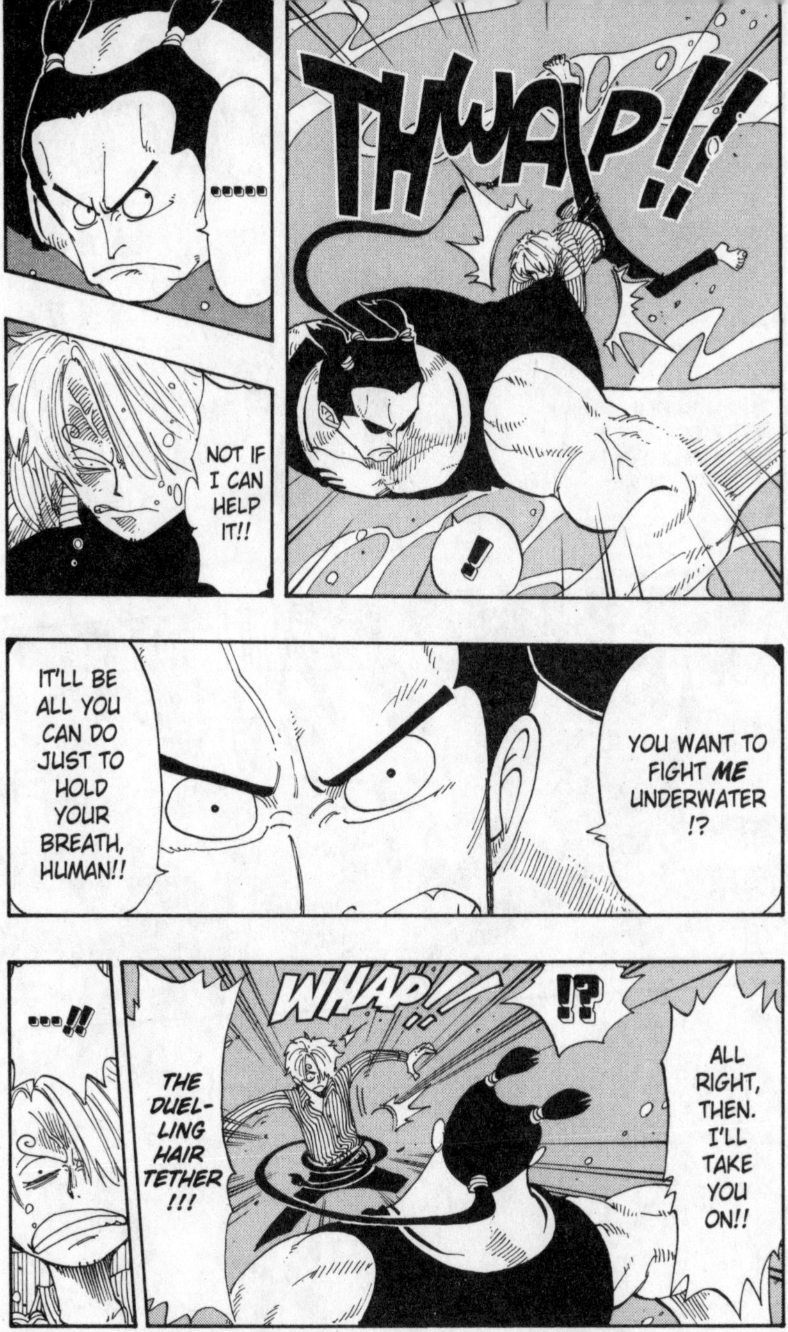
THWAP!!
!
.....
NOT IF I CAN HELP IT!!
YOU WANT TO FIGHT ME UNDERWATER!?
IT'LL BE ALL YOU CAN DO JUST TO HOLD YOUR BREATH, HUMAN!!
ALL RIGHT, THEN. I'LL TAKE YOU ON!!
!?
WHAP!!
THE DUELLING HAIR TETHER!!!
...!!

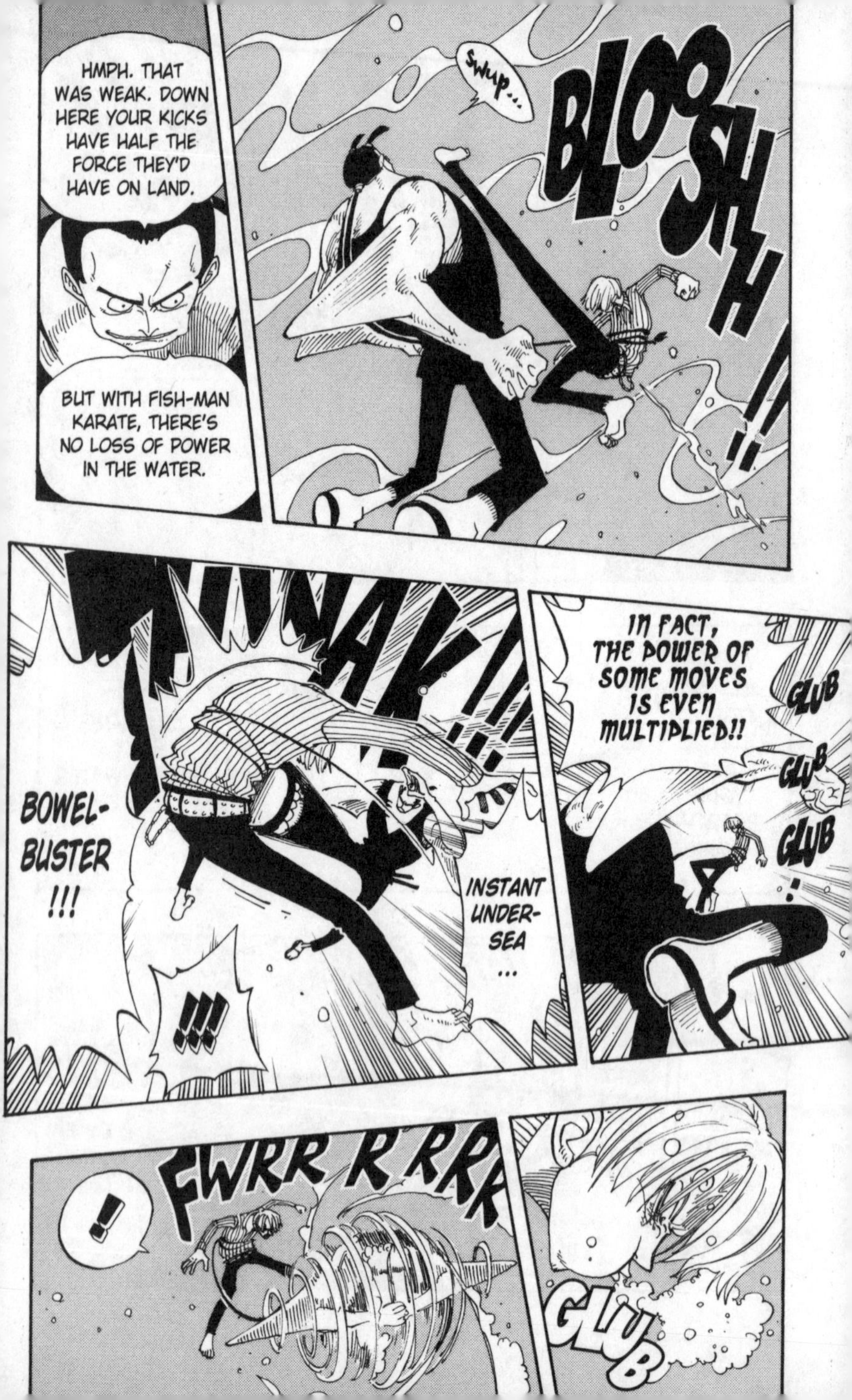
Swup...
BLOOSHH!!
HMPH. THAT WAS WEAK. DOWN HERE YOUR KICKS HAVE HALF THE FORCE THEY'D HAVE ON LAND.
BUT WITH FISH-MAN KARATE, THERE'S NO LOSS OF POWER IN THE WATER.
IN FACT, THE POWER OF SOME MOVES IS EVEN MULTIPLIED!!
GLUB
GLUB
GLUB
!
AK!!!!
INSTANT UNDER-SEA ...
BOWEL-BUSTER !!!
!!!
GLUB
GLUB
FWRR R RRR
!

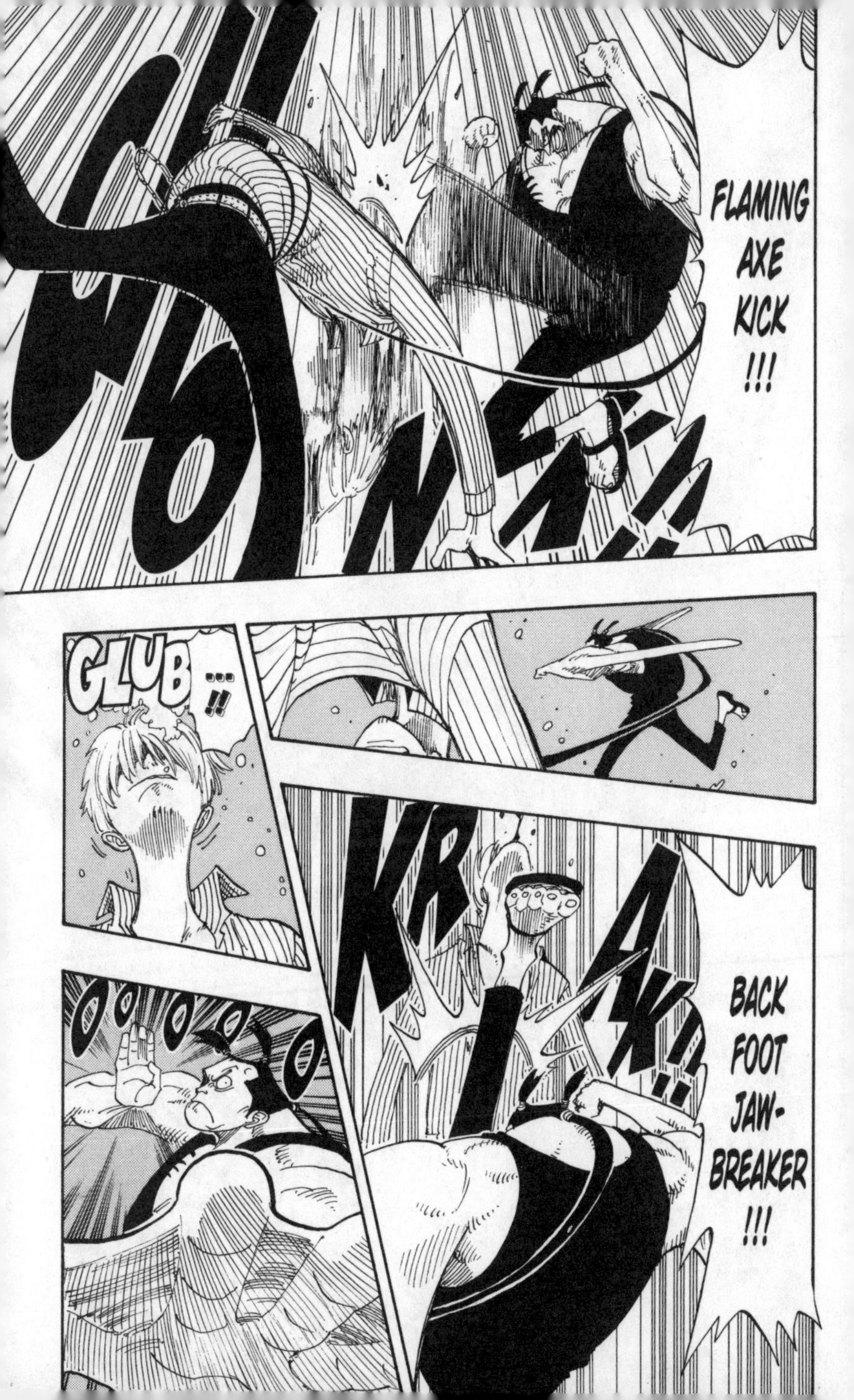
FLAMING AXE KICK!!!
GLUB...!!
KRAK!!
BACK FOOT JAW-BREAKER!!!

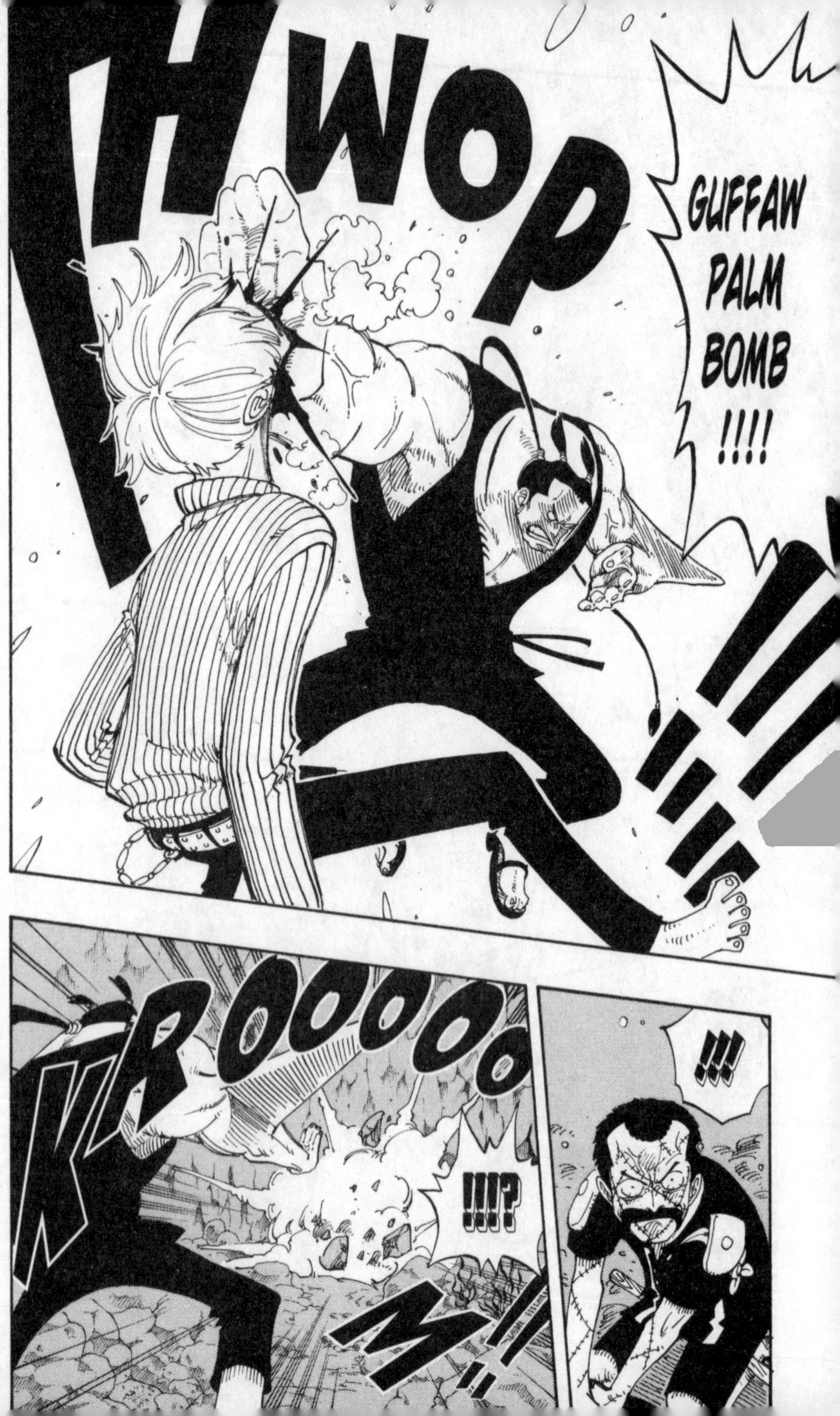
THWOP
GUFFAW PALM BOMB !!!!
KABOOOOOM!!
!!!?
!!!

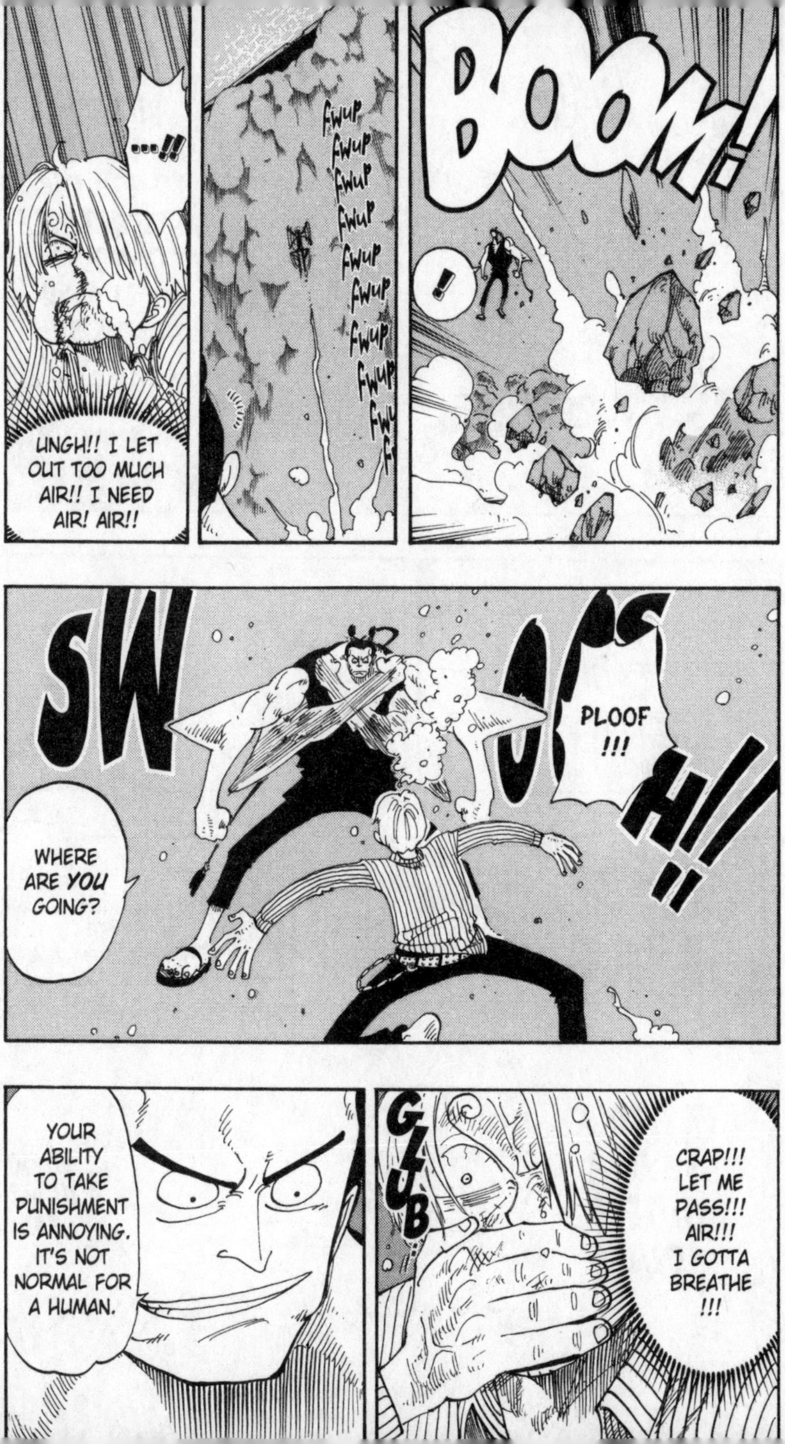
BOOM!
!
fwup fwup fwup fwup fwup fwup fwup fwup fwup
...!!
UNGH!! I LET OUT TOO MUCH AIR!! I NEED AIR! AIR!!
PLOOF !!!
SW
WHERE ARE YOU GOING?
CRAP!!! LET ME PASS!!! AIR!!! I GOTTA BREATHE !!!
GLUB
YOUR ABILITY TO TAKE PUNISHMENT IS ANNOYING. IT'S NOT NORMAL FOR A HUMAN.

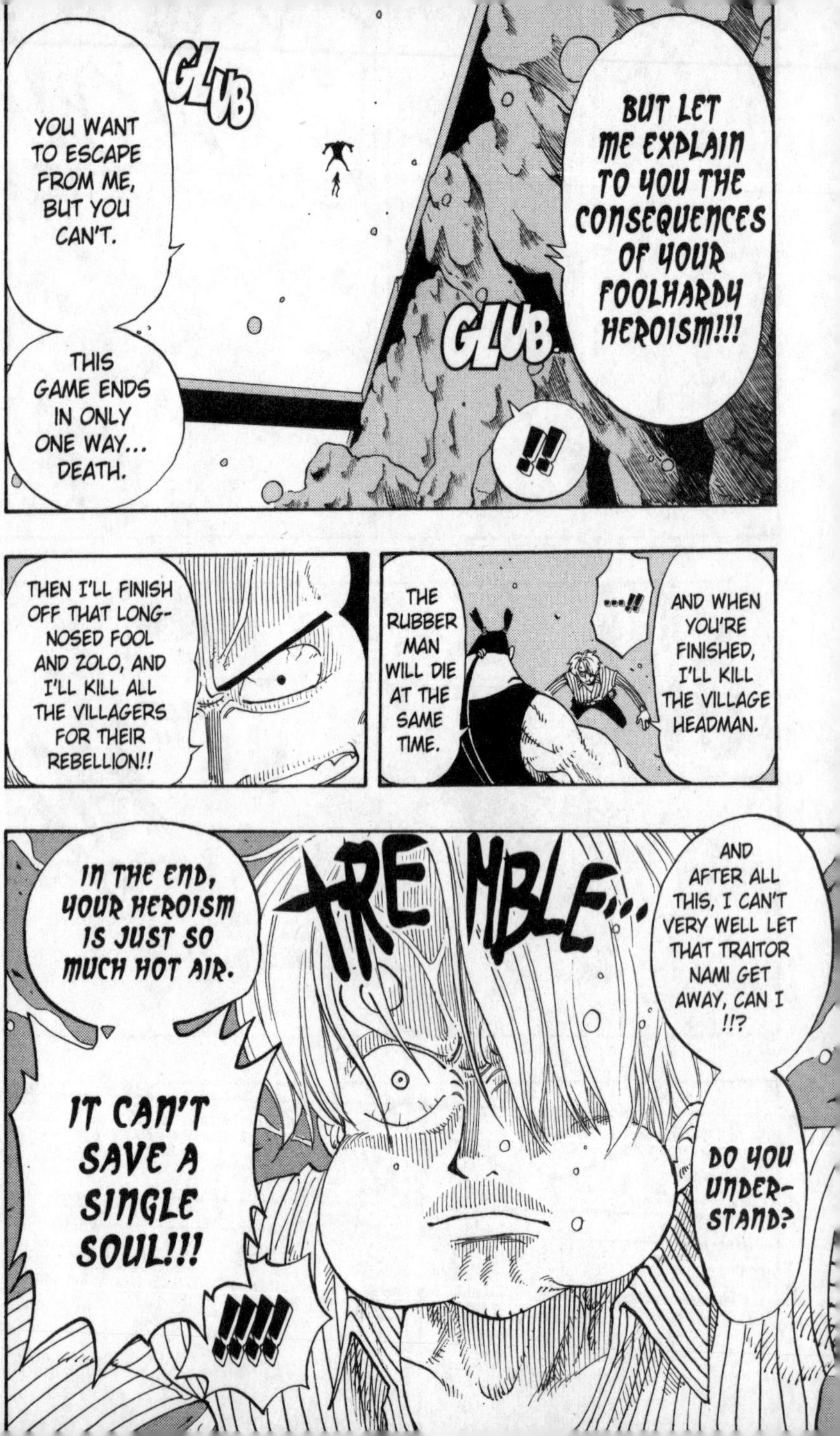
BUT LET ME EXPLAIN TO YOU THE CONSEQUENCES OF YOUR FOOLHARDY HEROISM!!!
GLUB
GLUB
!!
YOU WANT TO ESCAPE FROM ME, BUT YOU CAN'T.
THIS GAME ENDS IN ONLY ONE WAY... DEATH.
AND WHEN YOU'RE FINISHED, I'LL KILL THE VILLAGE HEADMAN.
...!!
THE RUBBER MAN WILL DIE AT THE SAME TIME.
THEN I'LL FINISH OFF THAT LONG-NOSED FOOL AND ZOLO, AND I'LL KILL ALL THE VILLAGERS FOR THEIR REBELLION!!
AND AFTER ALL THIS, I CAN'T VERY WELL LET THAT TRAITOR NAMI GET AWAY, CAN I !!?
DO YOU UNDER-STAND?
TREMBLE...
IN THE END, YOUR HEROISM IS JUST SO MUCH HOT AIR.
IT CAN'T SAVE A SINGLE SOUL!!!
!!!!

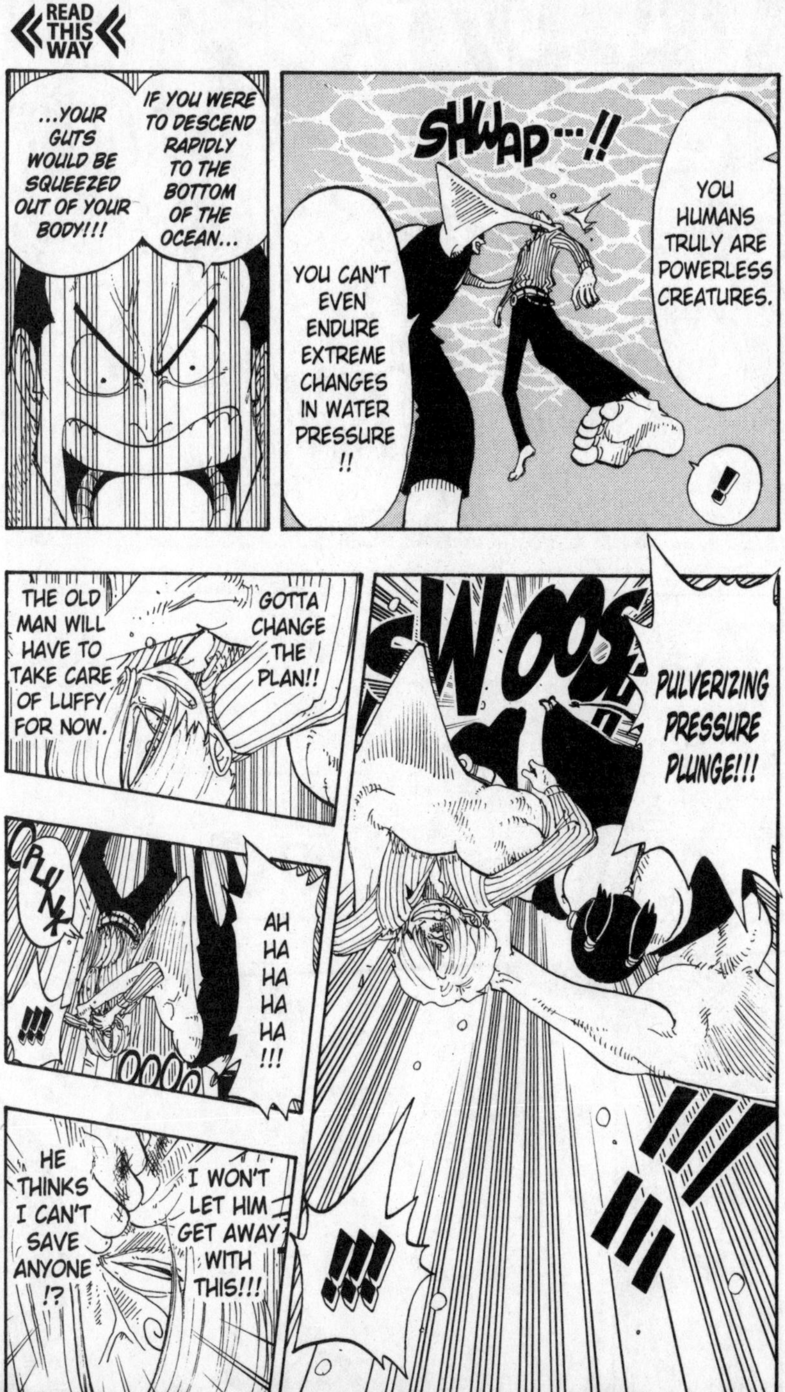
READ THIS WAY
SHWAP...!!
YOU HUMANS TRULY ARE POWERLESS CREATURES.
YOU CAN'T EVEN ENDURE EXTREME CHANGES IN WATER PRESSURE !!
!
IF YOU WERE TO DESCEND RAPIDLY TO THE BOTTOM OF THE OCEAN...
...YOUR GUTS WOULD BE SQUEEZED OUT OF YOUR BODY!!!
PULVERIZING PRESSURE PLUNGE!!!
!!!
GOTTA CHANGE THE PLAN!!
THE OLD MAN WILL HAVE TO TAKE CARE OF LUFFY FOR NOW.
CPLUNK
!!!
AH HA HA HA HA !!!
I WON'T LET HIM GET AWAY WITH THIS!!!
HE THINKS I CAN'T SAVE ANYONE !?

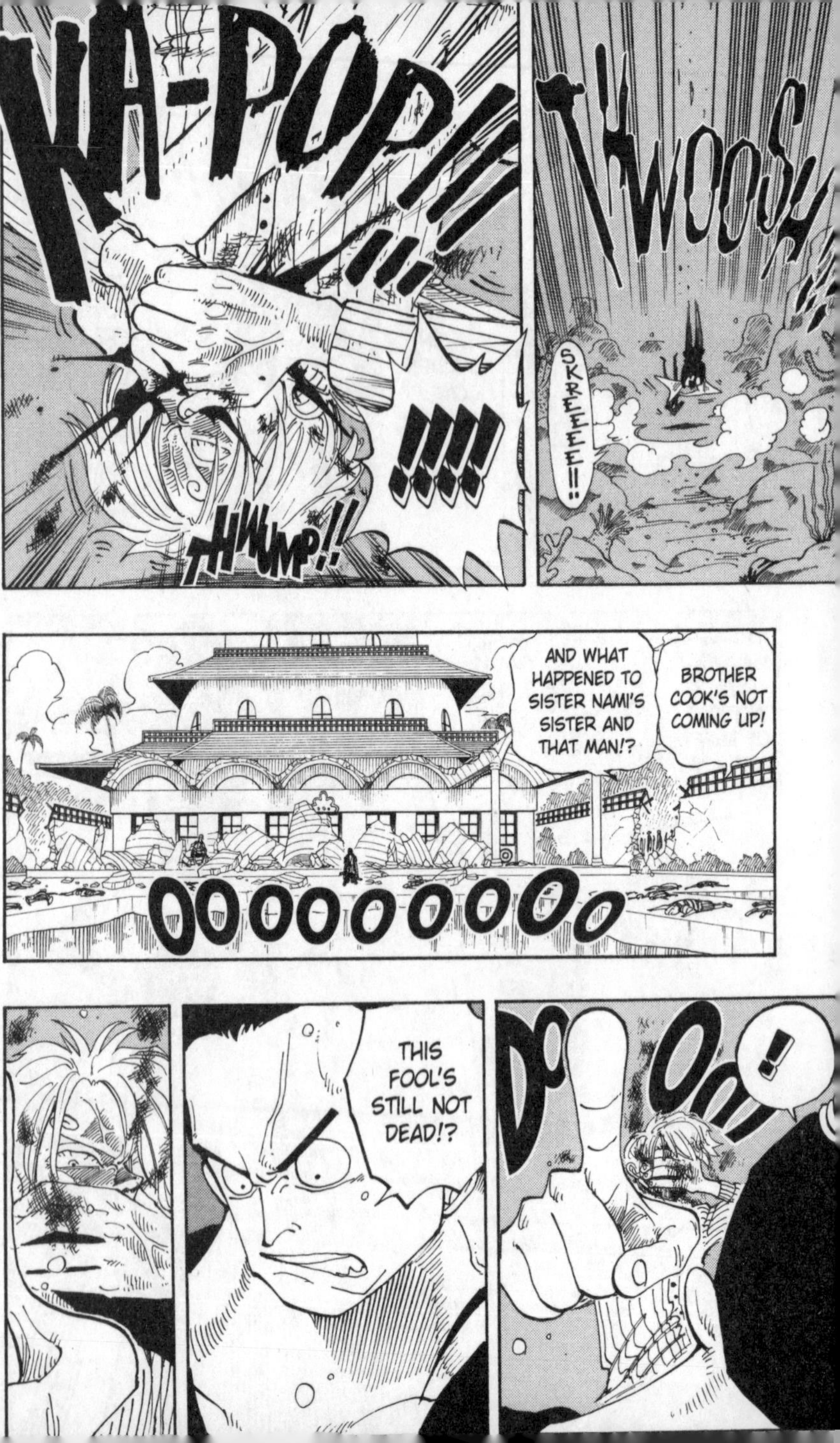
WHOOSH!!
SKREEEEE!!
KA-POP!!
!!!!
THWUMP!!
BROTHER COOK'S NOT COMING UP!
AND WHAT HAPPENED TO SISTER NAMI'S SISTER AND THAT MAN!?
OOOOOOOOOOO
DOOM!
THIS FOOL'S STILL NOT DEAD!?

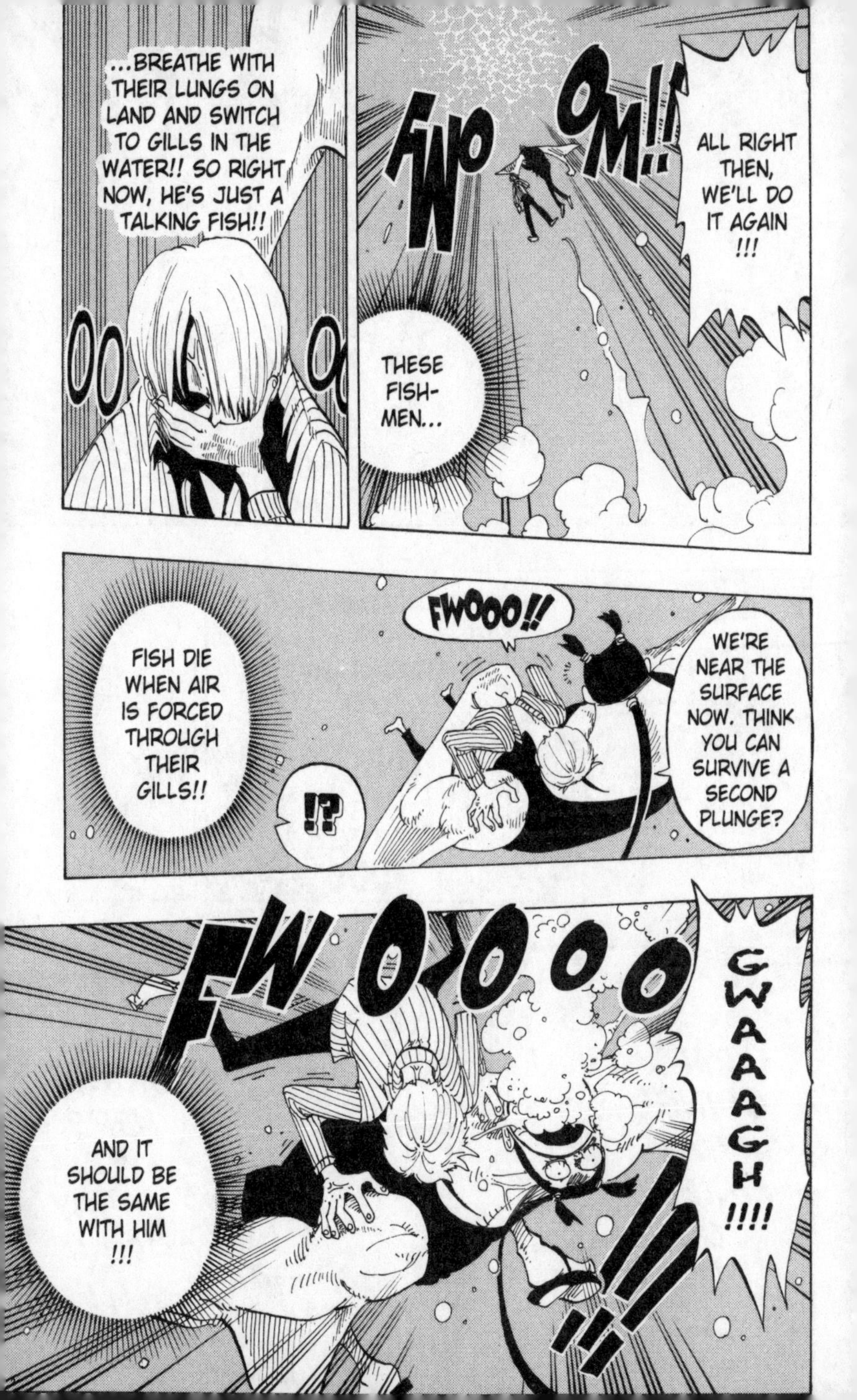
FWOOM!!
ALL RIGHT THEN, WE'LL DO IT AGAIN!!!
THESE FISH-MEN...
...BREATHE WITH THEIR LUNGS ON LAND AND SWITCH TO GILLS IN THE WATER!! SO RIGHT NOW, HE'S JUST A TALKING FISH!!
WE'RE NEAR THE SURFACE NOW. THINK YOU CAN SURVIVE A SECOND PLUNGE?
FWOOO!!
!?
FISH DIE WHEN AIR IS FORCED THROUGH THEIR GILLS!!
GWAAAGH!!!!
FWOOOO
AND IT SHOULD BE THE SAME WITH HIM!!!

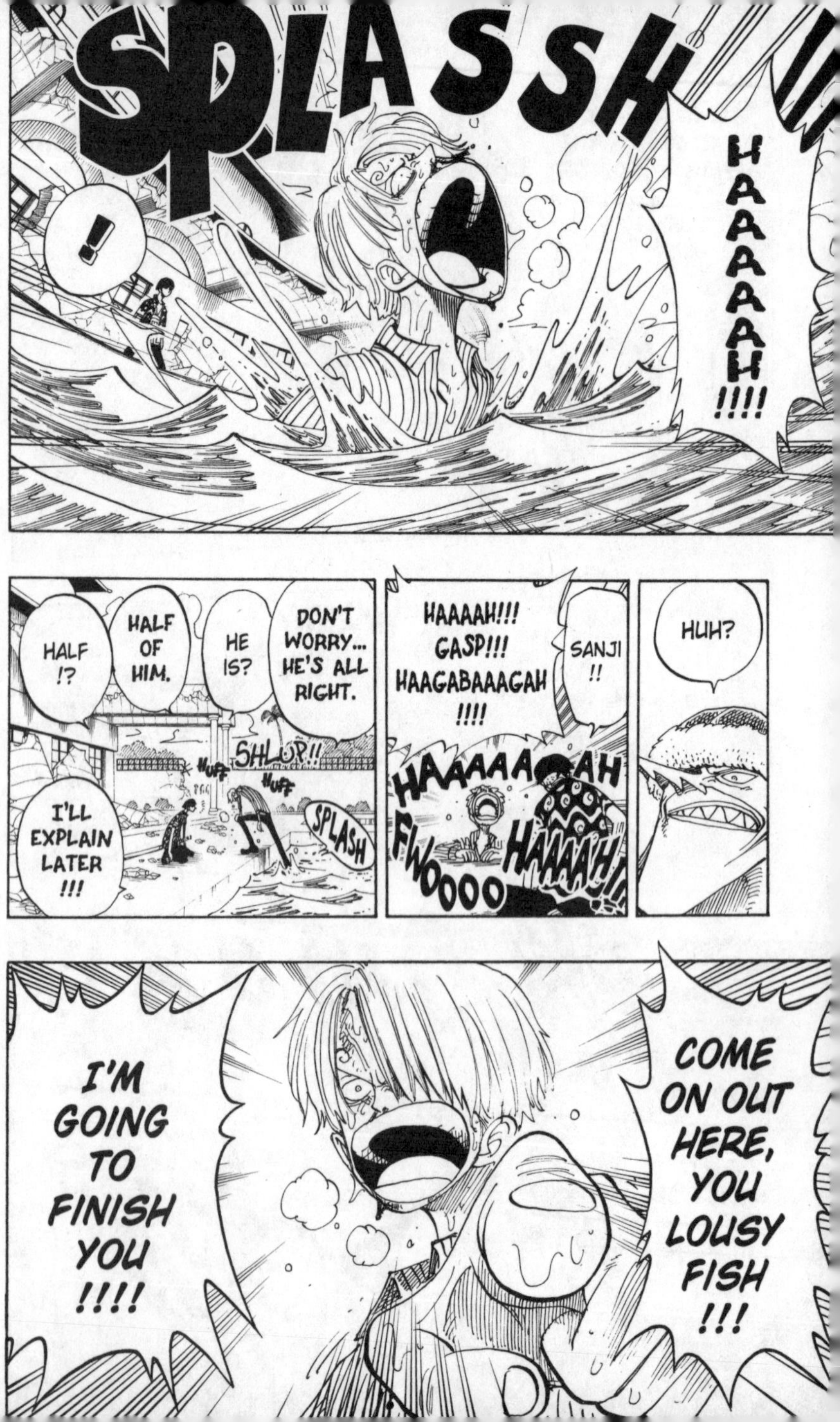
HAAAAAH!!!!
SPLASSH
!
HUH?
SANJI!!
HAAAAH!!! GASP!!! HAAGABAAAGAH!!!!
HAAAAAAH
HAAAAH!!
FWOOOO
DON'T WORRY... HE'S ALL RIGHT.
HE IS?
HALF OF HIM.
HALF!?
SHLUP!!
HUFF
HUFF
SPLASH
I'LL EXPLAIN LATER!!!
COME ON OUT HERE, YOU LOUSY FISH!!!
I'M GOING TO FINISH YOU!!!!

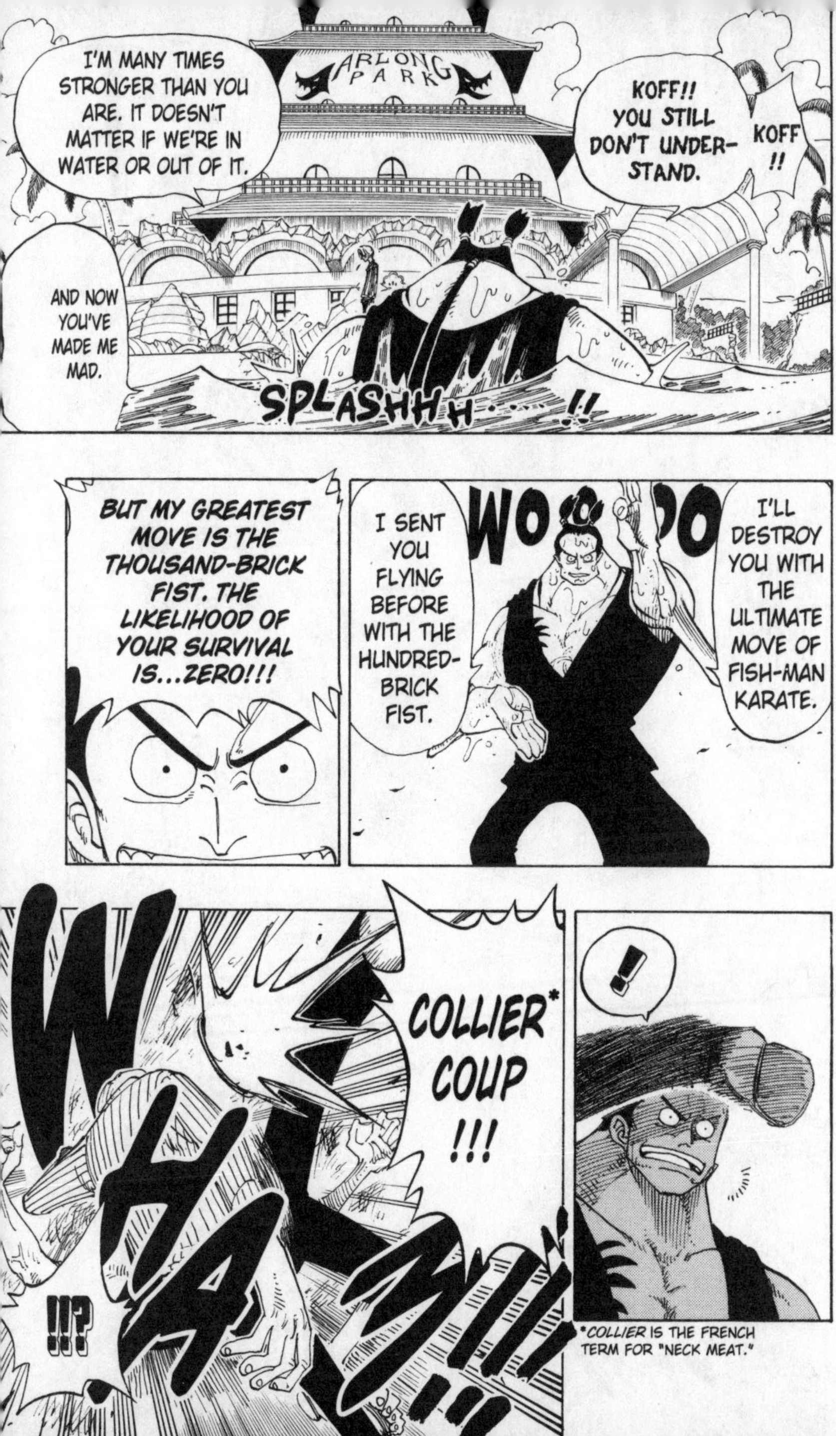
ARLONG PARK
KOFF!! YOU STILL DON'T UNDERSTAND.
KOFF !!
I'M MANY TIMES STRONGER THAN YOU ARE. IT DOESN'T MATTER IF WE'RE IN WATER OR OUT OF IT.
AND NOW YOU'VE MADE ME MAD.
SPLASHHH.....!!
I'LL DESTROY YOU WITH THE ULTIMATE MOVE OF FISH-MAN KARATE.
I SENT YOU FLYING BEFORE WITH THE HUNDRED-BRICK FIST.
BUT MY GREATEST MOVE IS THE THOUSAND-BRICK FIST. THE LIKELIHOOD OF YOUR SURVIVAL IS...ZERO!!!
!
COLLIER* COUP !!!
!!?

*COLLIER IS THE FRENCH TERM FOR "NECK MEAT."

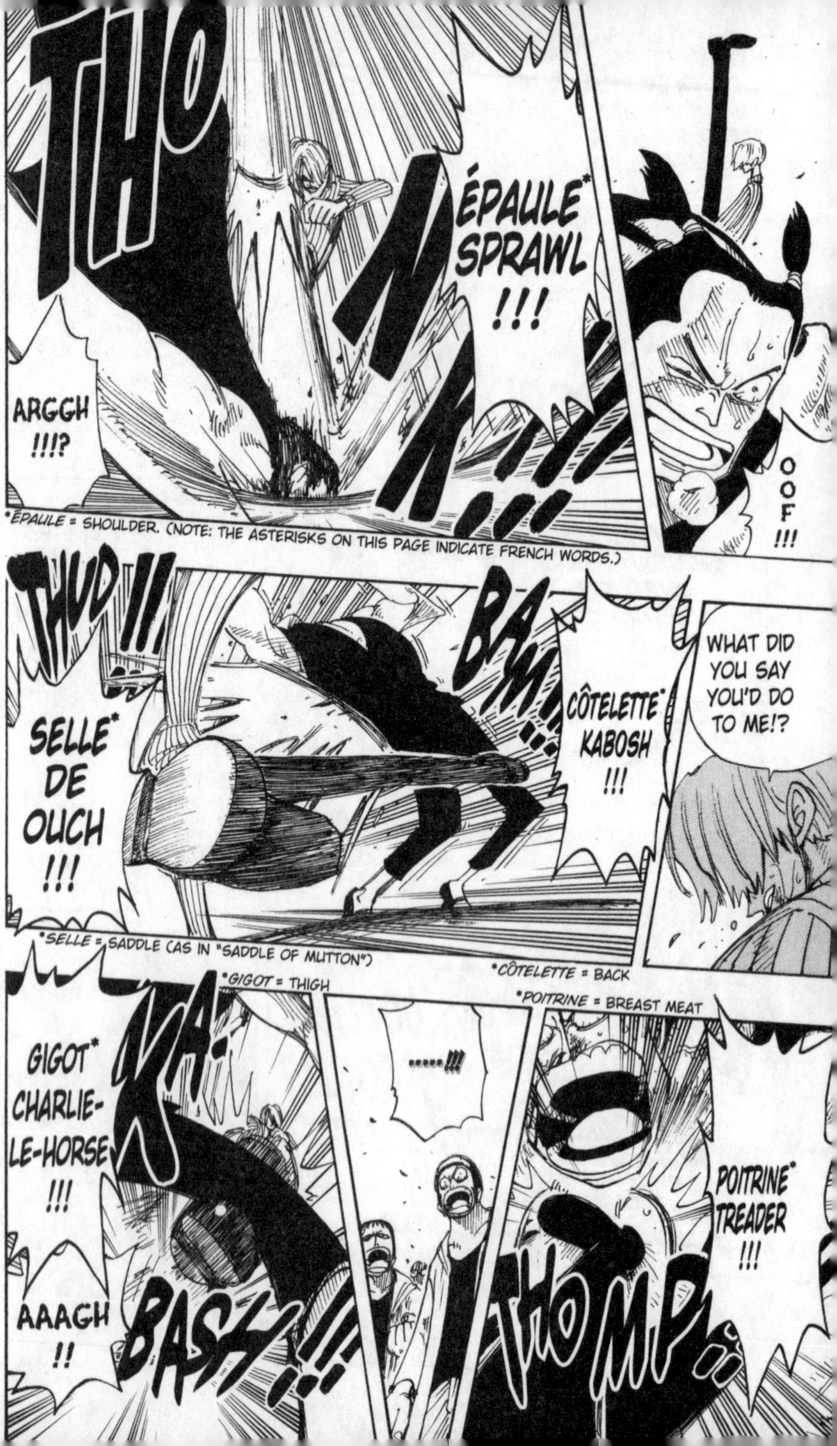
OOF !!!
ÉPAULE* SPRAWL !!!
THOM
ARGGH !!!?
*ÉPAULE = SHOULDER. (NOTE: THE ASTERISKS ON THIS PAGE INDICATE FRENCH WORDS.)
WHAT DID YOU SAY YOU'D DO TO ME!?
CÔTELETTE* KABOSH !!!
BAM..!!
SELLE* DE OUCH !!!
THUD!!
*SELLE = SADDLE (AS IN "SADDLE OF MUTTON")
*CÔTELETTE = BACK
POITRINE* TREADER !!!
THOMP..!
......!!!
GIGOT* CHARLIE-LE-HORSE !!!
KA-BASH..!!!
AAAGH !!
*GIGOT = THIGH
*POITRINE = BREAST MEAT

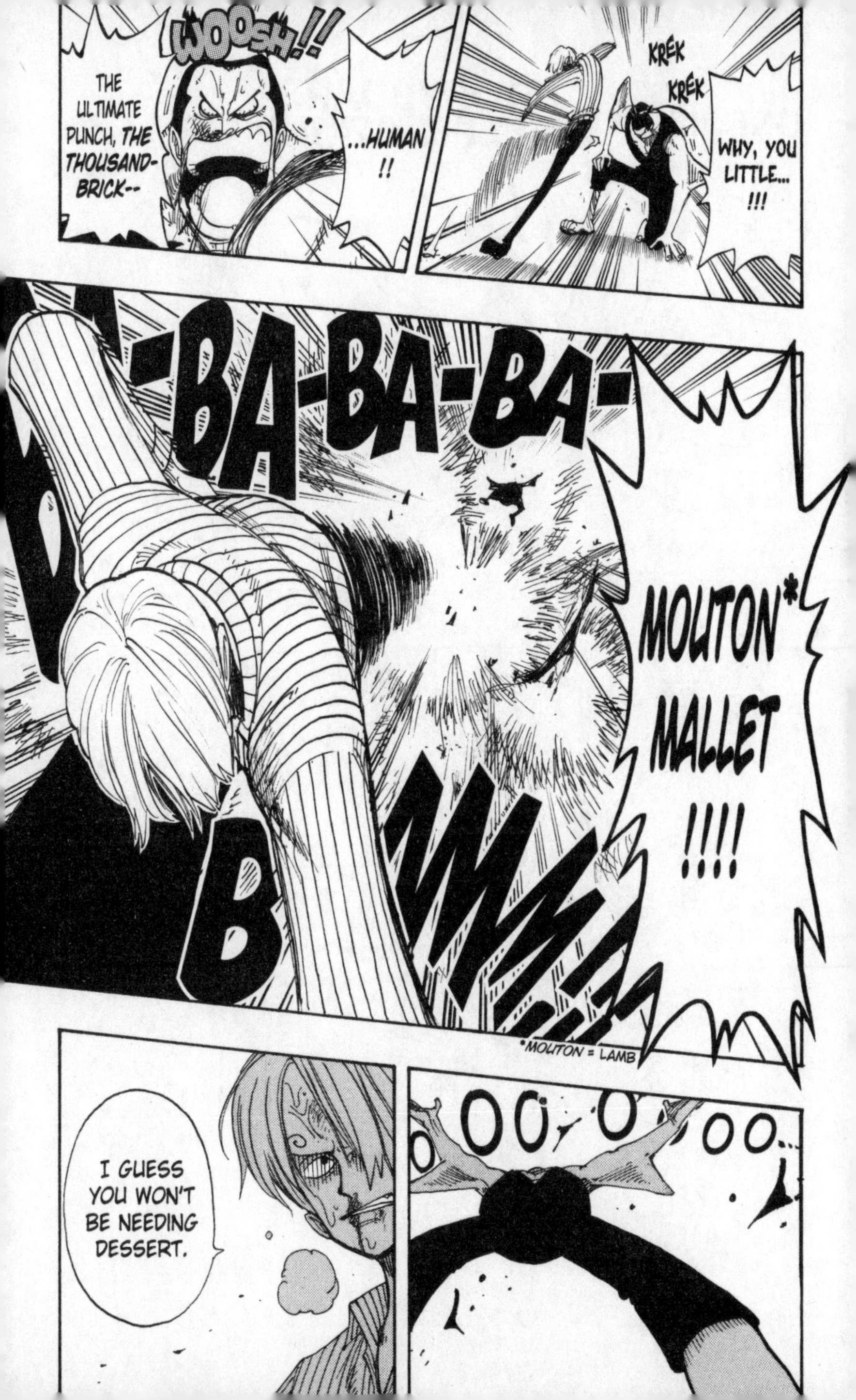
KREK
KREK
WHY, YOU LITTLE... !!!
WOOSH!!
THE ULTIMATE PUNCH, THE THOUSAND-BRICK--
...HUMAN !!
MOUTON* MALLET !!!!
-BA-BA-BA-
B
*MOUTON = LAMB
OOO...
I GUESS YOU WON'T BE NEEDING DESSERT.

ONE PIECE **STORYBOARD PRESENTATION!!** #13

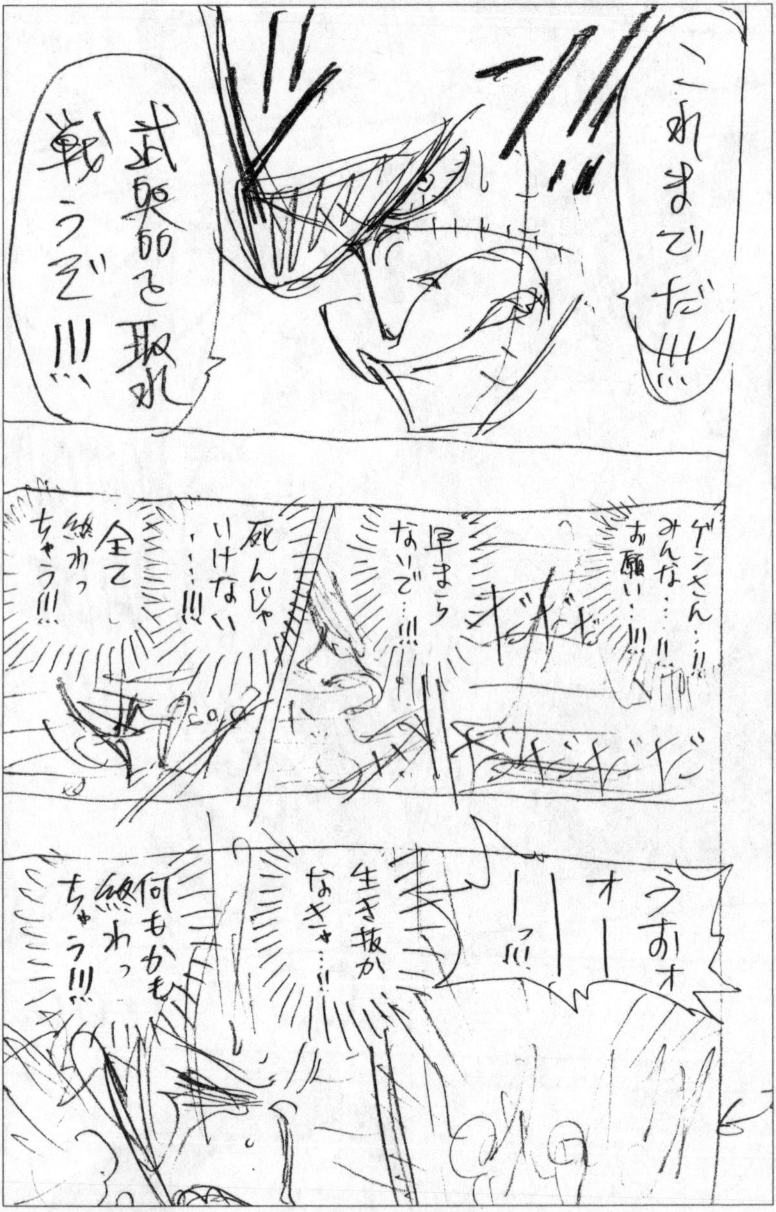

これまでだ!!!
武器を取れ 戦うぞ!!!
ゲンさん…!! みんな…お願い…!!!
早まらないで…!!!
死んじゃいけない……!!!
全て終わっちゃう!!!
うおオオ———!!!
生き抜かなきゃ…!!
何もかも終わっちゃう!!!

Chapter 87:
IT'S ALL OVER!!

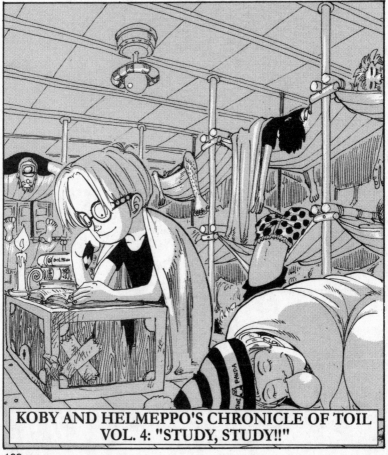

**KOBY AND HELMEPPO'S CHRONICLE OF TOIL
VOL. 4: "STUDY, STUDY!!"**

HACHI...

KUROOBI...

LOOKS LIKE WE'RE THE WINNERS OF THIS GAME.

LIKE I SAID, INSIGNIFICANT SMALL FRY.

HOW DARE YOU WIPE OUT MY MOST VALUABLE OFFICERS !?

WHO DO YOU THINK YOU ARE !!!?

I'LL HAVE TO GO BACK DOWN TO THE OCEAN FLOOR.

IT MEANS HE'S NOT DEAD... YET.

WHAT'S THAT MEAN?

YOU SAID LUFFY'S HALF-OKAY.

WHEEZE WHEEZE

KLAK

...THAT GUY ISN'T ABOUT TO LET ME.

BUT IT LOOKS LIKE...

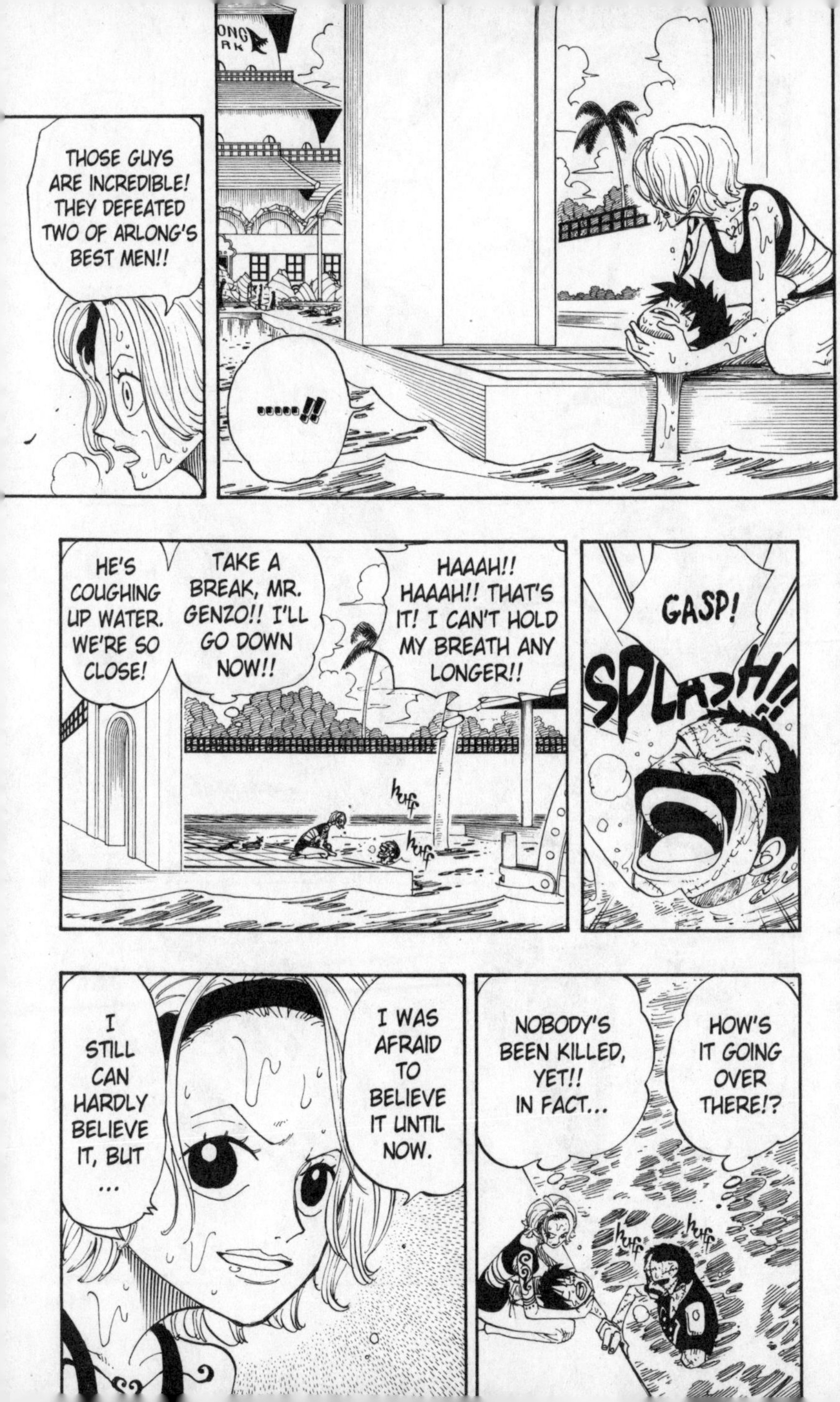
......!!
THOSE GUYS ARE INCREDIBLE! THEY DEFEATED TWO OF ARLONG'S BEST MEN!!
GASP!
SPLASH!!
HAAAH!! HAAAH!! THAT'S IT! I CAN'T HOLD MY BREATH ANY LONGER!!
TAKE A BREAK, MR. GENZO!! I'LL GO DOWN NOW!!
HE'S COUGHING UP WATER. WE'RE SO CLOSE!
huff
huff
HOW'S IT GOING OVER THERE!?
NOBODY'S BEEN KILLED, YET!! IN FACT...
huff
huff
I WAS AFRAID TO BELIEVE IT UNTIL NOW.
I STILL CAN HARDLY BELIEVE IT, BUT ...

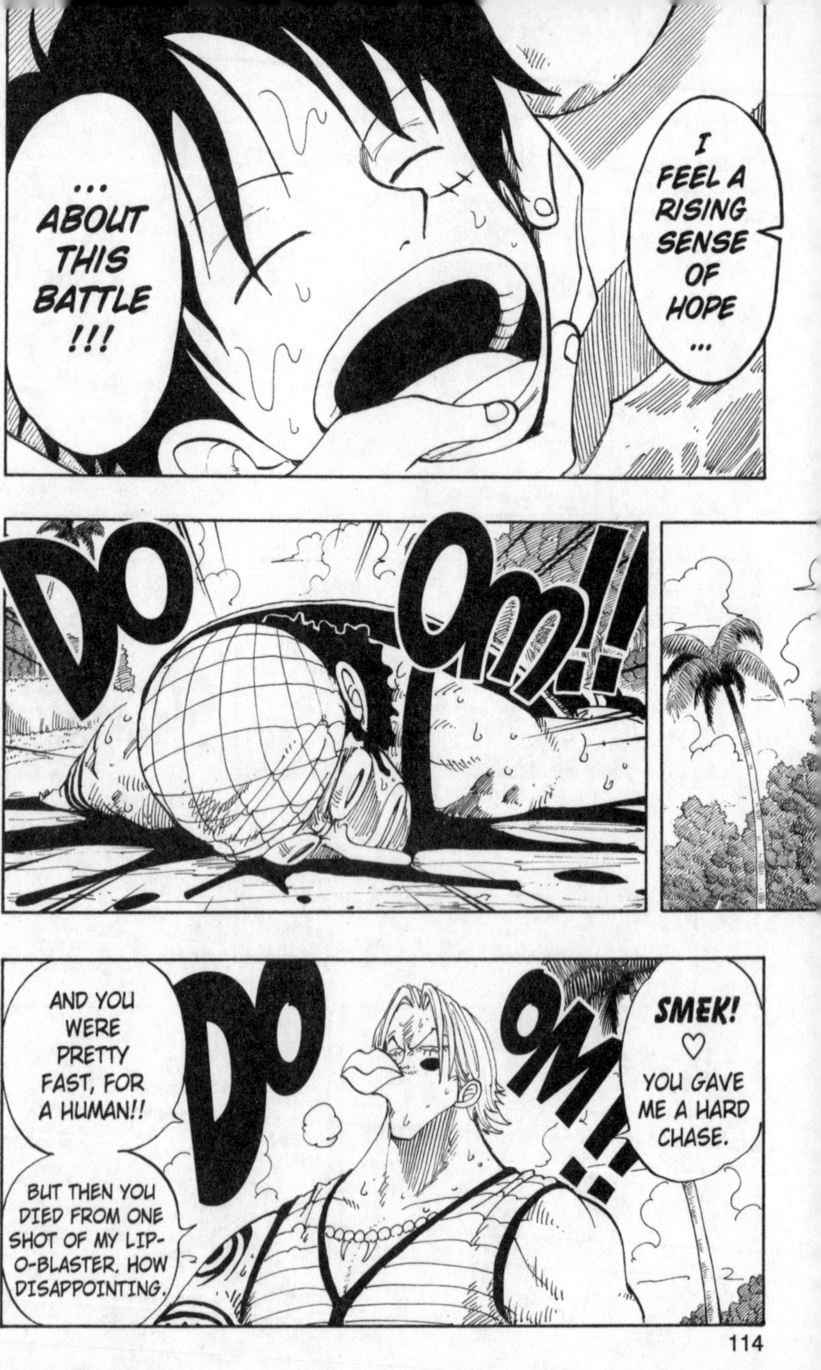
I FEEL A RISING SENSE OF HOPE ...
... ABOUT THIS BATTLE !!!
DOOM!!
SMEK! ♡ YOU GAVE ME A HARD CHASE.
DOOM!!
AND YOU WERE PRETTY FAST, FOR A HUMAN!!
BUT THEN YOU DIED FROM ONE SHOT OF MY LIPO-BLASTER. HOW DISAPPOINTING.

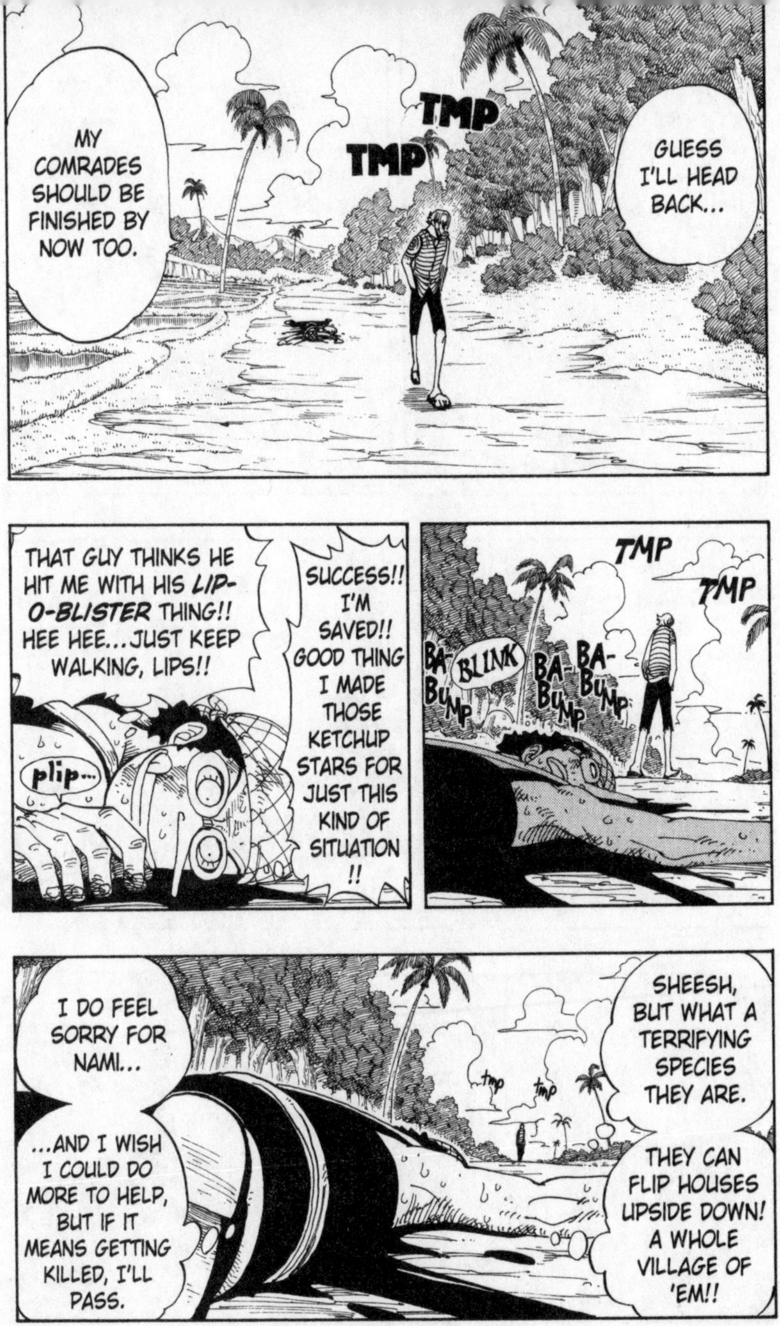
GUESS I'LL HEAD BACK...
TMP
TMP
MY COMRADES SHOULD BE FINISHED BY NOW TOO.
TMP
TMP
BA-BUMP
BA-BUMP
BLINK
BA-BUMP
SUCCESS!! I'M SAVED!! GOOD THING I MADE THOSE KETCHUP STARS FOR JUST THIS KIND OF SITUATION!!
THAT GUY THINKS HE HIT ME WITH HIS *LIP-O-BLISTER* THING!! HEE HEE...JUST KEEP WALKING, LIPS!!
plip...
SHEESH, BUT WHAT A TERRIFYING SPECIES THEY ARE.
THEY CAN FLIP HOUSES UPSIDE DOWN! A WHOLE VILLAGE OF 'EM!!
tmp
tmp
I DO FEEL SORRY FOR NAMI...
...AND I WISH I COULD DO MORE TO HELP, BUT IF IT MEANS GETTING KILLED, I'LL PASS.

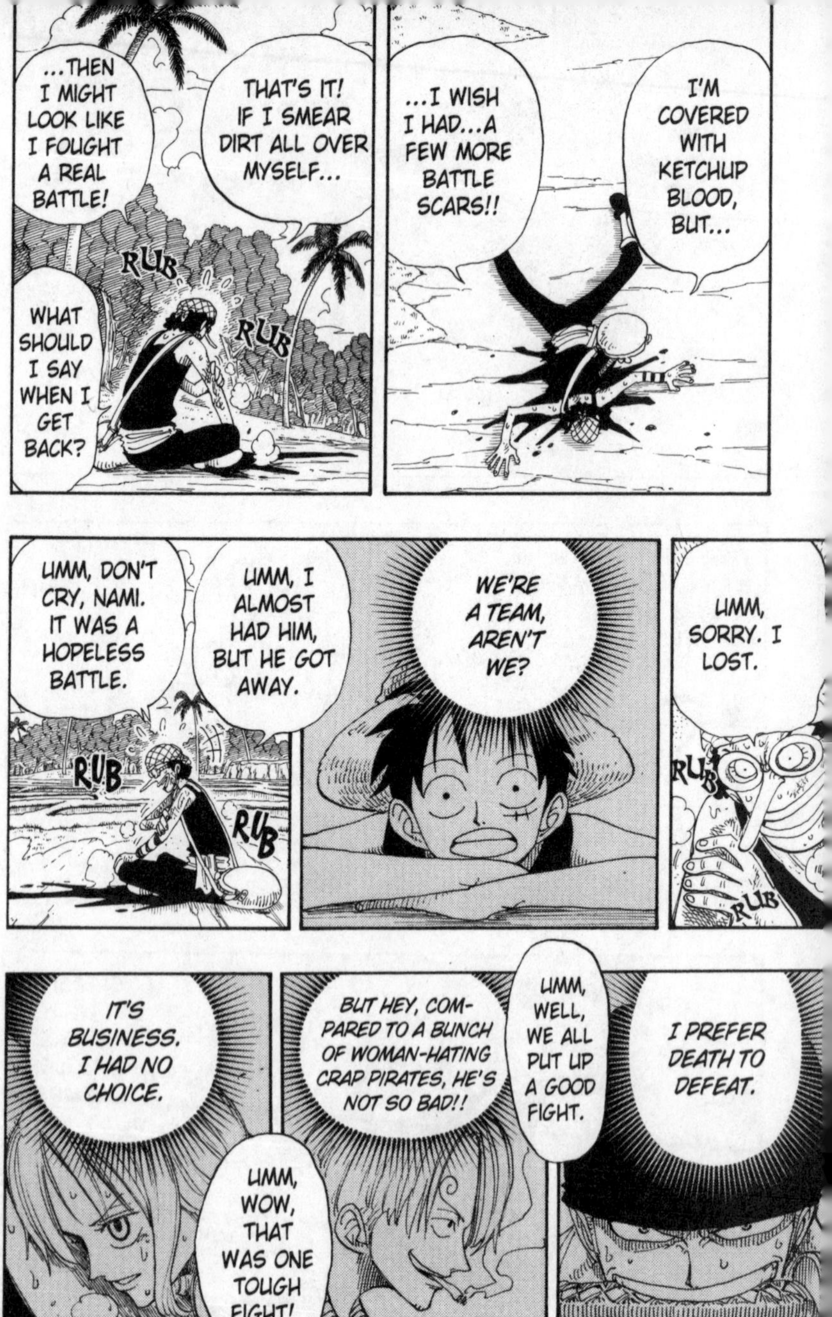
I'M COVERED WITH KETCHUP BLOOD, BUT...
...I WISH I HAD...A FEW MORE BATTLE SCARS!!
THAT'S IT! IF I SMEAR DIRT ALL OVER MYSELF...
...THEN I MIGHT LOOK LIKE I FOUGHT A REAL BATTLE!
RUB
RUB
WHAT SHOULD I SAY WHEN I GET BACK?
UMM, SORRY. I LOST.
RUB
RUB
WE'RE A TEAM, AREN'T WE?
UMM, I ALMOST HAD HIM, BUT HE GOT AWAY.
UMM, DON'T CRY, NAMI. IT WAS A HOPELESS BATTLE.
RUB
RUB
I PREFER DEATH TO DEFEAT.
UMM, WELL, WE ALL PUT UP A GOOD FIGHT.
BUT HEY, COMPARED TO A BUNCH OF WOMAN-HATING CRAP PIRATES, HE'S NOT SO BAD!!
UMM, WOW, THAT WAS ONE TOUGH FIGHT!
IT'S BUSINESS. I HAD NO CHOICE.

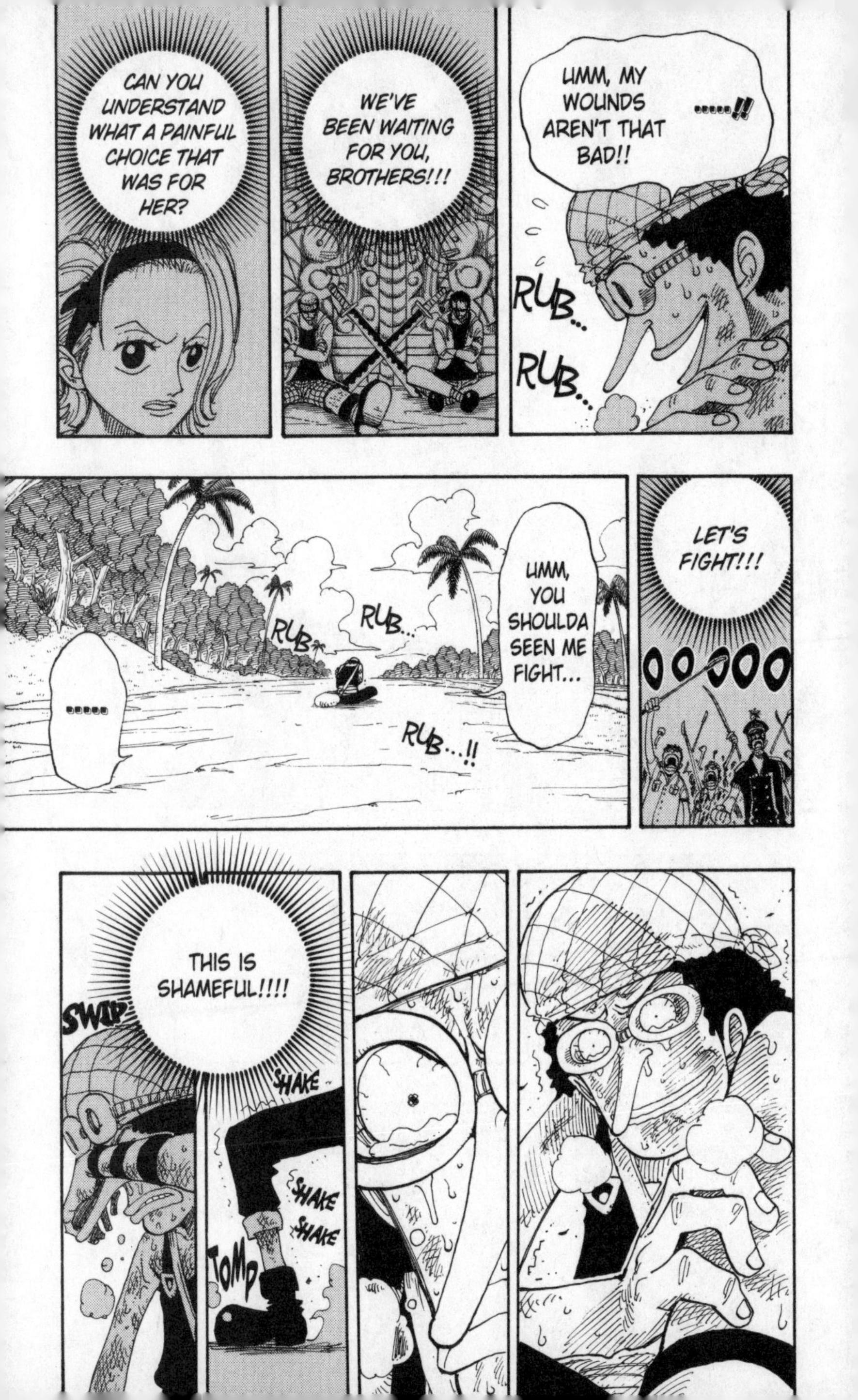
UMM, MY WOUNDS AREN'T THAT BAD!!
......!!
RUB...
RUB...
WE'VE BEEN WAITING FOR YOU, BROTHERS!!!
CAN YOU UNDERSTAND WHAT A PAINFUL CHOICE THAT WAS FOR HER?
LET'S FIGHT!!!
OOOOO
UMM, YOU SHOULDA SEEN ME FIGHT...
RUB...
RUB
RUB...!!
.....
SHAKE
SHAKE
SHAKE
TOMP
THIS IS SHAMEFUL!!!!
SWIP

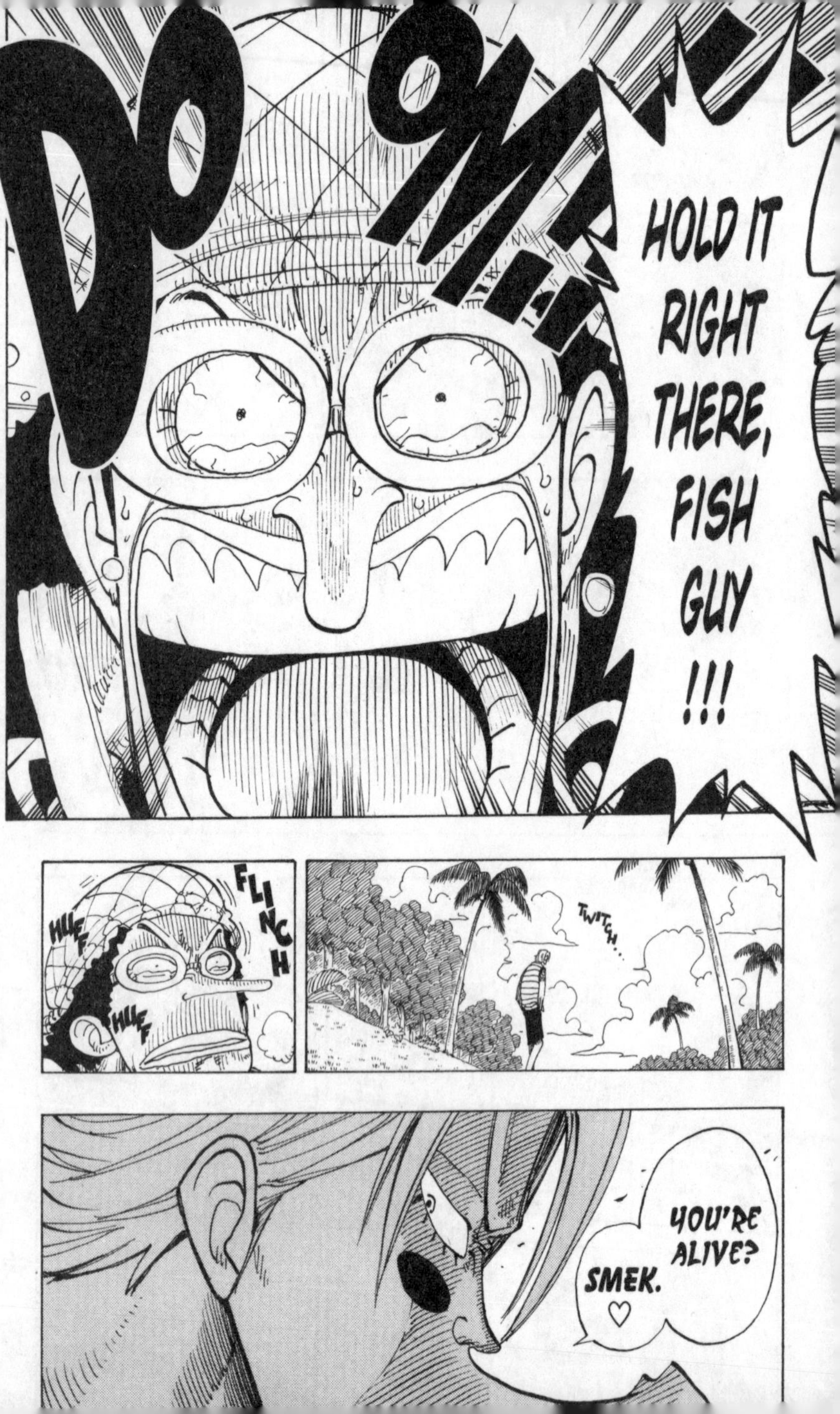
DOOM...
HOLD IT RIGHT THERE, FISH GUY !!!
TWITCH...
FLINCH
HUFF HUFF
YOU'RE ALIVE?
SMEK. ♡

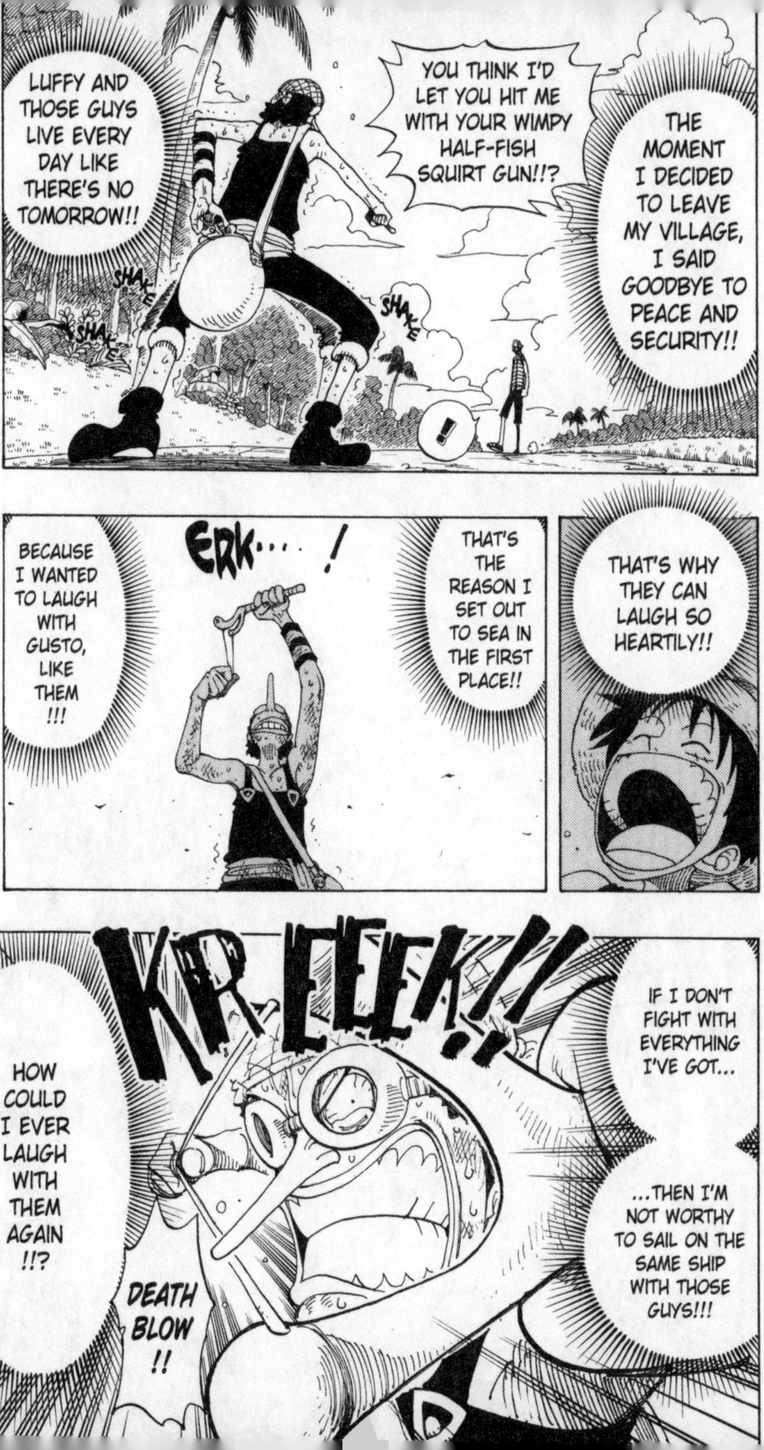
THE MOMENT I DECIDED TO LEAVE MY VILLAGE, I SAID GOODBYE TO PEACE AND SECURITY!!
YOU THINK I'D LET YOU HIT ME WITH YOUR WIMPY HALF-FISH SQUIRT GUN!!?
LUFFY AND THOSE GUYS LIVE EVERY DAY LIKE THERE'S NO TOMORROW!!
SHAKE
SHAKE
SHAKE
!
THAT'S WHY THEY CAN LAUGH SO HEARTILY!!
THAT'S THE REASON I SET OUT TO SEA IN THE FIRST PLACE!!
ERK...!
BECAUSE I WANTED TO LAUGH WITH GUSTO, LIKE THEM!!!
KR-EEEK!!
IF I DON'T FIGHT WITH EVERYTHING I'VE GOT...
...THEN I'M NOT WORTHY TO SAIL ON THE SAME SHIP WITH THOSE GUYS!!!
HOW COULD I EVER LAUGH WITH THEM AGAIN!!?
DEATH BLOW!!

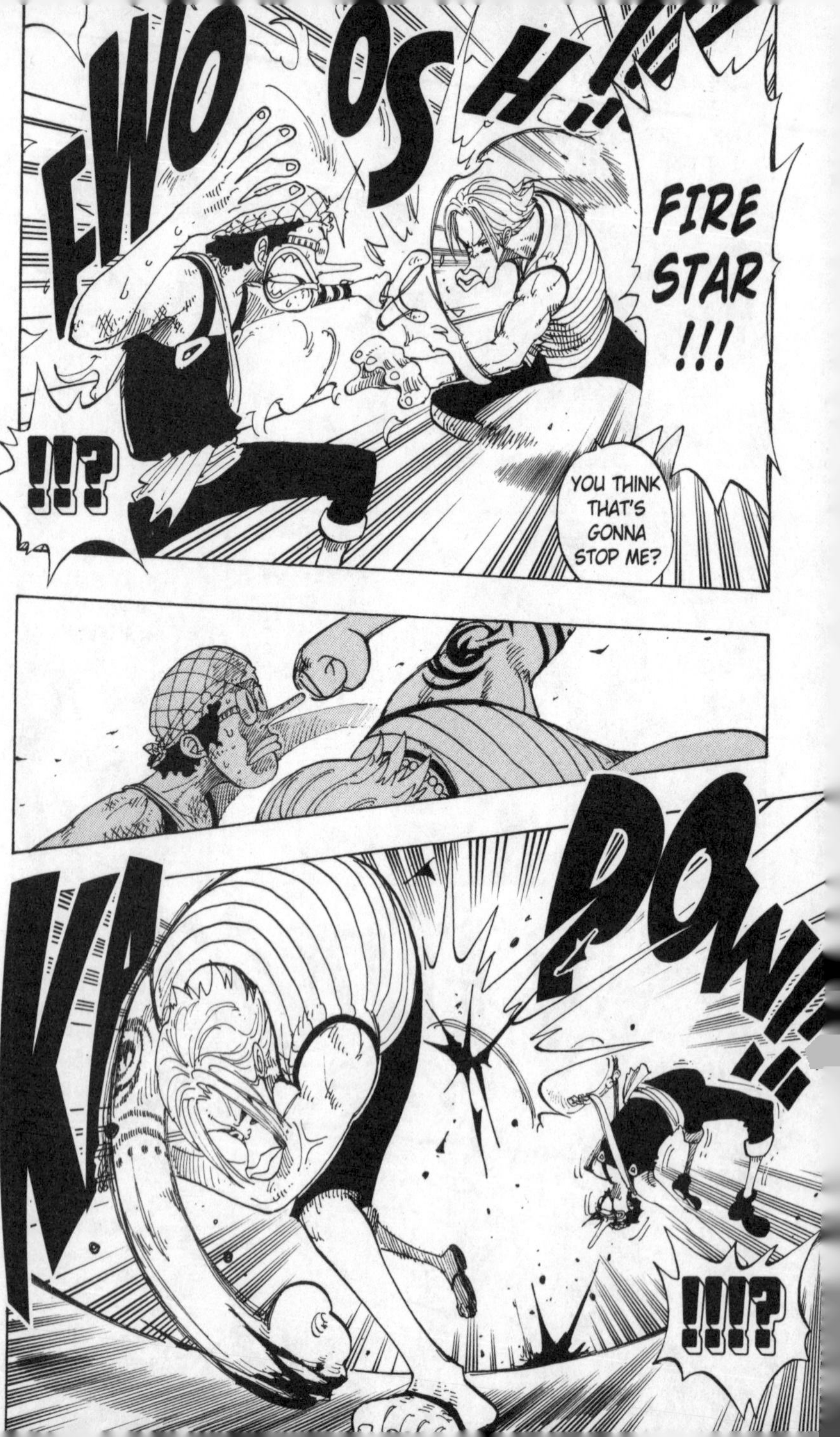
FIRE STAR!!!
FWOOSH!!
YOU THINK THAT'S GONNA STOP ME?
!!?
KA
POW!!
!!!?

READ THIS WAY

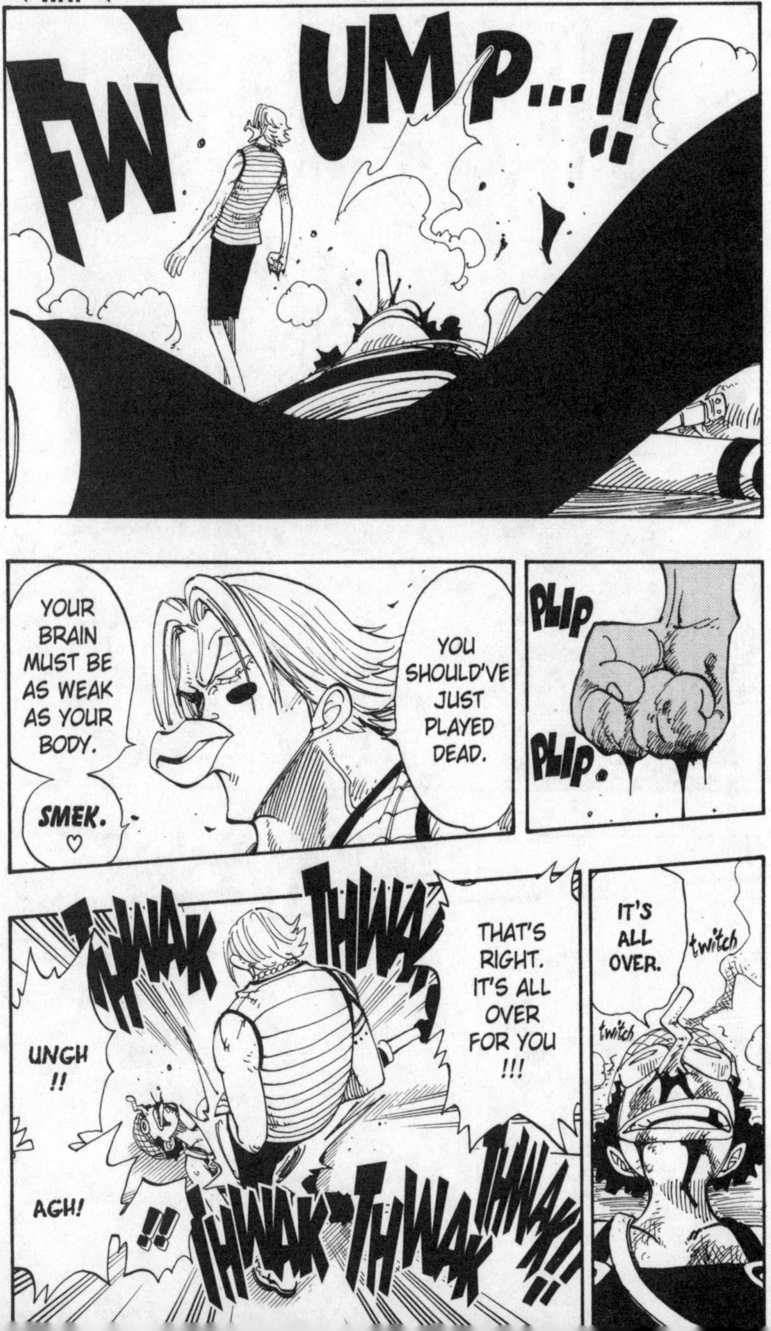
FWUMP...!!
PLIP
PLIP.
YOU SHOULD'VE JUST PLAYED DEAD.
YOUR BRAIN MUST BE AS WEAK AS YOUR BODY.
SMEK. ♡
IT'S ALL OVER.
twitch
twitch
THAT'S RIGHT. IT'S ALL OVER FOR YOU !!!
THWAK
THWAK
UNGH !!
AGH!
THWAK-THWAK THWAK!!

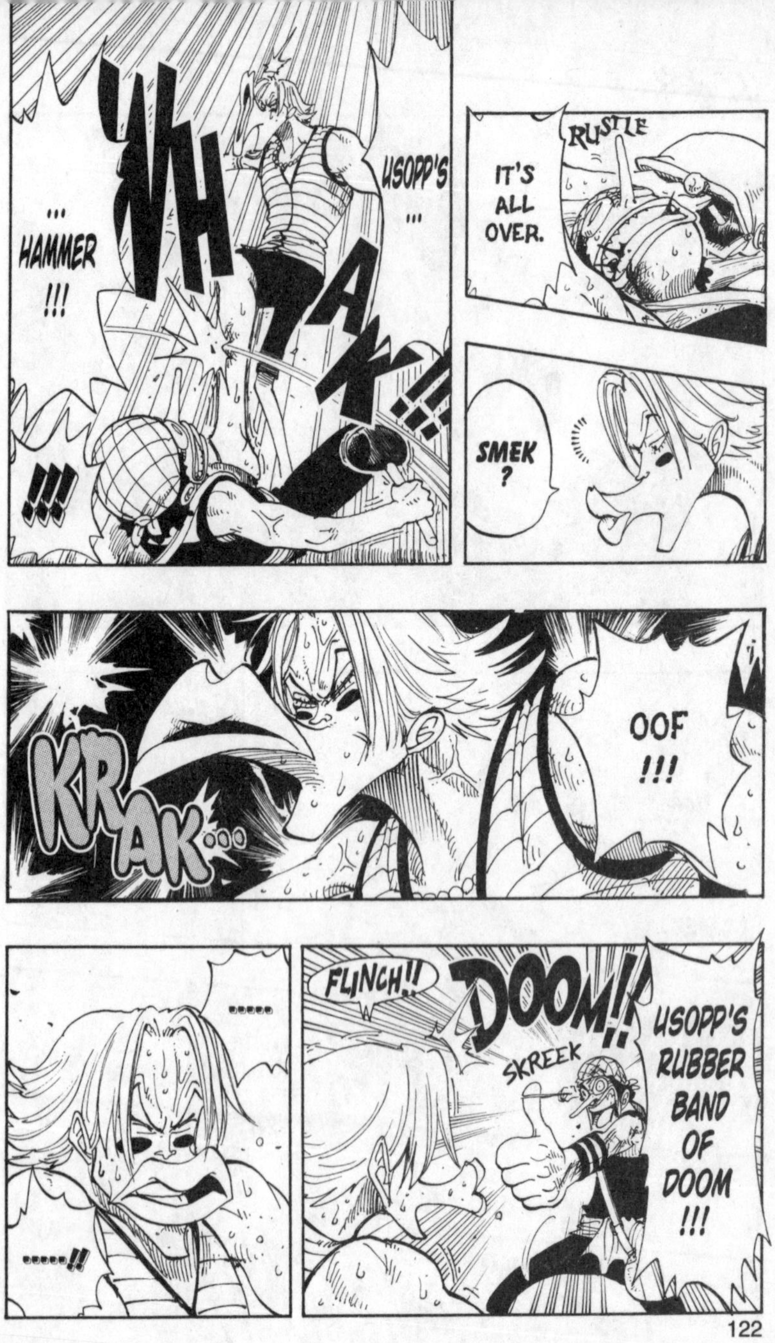
RUSTLE
IT'S ALL OVER.
SMEK ?
USOPP'S ...
... HAMMER !!!
WHAK!!!
!!!
OOF !!!
KRAK...
USOPP'S RUBBER BAND OF DOOM !!!
DOOM!!
SKREEK
FLINCH!!
......
......!!

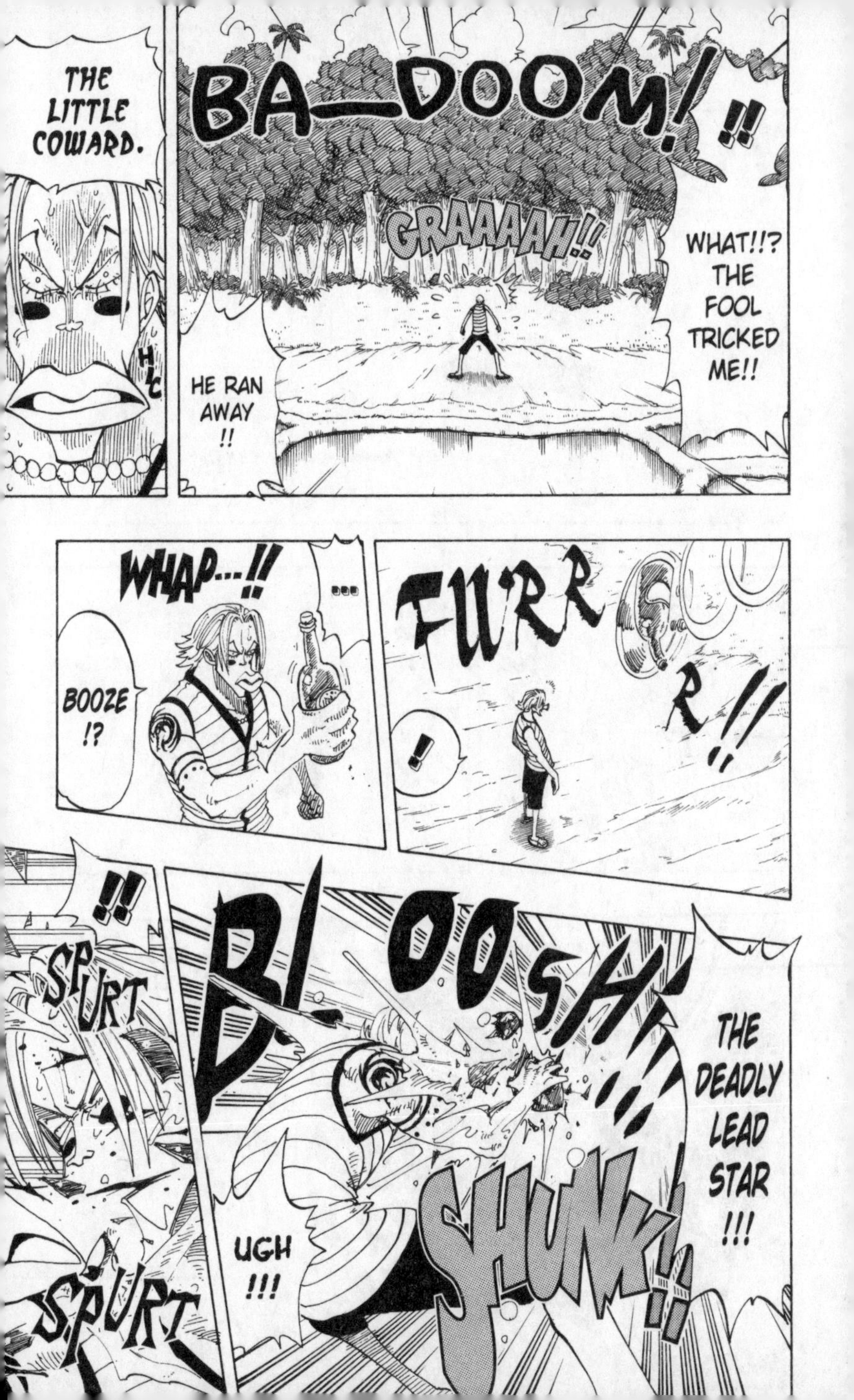
BA-DOOM!!!
GRAAAAH!!
WHAT!!? THE FOOL TRICKED ME!!
HE RAN AWAY !!
THE LITTLE COWARD.
HIC
FURRR!!
!
WHAP...!!
...
BOOZE !?
BLOOSH
THE DEADLY LEAD STAR !!!
SHUNK!!
UGH !!!
!!
SPURT
SPURT

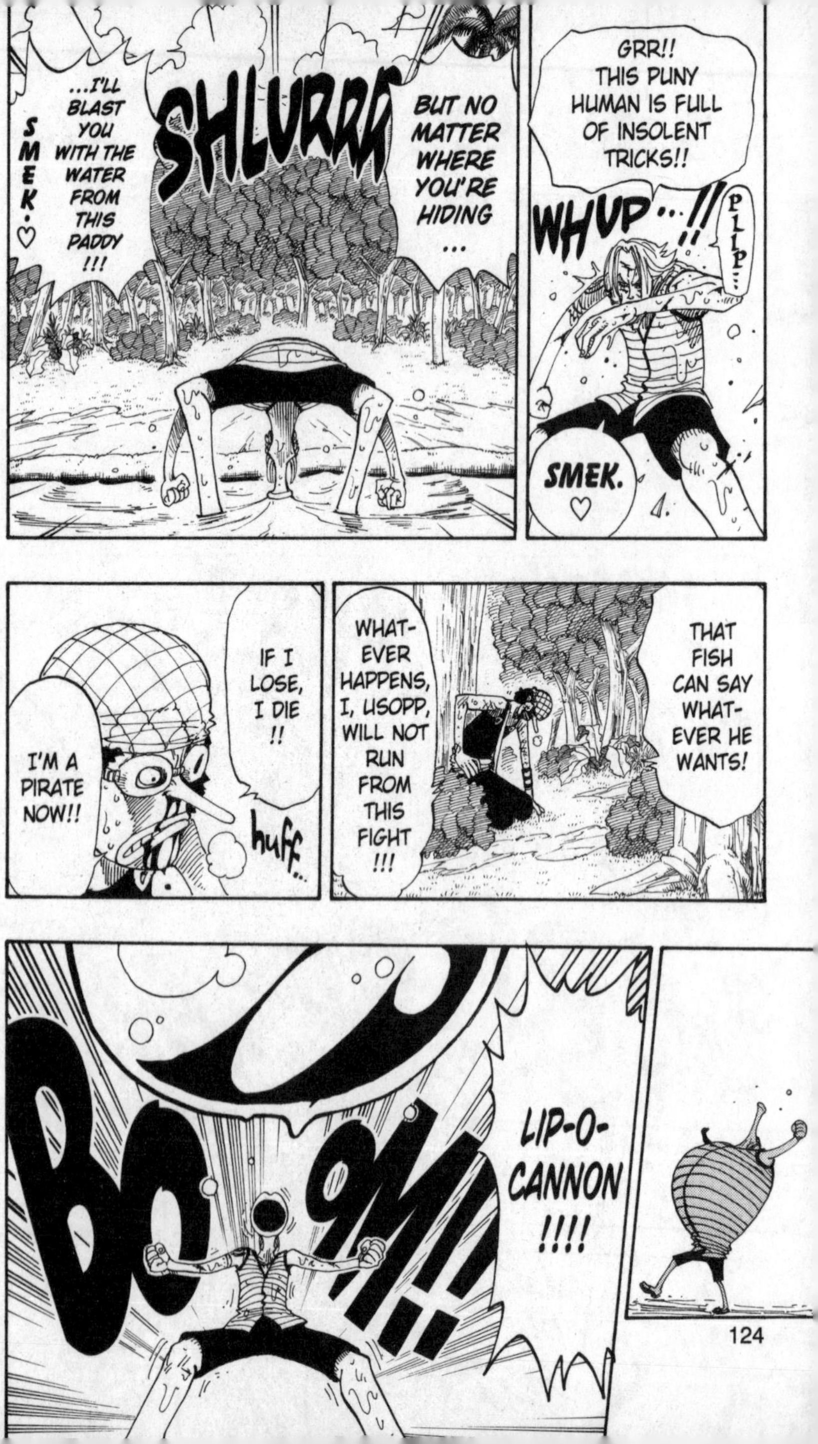
GRR!! THIS PUNY HUMAN IS FULL OF INSOLENT TRICKS!!
WHUP...!!
PLLP...
SMEK. ♡
BUT NO MATTER WHERE YOU'RE HIDING ...
SHLURRP
...I'LL BLAST YOU WITH THE WATER FROM THIS PADDY !!!
SMEK. ♡
THAT FISH CAN SAY WHATEVER HE WANTS!
WHAT-EVER HAPPENS, I, USOPP, WILL NOT RUN FROM THIS FIGHT !!!
IF I LOSE, I DIE !!
I'M A PIRATE NOW!!
huff..
LIP-O-CANNON !!!!
BOOM!!

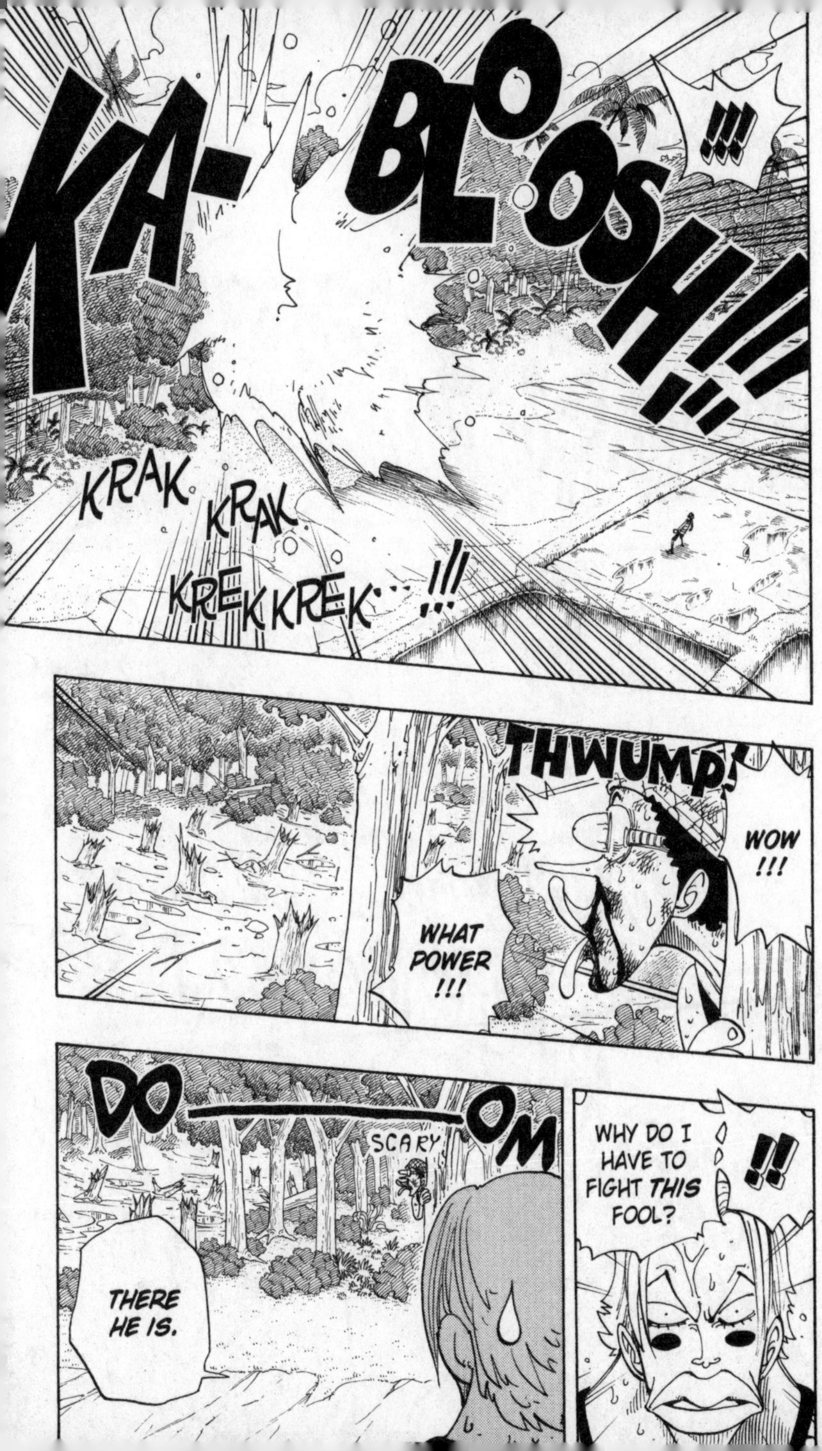
KA-BLOOSH!!!
KRAK KRAK
KREK KREK...!!!
THWUMP!
WOW !!!
WHAT POWER !!!
WHY DO I HAVE TO FIGHT THIS FOOL?
!!
DO———OM
SCARY
THERE HE IS.

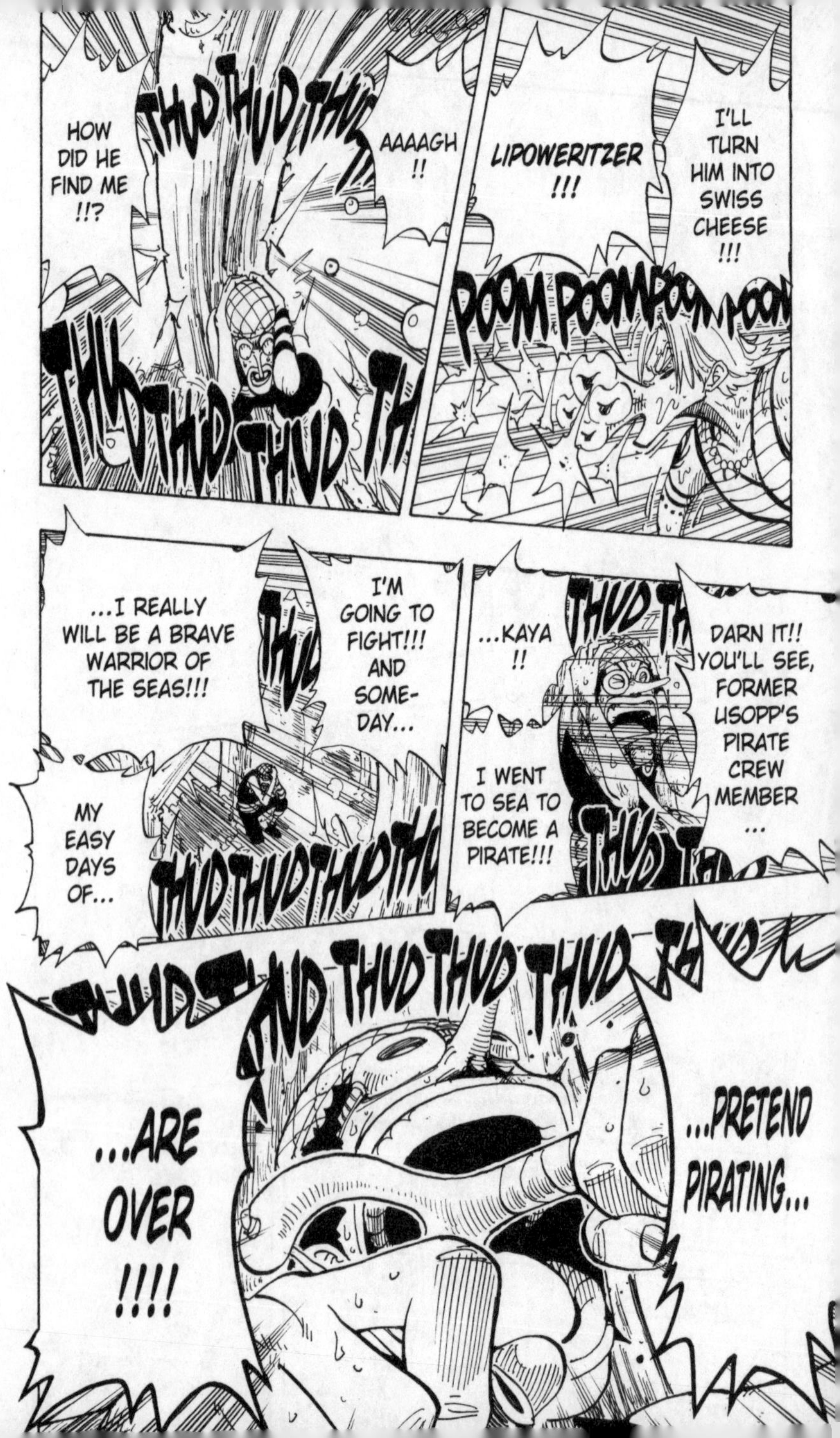
I'LL TURN HIM INTO SWISS CHEESE!!!
LIPOWERITZER!!!
POOM POOM POOM POOM
AAAAGH!!
HOW DID HE FIND ME!!?
THUD THUD THUD
THUD THUD THUD
DARN IT!! YOU'LL SEE, FORMER USOPP'S PIRATE CREW MEMBER...
...KAYA!!
I WENT TO SEA TO BECOME A PIRATE!!!
THUD
I'M GOING TO FIGHT!!! AND SOME-DAY...
...I REALLY WILL BE A BRAVE WARRIOR OF THE SEAS!!!
MY EASY DAYS OF...
THUD THUD THUD
THUD THUD THUD THUD
...PRETEND PIRATING...
...ARE OVER!!!!

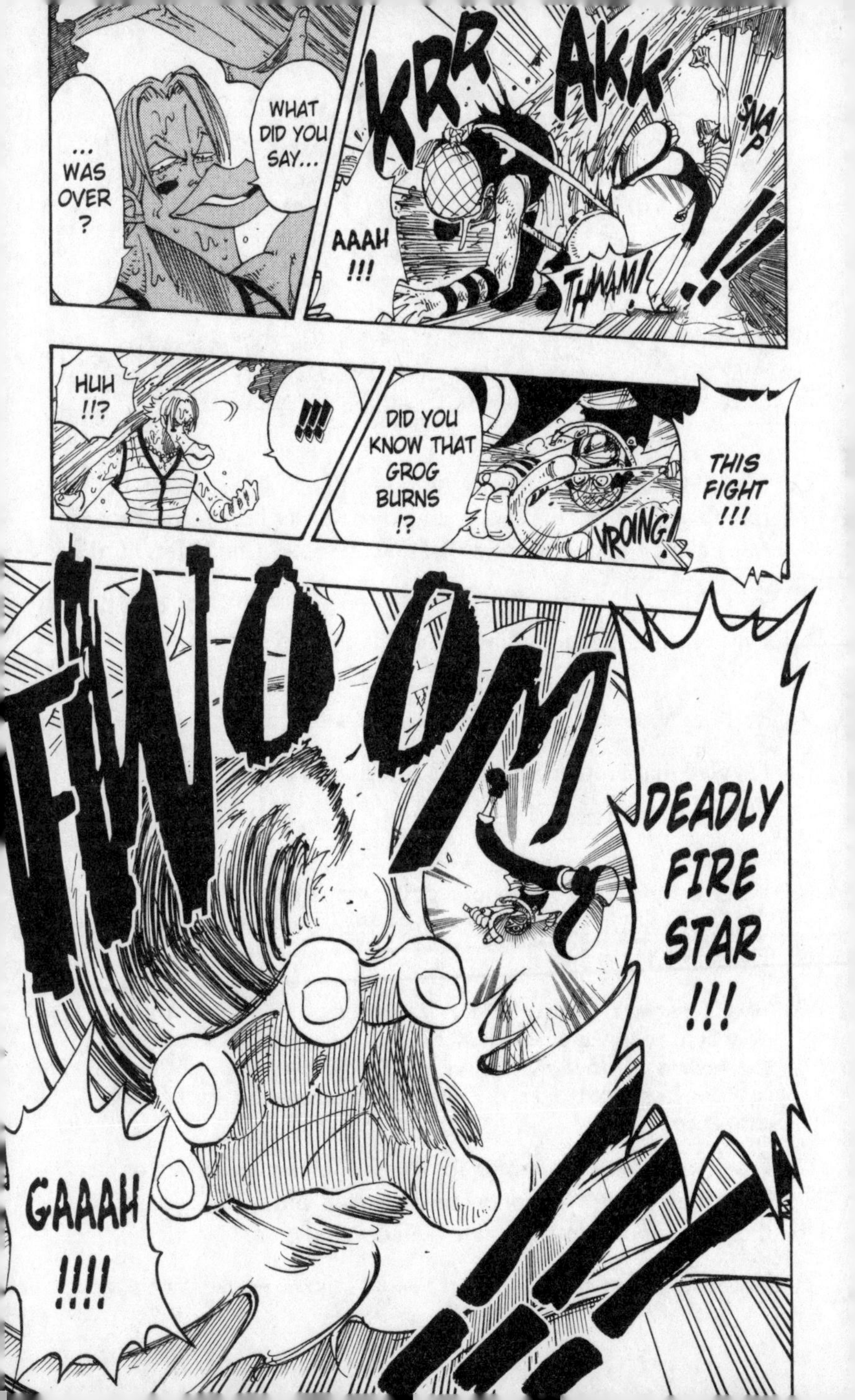
KRR AKK
SNAP
AAAH !!!
THWAM!
..!!
WHAT DID YOU SAY...
... WAS OVER ?
THIS FIGHT !!!
VROING!
DID YOU KNOW THAT GROG BURNS !?
!!!
HUH !!?
FWOOM
DEADLY FIRE STAR !!!
GAAAH !!!!

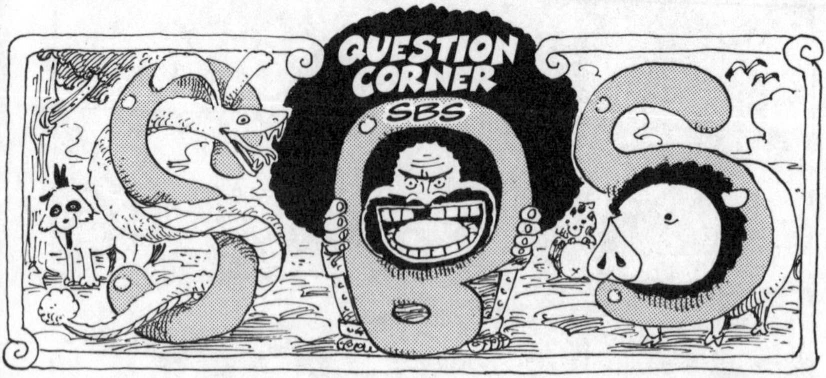
QUESTION CORNER
SBS

Q: Sensei! I thought up a new technique for Luffy. He stretches his mouth and eats up his enemy and later flushes him down the toilet along with his *oop! What do you think? Good idea, huh?

A: It stinks-o.

Q: I've got a question for Oda Sensei. Whaddaya call Belle-Mère's hairdo?

A: It's called "women are brave." Go to the beauty parlor and shout it out.

Q: I'm glad that brother Sanji is a ladies' man and not a "gentlemen's man."

A: Indeed.

Q: When Sanji is thinking about a girl, his cigarette smoke forms the shape of a heart. How does he do that? I want to do that too!! Please (x100) teach me!

A: Hmm. First you have to be over 20 years old. Then light a cigarette and take a deep puff of smoke. Let the smoke soak up the feelings of love that you've prepared in your lungs and exhale it from your mouth. The smoke will surely come out in the shape of a heart.

Q: I can't quite decide whether Yosaku and Johnny are strong or not. I'm within a frog's hair of being able to tell. But really, between those two and Helmeppo, who will develop more?

A: I have high hopes that, one day, Kaya will become an excellent doctor.

Chapter 88:
DIE!!!

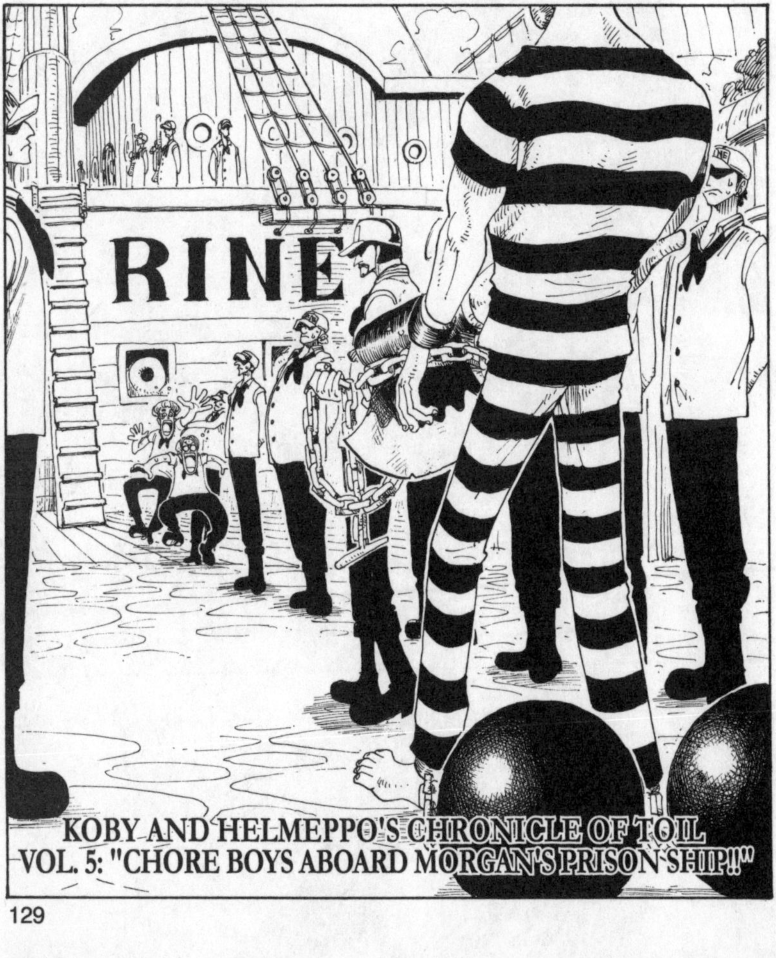
RINE
KOBY AND HELMEPPO'S CHRONICLE OF TOIL
VOL. 5: "CHORE BOYS ABOARD MORGAN'S PRISON SHIP!!"

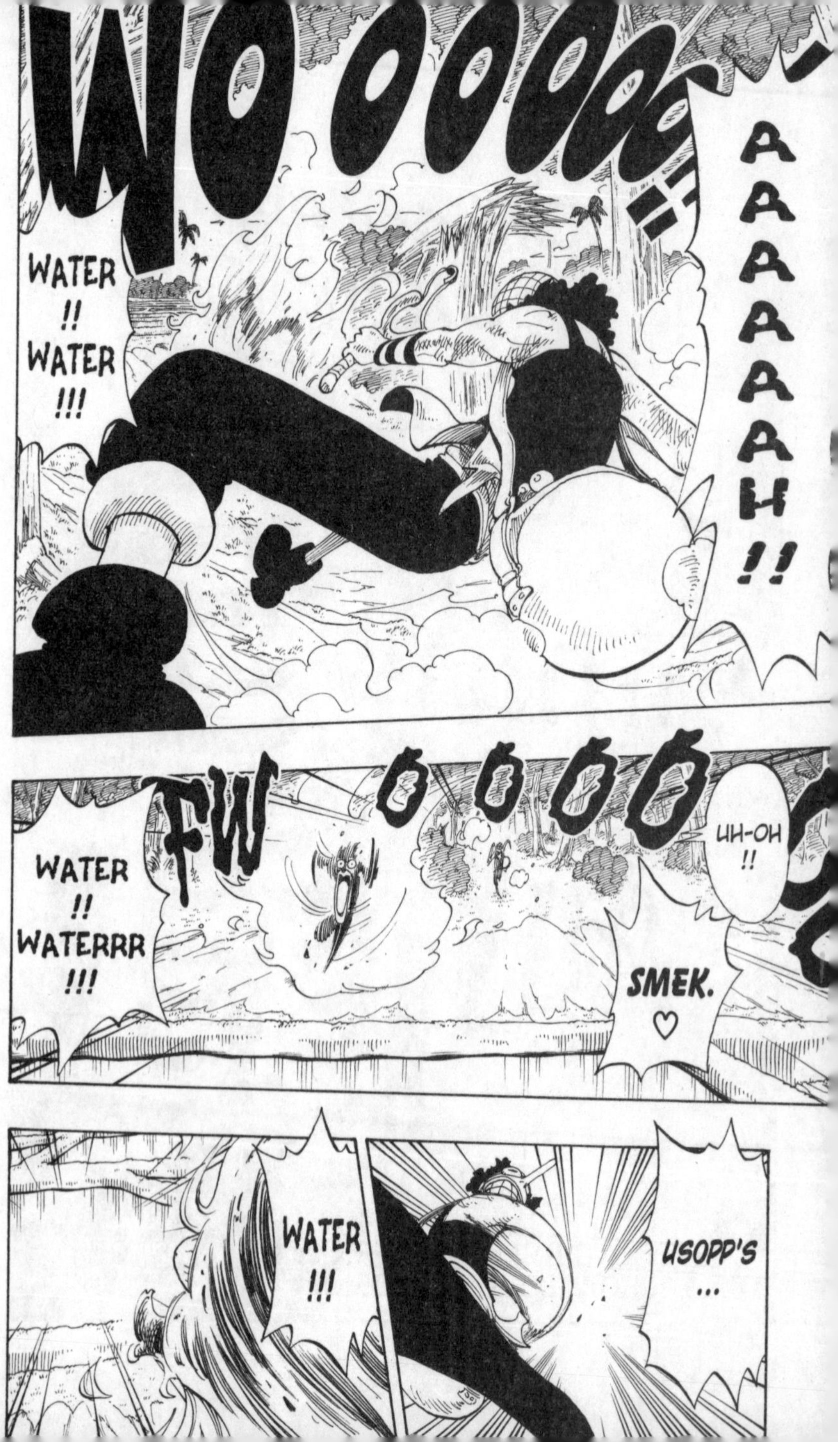
WOOOOO!!
AAAAAH!!
WATER!! WATER!!!
UH-OH!!
SMEK. ♡
FWOOOOO
WATER!! WATERRR!!!
USOPP'S ...
WATER!!!

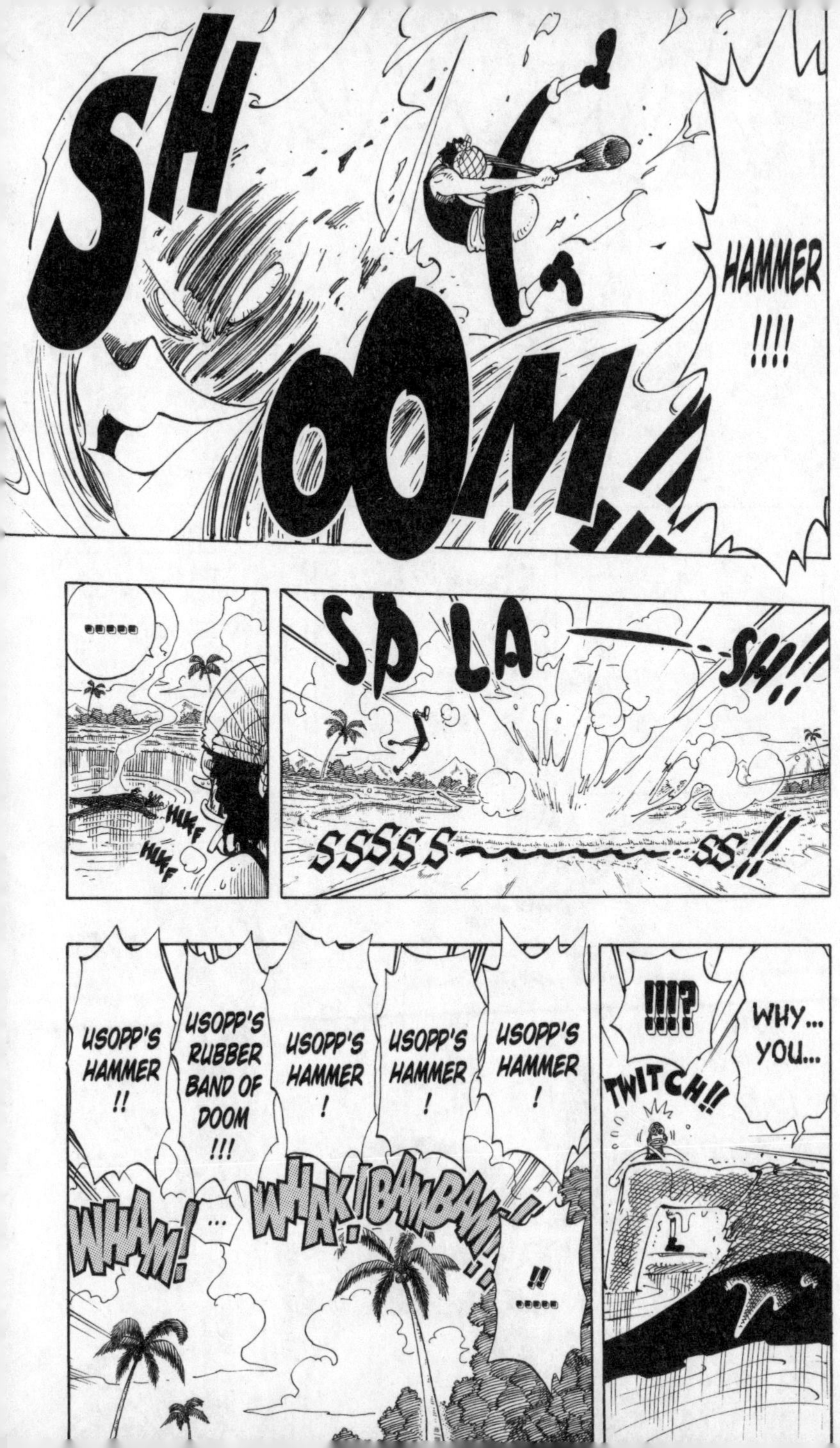
HAMMER !!!!
SHOOM!!
SPLA—SH!!
SSSSS—SS!!
.....
HUFF
HUFF
WHY... YOU...
!!!?
TWITCH!!
USOPP'S HAMMER !
USOPP'S HAMMER !
USOPP'S HAMMER !
USOPP'S RUBBER BAND OF DOOM !!!
USOPP'S HAMMER !!
!! .....
WHAK! BAMBAM!!
...
WHAM!

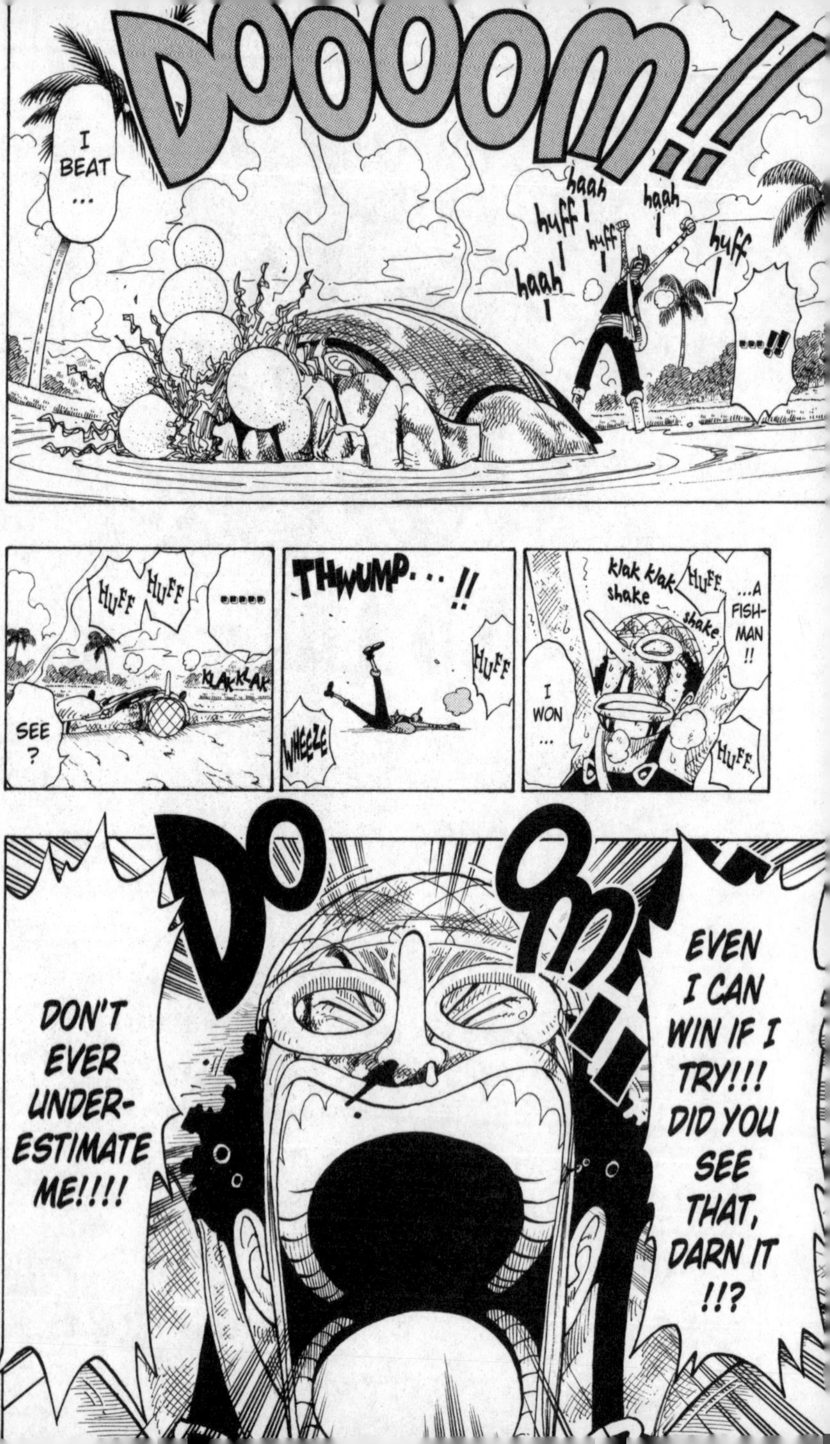
DOOOOM!!
haah huff huff haah haah huff
...!!
I BEAT ...
.....
HUFF HUFF
KLAK KLAK
SEE ?
THWUMP...!!
HUFF
WHEEZE
...A FISH-MAN !!
HUFF...
klak klak shake shake
I WON ...
HUFF...
DOOM!!
EVEN I CAN WIN IF I TRY!!! DID YOU SEE THAT, DARN IT !!?
DON'T EVER UNDER-ESTIMATE ME!!!!

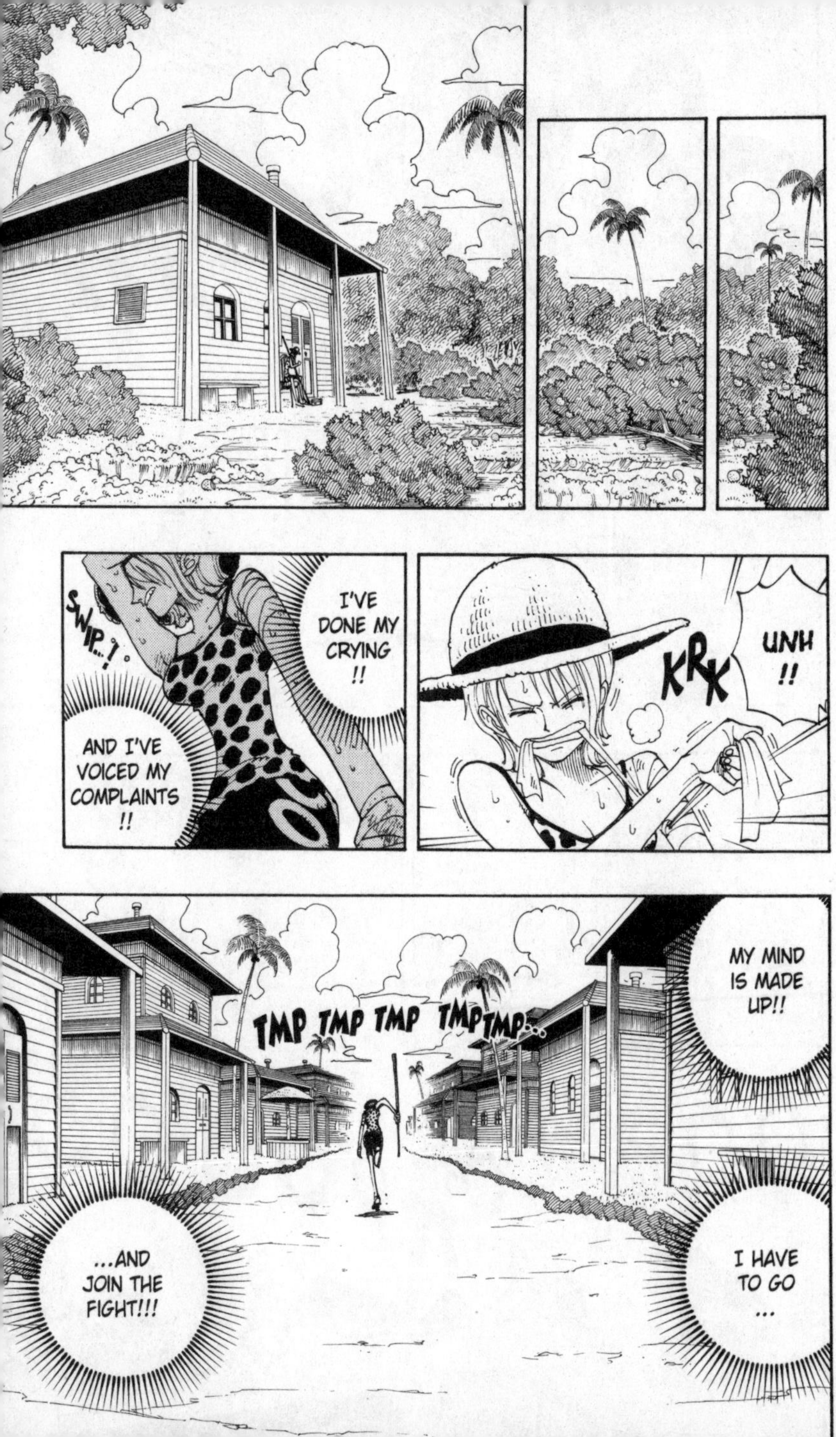
KRK
UNH!!
I'VE DONE MY CRYING!!
SWIP..!
AND I'VE VOICED MY COMPLAINTS!!
MY MIND IS MADE UP!!
TMP TMP TMP TMPTMP...
I HAVE TO GO...
...AND JOIN THE FIGHT!!!

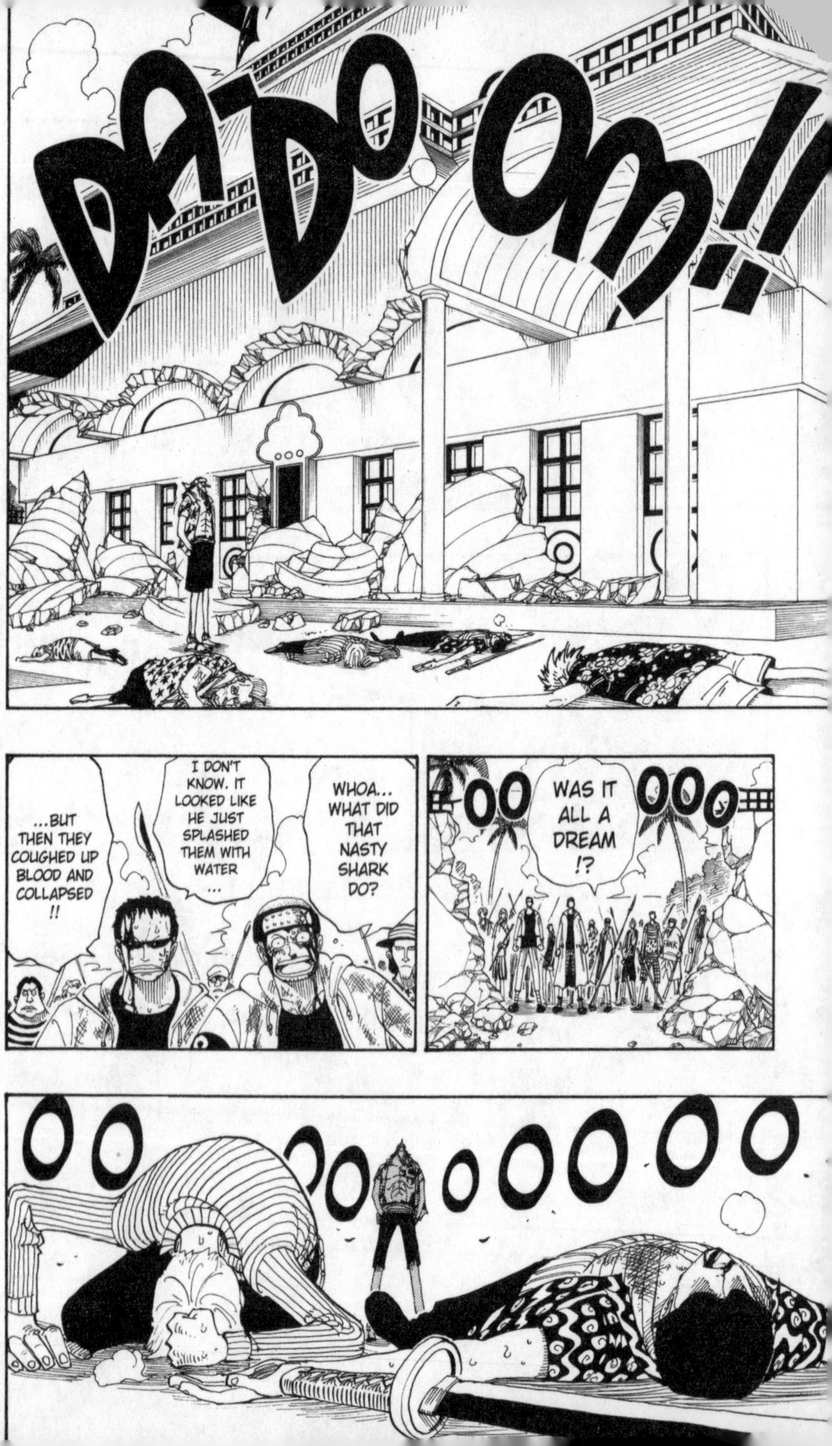
DADOOM!!
OOO
WAS IT ALL A DREAM !?
OOO
WHOA... WHAT DID THAT NASTY SHARK DO?
I DON'T KNOW. IT LOOKED LIKE HE JUST SPLASHED THEM WITH WATER ...
...BUT THEN THEY COUGHED UP BLOOD AND COLLAPSED !!
OOOOOOOOOOO

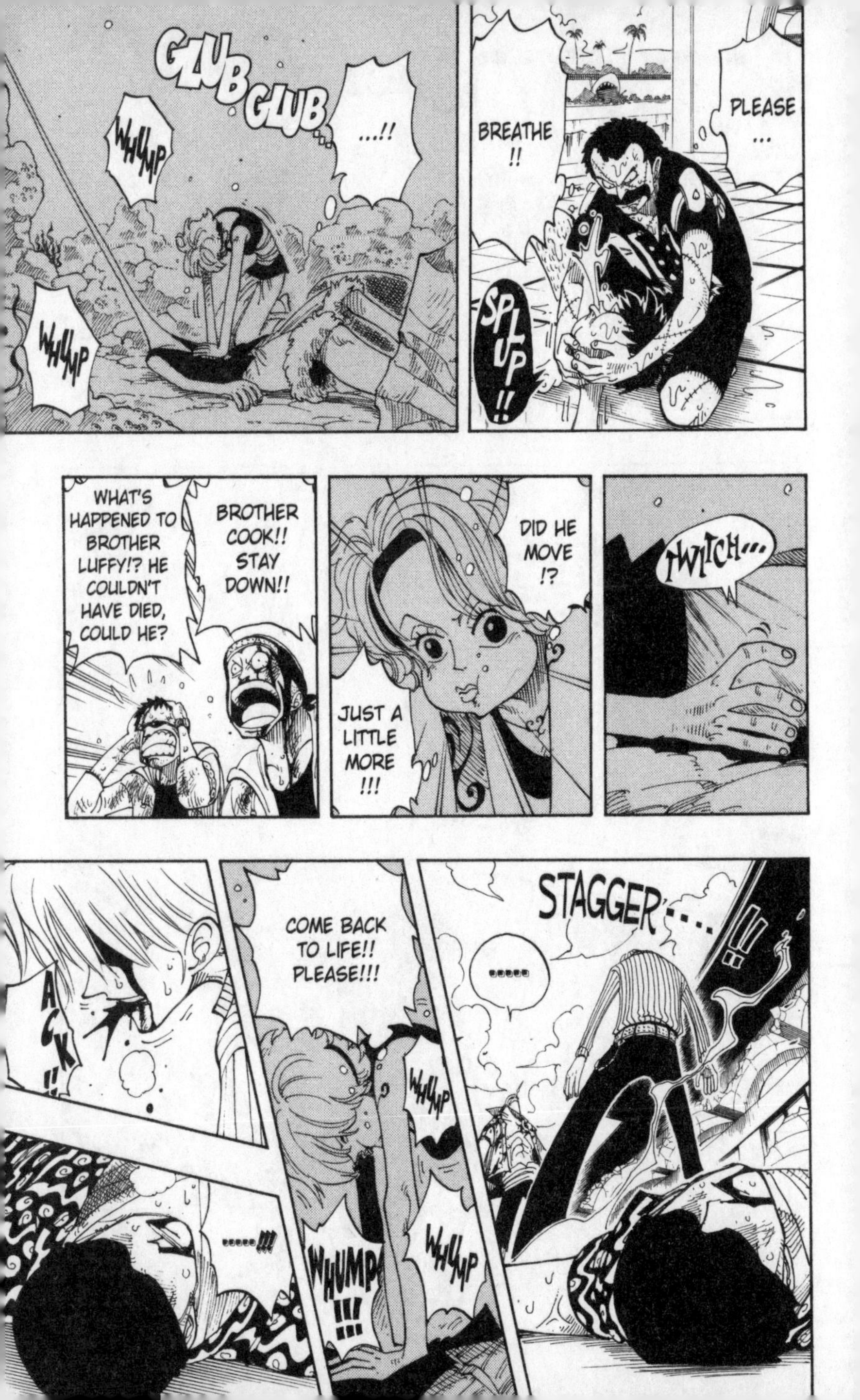
PLEASE...
BREATHE!!
SPLUP!!
...!!
GLUB GLUB
WHUMP
WHUMP
TWITCH...
DID HE MOVE!?
JUST A LITTLE MORE!!!
BROTHER COOK!! STAY DOWN!!
WHAT'S HAPPENED TO BROTHER LUFFY!? HE COULDN'T HAVE DIED, COULD HE?
STAGGER....
!!
......
COME BACK TO LIFE!! PLEASE!!!
WHUMP
WHUMP
WHUMP!!!
ACK!!
......!!!

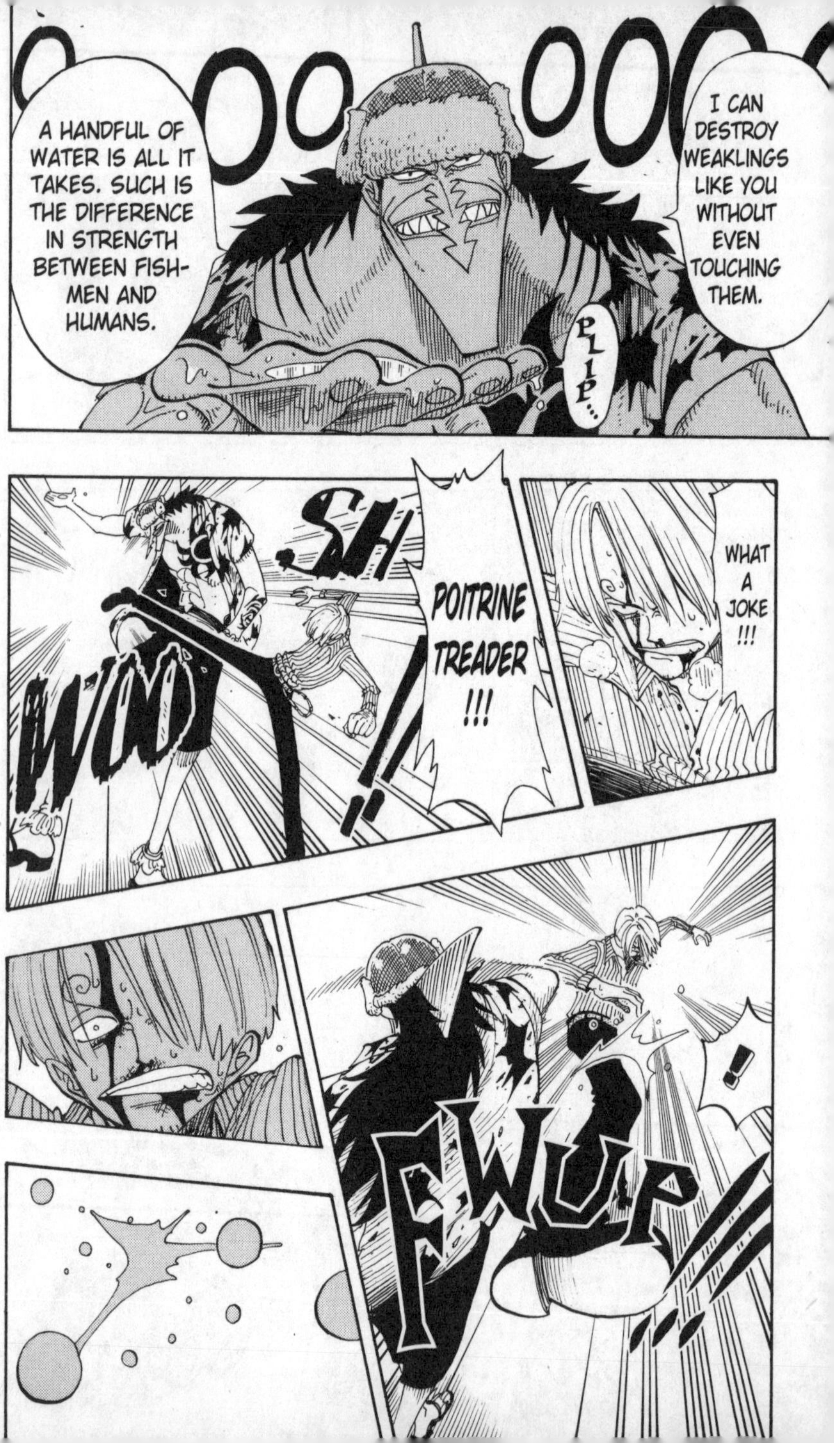
OOOO OOOO
I CAN DESTROY WEAKLINGS LIKE YOU WITHOUT EVEN TOUCHING THEM.
A HANDFUL OF WATER IS ALL IT TAKES. SUCH IS THE DIFFERENCE IN STRENGTH BETWEEN FISH-MEN AND HUMANS.
PLIP...
WHAT A JOKE!!!
POITRINE TREADER!!!
SH
WM
!
FWUP!!

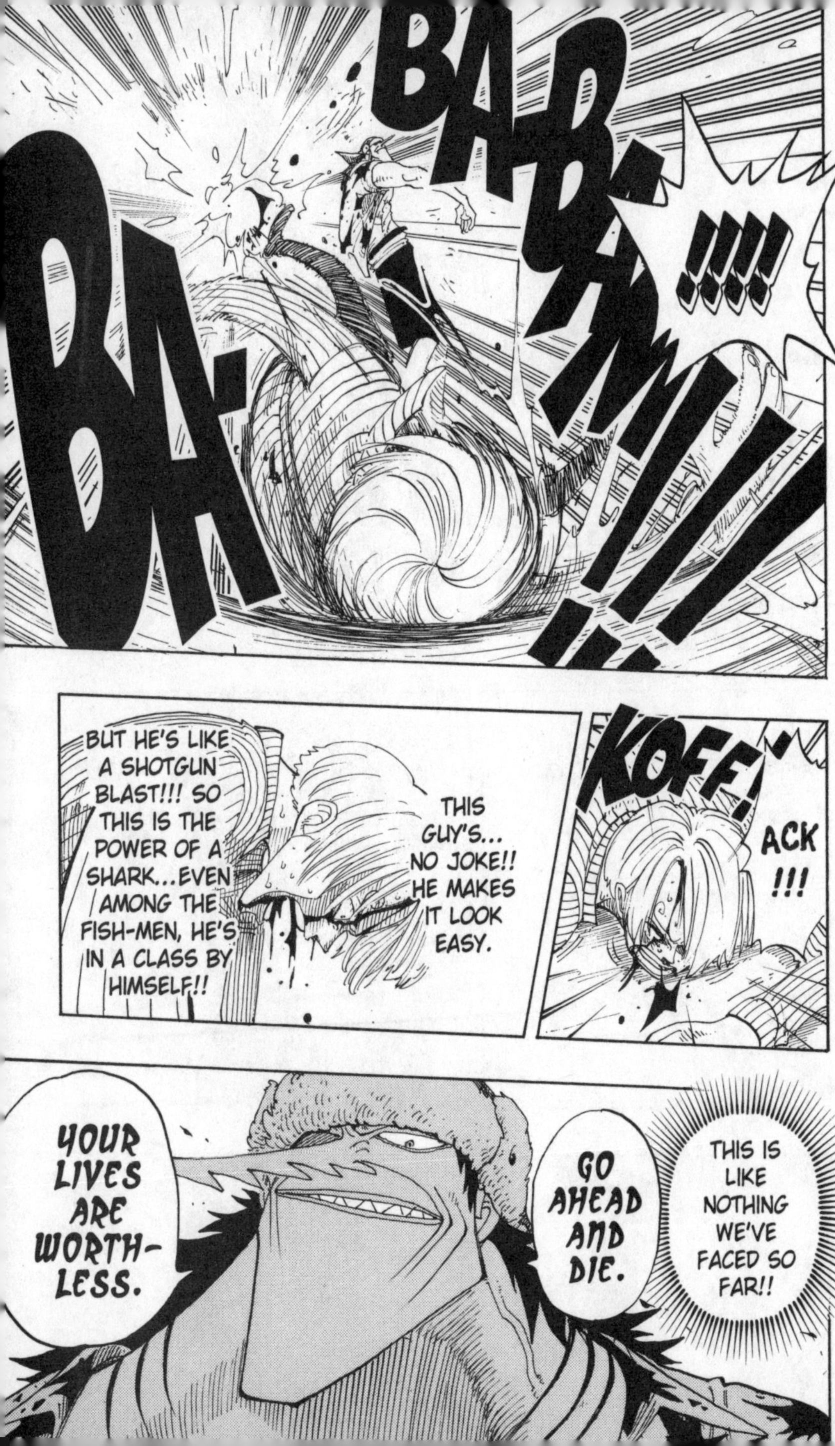
BA-BAM!!!!
BA
KOFF!
ACK!!!
THIS GUY'S... NO JOKE!! HE MAKES IT LOOK EASY.
BUT HE'S LIKE A SHOTGUN BLAST!!! SO THIS IS THE POWER OF A SHARK...EVEN AMONG THE FISH-MEN, HE'S IN A CLASS BY HIMSELF!!
THIS IS LIKE NOTHING WE'VE FACED SO FAR!!
GO AHEAD AND DIE.
YOUR LIVES ARE WORTH-LESS.

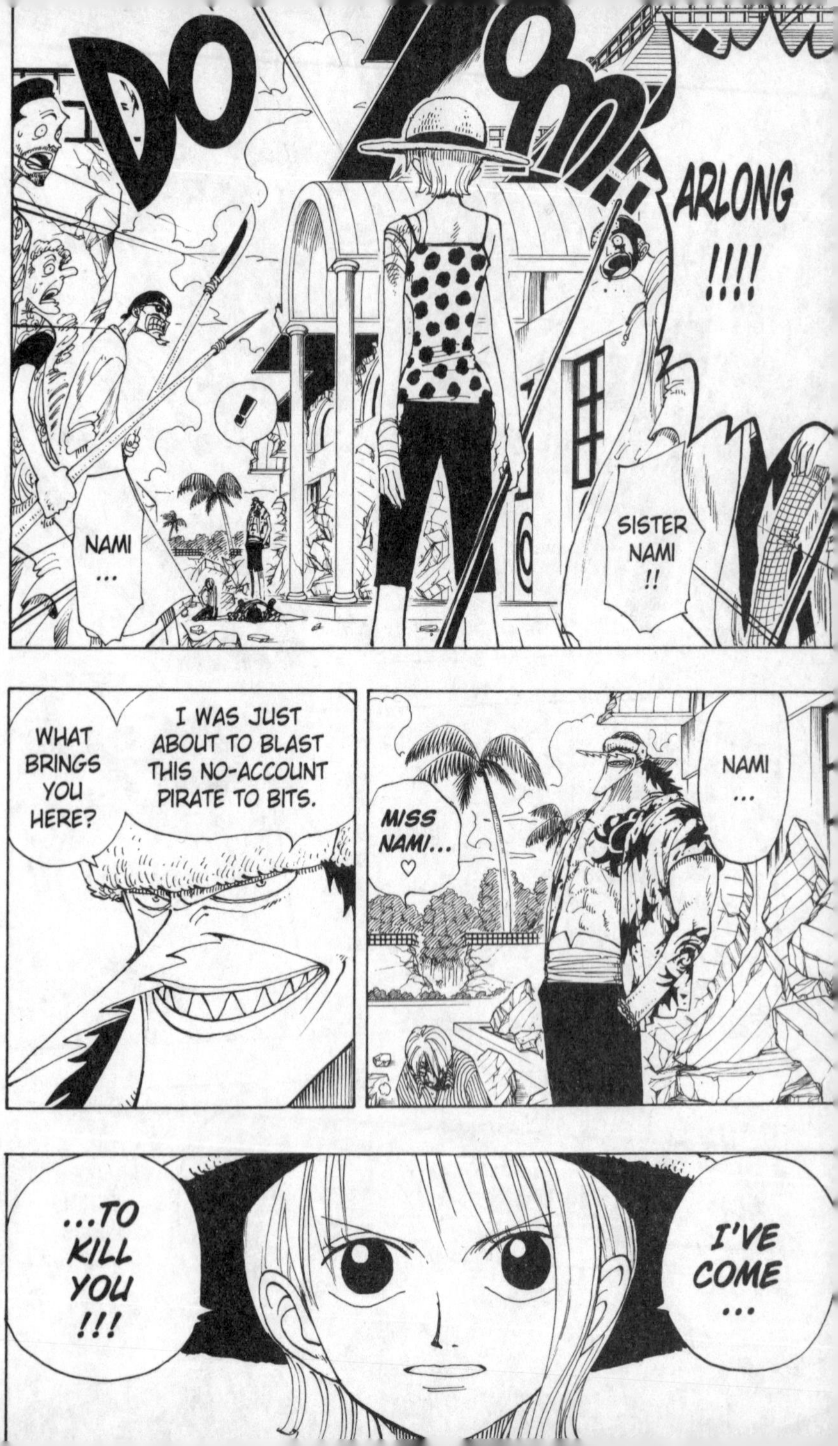
ARLONG !!!!
SISTER NAMI !!
NAMI ...
NAMI ...
MISS NAMI... ♡
I WAS JUST ABOUT TO BLAST THIS NO-ACCOUNT PIRATE TO BITS.
WHAT BRINGS YOU HERE?
I'VE COME ...
...TO KILL YOU !!!

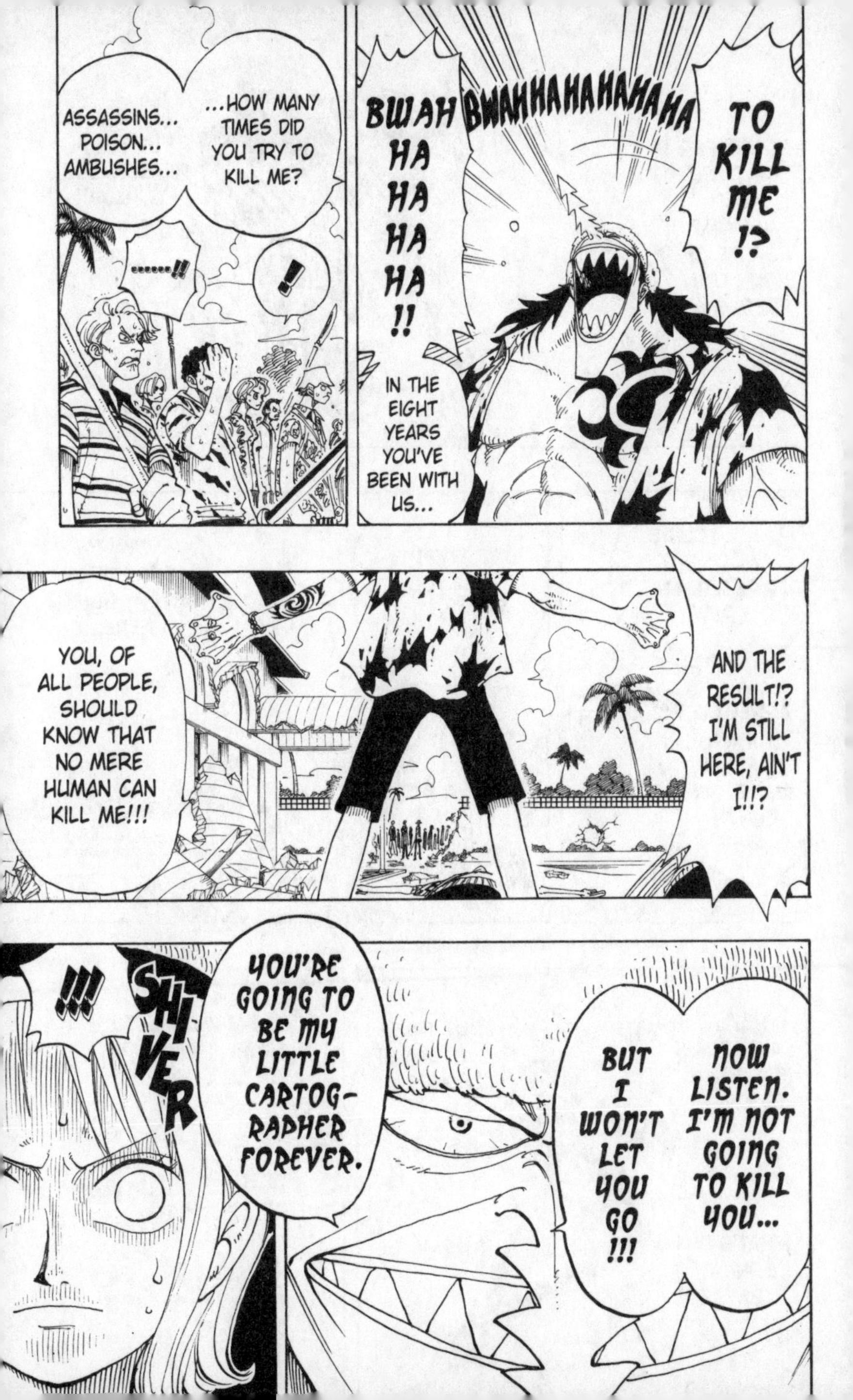
TO KILL ME!?
BWAH BWAHHAHAHAHAHAHA HA HA HA HA!!
IN THE EIGHT YEARS YOU'VE BEEN WITH US...
...HOW MANY TIMES DID YOU TRY TO KILL ME?
ASSASSINS... POISON... AMBUSHES...
......!!
!
AND THE RESULT!? I'M STILL HERE, AIN'T I!!?
YOU, OF ALL PEOPLE, SHOULD KNOW THAT NO MERE HUMAN CAN KILL ME!!!
NOW LISTEN. I'M NOT GOING TO KILL YOU...
BUT I WON'T LET YOU GO!!!
YOU'RE GOING TO BE MY LITTLE CARTOG-RAPHER FOREVER.
SHIVER
!!!

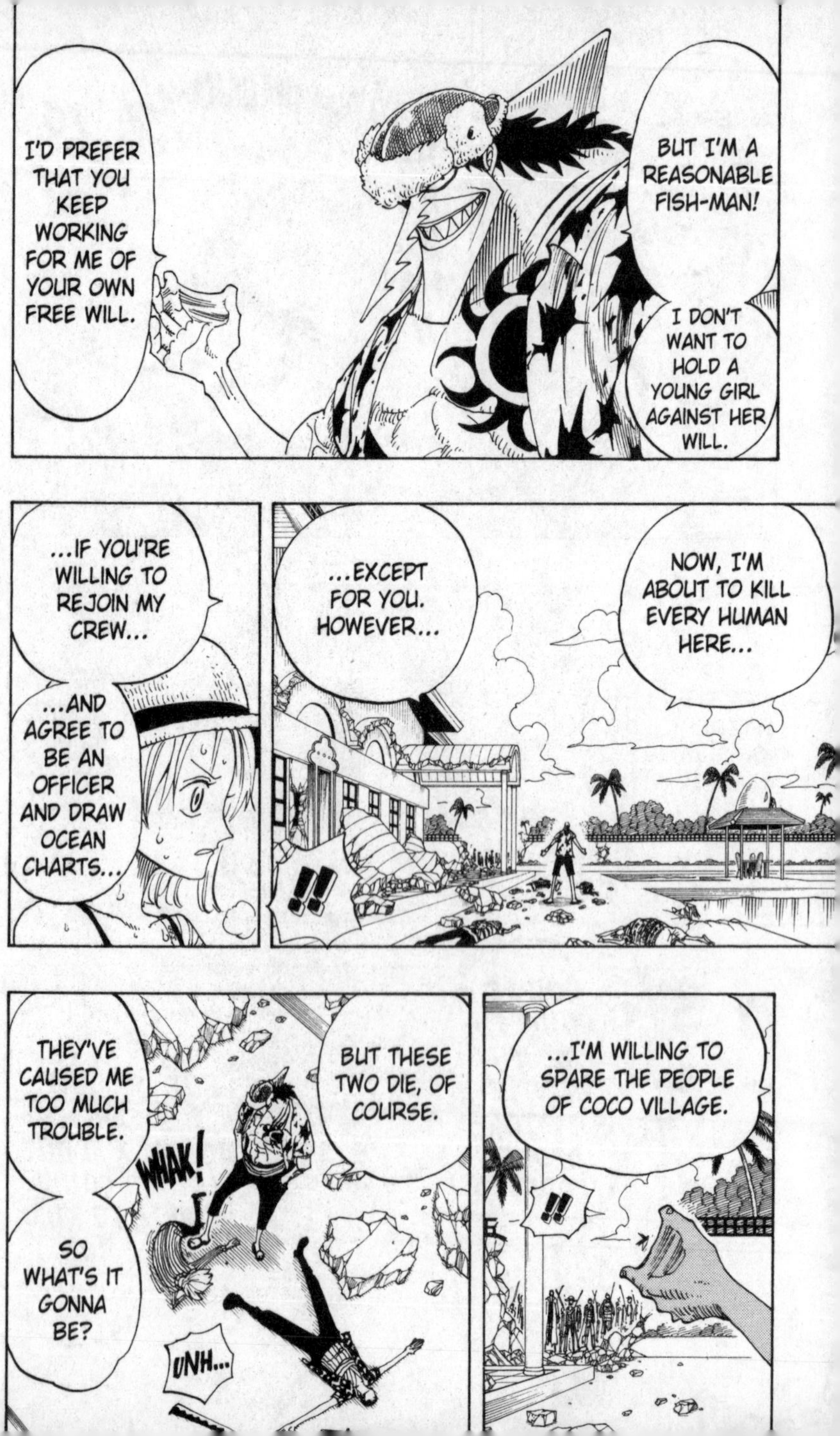
BUT I'M A REASONABLE FISH-MAN!
I DON'T WANT TO HOLD A YOUNG GIRL AGAINST HER WILL.
I'D PREFER THAT YOU KEEP WORKING FOR ME OF YOUR OWN FREE WILL.
NOW, I'M ABOUT TO KILL EVERY HUMAN HERE...
...EXCEPT FOR YOU. HOWEVER...
!!
...IF YOU'RE WILLING TO REJOIN MY CREW...
...AND AGREE TO BE AN OFFICER AND DRAW OCEAN CHARTS...
...I'M WILLING TO SPARE THE PEOPLE OF COCO VILLAGE.
!!
BUT THESE TWO DIE, OF COURSE.
THEY'VE CAUSED ME TOO MUCH TROUBLE.
WHAK!
SO WHAT'S IT GONNA BE?
UNH...

...YOU CAN SEE WHAT A TRAGIC MISTAKE THAT WOULD BE!!

OR STICK WITH THESE WEAKLINGS AND TRY TO FIGHT ME TOGETHER!!

COME BACK TO ME NOW AND SAVE YOUR BELOVED VILLAGERS...

GULP....!!

BUT IF YOU LOOK AT THE SHAPE THESE TWO ARE IN...

ARE YOU MY SHIP-MATE...

WELL, NAMI!!?

...OR THEIRS?

BUT IF I SAY I'M ARLONG'S, ALL OF THE VILLAGERS WILL BE SPARED!! IS IT UP TO ME TO DECIDE WHO LIVES AND WHO DIES!!?

IF I SAY I'M LUFFY AND ZOLO'S SHIPMATE, EVERYONE MAY GET KILLED.

I HAVE TO BELIEVE IN THEM!!!

THAT'S DIRTY!! HE'S GONNA KEEP NAMI NO MATTER WHAT SHE DECIDES!!

...!!

BUT...I...

OKAY !!!!

...WITH ME!!!

FIGHT AND DIE...

I'M SORRY, EVERYONE !!!

!?

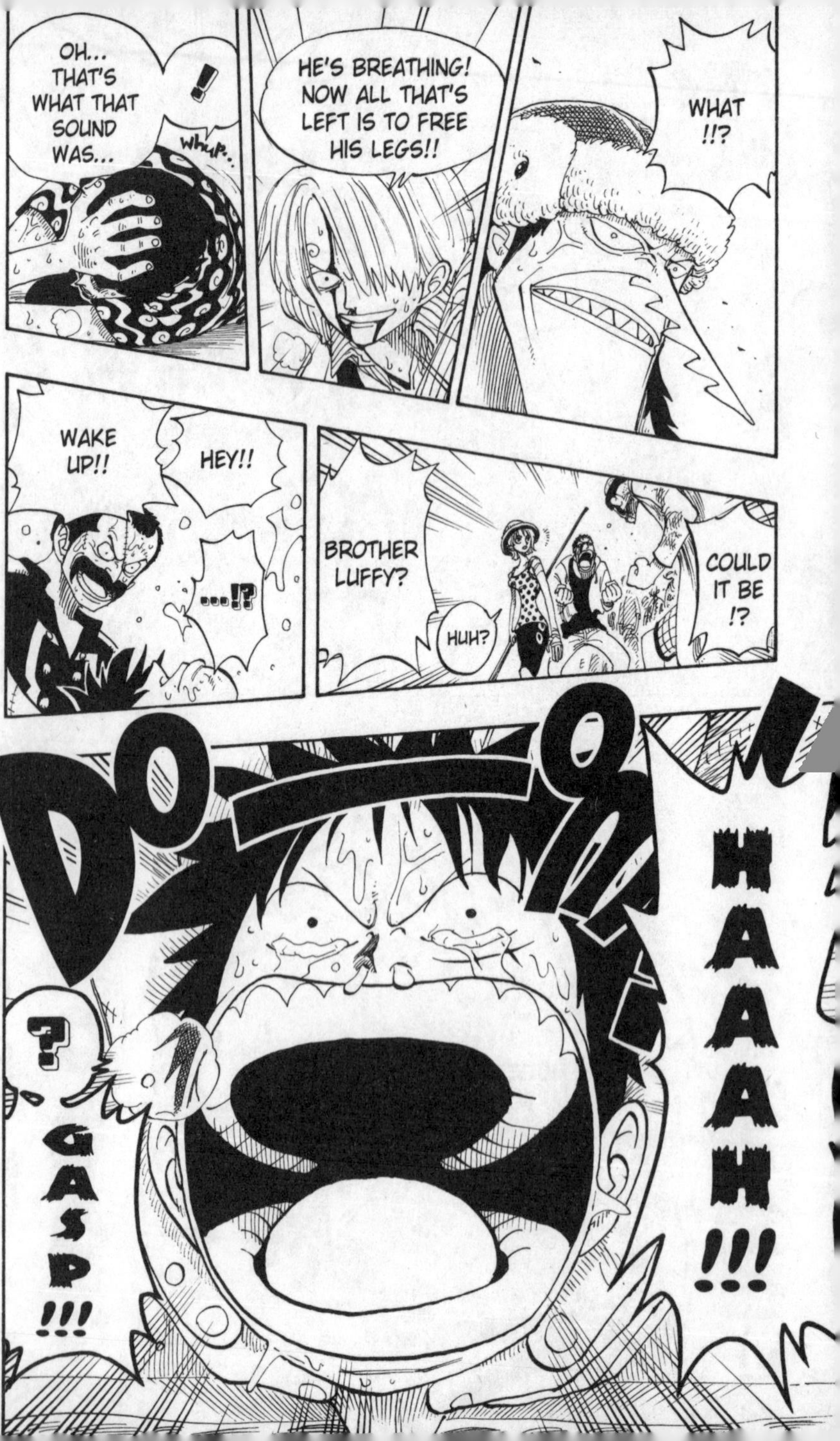
WHAT !!?
HE'S BREATHING! NOW ALL THAT'S LEFT IS TO FREE HIS LEGS!!
!
Whup..
OH... THAT'S WHAT THAT SOUND WAS...
COULD IT BE !?
HUH?
BROTHER LUFFY?
HEY!!
WAKE UP!!
...!?
HAAAAH!!!
?
GASP!!!

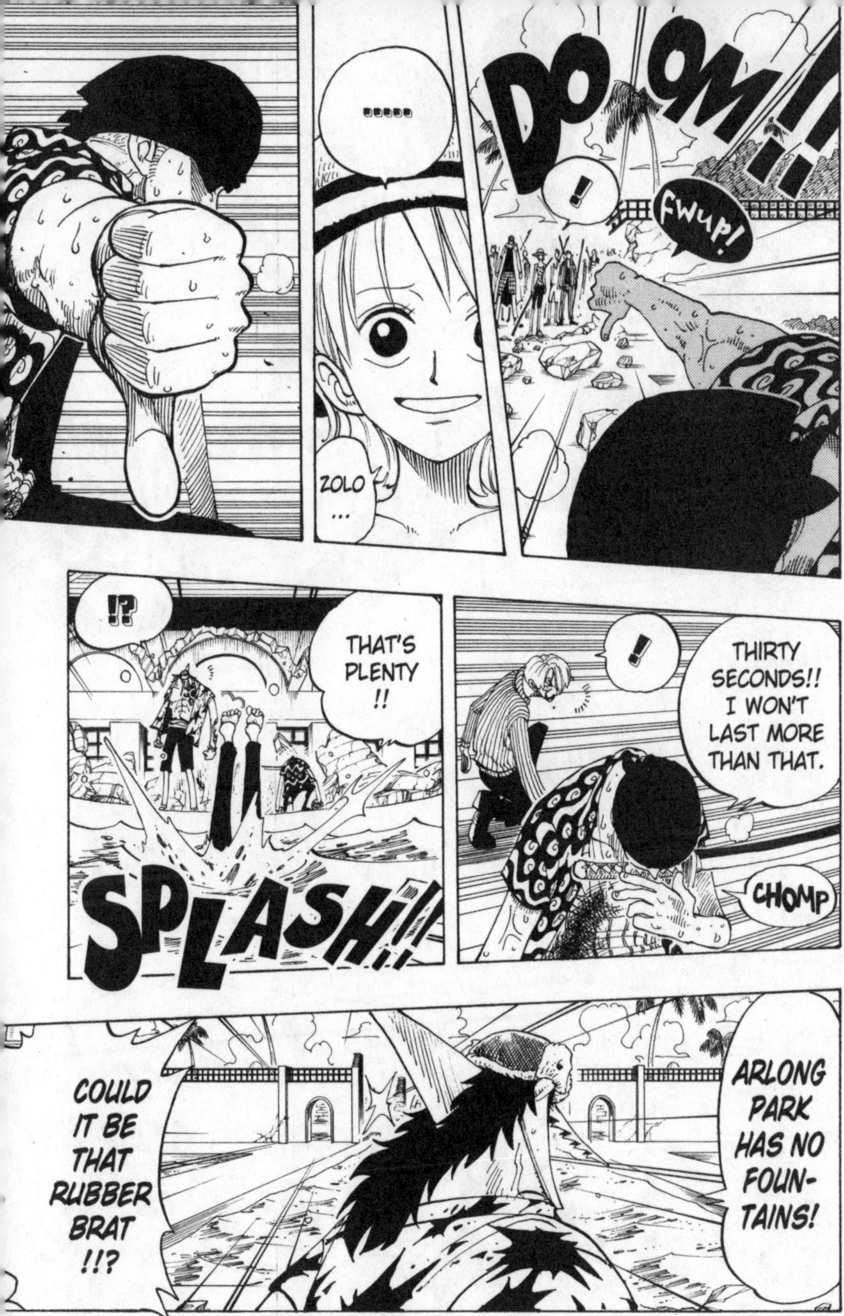
DOOM!!
!
FWUP!
.....
ZOLO...
!
THIRTY SECONDS!! I WON'T LAST MORE THAN THAT.
CHOMP
!?
THAT'S PLENTY!!
SPLASH!!
ARLONG PARK HAS NO FOUN-TAINS!
COULD IT BE THAT RUBBER BRAT!!?

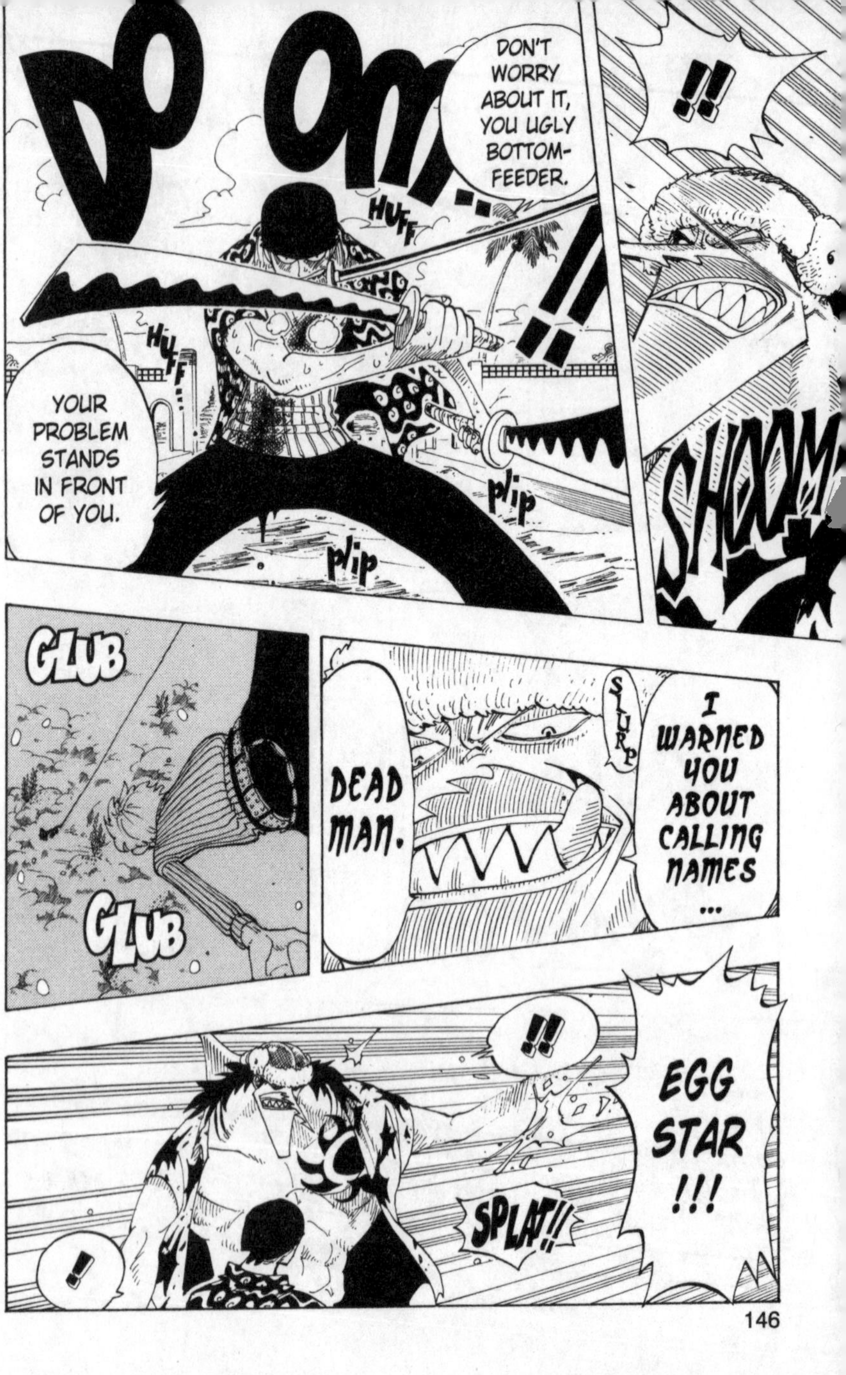
!!
SHOOM
DO ON...
DON'T WORRY ABOUT IT, YOU UGLY BOTTOM-FEEDER.
!!
HUFF
HUFF...
YOUR PROBLEM STANDS IN FRONT OF YOU.
plip
plip
SLURP
I WARNED YOU ABOUT CALLING NAMES ...
DEAD MAN.
GLUB
GLUB
!!
EGG STAR !!!
SPLAT!!
!

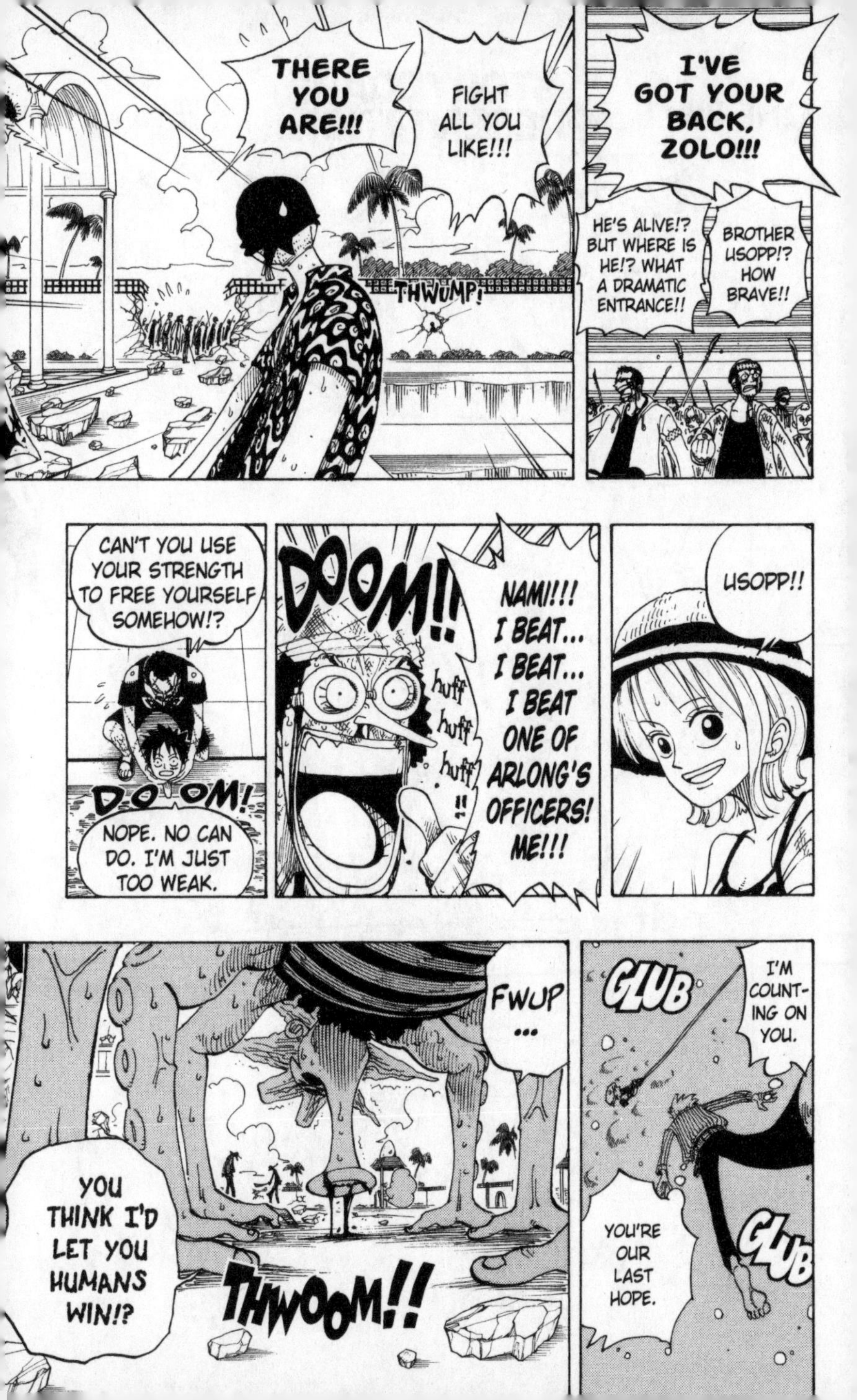
I'VE GOT YOUR BACK, ZOLO!!!
BROTHER USOPP!? HOW BRAVE!!
HE'S ALIVE!? BUT WHERE IS HE!? WHAT A DRAMATIC ENTRANCE!!
FIGHT ALL YOU LIKE!!!
THERE YOU ARE!!!
THWUMP!
USOPP!!
NAMI!!! I BEAT... I BEAT... I BEAT ONE OF ARLONG'S OFFICERS! ME!!!
DOOM!!
huff huff huff!!
CAN'T YOU USE YOUR STRENGTH TO FREE YOURSELF SOMEHOW!?
DOOM!
NOPE. NO CAN DO. I'M JUST TOO WEAK.
GLUB
I'M COUNTING ON YOU.
YOU'RE OUR LAST HOPE.
GLUB
FWUP ...
YOU THINK I'D LET YOU HUMANS WIN!?
THWOOM!!

ONE PIECE **STORYBOARD PRESENTATION!!** **#14**

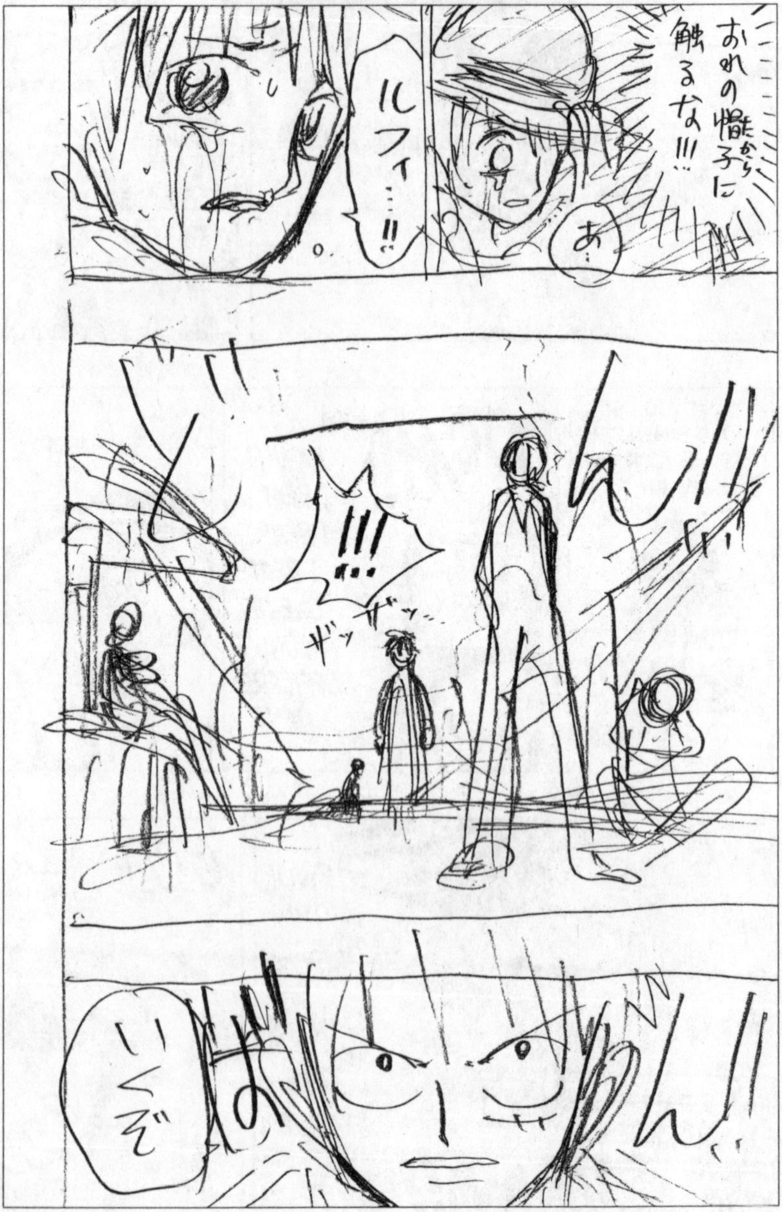
おれの帽子に触るな!!!
あ…
ルフィ…!!
ど
ん!!
!!!
ザッ
ザザッ…
ば
ん!!
いくぞ

Chapter 89:
TRADE-OFF

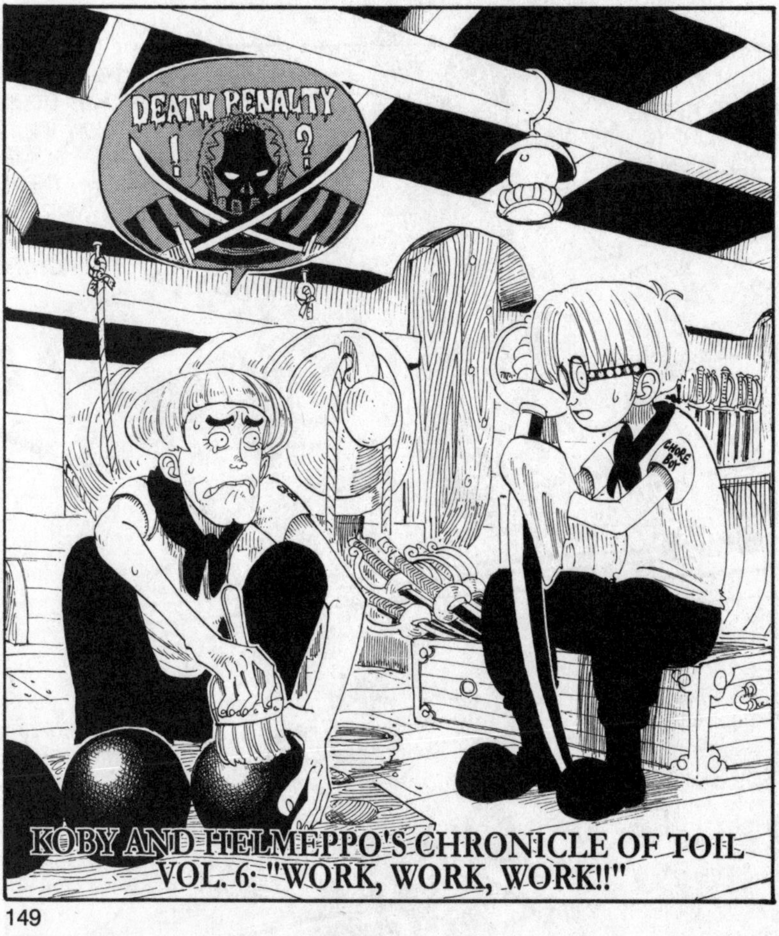
DEATH PENALTY
! ?
CHORE BOY
KOBY AND HELMEPPO'S CHRONICLE OF TOIL
VOL. 6: "WORK, WORK, WORK!!"

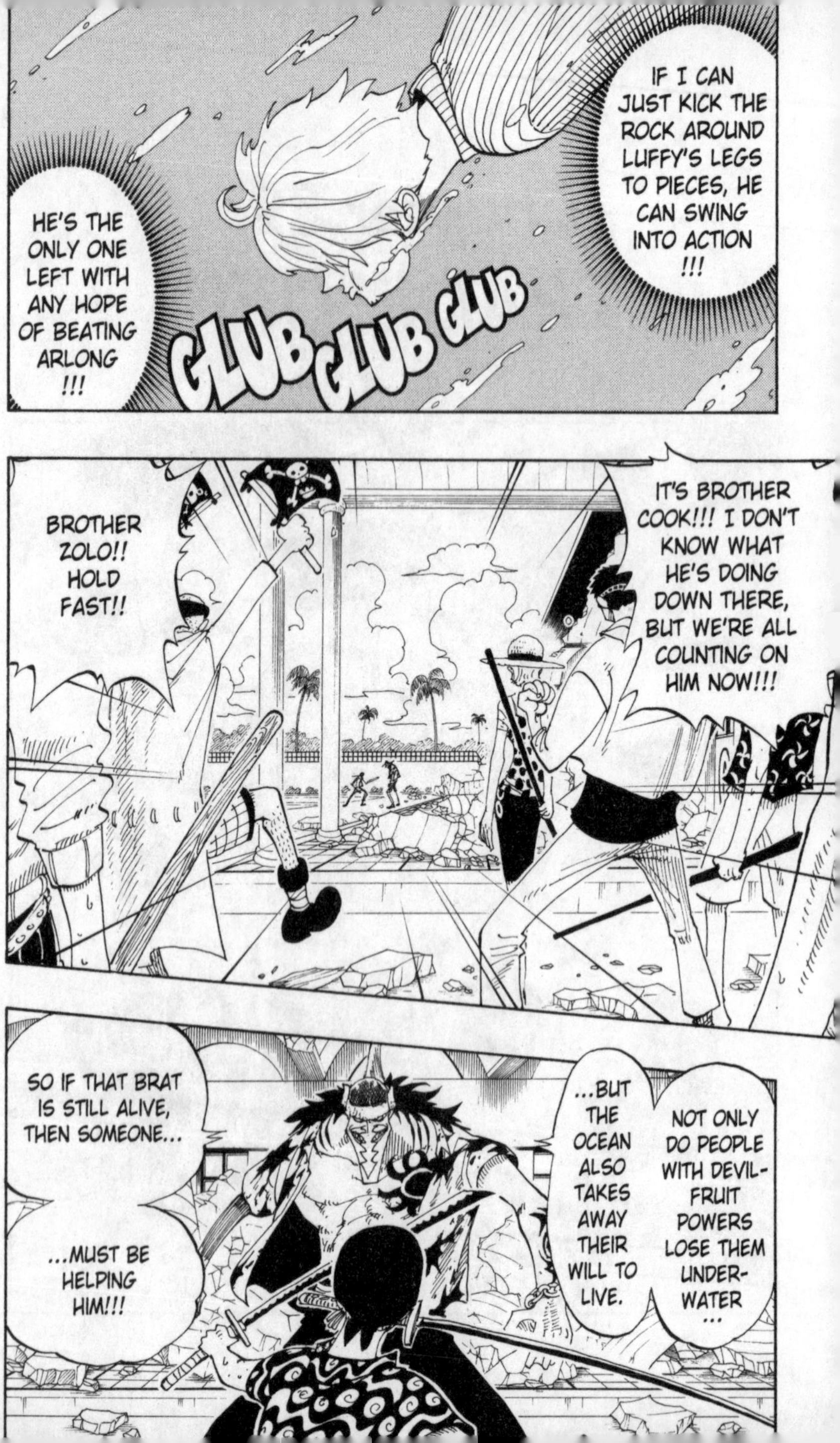
IF I CAN JUST KICK THE ROCK AROUND LUFFY'S LEGS TO PIECES, HE CAN SWING INTO ACTION !!!
HE'S THE ONLY ONE LEFT WITH ANY HOPE OF BEATING ARLONG !!!
GLUB GLUB GLUB
IT'S BROTHER COOK!!! I DON'T KNOW WHAT HE'S DOING DOWN THERE, BUT WE'RE ALL COUNTING ON HIM NOW!!!
BROTHER ZOLO!! HOLD FAST!!
NOT ONLY DO PEOPLE WITH DEVIL-FRUIT POWERS LOSE THEM UNDER-WATER ...
...BUT THE OCEAN ALSO TAKES AWAY THEIR WILL TO LIVE.
SO IF THAT BRAT IS STILL ALIVE, THEN SOMEONE...
...MUST BE HELPING HIM!!!

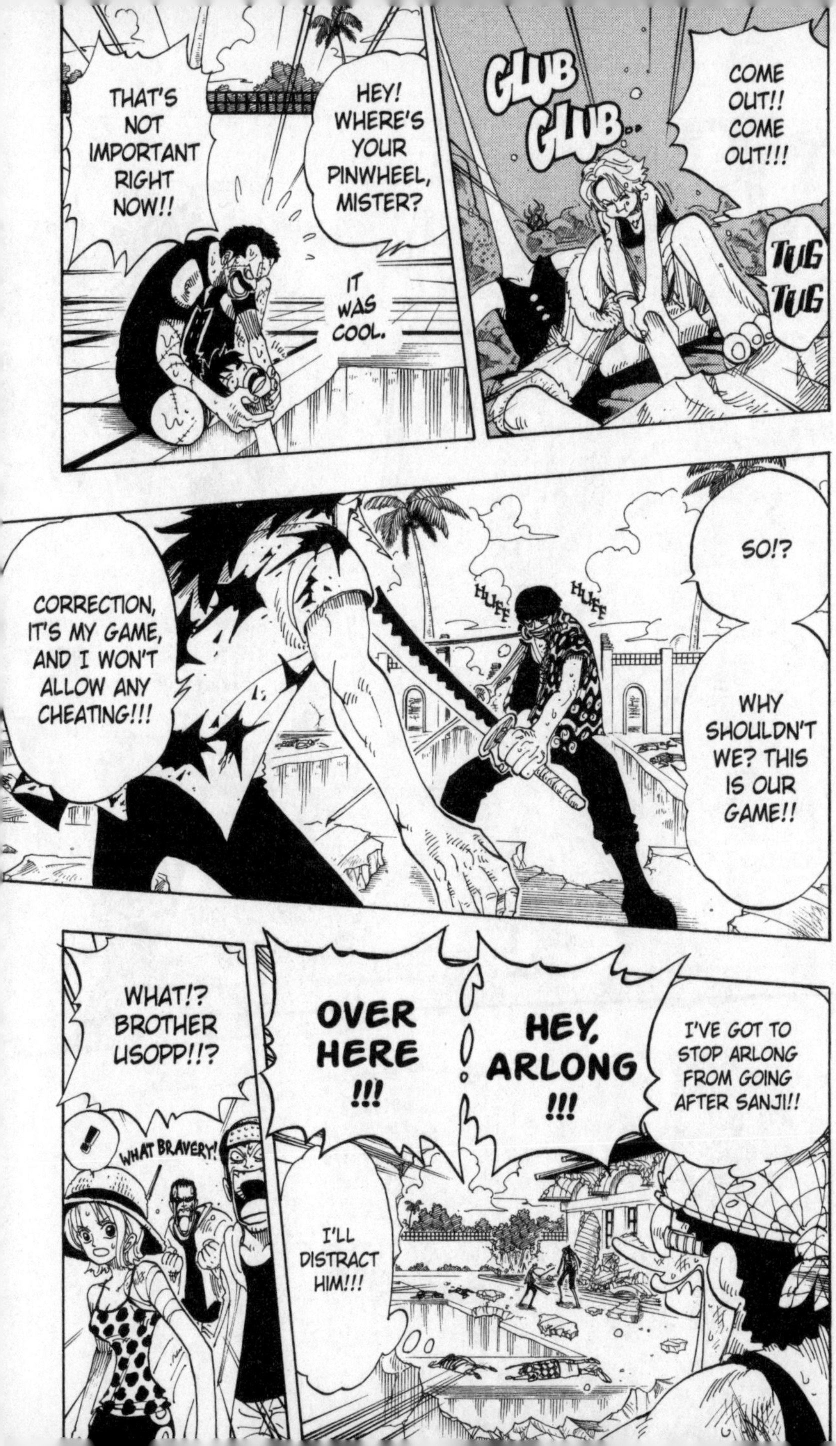
GLUB GLUB..
COME OUT!! COME OUT!!!
TUG TUG
HEY! WHERE'S YOUR PINWHEEL, MISTER?
THAT'S NOT IMPORTANT RIGHT NOW!!
IT WAS COOL.
SO!?
WHY SHOULDN'T WE? THIS IS OUR GAME!!
HUFF HUFF
CORRECTION, IT'S MY GAME, AND I WON'T ALLOW ANY CHEATING!!!
I'VE GOT TO STOP ARLONG FROM GOING AFTER SANJI!!
HEY, ARLONG!!!
OVER HERE!!!
I'LL DISTRACT HIM!!!
WHAT!? BROTHER USOPP!!?
!
WHAT BRAVERY!

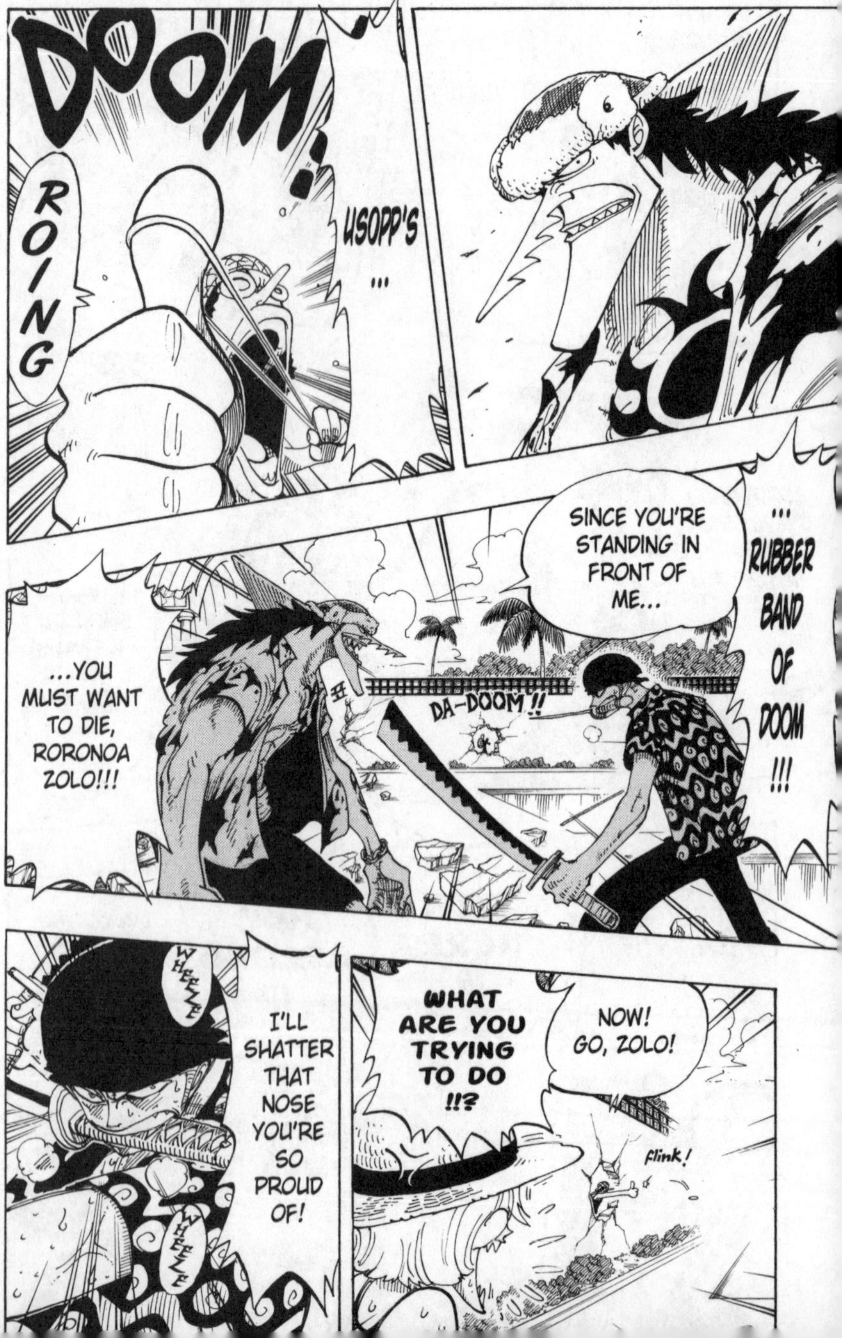
DOOM
USOPP'S ...
ROING
... RUBBER BAND OF DOOM !!!
SINCE YOU'RE STANDING IN FRONT OF ME...
DA-DOOM!!
...YOU MUST WANT TO DIE, RORONOA ZOLO!!!
NOW! GO, ZOLO!
WHAT ARE YOU TRYING TO DO !!?
flink!
I'LL SHATTER THAT NOSE YOU'RE SO PROUD OF!
WHEEZE
WHEEZE

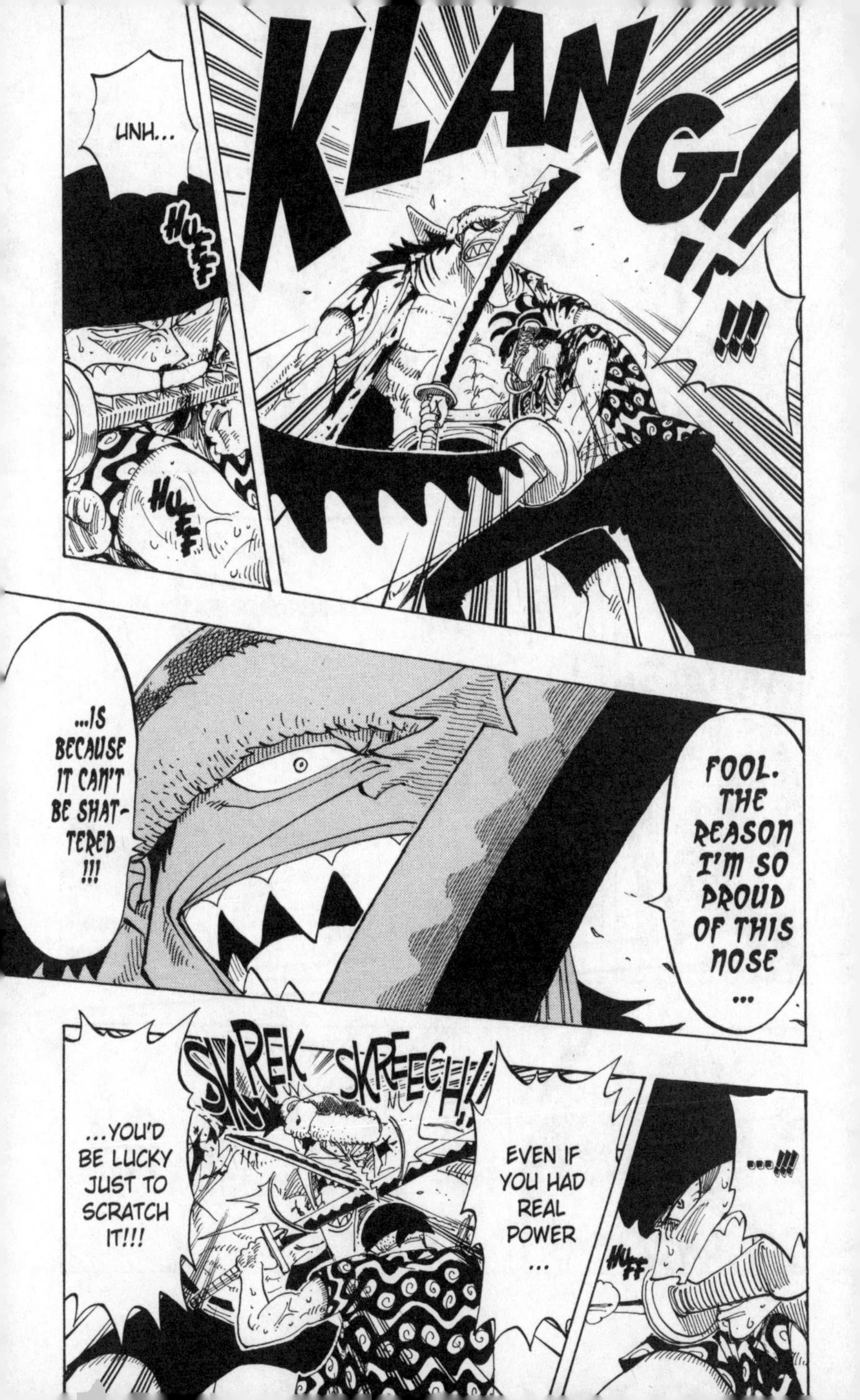

KLANG!!
!!!
UNH...
HUFF
HUFF
FOOL. THE REASON I'M SO PROUD OF THIS NOSE ...
...IS BECAUSE IT CAN'T BE SHATTERED !!!
...!!!
HUFF
EVEN IF YOU HAD REAL POWER ...
SKREK SKREECH!!
...YOU'D BE LUCKY JUST TO SCRATCH IT!!!

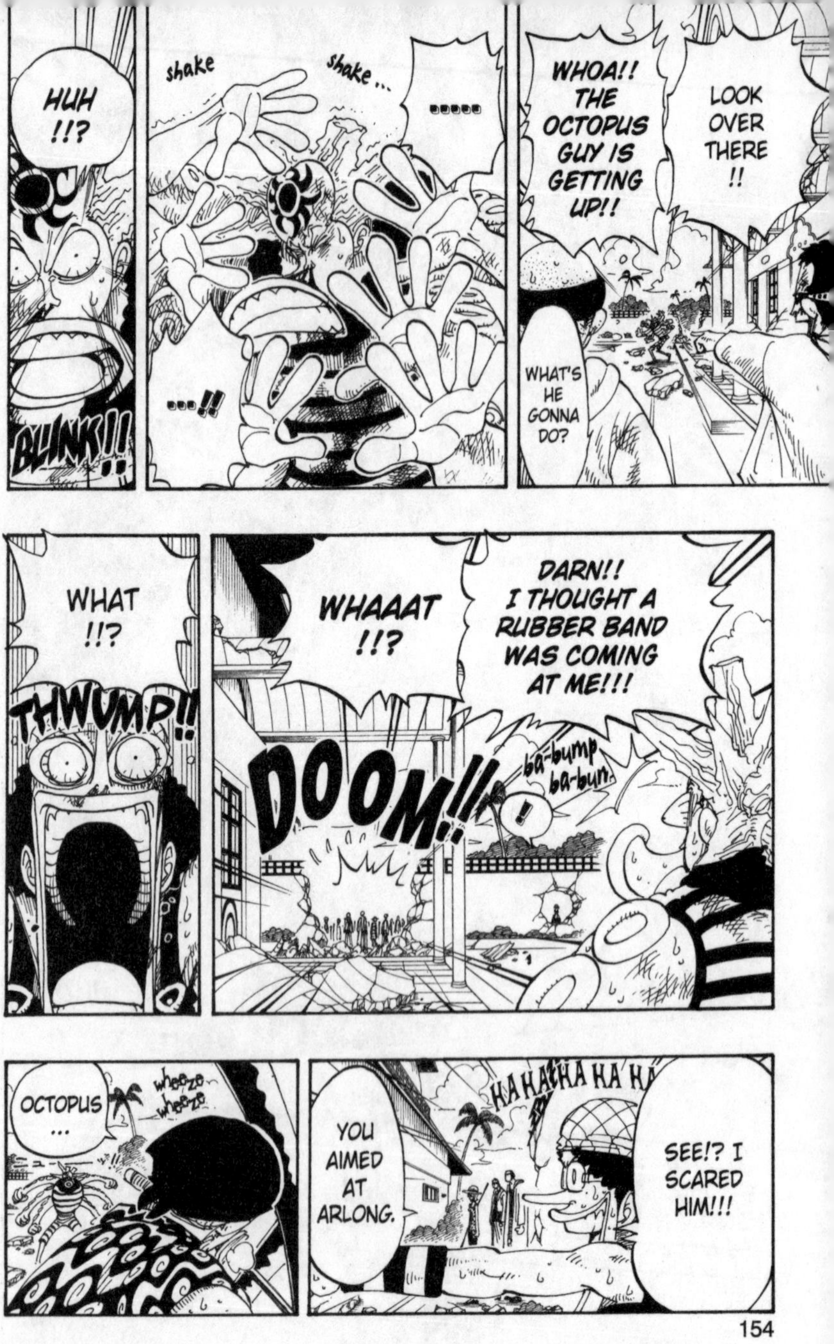
LOOK OVER THERE !!
WHOA!! THE OCTOPUS GUY IS GETTING UP!!
WHAT'S HE GONNA DO?
shake
shake ...
.....
...!!
HUH !!?
BLINK!!
DARN!! I THOUGHT A RUBBER BAND WAS COMING AT ME!!!
WHAAAT !!?
DOOM!!
ba-bump ba-bun
!
WHAT !!?
THWUMP!!
HA HA HA HA HA HA
SEE!? I SCARED HIM!!!
YOU AIMED AT ARLONG.
OCTOPUS ...
wheeze wheeze

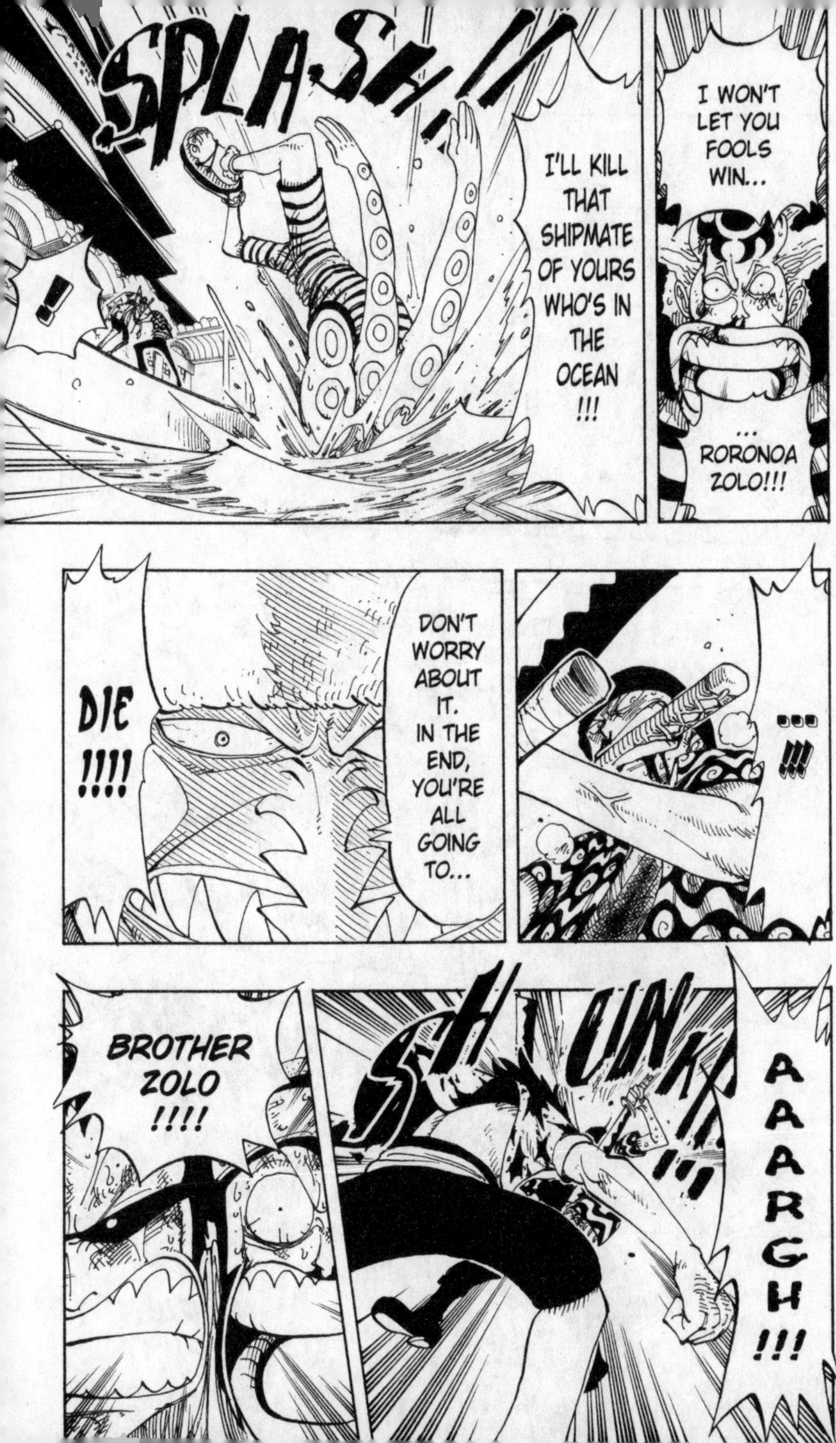
I WON'T LET YOU FOOLS WIN...
...RORONOA ZOLO!!!
I'LL KILL THAT SHIPMATE OF YOURS WHO'S IN THE OCEAN!!!
SPLASH!!
!
...!!!
DON'T WORRY ABOUT IT. IN THE END, YOU'RE ALL GOING TO...
DIE!!!!
AAAARGH!!!
SHUNK!!!
BROTHER ZOLO!!!!

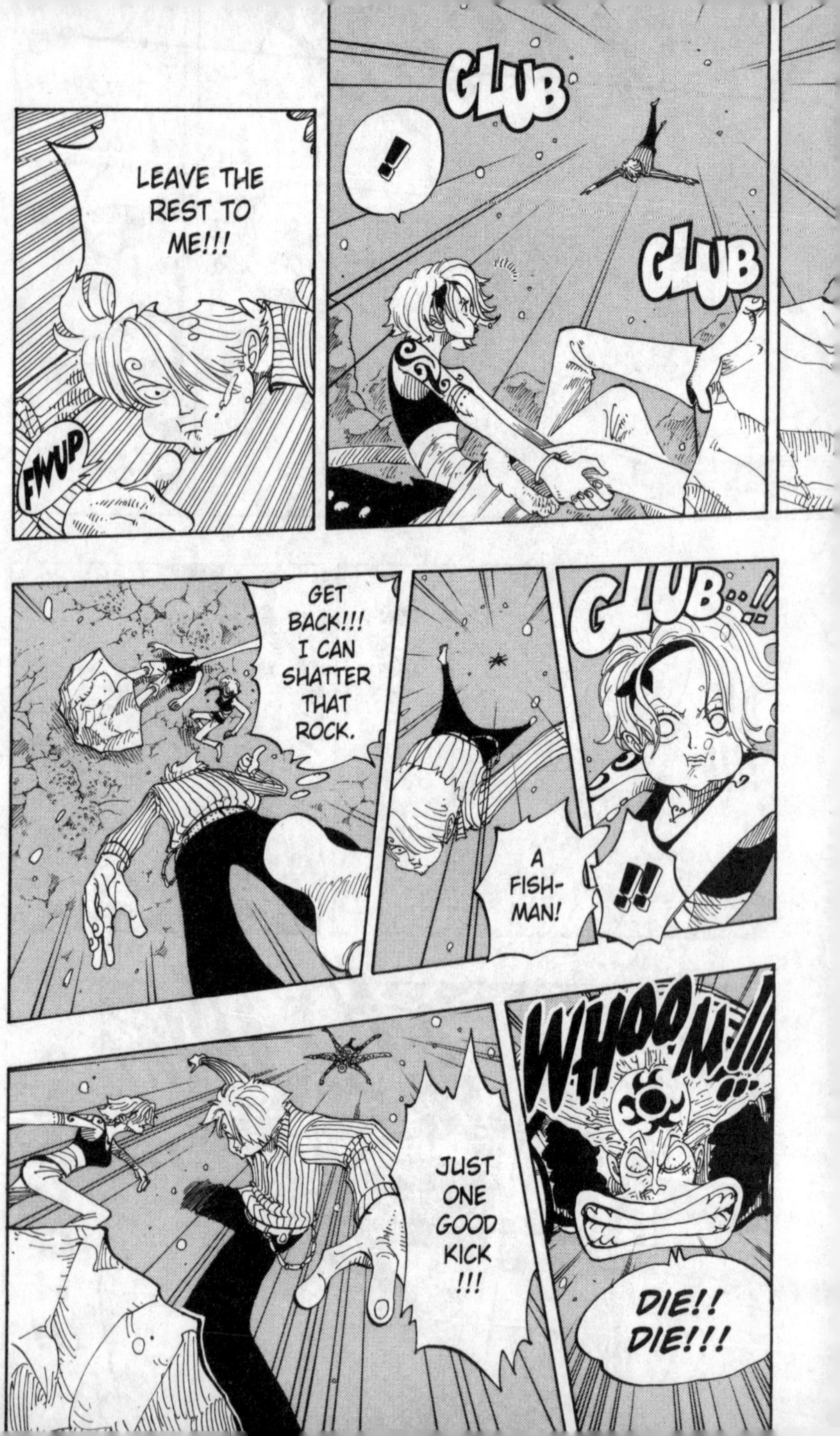
GLUB
!
GLUB
LEAVE THE REST TO ME!!!
FWUP
GLUB..!!
!!
A FISH-MAN!
GET BACK!!! I CAN SHATTER THAT ROCK.
WHOOM!!!
DIE!! DIE!!!
JUST ONE GOOD KICK !!!

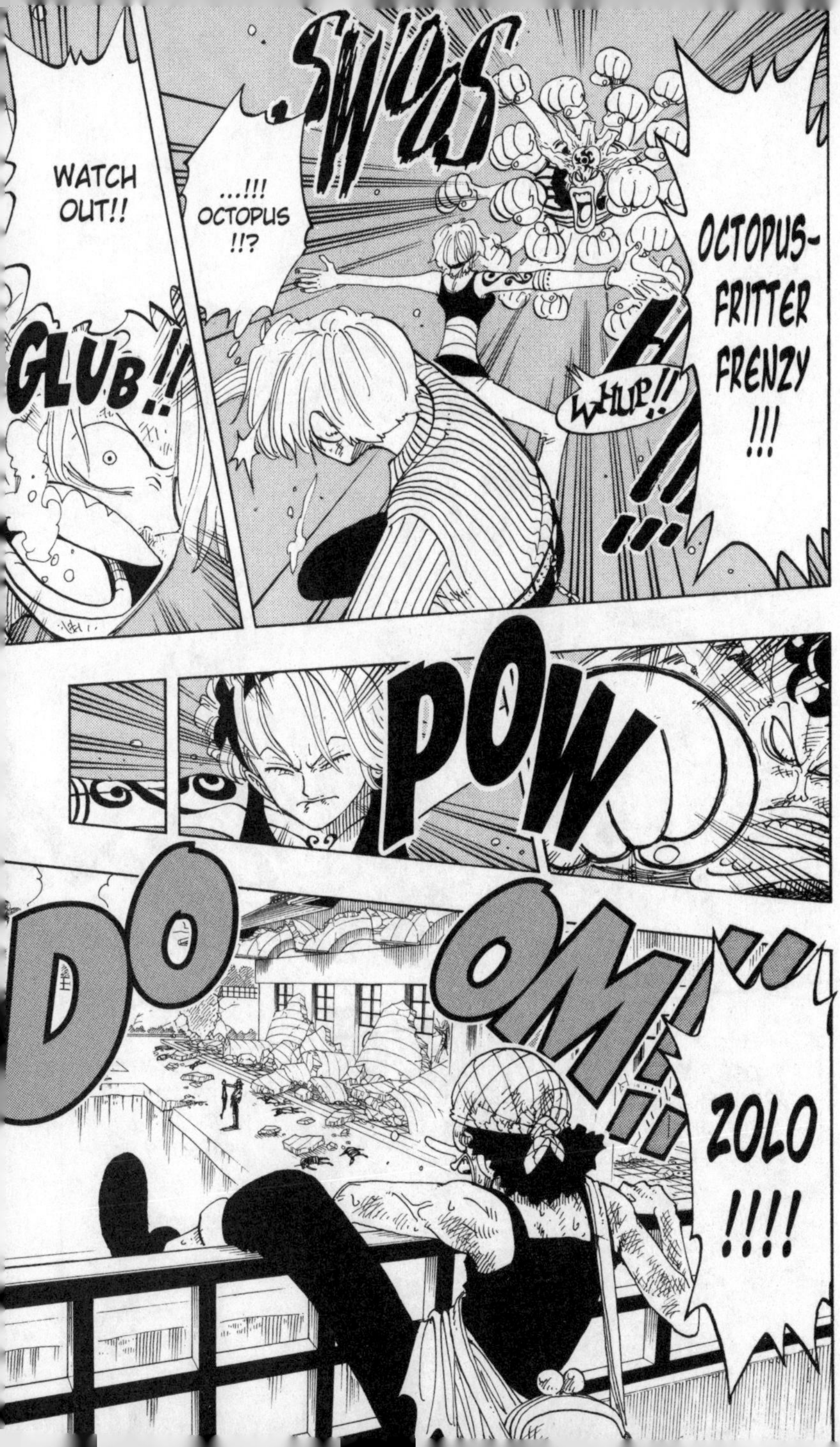
OCTOPUS-FRITTER FRENZY !!!
WHUP!!
SWOS
...!!! OCTOPUS !!?
WATCH OUT!!
GLUB!!
POW
DOOM!!
ZOLO !!!!

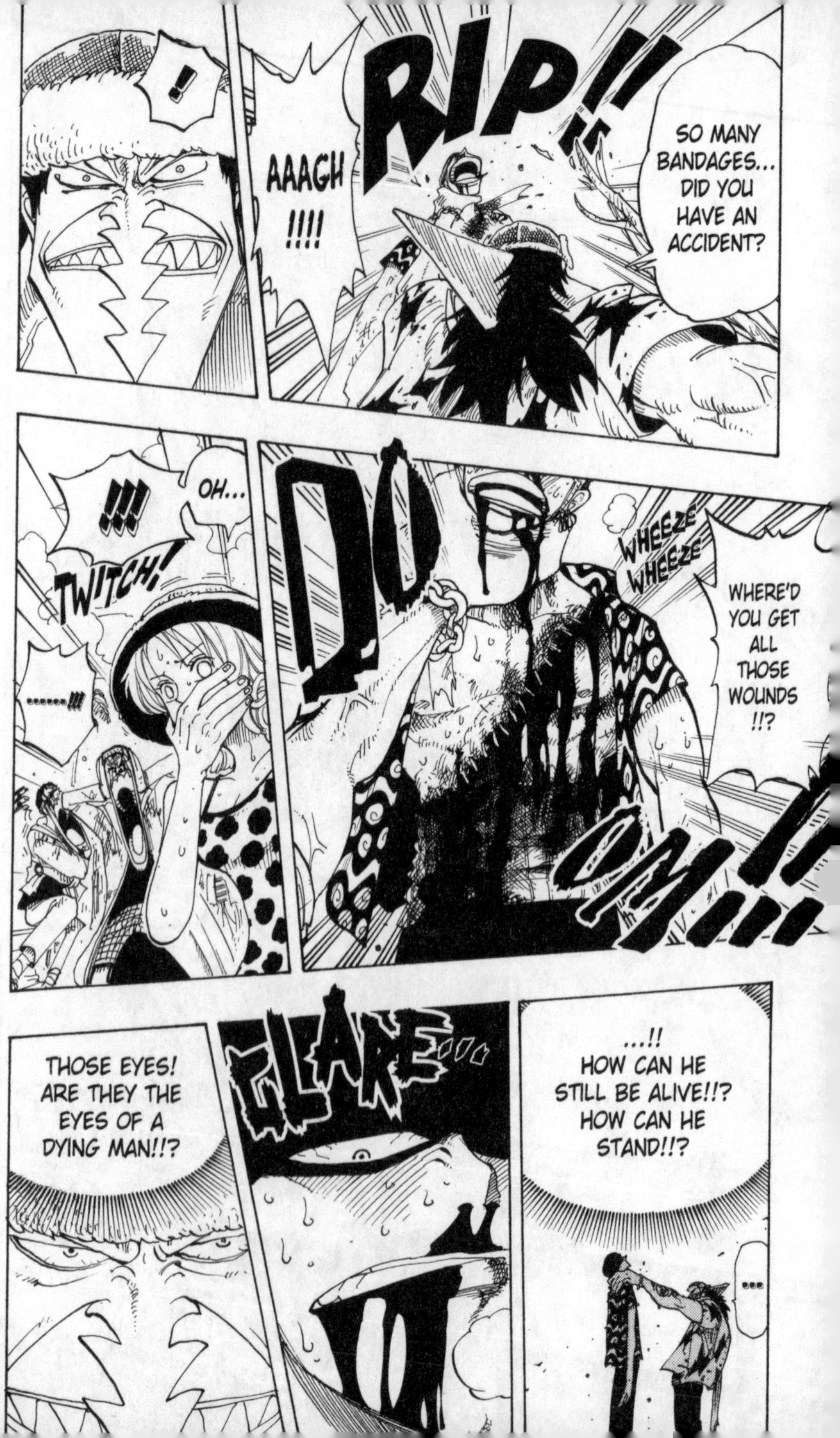
RIP!!
SO MANY BANDAGES... DID YOU HAVE AN ACCIDENT?
AAAGH !!!!
!
WHERE'D YOU GET ALL THOSE WOUNDS !!?
WHEEZE WHEEZE
DO
OM...!!
OH...
!!!
TWITCH!
......!!!
...!! HOW CAN HE STILL BE ALIVE!!? HOW CAN HE STAND!!?
...
GLARE...
THOSE EYES! ARE THEY THE EYES OF A DYING MAN!!?

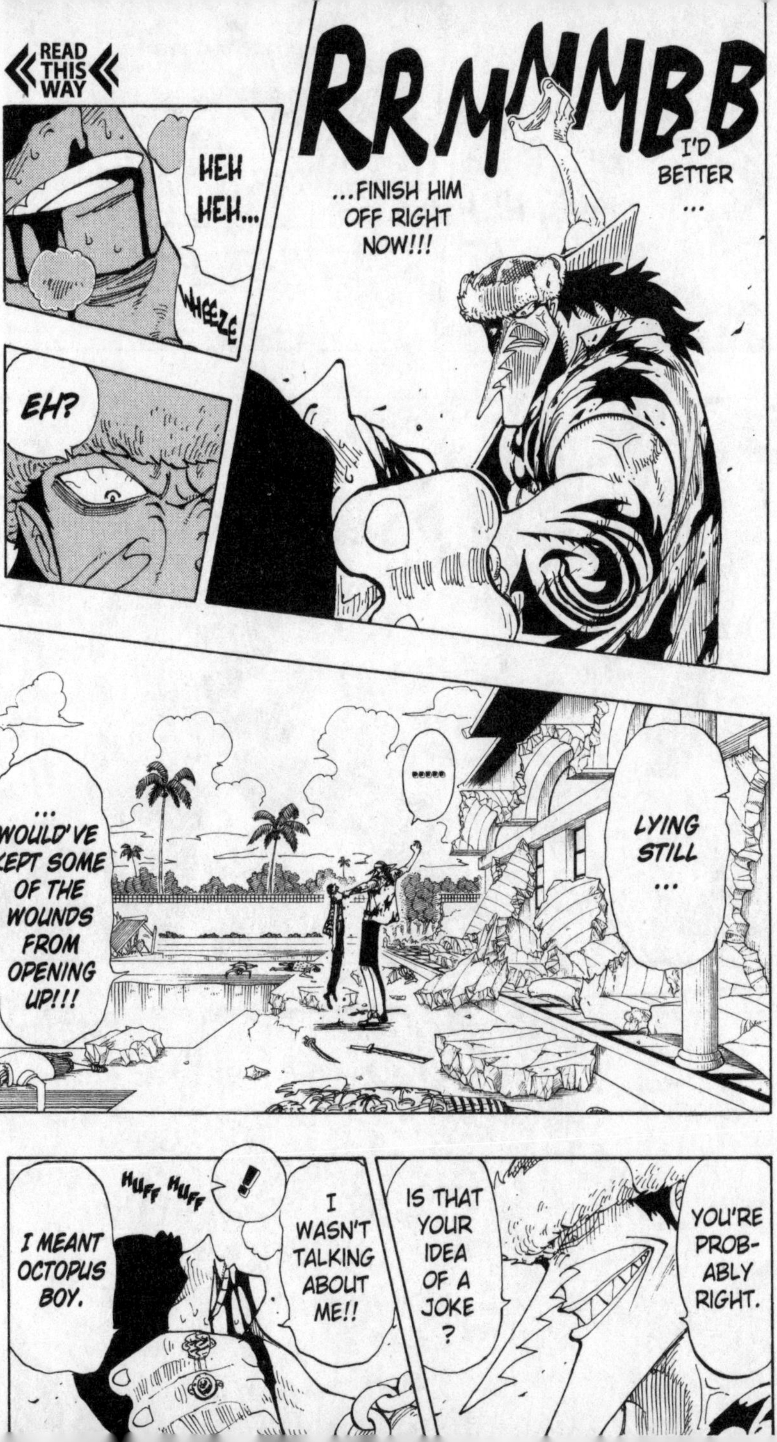
READ THIS WAY
RRMMMBB
I'D BETTER ...
...FINISH HIM OFF RIGHT NOW!!!
HEH HEH...
WHEEZE
EH?
LYING STILL ...
.....
...WOULD'VE KEPT SOME OF THE WOUNDS FROM OPENING UP!!!
YOU'RE PROB-ABLY RIGHT.
IS THAT YOUR IDEA OF A JOKE ?
I WASN'T TALKING ABOUT ME!!
!
HUFF HUFF
I MEANT OCTOPUS BOY.

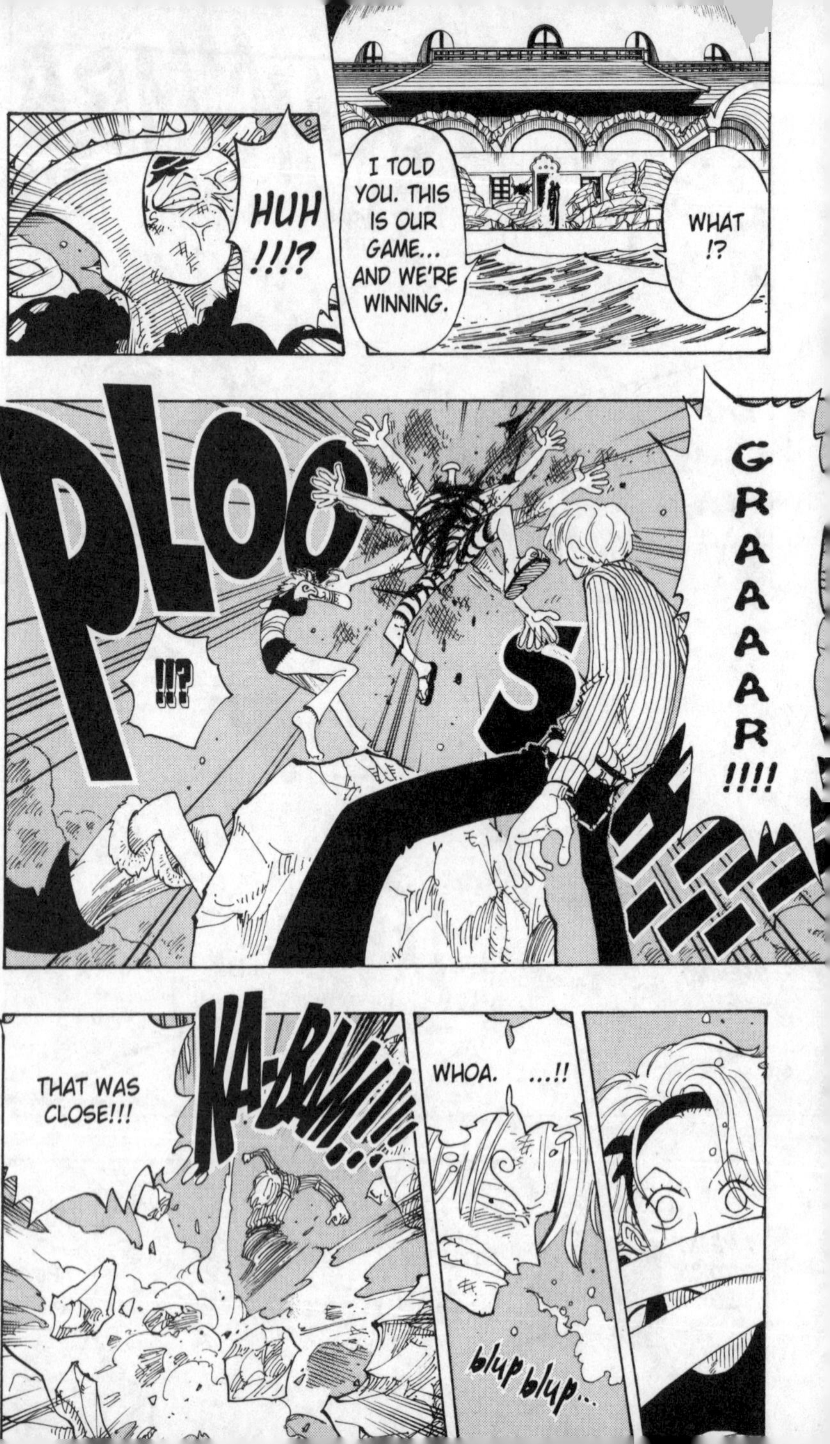
WHAT !?
I TOLD YOU. THIS IS OUR GAME... AND WE'RE WINNING.
HUH !!!?
GRAAAAR !!!!
PLOO
S
!!?
...!!
WHOA.
blup blup...
KA-BAM!!!!
THAT WAS CLOSE!!!

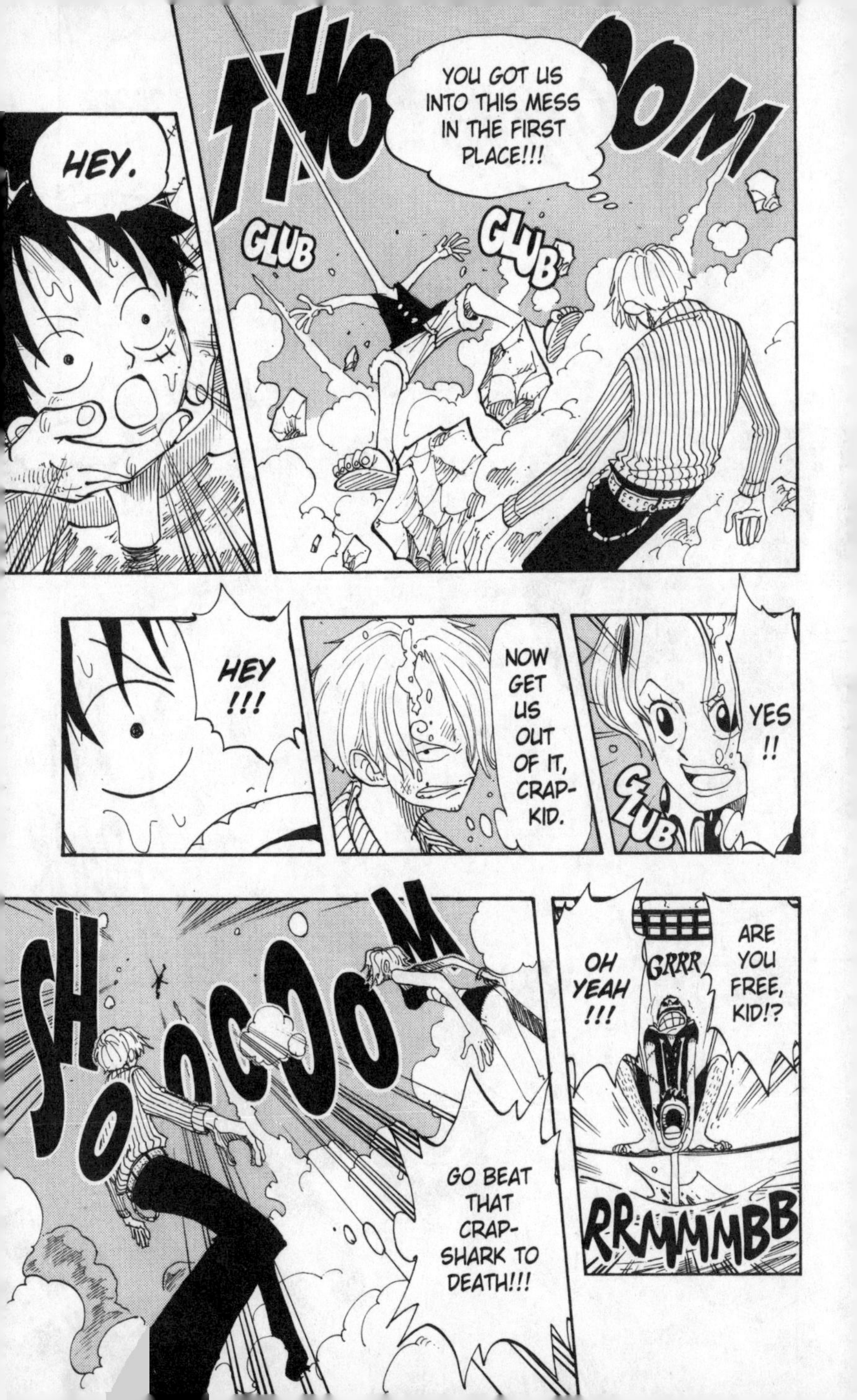
THO OOM
YOU GOT US INTO THIS MESS IN THE FIRST PLACE!!!
GLUB
GLUB
HEY.
YES!!
GLUB
NOW GET US OUT OF IT, CRAP-KID.
HEY!!!
ARE YOU FREE, KID!?
GRRR
OH YEAH!!!
RRMMMBB
SHOOOOOOM
GO BEAT THAT CRAP-SHARK TO DEATH!!!

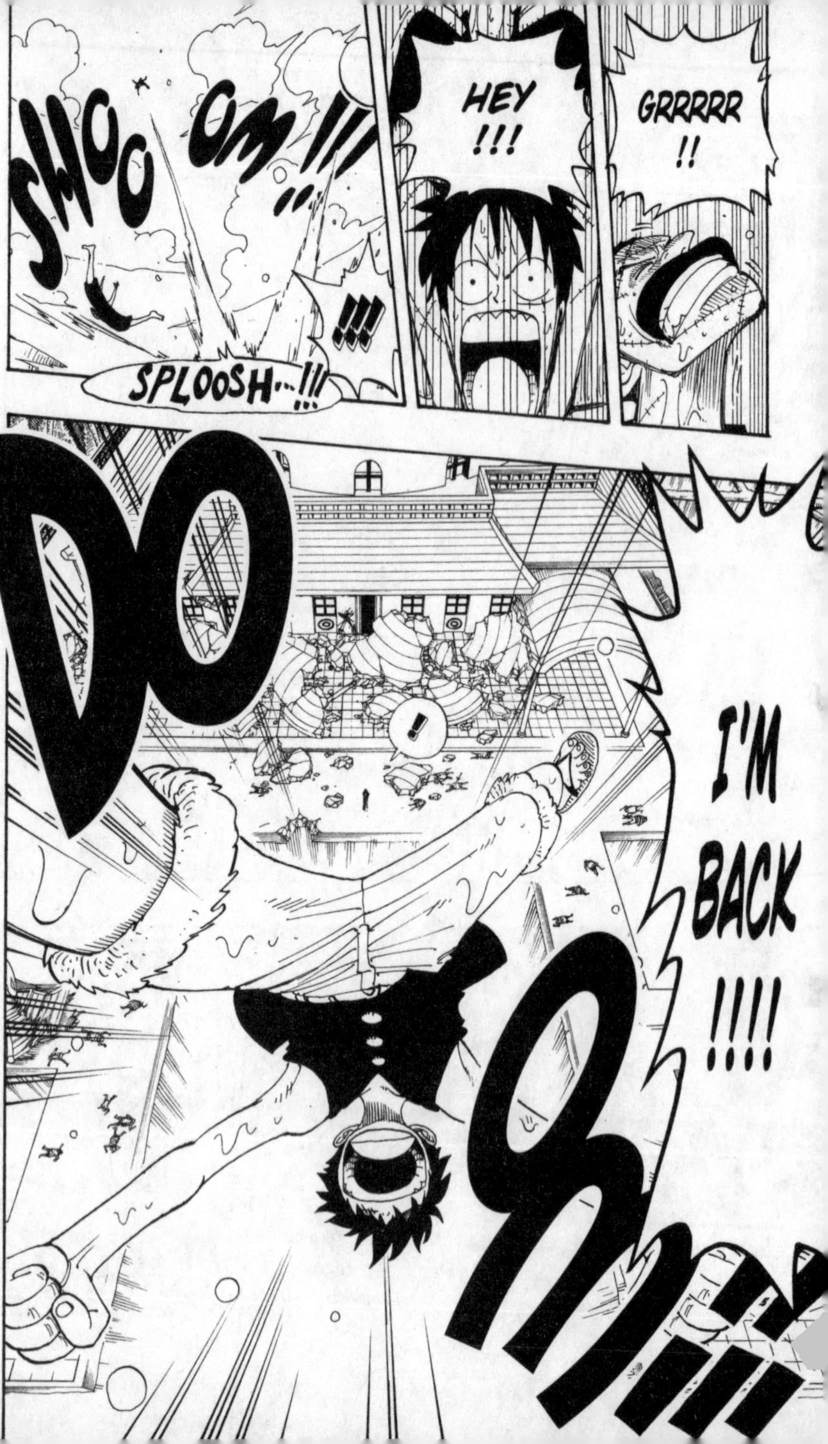
GRRRRR !!
HEY !!!
SHOOOM!!!
SPLOOSH...!!!
I'M BACK !!!!
DOOOM

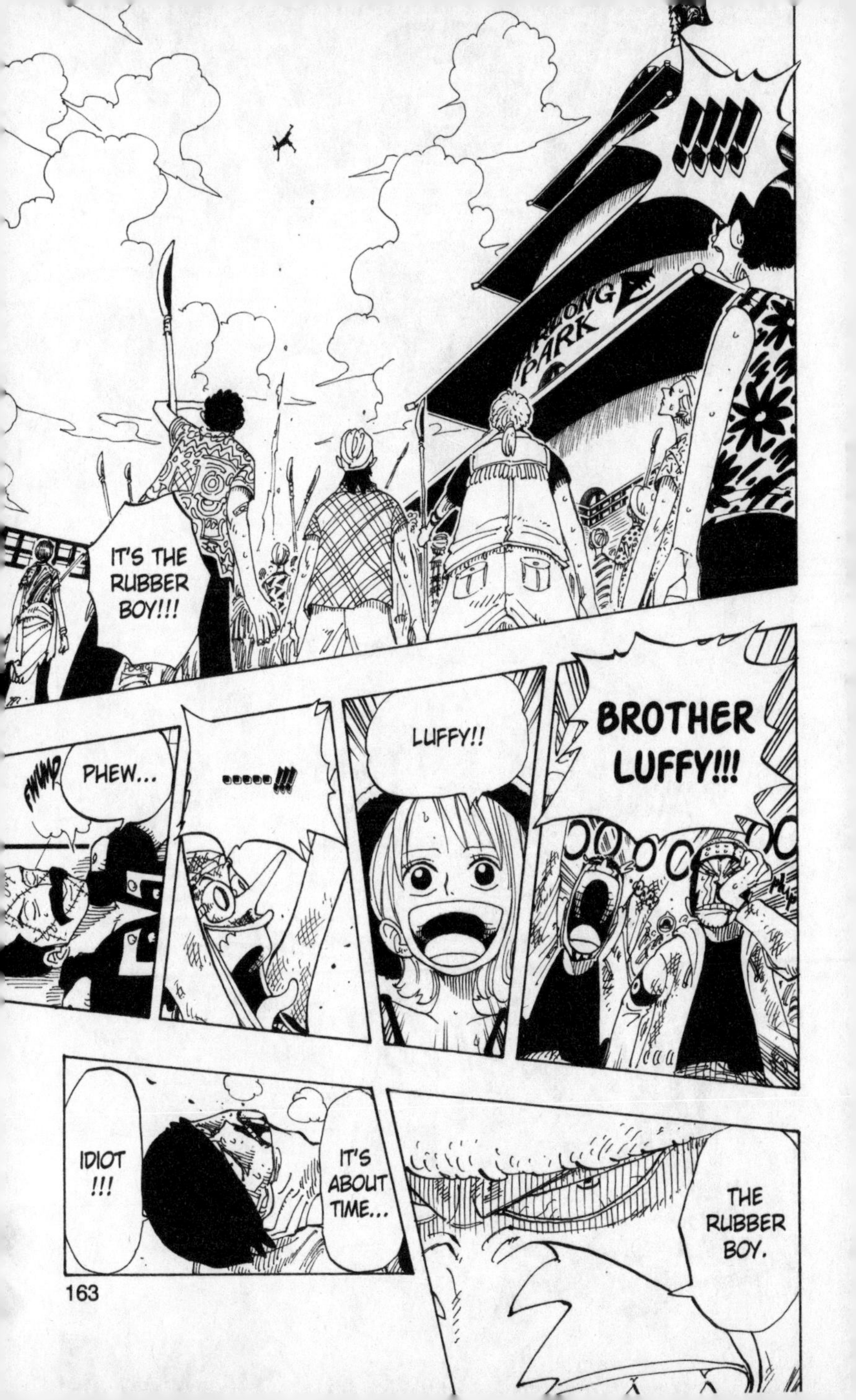
!!!!
AFLONG PARK
IT'S THE RUBBER BOY!!!
BROTHER LUFFY!!!
LUFFY!!
.....!!!
PHEW...
FWUMP
THE RUBBER BOY.
IT'S ABOUT TIME...
IDIOT !!!

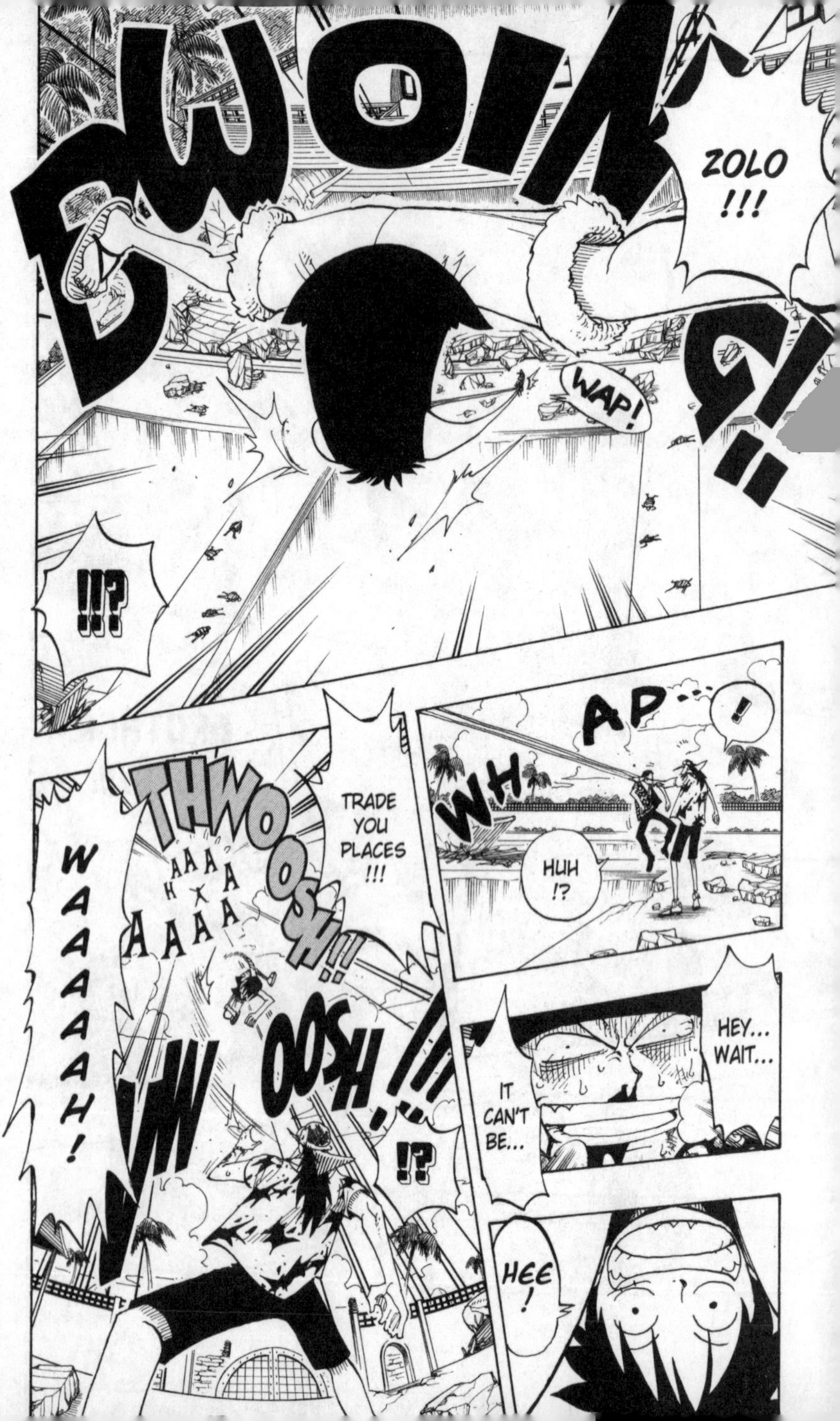
ZOLO !!!
WAP!
!!?
WHAP---
!
HUH !?
HEY... WAIT...
IT CAN'T BE...
HEE!
TRADE YOU PLACES !!!
THWOOSH!!
WAAAAAAAAH!
WHOOSH!!!
!?

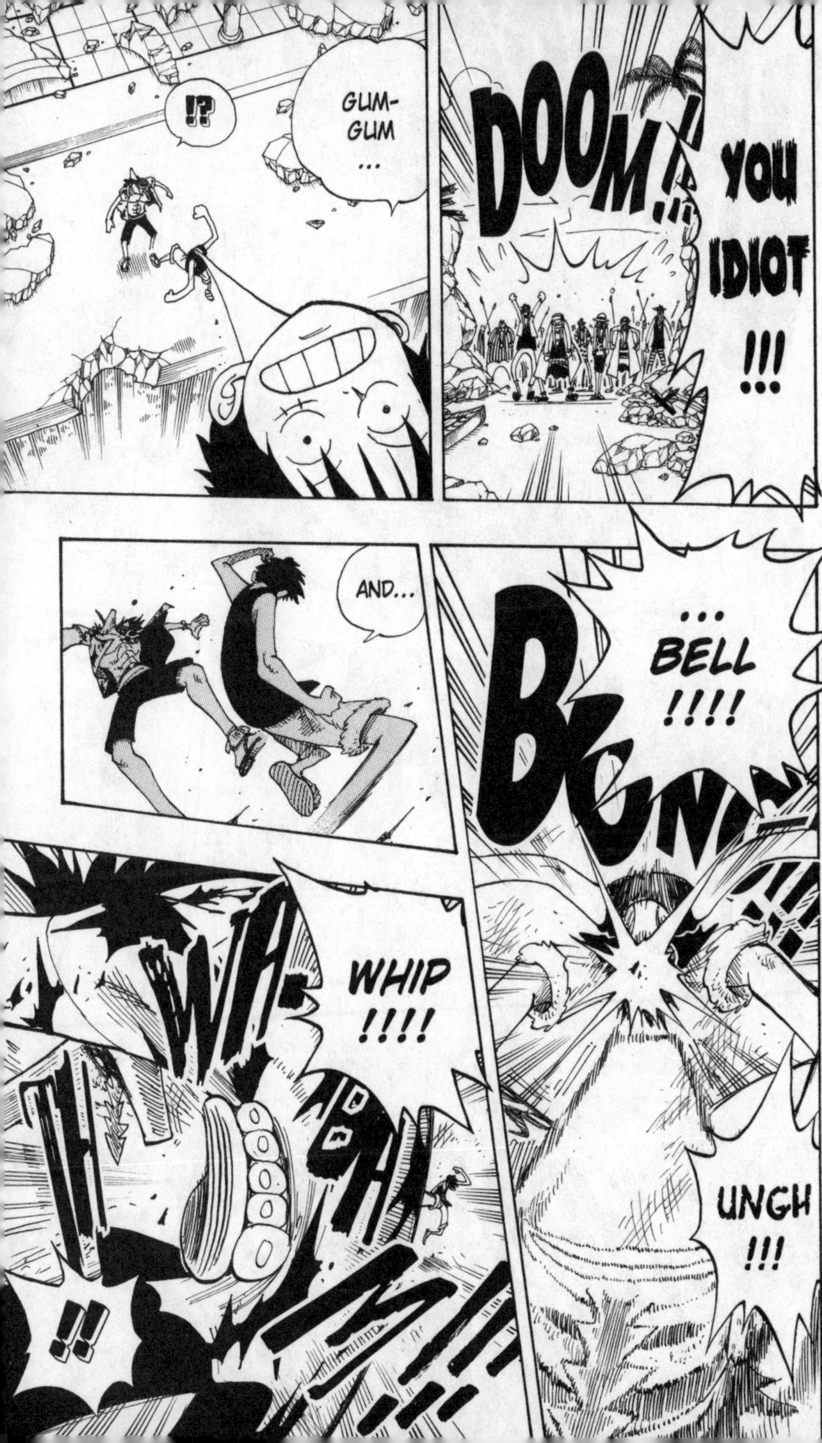
DOOM!!!
YOU IDIOT !!!
GUM-GUM ...
!?
AND...
WHIP !!!!
!!
... BELL !!!!
UNGH !!!

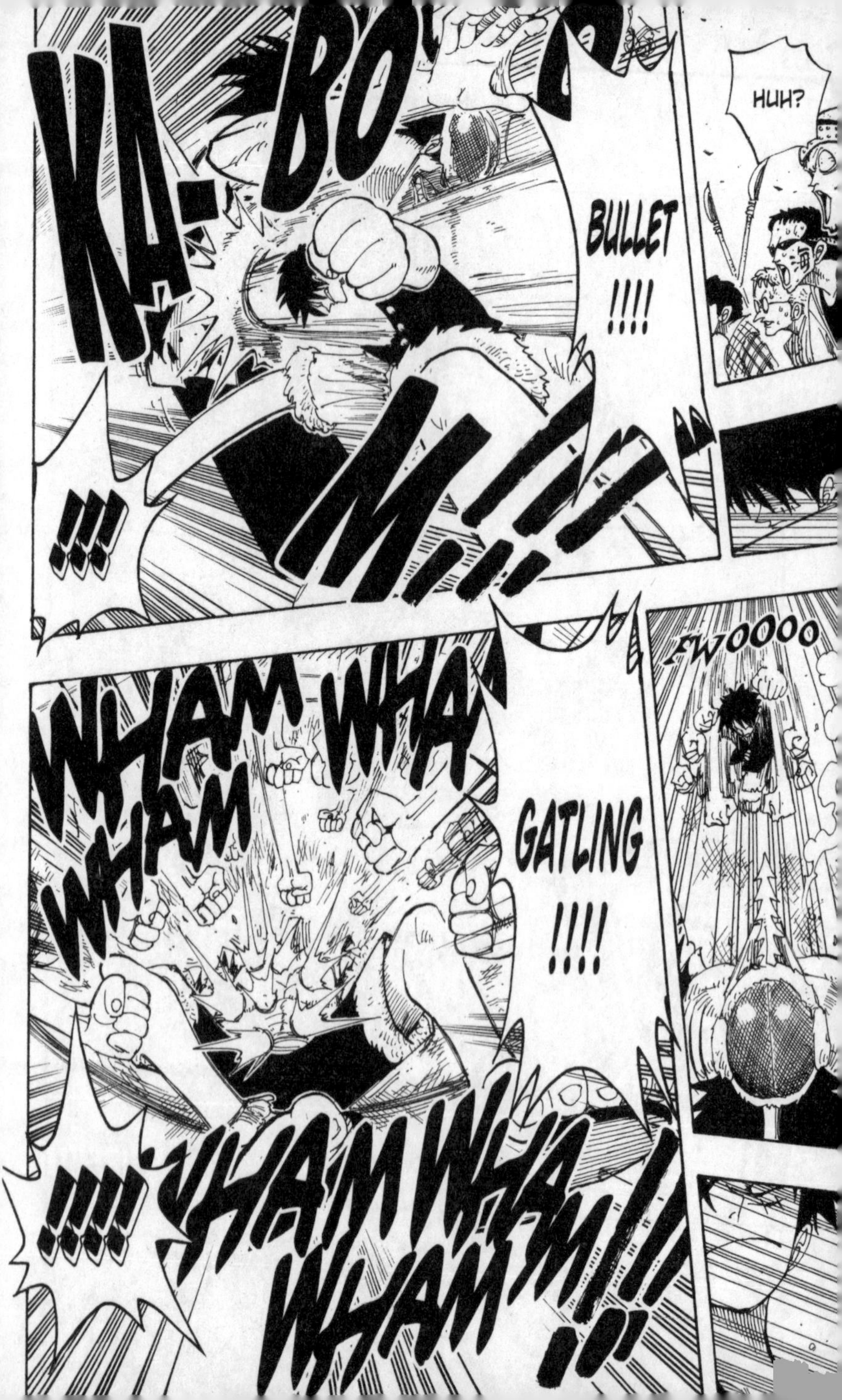
HUH?
BULLET !!!!
KA-BOOM!!!!
FWOOOO
GATLING !!!!
WHAM WHAM WHAM WHAM
WHAM WHAM WHAM!!!!

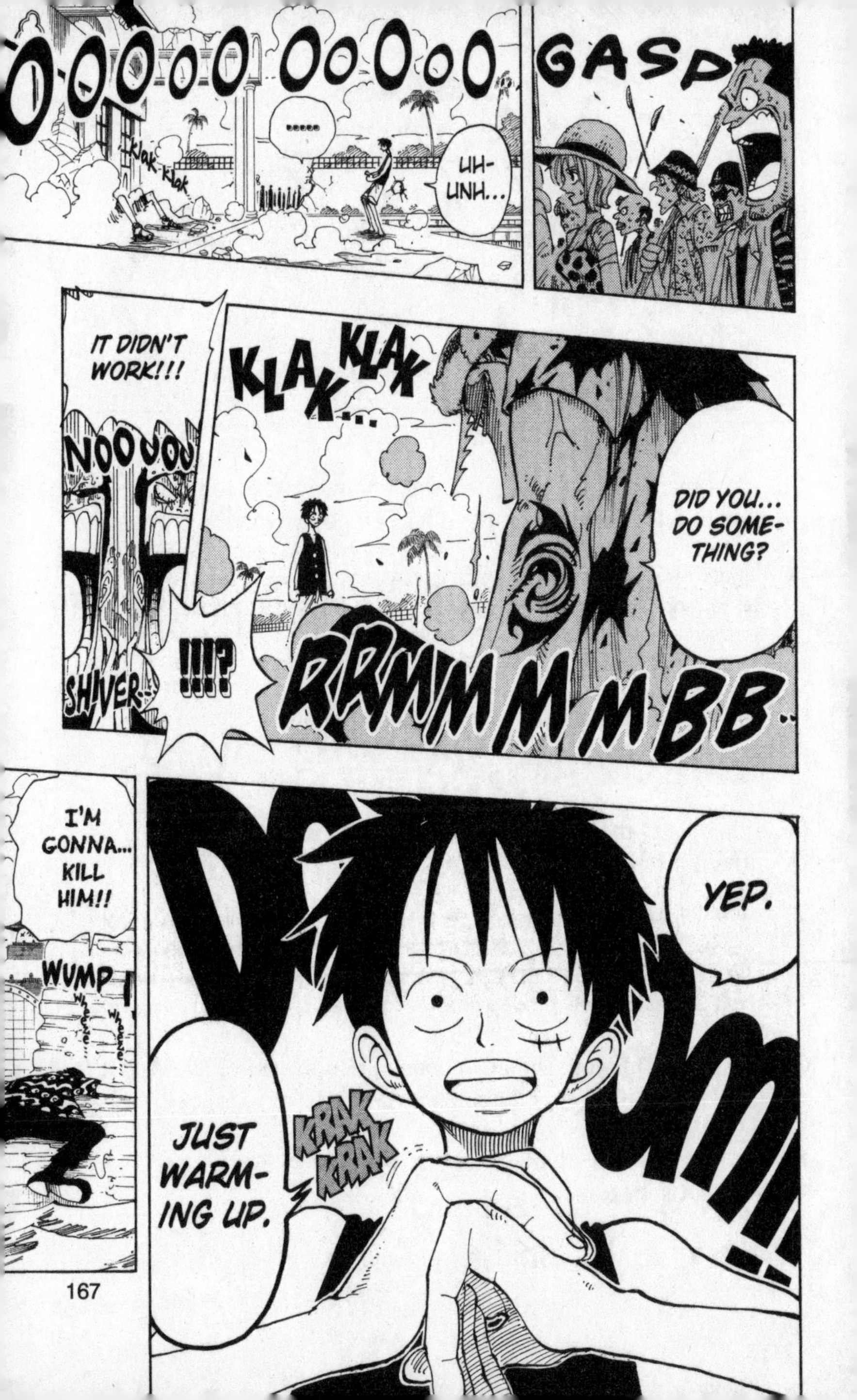
GASP
O-O-O-O-O OO-O-O-O
KLAK-KLAK
.....
UH-UNH...
KLAK KLAK...
DID YOU... DO SOMETHING?
RRMMMMBB..
!!!?
IT DIDN'T WORK!!!
NOOOOO
SHIVER
YEP.
KRAK KRAK
JUST WARMING UP.
I'M GONNA... KILL HIM!!
WUMP
wheeze...
wheeze...

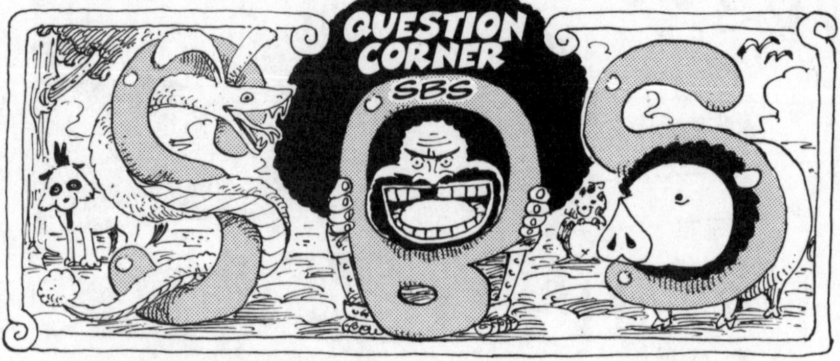
QUESTION CORNER
SBS

Q: After reading your manga, Sensei, I'm inspired to follow my dream. My dream is to build a big bridge in America.

A: That's nice. A young man with dreams. I like that. All right then, do it. And if anyone gets in your way I'll go and--wearing hard leather boots--stomp on the pinky toe of his foot, so don't worry. Go for it.

Q: Knock, knock, Oda Sensei. Oda-body home!!?

A: Give me a break.

Q: When Patty the Cook says "I'm turniply saucy," what does it mean?

A: "I'm terribly sorry." He tends to make things sound like food. For example, he might say: "He's quite a man. He did lettuce of ham-glazing a-cheese-mints. Peas apple-aud him." But if *you* say things like that, people will probably look at you funny.

Q: A question for you. Is there a bone in Usopp's nose? I've seen it bend so many times. Like *squish*.

A: I've never seen that. Bend...like *squish*? How absurd...

Whoa!! It does bend!!!

Here ends SBS!!

Chapter 90:
WHAT CAN YOU DO?

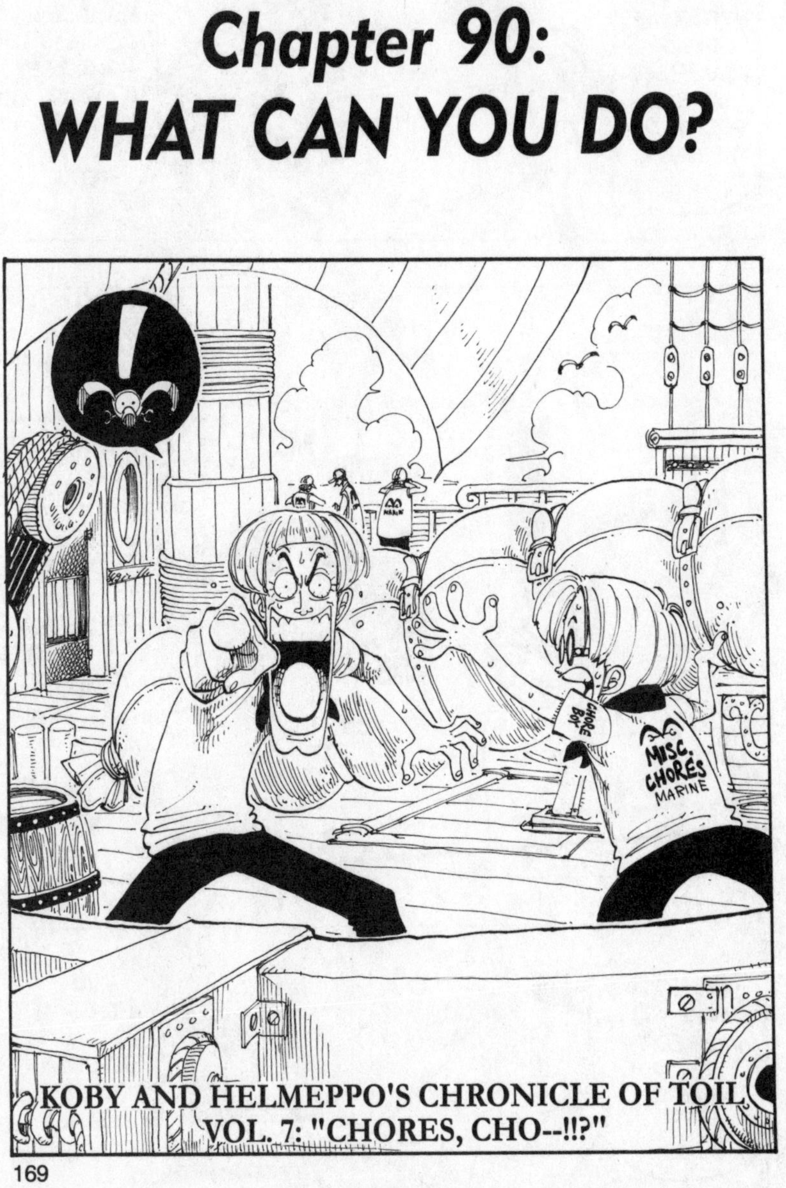
!
CHORE BOY
MISC. CHORES MARINE

KOBY AND HELMEPPO'S CHRONICLE OF TOIL
VOL. 7: "CHORES, CHO--!!?"

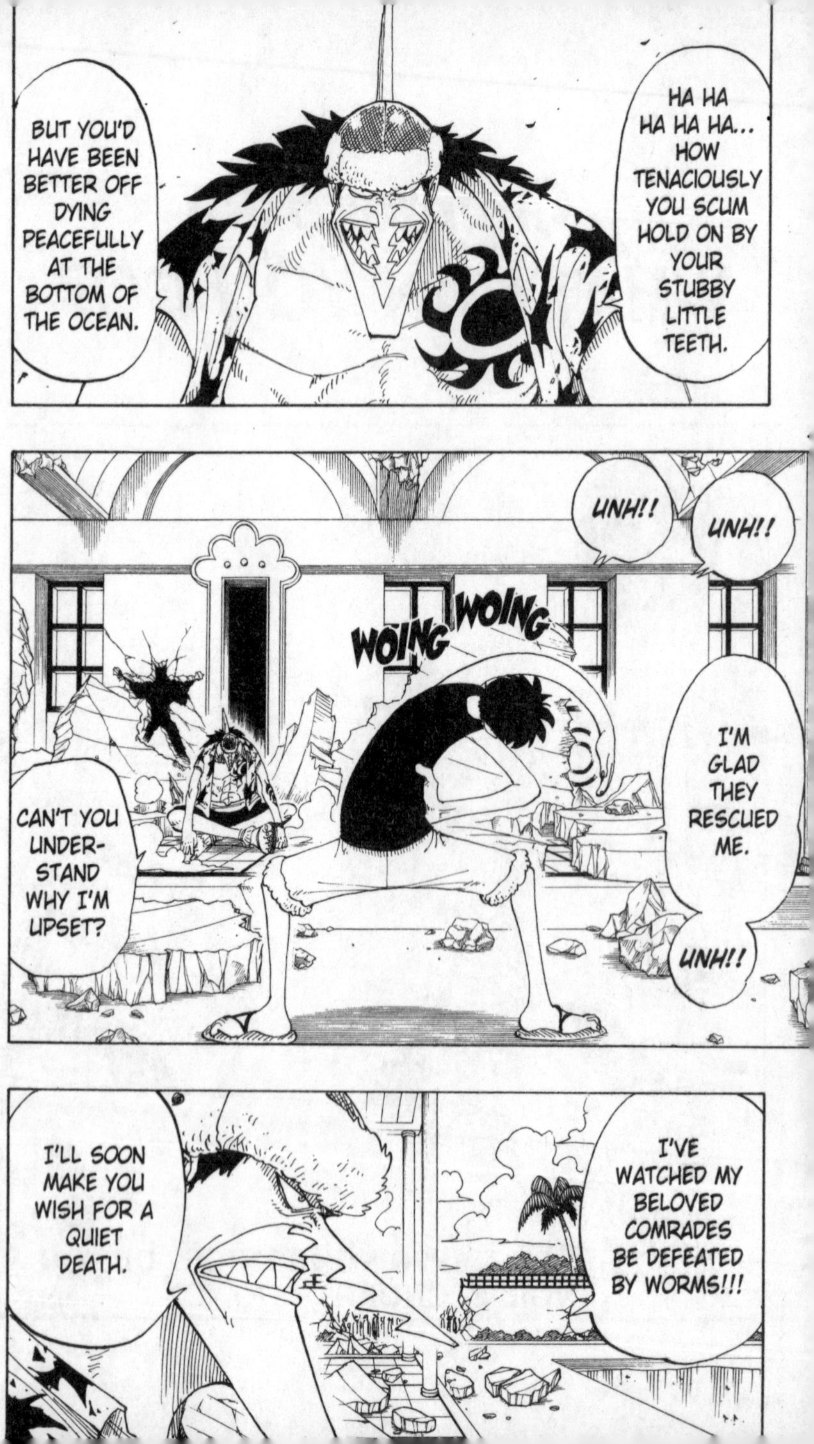
HA HA HA HA HA... HOW TENACIOUSLY YOU SCUM HOLD ON BY YOUR STUBBY LITTLE TEETH.
BUT YOU'D HAVE BEEN BETTER OFF DYING PEACEFULLY AT THE BOTTOM OF THE OCEAN.
UNH!!
UNH!!
WOING
WOING
I'M GLAD THEY RESCUED ME.
UNH!!
CAN'T YOU UNDER-STAND WHY I'M UPSET?
I'VE WATCHED MY BELOVED COMRADES BE DEFEATED BY WORMS!!!
I'LL SOON MAKE YOU WISH FOR A QUIET DEATH.

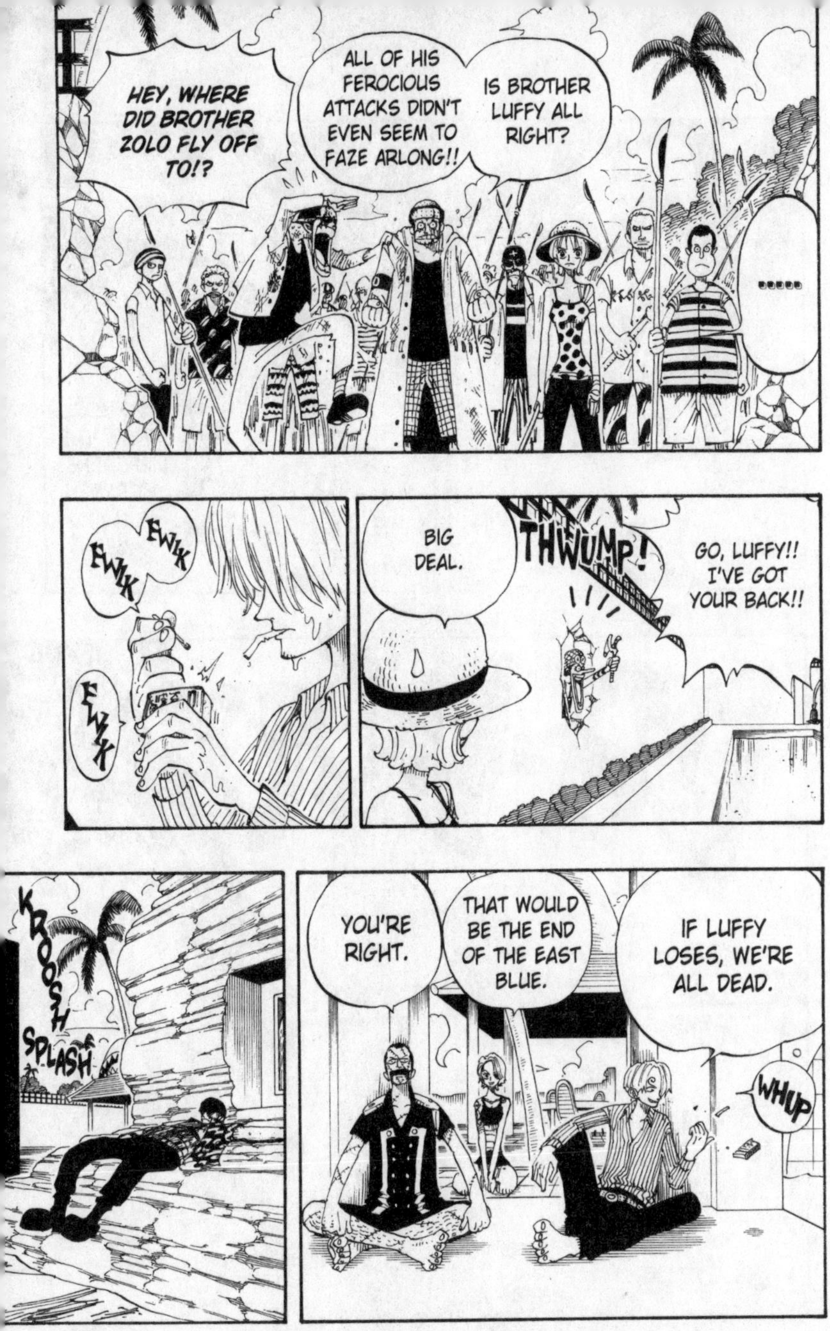
.....
IS BROTHER LUFFY ALL RIGHT?
ALL OF HIS FEROCIOUS ATTACKS DIDN'T EVEN SEEM TO FAZE ARLONG!!
HEY, WHERE DID BROTHER ZOLO FLY OFF TO!?
GO, LUFFY!! I'VE GOT YOUR BACK!!
THWUMP!
BIG DEAL.
FWIK
FWIK
FWIK
WHUP
IF LUFFY LOSES, WE'RE ALL DEAD.
THAT WOULD BE THE END OF THE EAST BLUE.
YOU'RE RIGHT.
KROOSH
SPLASH

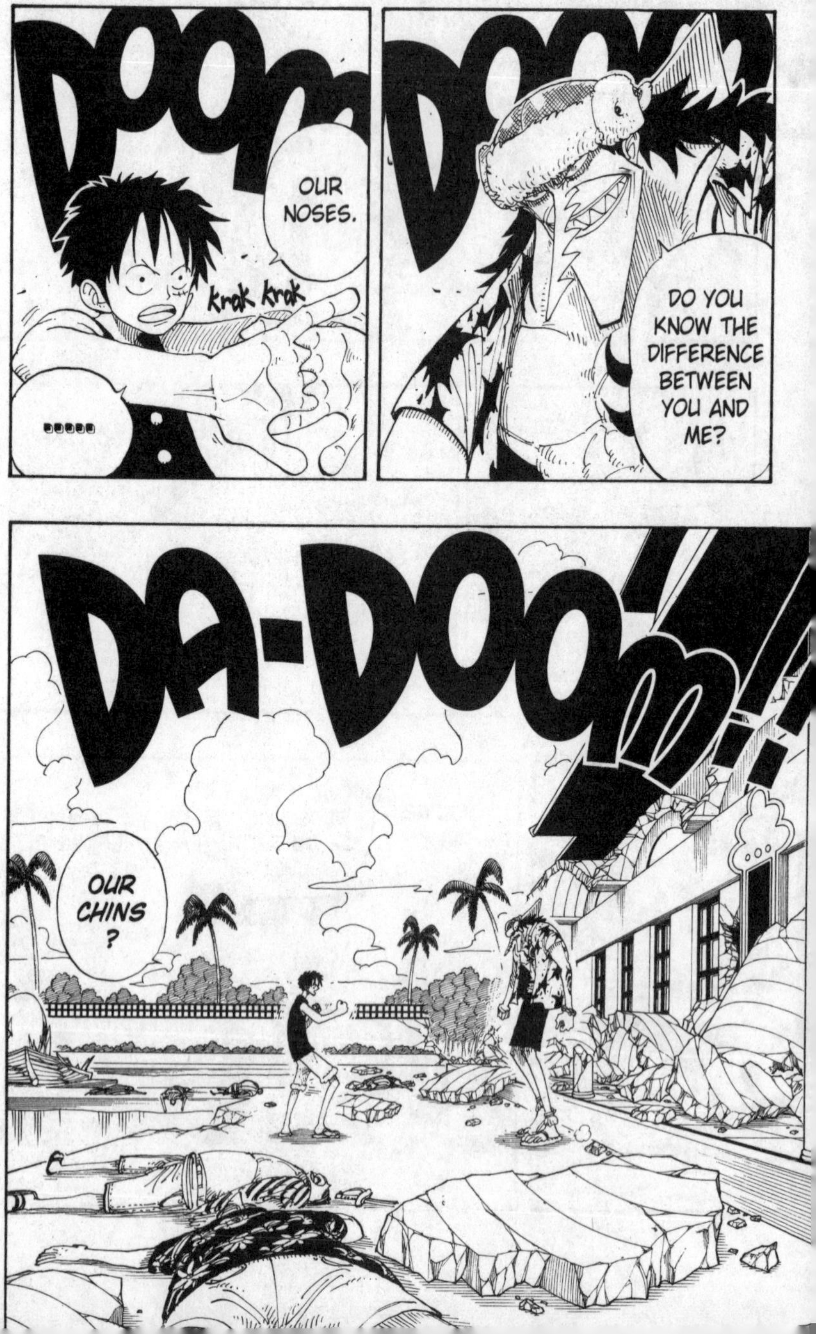
DOOM
DO YOU KNOW THE DIFFERENCE BETWEEN YOU AND ME?
DOOM
OUR NOSES.
krak krak
.....
DA-DOOM!!
OUR CHINS ?

READ THIS WAY

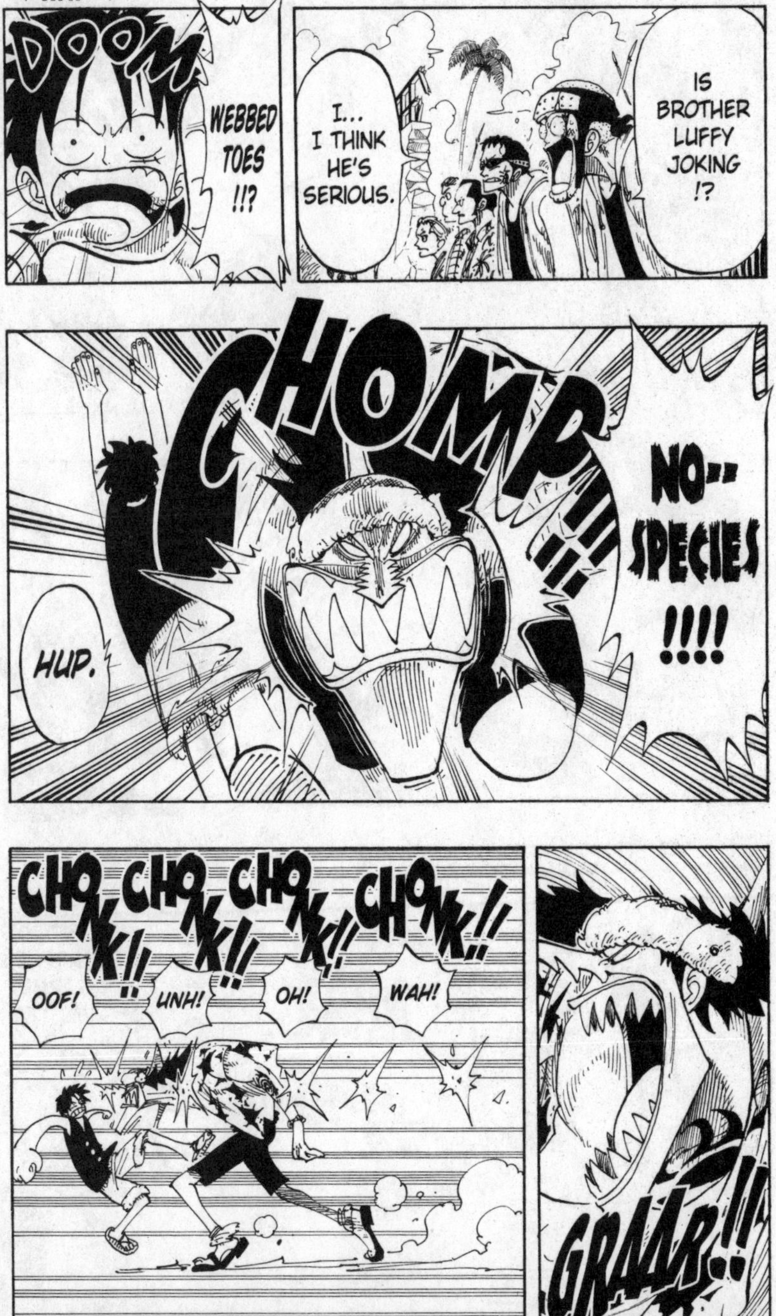
IS BROTHER LUFFY JOKING !?
I... I THINK HE'S SERIOUS.
DOOM
WEBBED TOES !!?
CHOMP!!!!
NO-- SPECIES !!!!
HUP.
GRAAR!!
CHONK!!
WAH!
CHONK!!
OH!
CHONK!!
UNH!
CHONK!!
OOF!

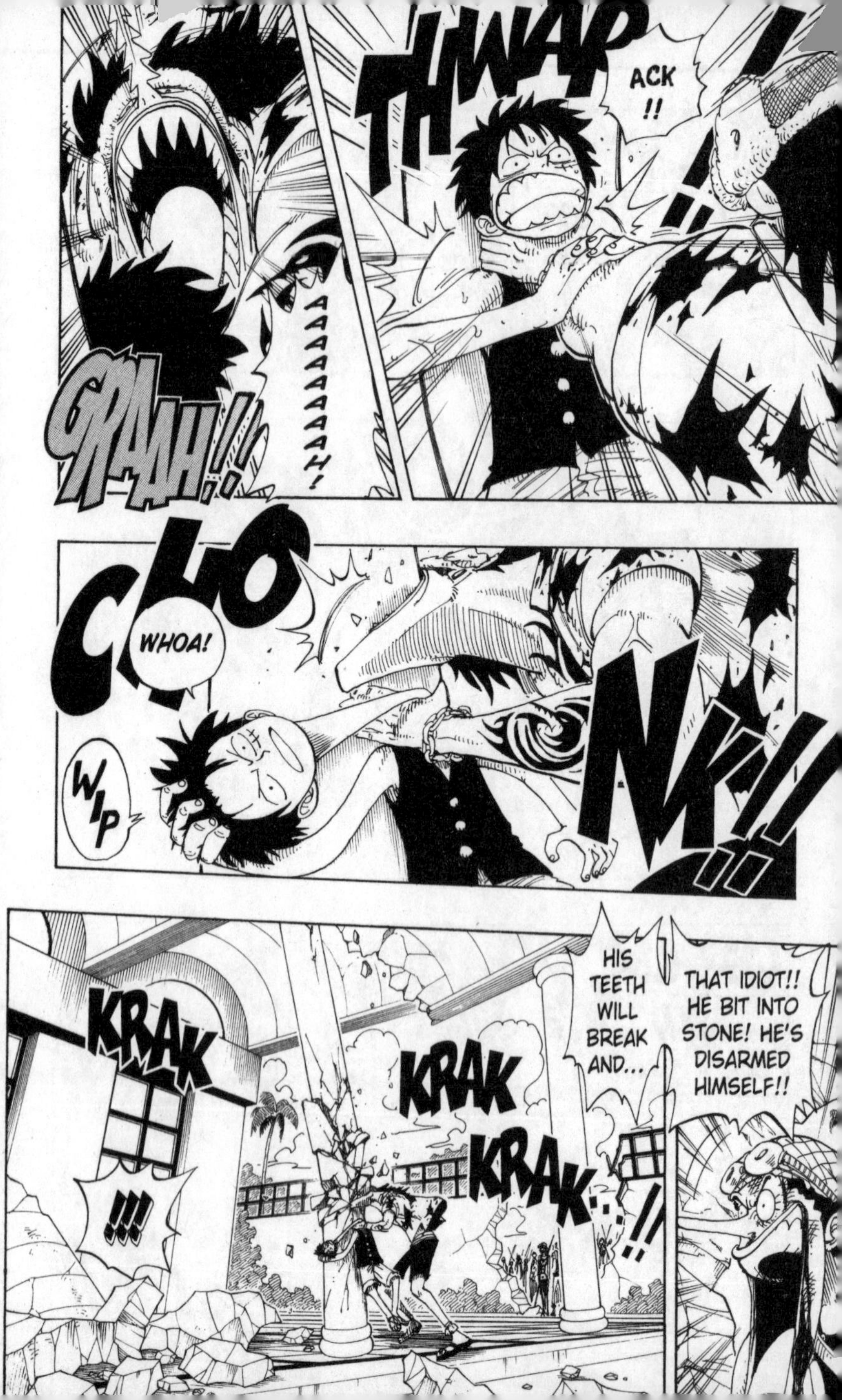
THWAP!!
ACK!!
AAAAAAAAAAAH!
GRAAH!!!
CHOMP!!
WHOA!
WIP
THAT IDIOT!! HE BIT INTO STONE! HE'S DISARMED HIMSELF!!
HIS TEETH WILL BREAK AND...
KRAK KRAK KRAK...!!
KRAK
!!!

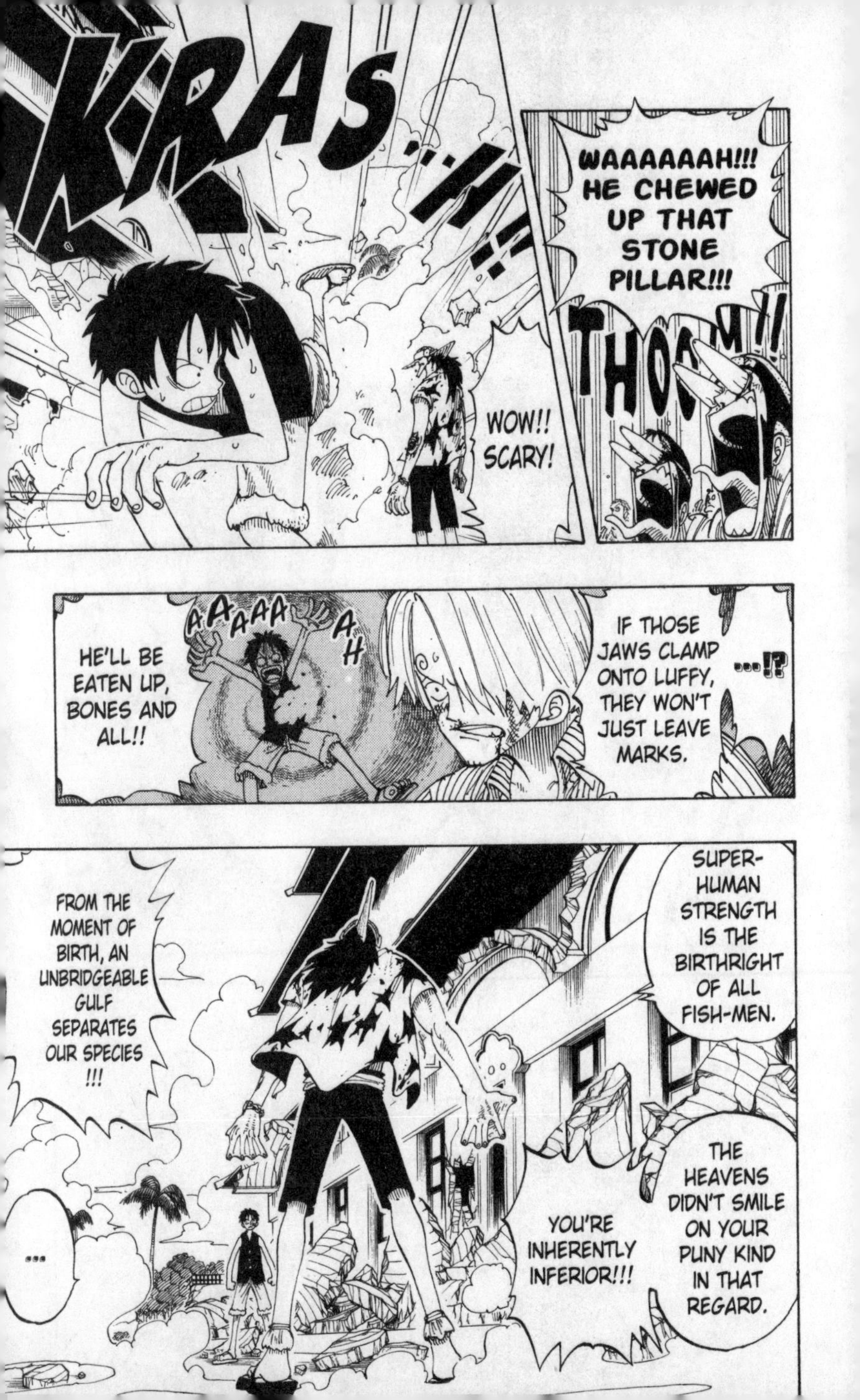
WAAAAAAH!!! HE CHEWED UP THAT STONE PILLAR!!!
KRASH!!
WOW!! SCARY!
...!?
IF THOSE JAWS CLAMP ONTO LUFFY, THEY WON'T JUST LEAVE MARKS.
AAAAAAH
HE'LL BE EATEN UP, BONES AND ALL!!
SUPER-HUMAN STRENGTH IS THE BIRTHRIGHT OF ALL FISH-MEN.
FROM THE MOMENT OF BIRTH, AN UNBRIDGEABLE GULF SEPARATES OUR SPECIES!!!
THE HEAVENS DIDN'T SMILE ON YOUR PUNY KIND IN THAT REGARD.
YOU'RE INHERENTLY INFERIOR!!!
...

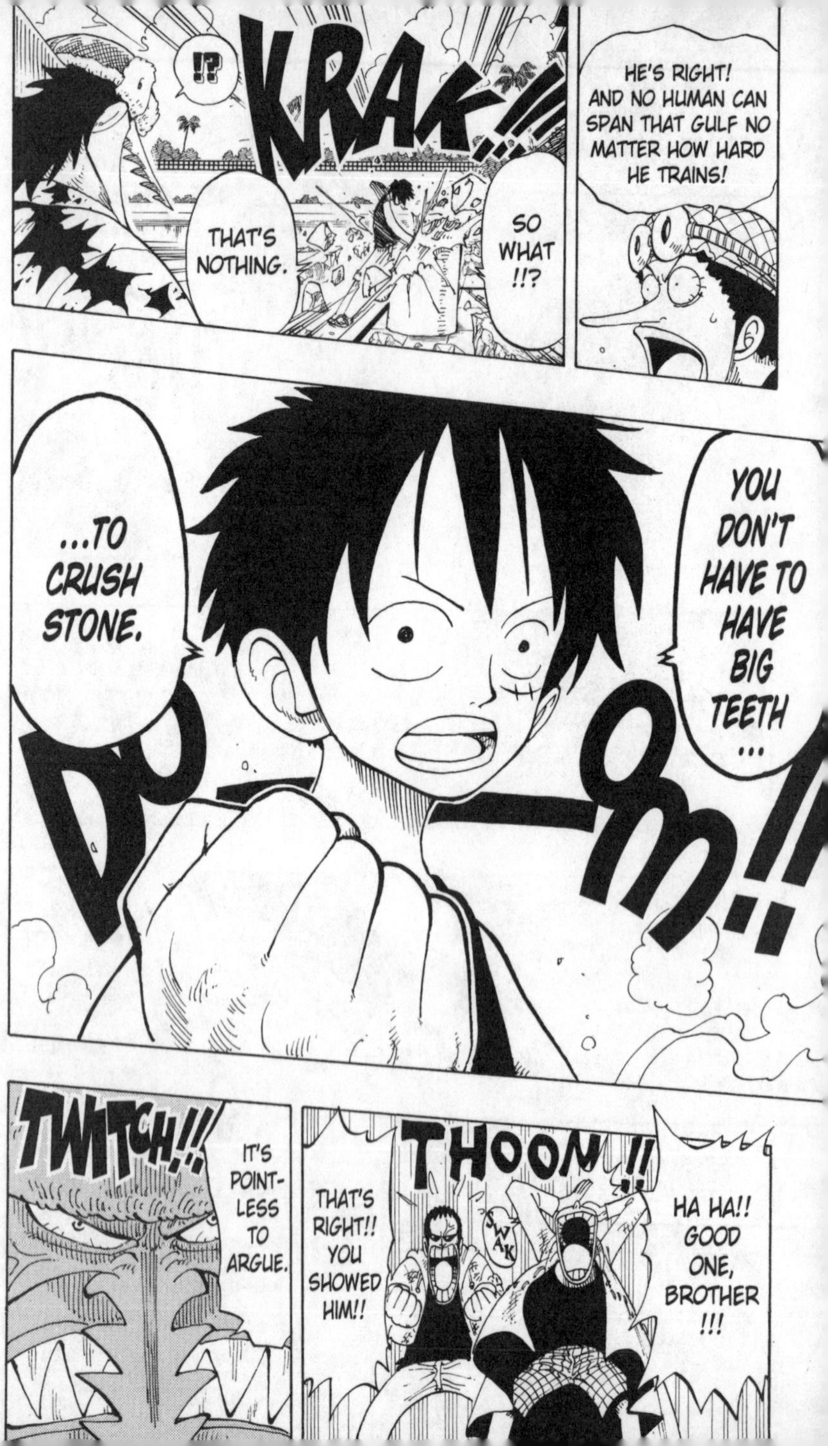
HE'S RIGHT! AND NO HUMAN CAN SPAN THAT GULF NO MATTER HOW HARD HE TRAINS!
KRAK!!!
!?
SO WHAT !!?
THAT'S NOTHING.
YOU DON'T HAVE TO HAVE BIG TEETH ...
DO-OM!!
...TO CRUSH STONE.
THOON!!
HA HA!! GOOD ONE, BROTHER !!!
SWAK
THAT'S RIGHT!! YOU SHOWED HIM!!
TWITCH!!
IT'S POINT-LESS TO ARGUE.

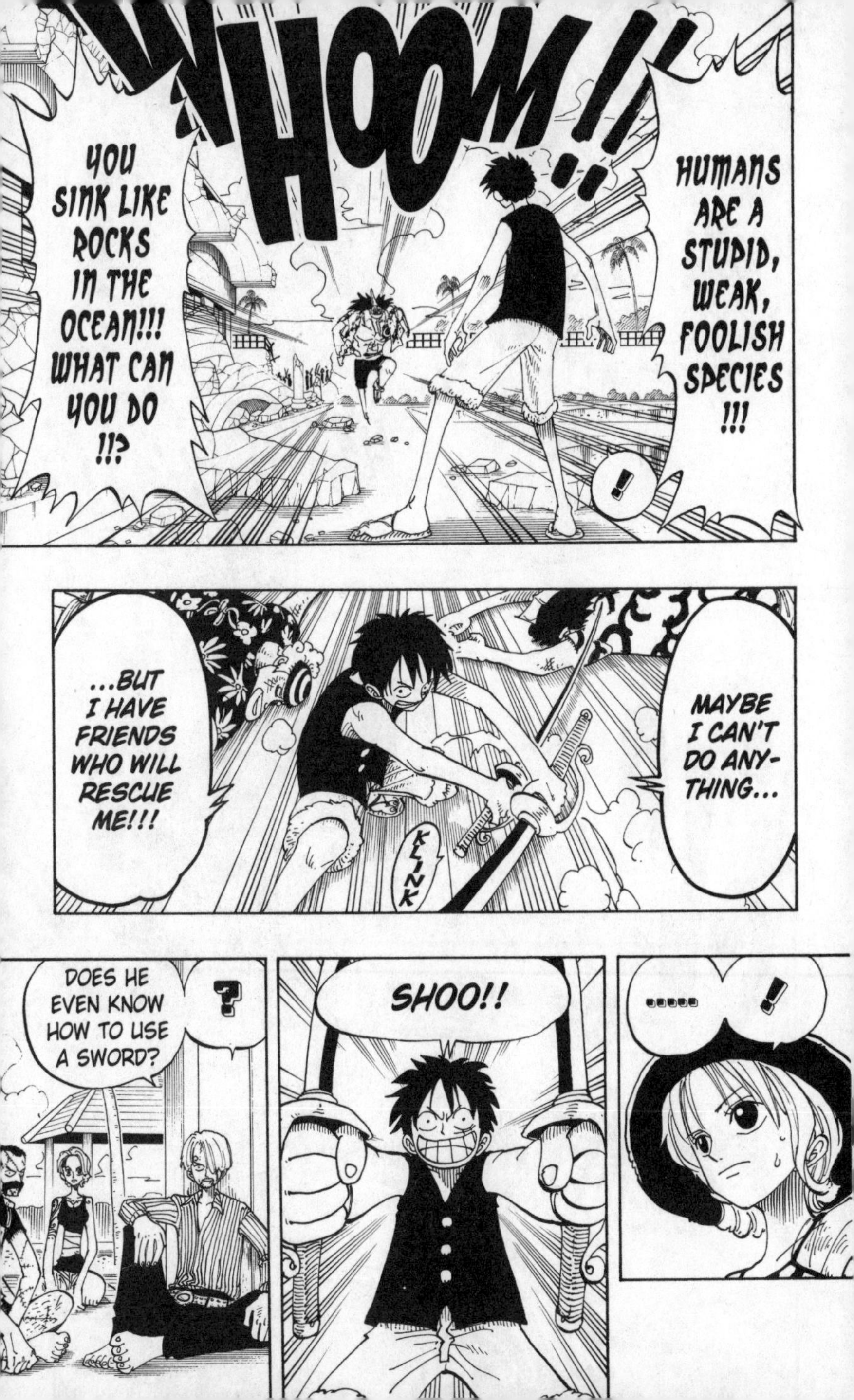
WHOOM!!
HUMANS ARE A STUPID, WEAK, FOOLISH SPECIES!!!
YOU SINK LIKE ROCKS IN THE OCEAN!!! WHAT CAN YOU DO!!?
!
MAYBE I CAN'T DO ANYTHING...
...BUT I HAVE FRIENDS WHO WILL RESCUE ME!!!
KLINK
.....
!
SHOO!!
?
DOES HE EVEN KNOW HOW TO USE A SWORD?

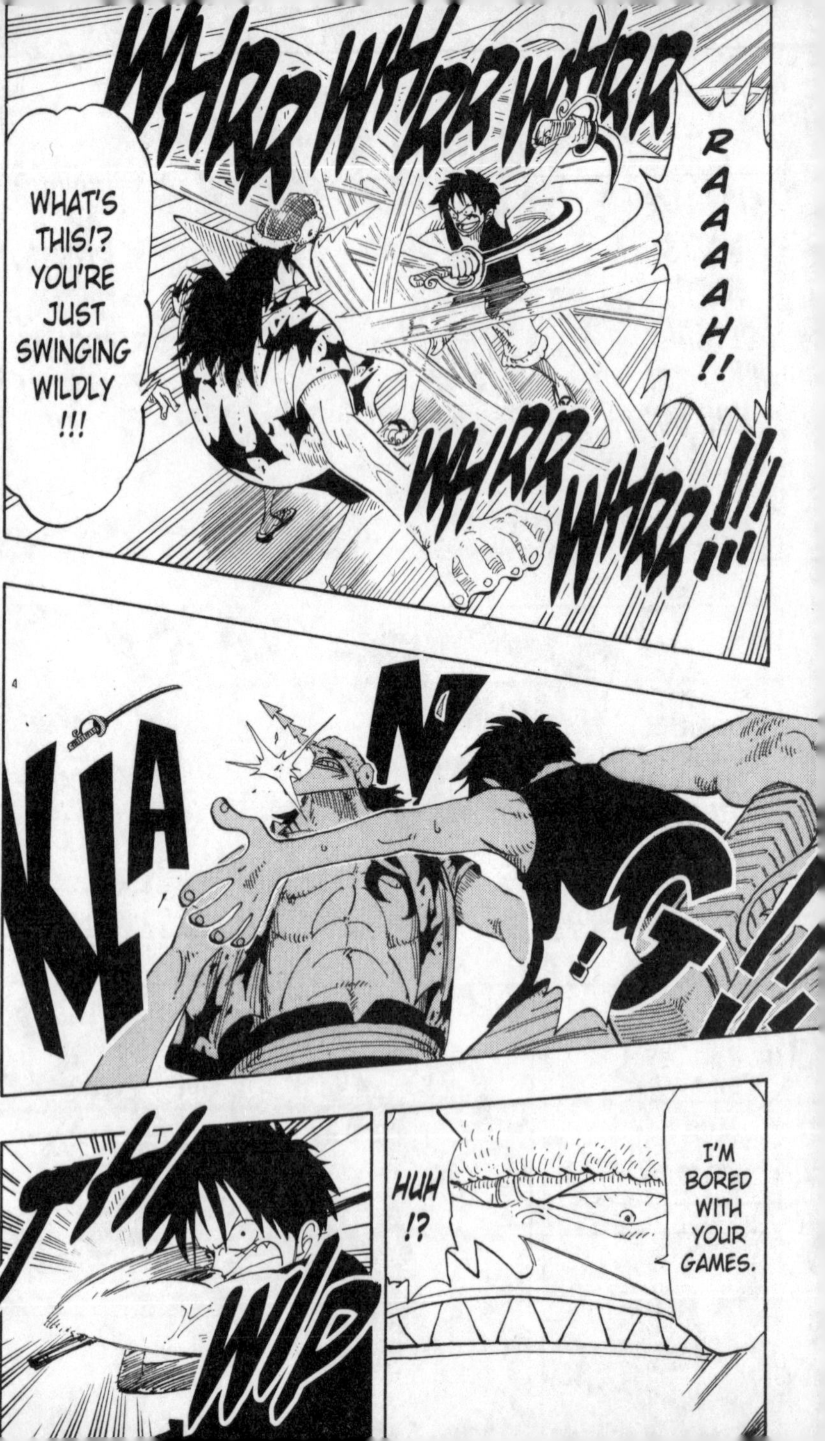
WHRR WHRR WHRR
RAAAAAH!!
WHAT'S THIS!? YOU'RE JUST SWINGING WILDLY !!!
WHRR WHRR!!
I'M BORED WITH YOUR GAMES.
HUH !?
THWIP

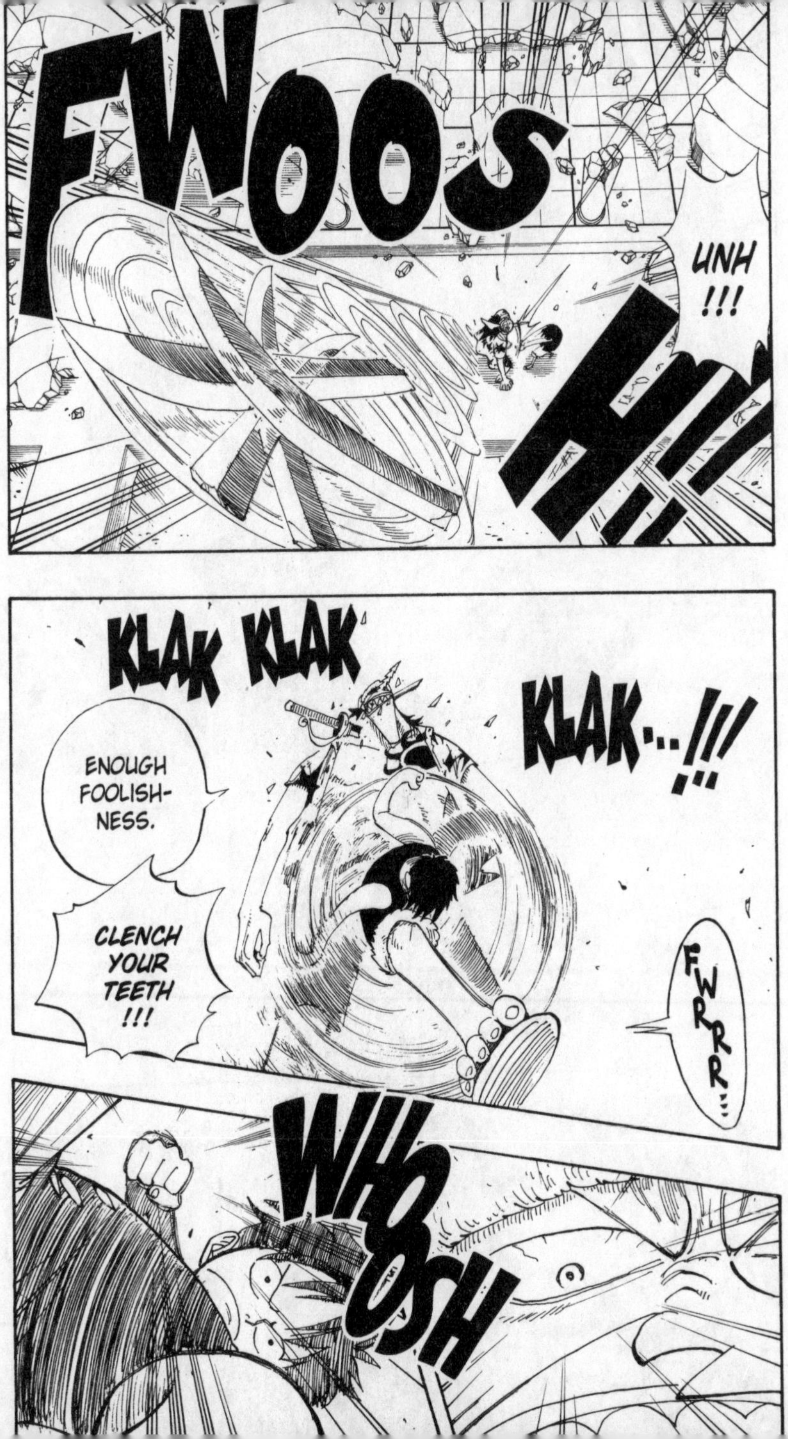
FWOOSH!!
UNH!!!
KLAK KLAK KLAK...!!!
ENOUGH FOOLISH-NESS.
CLENCH YOUR TEETH!!!
FWRRR...
WHOOSH

WHAT!!?

DOOM!!

GWAAAAH!!!

HE SHATTERED ARLONG'S TEETH!!!!

HUH? WHAT'S HE ON ABOUT?

THOOM

SPLASH!

I DON'T KNOW HOW TO USE A SWORD, SHARK FACE!!!

DOOM!

I DON'T KNOW HOW TO NAVIGATE EITHER!!!

I KNOW I CAN'T LIVE WITHOUT HELP FROM A LOT OF PEOPLE!!!

HEY.

AND I CAN'T TELL LIES!!

FWUP

I CAN'T COOK!!

WHAT A BURDEN IT MUST BE FOR YOUR CREW TO HAVE SUCH AN IDIOT FOR A CAPTAIN.

I DON'T KNOW WHY THEY FIGHT SO DESPERATELY TO SAVE YOU.

BWAH HA HA HA HA... WHAT A CLEVER BOY YOU ARE TO ADMIT YOUR OWN HELPLESS-NESS!!!

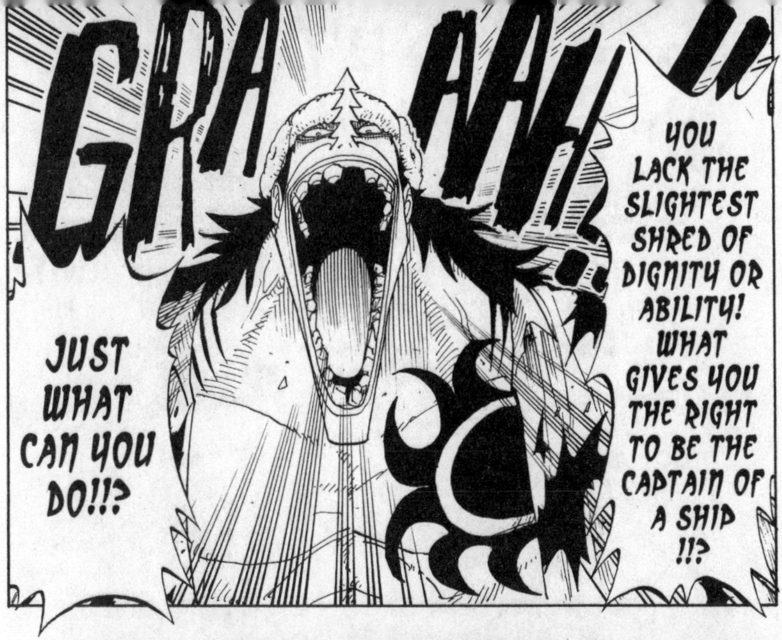
GRA AAH!!
YOU LACK THE SLIGHTEST SHRED OF DIGNITY OR ABILITY! WHAT GIVES YOU THE RIGHT TO BE THE CAPTAIN OF A SHIP !!?
JUST WHAT CAN YOU DO!!?
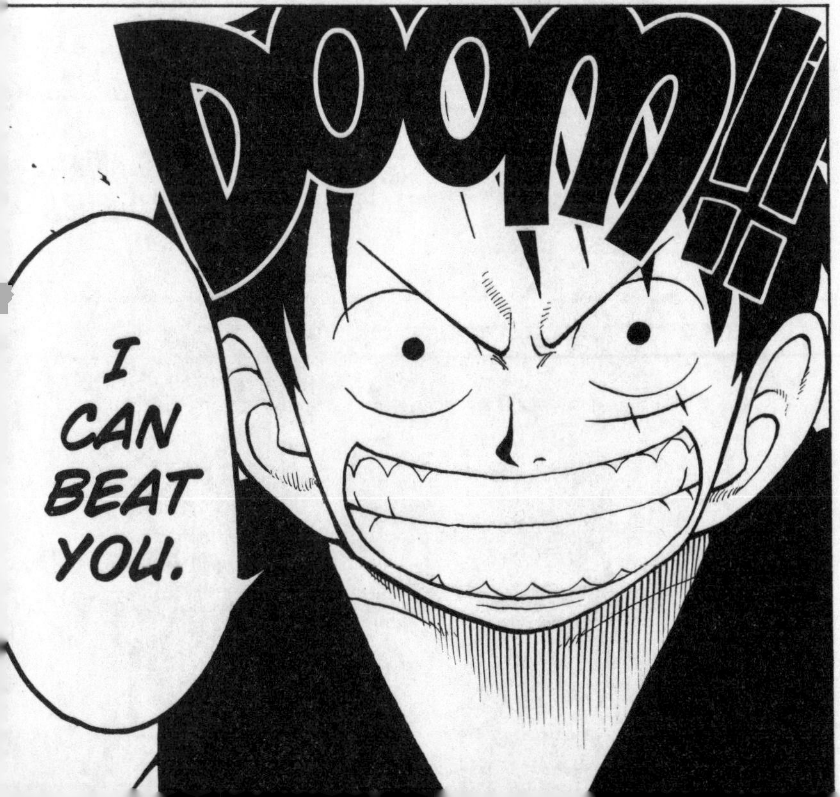
DOOON!!
I CAN BEAT YOU.

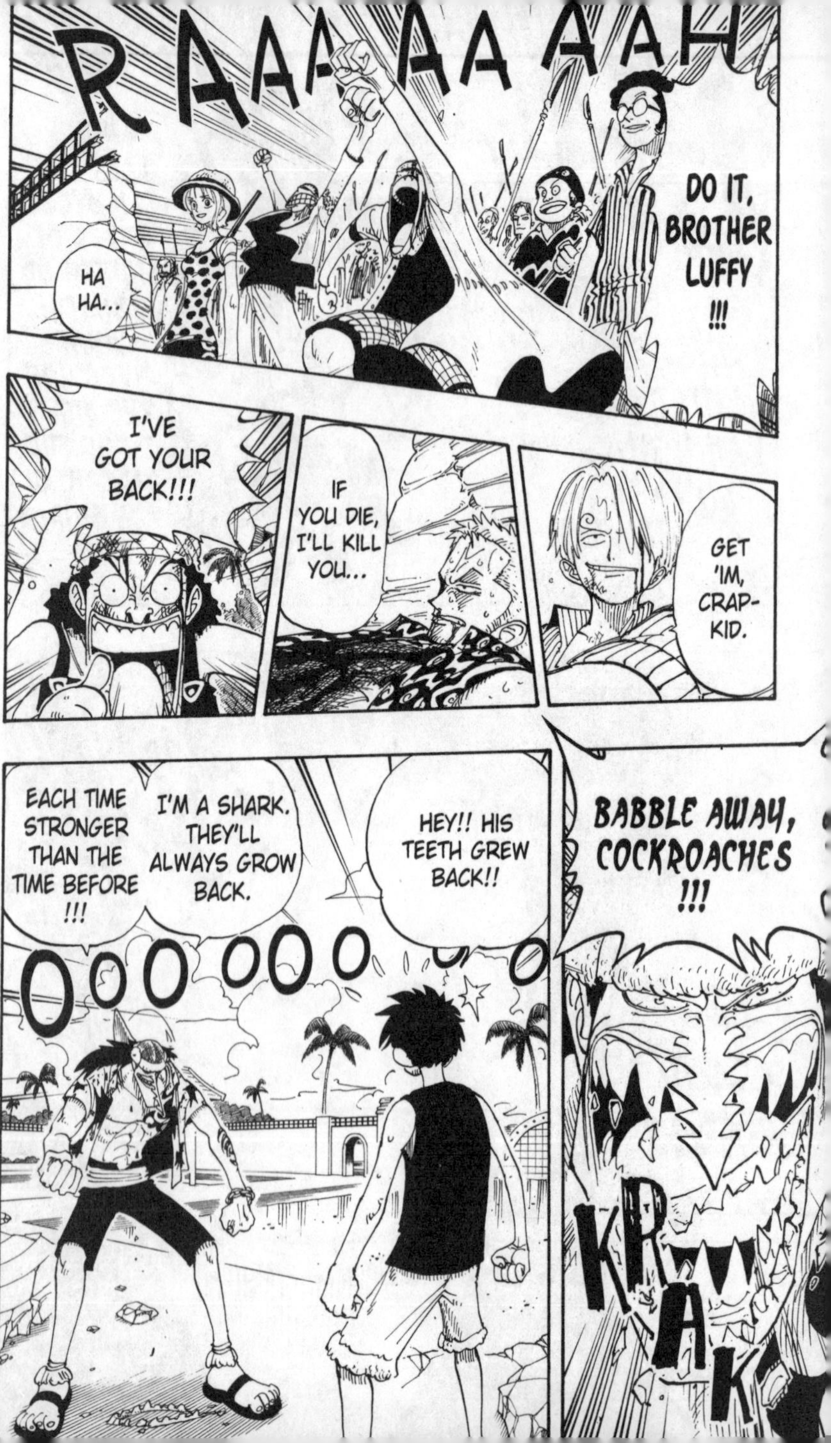
RAAAAAAAH
DO IT, BROTHER LUFFY!!!
HA HA...
GET 'IM, CRAP-KID.
IF YOU DIE, I'LL KILL YOU...
I'VE GOT YOUR BACK!!!
BABBLE AWAY, COCKROACHES!!!
KRAK
HEY!! HIS TEETH GREW BACK!!
I'M A SHARK. THEY'LL ALWAYS GROW BACK.
EACH TIME STRONGER THAN THE TIME BEFORE!!!
OOOOOOOO

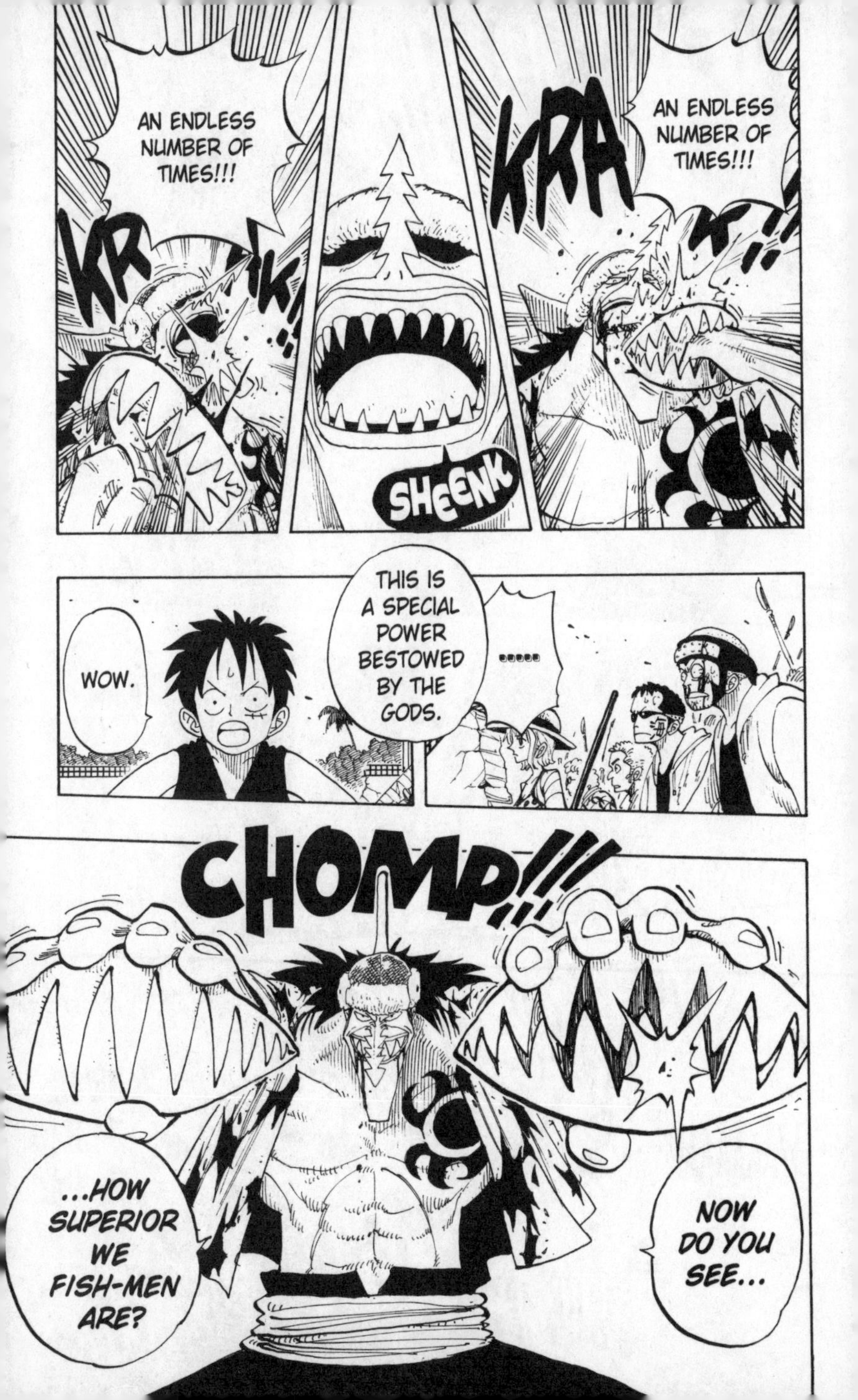
AN ENDLESS NUMBER OF TIMES!!!
KRAK!!
SHEENK
AN ENDLESS NUMBER OF TIMES!!!
KRKK!!
THIS IS A SPECIAL POWER BESTOWED BY THE GODS.
......
WOW.
CHOMP!!!
NOW DO YOU SEE...
...HOW SUPERIOR WE FISH-MEN ARE?

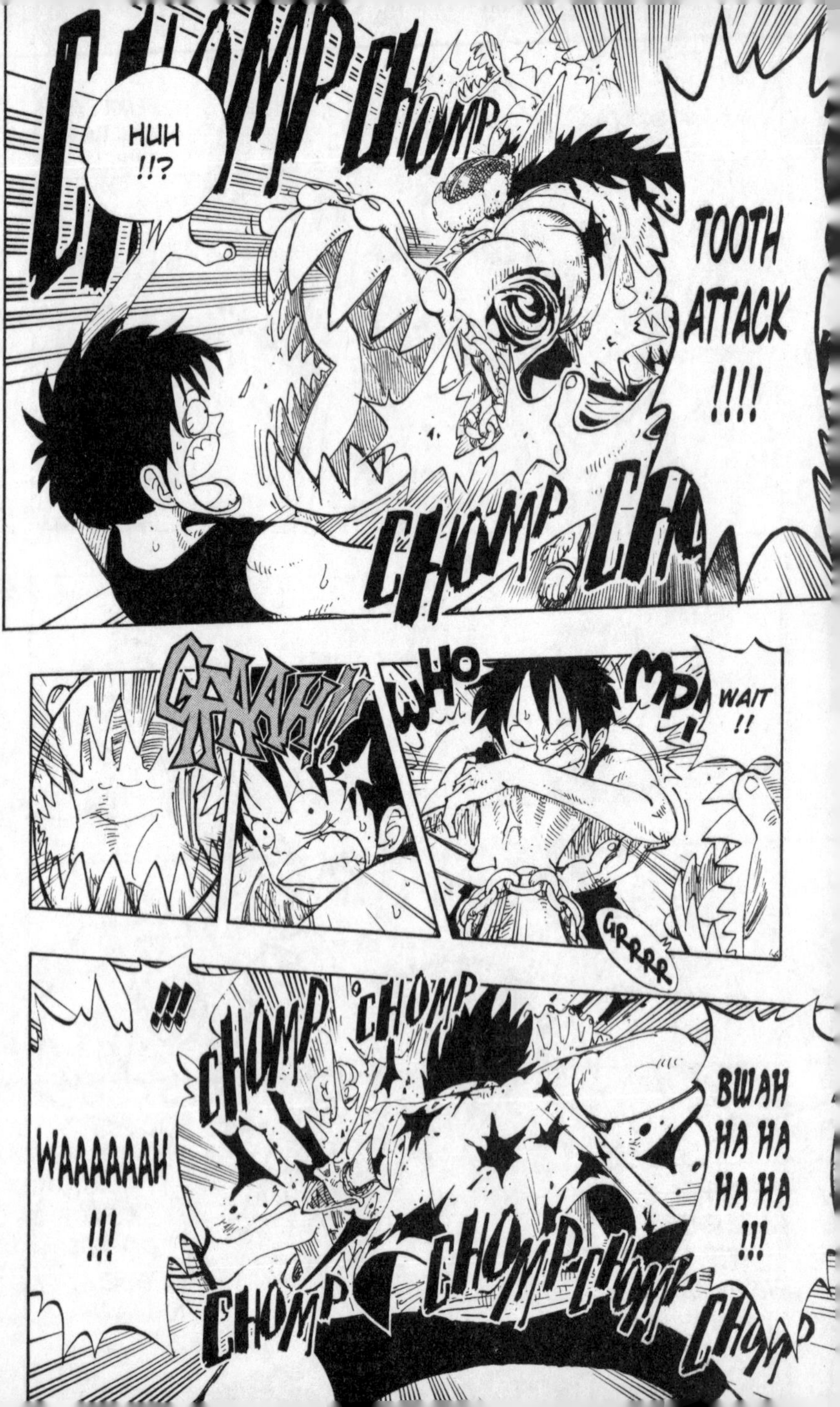
TOOTH ATTACK !!!!
CHOMP CHOMP
HUH !!?
CHOMP
WAIT !!
WHOMP!
GRRRR
GAAAH!!
BWAH HA HA HA HA !!!
CHOMP CHOMP
!!!
WAAAAAAH !!!
CHOMP CHOMP CHOMP CHOMP

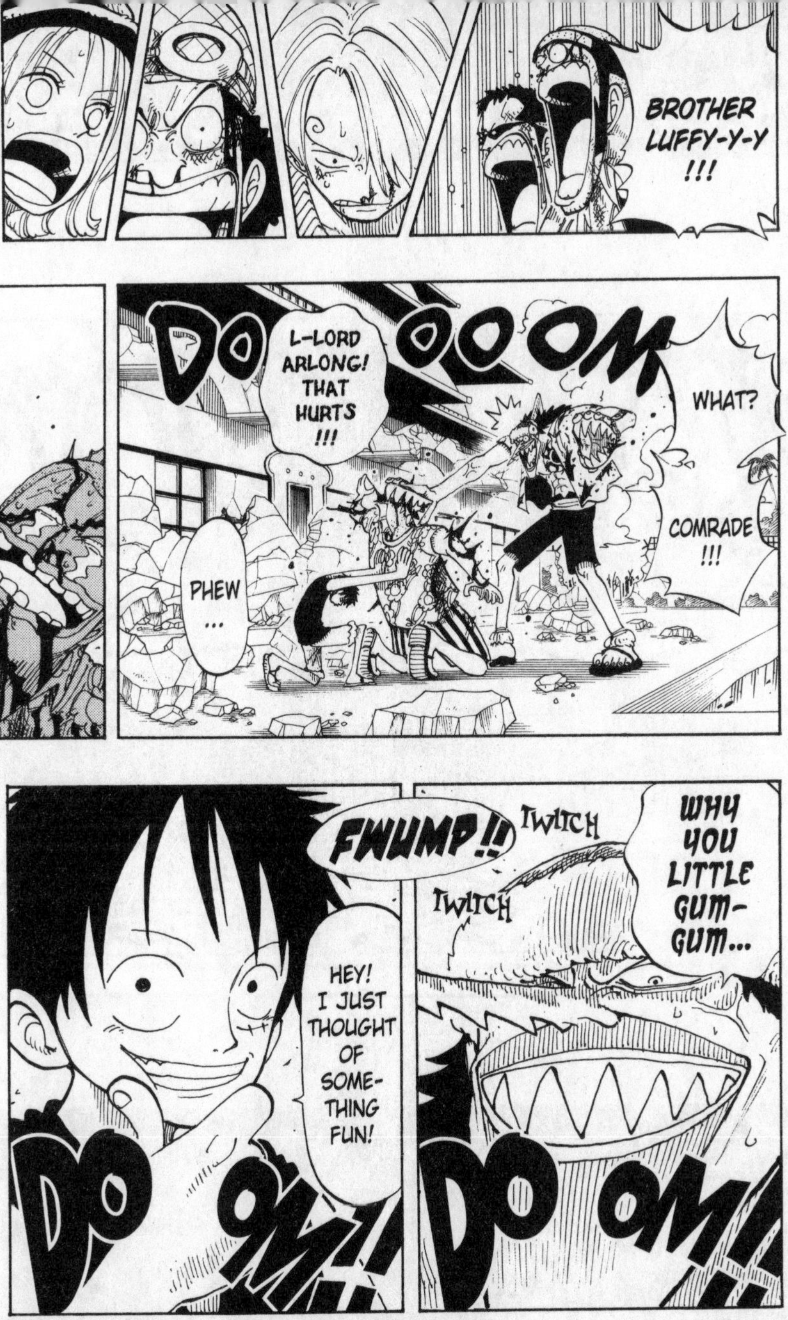

BROTHER LUFFY-Y-Y!!!
DOOOOM
WHAT?
COMRADE!!!
L-LORD ARLONG! THAT HURTS!!!
PHEW...
TWITCH
TWITCH
WHY YOU LITTLE GUM-GUM...
DOOM!!
FWUMP!!
HEY! I JUST THOUGHT OF SOME-THING FUN!
DOOM!!

 TO BE CONTINUED IN *ONE PIECE*, VOL. 11!

COMING NEXT VOLUME:

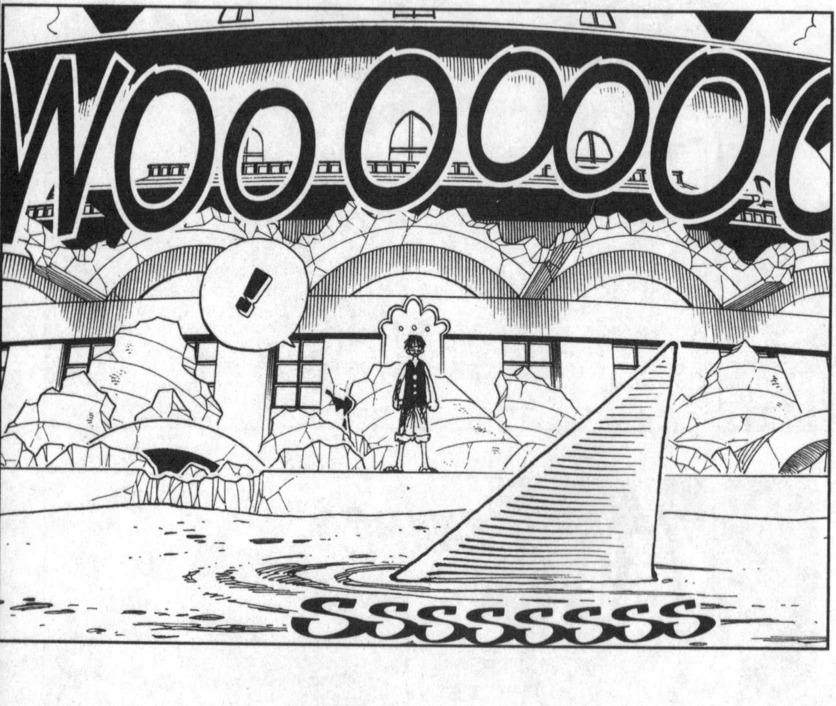
WOOOOOO
!
SSSSSSSS

Luffy's fun idea makes him more than an ideal match for the toothsome Captain Arlong. During a brief lull in their pitched battle, Luffy learns the unhappy tale behind Arlong Park's map room and takes it upon himself to demolish it completely, along with Arlong Park itself!

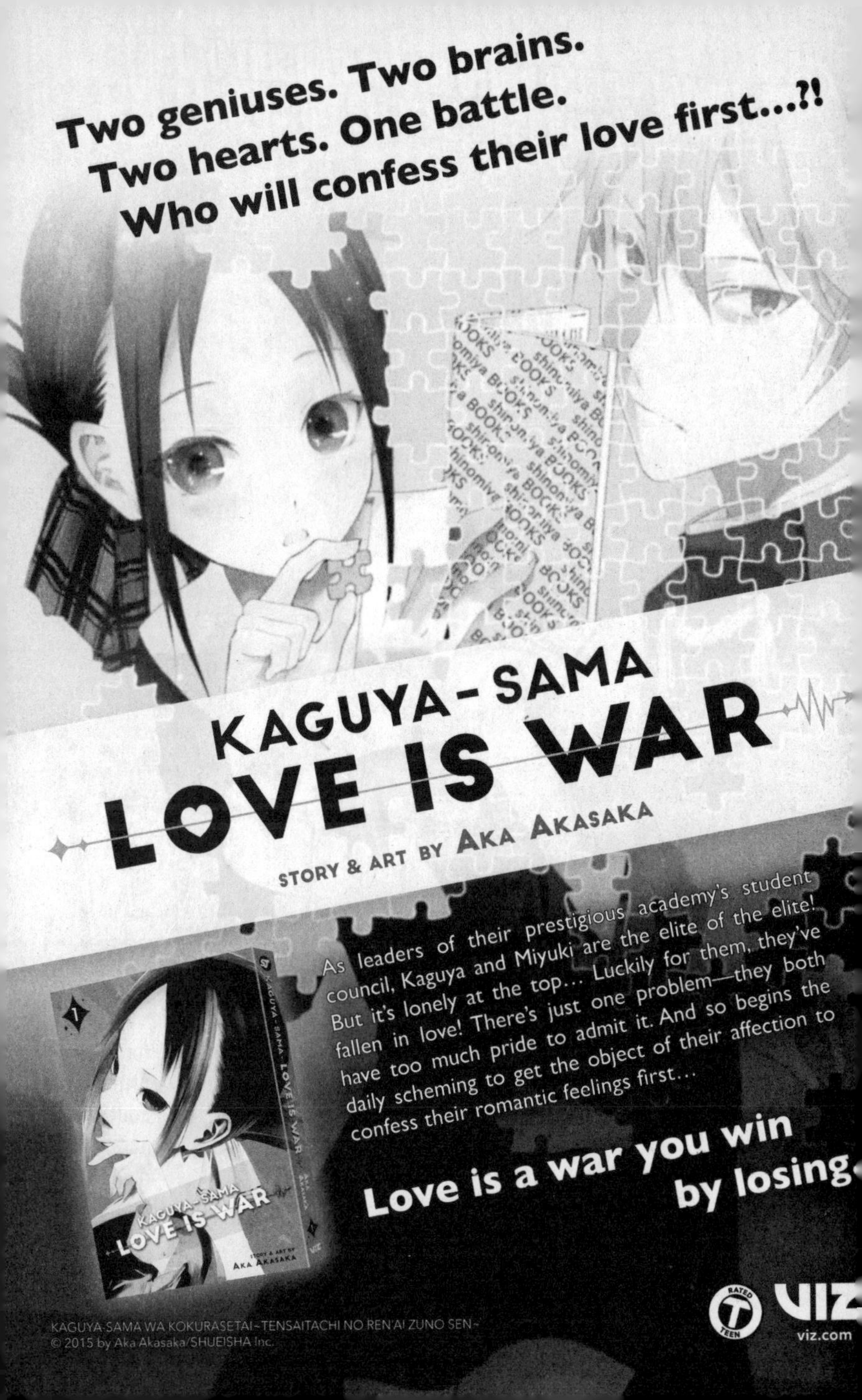
Two geniuses. Two brains.
Two hearts. One battle.
Who will confess their love first...?!
KAGUYA-SAMA
LOVE IS WAR
STORY & ART BY AKA AKASAKA
As leaders of their prestigious academy's student council, Kaguya and Miyuki are the elite of the elite! But it's lonely at the top... Luckily for them, they've fallen in love! There's just one problem—they both have too much pride to admit it. And so begins the daily scheming to get the object of their affection to confess their romantic feelings first...
Love is a war you win by losing.
KAGUYA-SAMA
LOVE IS WAR
STORY & ART BY
AKA AKASAKA
RATED T TEEN
VIZ
viz.com
KAGUYA-SAMA WA KOKURASETAI~TENSAITACHI NO REN'AI ZUNO SEN~
© 2015 by Aka Akasaka/SHUEISHA Inc.

You're Reading in the Wrong Direction!!

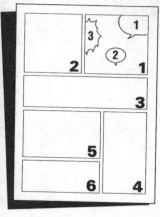

Whoops! Guess what? You're starting at the wrong end of the comic!

...It's true! In keeping with the original Japanese format, **One Piece** is meant to be read from right to left, starting in the upper-right corner.

Unlike English, which is read from left to right, Japanese is read from right to left, meaning that action, sound effects and word-balloon order are completely reversed... something which can make readers unfamiliar with Japanese feel pretty backwards themselves. For this reason, manga or Japanese comics published in the U.S. in English have sometimes been published "flopped"— that is, printed in exact reverse order, as though seen from the other side of a mirror.

By flopping pages, U.S. publishers can avoid confusing readers, but the compromise is not without its downside. For one thing, a character in a flopped manga series who once wore in the original Japanese version a T-shirt emblazoned with "M A Y" (as in "the merry month of") now wears one which reads "Y A M"! Additionally, many manga creators in Japan are themselves unhappy with the process, as some feel the mirror-imaging of their art skews their original intentions.

We are proud to bring you Eiichiro Oda's **One Piece** in the original unflopped format. For now, though, turn to the other side of the book and let the journey begin...!

–Editor

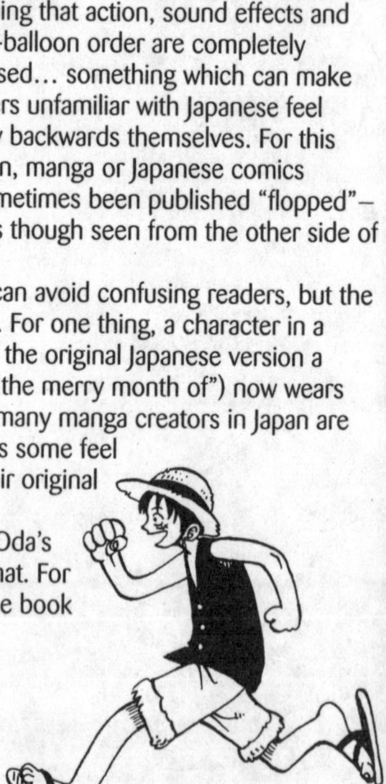